Essential SNMP

Other resources from O'Reilly

SECOND EDITION

Essential SNMP

Douglas R. Mauro and Kevin J. Schmidt

O'REILLY®

Beijing · Cambridge · Farnham · Köln · Paris · Sebastopol · Taipei · Tokyo

Essential SNMP, Second Edition

by Douglas R. Mauro and Kevin J. Schmidt

Copyright © 2005, 2001 O'Reilly Media, Inc. All rights reserved.
Printed in the United States of America.

Published by O'Reilly Media, Inc., 1005 Gravenstein Highway North, Sebastopol, CA 95472.

O'Reilly books may be purchased for educational, business, or sales promotional use. Online editions are also available for most titles (*safari.oreilly.com*). For more information, contact our corporate/institutional sales department: (800) 998-9938 or *corporate@oreilly.com*.

Editors:	Michael Loukides and Debra Cameron
Production Editor:	Darren Kelly
Cover Designer:	Ellie Volckhausen
Interior Designer:	David Futato

Printing History:

July 2001:	First Edition.
September 2005:	Second Edition.

Nutshell Handbook, the Nutshell Handbook logo, and the O'Reilly logo are registered trademarks of O'Reilly Media, Inc. *Essential SNMP*, the image of red deer, and related trade dress are trademarks of O'Reilly Media, Inc.

Many of the designations used by manufacturers and sellers to distinguish their products are claimed as trademarks. Where those designations appear in this book, and O'Reilly Media, Inc. was aware of a trademark claim, the designations have been printed in caps or initial caps.

While every precaution has been taken in the preparation of this book, the publisher and authors assume no responsibility for errors or omissions, or for damages resulting from the use of the information contained herein.

 This book uses RepKover,™ a durable and flexible lay-flat binding.

ISBN: 0-596-00840-6
ISBN13: 978-0-596-00840-6
[M]   [06/07]

Table of Contents

Preface

The Simple Network Management Protocol (SNMP) is an Internet-standard proto-col for managing devices on IP networks. Many kinds of devices support SNMP, including routers, switches, servers, workstations, printers, modem racks, and unin-terruptible power supplies (UPSs). The ways you can use SNMP range from the mundane to the exotic: it's fairly simple to use SNMP to monitor the health of your routers, servers, and other pieces of network hardware, but you can also use it to control your network devices, page someone, or take other automatic actions if prob-lems arise. The information you can monitor ranges from relatively simple and stan-dardized items, like the amount of traffic flowing into or out of an interface, to more esoteric hardware- and vendor-specific items, like the air temperature inside a router.

Given that there are already a number of books about SNMP in print, why write another one? Although there are many books on SNMP, there's a lack of books aimed at the practicing network or system administrator. Many books cover how to implement SNMP or discuss the protocol at a fairly abstract level, but none really answers the network administrator's most basic questions: how can I best put SNMP to work on my network? How can I make managing my network easier?

We provide a brief overview of the SNMP protocol in Chapters 2 and 3 and then spend a few chapters discussing issues such as hardware requirements and the sorts of tools that are available for use with SNMP. However, the bulk of this book is devoted to discussing, with real examples, how to use SNMP for system and net-work administration tasks.

Most newcomers to SNMP ask some or all of the following questions:

- What exactly is SNMP?
- How can I, as a system or network administrator, benefit from SNMP?
- What is a MIB?
- What is an OID?
- What is a community string?

- What is a trap?
- I've heard that SNMP is insecure. Is this true?
- Do any of my devices support SNMP? If so, how can I tell if they are configured properly?
- How do I go about gathering SNMP information from a device?
- I have a limited budget for purchasing network management software. What sort of free/open source software is available?
- Is there an SNMP Perl module that I can use to write cool scripts?
- Can I use Java™ to work with SNMP?

This book answers all these questions and more. Our goal is to demystify SNMP and make it more accessible to a wider range of users.

Audience for This Book

This book is intended for system and network administrators who could benefit from using SNMP to manage their equipment but who have little or no experience with SNMP or SNMP applications. In our experience, almost any network, no matter how small, can benefit from using SNMP. If you're a Perl programmer, this book will give you some ideas about how to write scripts that use SNMP to help manage your network. If you're not a Perl user, you can use many of the other tools we present, ranging from Net-SNMP (an open source collection of command-line tools) to Hewlett-Packard's OpenView (a high-end, high-priced network management platform).

Organization

Chapter 1, *Introduction to SNMP and Network Management*, provides a nontechnical overview of network management with SNMP. We introduce the different versions of SNMP, managers and agents, network management concepts, and change management techniques.

Chapter 2, *SNMPv1 and SNMPv2*, discusses the technical details of SNMP versions 1 and 2. We look at the Structure of Management Information (SMI) and the Management Information Base (MIB) and discuss how SNMP actually works—how management information is sent and received over the network.

Chapter 3, *SNMPv3*, discusses SNMP version 3, which is now a full standard that provides robust security for SNMP.

Chapter 4, *NMS Architectures*, helps you to think through strategies for deploying SNMP.

Chapter 5, *Configuring Your NMS*, provides a basic understanding of what to expect when installing NMS software by looking at two NMS packages, HP's OpenView and Castle Rock's SNMPc.

Chapter 6, *Configuring SNMP Agents*, describes how to configure several SNMP agents for Unix and Windows, including the Net-SNMP agent. To round out the chapter, we discuss how to configure the embedded agents on two network devices: the Cisco SNMP agent and the APC Symetra SNMP agent.

Chapter 7, *Polling and Setting*, shows how you can use command-line tools and Perl to gather (poll) SNMP information and change (set) the state of a managed device.

Chapter 8, *Polling and Thresholds*, discusses how to configure OpenView and SNMPc to gather SNMP information via polling. This chapter also discusses RMON configuration on a Cisco router.

Chapter 9, *Traps*, examines how to send and receive traps using command-line tools, Perl, OpenView, and other management applications.

Chapter 10, *Extensible SNMP Agents*, shows how several popular SNMP agents can be extended. Extensible agents provide end users with a means to extend the operation of an agent without having access to the agent's source code.

Chapter 11, *Adapting SNMP to Fit Your Environment*, is geared toward Perl-savvy system administrators. We provide Perl scripts that demonstrate how to perform some common system administration tasks with SNMP.

Chapter 12, *MRTG*, introduces one of the most widely used open source SNMP applications, the Multi Router Traffic Grapher (MRTG). MRTG provides network administrators with web-based usage graphs of router interfaces and can be configured to graph many other kinds of data.

Chapter 13, *RRDtool and Cricket*, introduces RRDtool and Cricket. Used together, these tools provide graphing techniques like those in MRTG, but with added flexibility.

Chapter 14, *Java and SNMP*, discusses how to use Java to build SNMP applications.

Appendix A, *Using Input and Output Octets*, discusses how to use OpenView to graph input and output octets.

Appendix B, *More on OpenView's NNM*, discusses how to graph external data with Network Node Manager (NNM), add menu items to NNM, configure user profiles, and use NNM as a centralized communication interface.

Appendix C, *Net-SNMP Tools*, summarizes the usage of the Net-SNMP command-line tools.

Appendix D, *SNMP RFCs*, provides an authoritative list of the various RFC numbers that pertain to SNMP.

Appendix E, *SNMP Support for Perl*, is a good summary of the SNMP Perl module used throughout the book along with an introduction to the Net-SNMP Perl module.

Appendix F, *Network Management Software*, presents an overview of network management software by category.

Appendix G, *Open Source Monitoring Software*, introduces some commonly used open source network management and monitoring tools.

Appendix H, *Network Troubleshooting Primer*, provides a primer on tools that can aid in network troubleshooting.

What's New in This Edition

This second edition has been thoroughly revised and expanded. It includes the following new features:

- Chapter 1 includes coverage of the concepts behind network management and change management.

- Chapter 2 provides packet traces of the various SNMP operations.

- Chapter 3 provides coverage of SNMPv3. This chapter was an appendix in the first edition; it has been expanded to a full chapter.

- SNMPc coverage has been expanded in Chapters 5 and 9.

- Chapter 11 explains the use of scripts for a variety of tasks. This chapter has doubled in size to include many new scripts. You'll find scripts for service monitoring techniques for SMTP, POP3, HTTP, and DNS, a Perl-based SNMP agent, switch port control, usage of the Cisco Ping MIB, and a section on wireless access point (WAP) monitoring.

- Chapter 13, new in this edition, discusses RRDtool and Cricket.

- Chapter 14, also new in this edition, is devoted to showing how Java can be used to create SNMP applications.

- Appendix E provides a brief overview of Net-SNMP's Perl module.

- Appendix G provides details on the most commonly used open source tools for network management and monitoring.

- Appendix H introduces the most commonly used network troubleshooting tools.

Example Programs

All the example programs in this book are available from this book's web page at *http://www.oreilly.com/catalog/esnmp2/*.

Using Code Examples

This book is here to help you get your job done. In general, you may use the code in this book in your programs and documentation. You do not need to contact O'Reilly for permission unless you're reproducing a significant portion of the code. For example, writing a program that uses several chunks of code from this book does not require permission. Selling or distributing a CD-ROM of examples from O'Reilly books *does* require permission. Answering a question by citing this book and quoting example code does not require permission. Incorporating a significant amount of example code from this book into your product's documentation *does* require permission.

We appreciate, but do not require, attribution. An attribution usually includes the title, author, publisher, and ISBN. For example: "*Essential SNMP*, Second Edition, by Douglas R. Mauro and Kevin J. Schmidt. Copyright 2005 O'Reilly Media, Inc., 0-596-00840-6."

If you feel your use of code examples falls outside fair use or the permission given above, feel free to contact us at *permissions@oreilly.com*.

Conventions Used in This Book

The following typographical conventions are used in this book:

Italic
> Used for object IDs, URLs, filenames, and directory names. It is also used for emphasis and for the first use of technical terms.

`Constant width`
> Used for examples, object definitions, literal values, textual conventions, and datatypes. It is also used to show source code, the contents of files, and the output of commands.

`Constant width bold`
> Used in interactive examples to show commands or text that would be typed literally by the user. It is also used to emphasize when something, usually in source code or file-contents examples, has been added to or changed from a previous example.

`Constant width italic`
> Used for replaceable parameter names in command syntax.

 Indicates a tip, suggestion, or general note.

Indicates a warning or caution.

Comments and Questions

Please address comments and questions concerning this book to the publisher:

O'Reilly Media, Inc.
1005 Gravenstein Highway North
Sebastopol, CA 95472
(800) 998-9938 (in the United States or Canada)
(707) 829-0515 (international/local)
(707) 829-0104 (fax)

There is a web page for this book, which lists errata, code examples, reviews, and any additional information. You can access this page at:

http://www.oreilly.com/catalog/esnmp2/

To comment or ask technical questions about this book, send email to:

bookquestions@oreilly.com

For more information about books, conferences, software, Resource Centers, and the O'Reilly Network, see the O'Reilly web site at:

http://www.oreilly.com

Safari® Enabled

 When you see a Safari® Enabled icon on the cover of your favorite technology book, it means the book is available online through the O'Reilly Network Safari Bookshelf.

Safari offers a solution that's better than e-books. It's a virtual library that lets you easily search thousands of top technology books, cut and paste code samples, download chapters, and find quick answers when you need the most accurate, current information. Try it for free at *http://safari.oreilly.com*.

Acknowledgments for the Second Edition

Deb Cameron deserves a big thank you for shepherding this second edition from beginning to end. Her diligence and effort helped keep us on track. Dr. Robert Minch, professor at Boise State University, provided valuable suggestions for the second edition. Bobby Krupczak, Ph.D., once again provided feedback on the Concord SystemEDGE agent. Frank Fock was kind enough to provide comments on the Java and SNMP chapter. Max Baker provided the idea for the channel-setting algorithm presented in Chapter 11. Jim Boney graciously volunteered the use of his Cisco routers. Castle Rock Computing was gracious enough to provide us with a copy of SNMPc for the second edition of this book; special thanks go to Castle Rock's John Maytum for coordinating our access to SNMPc.

We are grateful for input from Jason Briggs, Bill Horsfall, and Jason Weiss, who reviewed new material for this second edition under a very tight schedule.

Douglas

For years I worked as a system and network administrator and often faced the question, "How are things running?" This is what led me to SNMP and eventually to the idea for this book. Of course, I would like to thank Kevin for his hard work and dedication. Special thanks go to three special people in my life: my wife, Amy, and our children, Kari and Matthew, for putting up with my long absences while I was writing in the computer room. Thanks also go to my family and friends, who provided support and encouragement.

Kevin

Working on the second edition has been a great joy. The first edition has been out for almost four years, and in this time I have thought about what I wanted to add if someday O'Reilly wanted a second edition written. So, a thank you goes to O'Reilly for giving me the chance to update this book. I would like to thank Douglas for allowing me to once again work on the book with him. Finally, I would like to thank Danette, my loving and generous wife, for allowing me the time I needed to complete this project. Without her support, I would not have made it through the process.

Acknowledgments for the First Edition

It would be an understatement to say that this book was a long time in the making. It would never have been published without the patience and support of Michael Loukides. Thanks Mike! We would also like to thank the individuals who provided us with valuable technical review feedback and general help and guidance: Mike DeGraw-Bertsch at O'Reilly; Donald Cooley at Global Crossing; Jacob Kirsch at Sun Microsystems, Inc.; Bobby Krupczak, Ph.D., at Concord Communications; John Reinhardt at Road Runner; Patrick Bailey and Rob Sweet at Netrail; and Jürgen Schönwälder at the Technical University of Braunschweig. Rob Romano, a talented graphic artist at O'Reilly, deserves a thank you for making the figures throughout the book look great. Finally, thanks to Jim Sumser, who took the project over in its final stages, and to Rachel Wheeler, the production editor, for putting this book together.

## CHAPTER 1

Introduction to SNMP and Network Management

In today's complex network of routers, switches, and servers, it can seem like a daunting task to manage all the devices on your network and make sure they're not only up and running but also performing optimally. This is where the Simple Network Management Protocol (SNMP) can help. SNMP was introduced in 1988 to meet the growing need for a standard for managing Internet Protocol (IP) devices. SNMP provides its users with a "simple" set of operations that allows these devices to be managed remotely.

This book is aimed toward system administrators who would like to begin using SNMP to manage their servers or routers, but who lack the knowledge or understanding to do so. We try to give you a basic understanding of what SNMP is and how it works; beyond that, we show you how to put SNMP into practice, using a number of widely available tools. Above all, we want this to be a practical book—a book that helps you keep track of what your network is doing.

This chapter introduces SNMP, network management, and change management. Obviously, SNMP is the focus of this book, but having an understanding of general network management concepts will make you better prepared to use SNMP to manage your network.

What Is SNMP?

The core of SNMP is a simple set of operations (and the information these operations gather) that gives administrators the ability to change the state of some SNMP-based device. For example, you can use SNMP to shut down an interface on your router or check the speed at which your Ethernet interface is operating. SNMP can even monitor the temperature on your switch and warn you when it is too high.

SNMP usually is associated with managing routers, but it's important to understand that it can be used to manage many types of devices. While SNMP's predecessor, the Simple Gateway Management Protocol (SGMP), was developed to manage Internet routers, SNMP can be used to manage Unix systems, Windows systems, printers, modem racks, power supplies, and more. Any device running software that allows the retrieval of SNMP information can be managed. This includes not only physical devices but also software, such as web servers and databases.

Another aspect of network management is network monitoring; that is, monitoring an entire network as opposed to individual routers, hosts, and other devices. Remote Network Monitoring (RMON) was developed to help us understand how the network itself is functioning, as well as how individual devices on the network are affecting the network as a whole. It can be used to monitor not only LAN traffic, but WAN interfaces as well. We discuss RMON in more detail later in this chapter and in Chapter 2.

RFCs and SNMP Versions

The Internet Engineering Task Force (IETF) is responsible for defining the standard protocols that govern Internet traffic, including SNMP. The IETF publishes Requests for Comments (RFCs), which are specifications for many protocols that exist in the IP realm. Documents enter the standards track first as *proposed* standards, then move to *draft* status. When a final draft is eventually approved, the RFC is given *standard* status—although there are fewer completely approved standards than you might think. Two other standards-track designations, *historical* and *experimental*, define (respectively) a document that has been replaced by a newer RFC and a document that is not yet ready to become a standard. The following list includes all the current SNMP versions and the IETF status of each (see Appendix D for a full list of the SNMP RFCs):

- SNMP Version 1 (SNMPv1) is the initial version of the SNMP protocol. It's defined in RFC 1157 and is a historical IETF standard. SNMPv1's security is based on communities, which are nothing more than passwords: plain-text strings that allow any SNMP-based application that knows the strings to gain access to a device's management information. There are typically three communities in SNMPv1: *read-only*, *read-write*, and *trap*. It should be noted that while SNMPv1 is historical, it is still the primary SNMP implementation that many vendors support.

- SNMP version 2 (SNMPv2) is often referred to as community-string-based SNMPv2. This version of SNMP is technically called SNMPv2c, but we will refer to it throughout this book simply as SNMPv2. It's defined in RFC 3416, RFC 3417, and RFC 3418.

- SNMP version 3 (SNMPv3) is the latest version of SNMP. Its main contribution to network management is security. It adds support for strong authentication and private communication between managed entities. In 2002, it finally made the transition from draft standard to full standard. The following RFCs define the standard: RFC 3410, RFC 3411, RFC 3412, RFC 3413, RFC 3414, RFC 3415, RFC 3416, RFC 3417, RFC 3418, and RFC 2576. Chapter 3 provides a thorough treatment of SNMPv3 and Chapter 6 goes through the SNMPv3 agent configuration for Net-SNMP and Cisco. While it is good news that SNMPv3 is a full standard, vendors are notoriously slow at adopting new versions of a protocol. While SNMPv1 has been transitioned to historical, the vast majority of vendor implementations of SNMP are SNMPv1 implementations. Some large infrastructure vendors like Cisco have supported SNMPv3 for quite some time, and we will undoubtedly begin to see more vendors move to SNMPv3 as customers insist on more secure means of managing networks.

The official site for RFCs is *http://www.ietf.org/rfc.html*. One of the biggest problems with RFCs, however, is finding the one you want. It is a little easier to navigate the RFC index at Ohio State University (*http://www.cse.ohio-state.edu/cs/Services/rfc/index.html*).

Managers and Agents

In the previous sections, we've vaguely referred to SNMP-capable devices and network management stations. Now it's time to describe what these two things really are. In the world of SNMP, there are two kind of entities: managers and agents. A *manager* is a server running some kind of software system that can handle management tasks for a network. Managers are often referred to as Network Management Stations (NMSs).[*] An NMS is responsible for polling and receiving traps from agents in the network. A *poll*, in the context of network management, is the act of querying an agent (router, switch, Unix server, etc.) for some piece of information. This information can be used later to determine if some sort of catastrophic event has occurred. A *trap* is a way for the agent to tell the NMS that something has happened. Traps are sent asynchronously, not in response to queries from the NMS. The NMS is further responsible for performing an action[†] based upon the information it receives from the agent. For example, when your T1 circuit to the Internet goes down, your router can send a trap to your NMS. In turn, the NMS can take some action, perhaps paging you to let you know that something has happened.

The second entity, the *agent*, is a piece of software that runs on the network devices you are managing. It can be a separate program (a daemon, in Unix language), or it can be incorporated into the operating system (for example, Cisco's IOS on a router, or the low-level operating system that controls a UPS). Today, most IP devices come with some kind of SNMP agent built in. The fact that vendors are willing to implement agents in many of their products makes the system administrator's or network manager's job easier. The agent provides management information to the NMS by keeping track of various operational aspects of the device. For example, the agent on a router is able to keep track of the state of each of its interfaces: which ones are up,

[*] See Appendix F for a listing of some popular NMS applications.
[†] Note that the NMS is preconfigured to perform this action.

which ones are down, etc. The NMS can query the status of each interface and take appropriate action if any of them are down. When the agent notices that something bad has happened, it can send a trap to the NMS. This trap originates from the agent and is sent to the NMS, where it is handled appropriately. Some devices will send a corresponding "all clear" trap when there is a transition from a bad state to a good state. This can be useful in determining when a problem situation has been resolved. Figure 1-1 shows the relationship between the NMS and an agent.

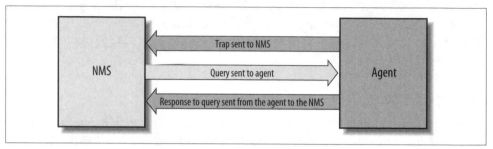

Figure 1-1. Relationship between an NMS and an agent

It's important to keep in mind that polls and traps can happen at the same time. There are no restrictions on when the NMS can query the agent or when the agent can send a trap.

The Structure of Management Information and MIBs

The Structure of Management Information (SMI) provides a way to define managed objects and their behavior. An agent has in its possession a list of the objects that it tracks. One such object is the operational status of a router interface (for example, *up*, *down*, or *testing*). This list collectively defines the information the NMS can use to determine the overall health of the device on which the agent resides.

The Management Information Base (MIB) can be thought of as a database of managed objects that the agent tracks. Any sort of status or statistical information that can be accessed by the NMS is defined in a MIB. The SMI provides a way to define managed objects while the MIB is the definition (using the SMI syntax) of the objects themselves. Like a dictionary, which shows how to spell a word and then gives its meaning or definition, a MIB defines a textual name for a managed object and explains its meaning. Chapter 2 goes into more technical detail about MIBs and the SMI.

An agent may implement many MIBs, but all agents implement a particular MIB called MIB-II[*] (RFC 1213). This standard defines variables for things such as inter-

---

[*] MIB-I is the original version of this MIB, but it is no longer referred to since MIB-II enhances it.

face statistics (interface speeds, MTU, octets* sent, octets received, etc.) as well as various other things pertaining to the system itself (system location, system contact, etc.). The main goal of MIB-II is to provide general TCP/IP management information. It doesn't cover every possible item a vendor may want to manage within its particular device.

What other kinds of information might be useful to collect? First, many draft and proposed standards have been developed to help manage things such as frame relay, ATM, FDDI, and services (mail, Domain Name System (DNS), etc.). A sampling of these MIBs and their RFC numbers includes:

- ATM MIB (RFC 2515)
- Frame Relay DTE Interface Type MIB (RFC 2115)
- BGP Version 4 MIB (RFC 1657)
- RDBMS MIB (RFC 1697)
- RADIUS Authentication Server MIB (RFC 2619)
- Mail Monitoring MIB (RFC 2789)
- DNS Server MIB (RFC 1611)

But that's far from the entire story, which is why vendors, and individuals, are allowed to define MIB variables for their own use.† For example, consider a vendor that is bringing a new router to market. The agent built into the router will respond to NMS requests (or send traps to the NMS) for the variables defined by the MIB-II standard; it probably also implements MIBs for the interface types it provides (e.g., RFC 2515 for ATM and RFC 2115 for Frame Relay). In addition, the router may have some significant new features that are worth monitoring but are not covered by any standard MIB. So, the vendor defines its own MIB (sometimes referred to as a *proprietary MIB*) that implements managed objects for the status and statistical information of its new router.

 Simply loading a new MIB into your NMS does not necessarily allow you to retrieve the data/values/objects, etc., defined within that MIB. You need to load only those MIBs supported by the agents from which you're requesting queries (e.g., snmpget, snmpwalk). Feel free to load additional MIBs for future device support, but don't panic when your device doesn't answer (and possibly returns errors for) these unsupported MIBs.

---

* An octet is an 8-bit quantity, which is the fundamental unit of transfer in TCP/IP networks.
† This topic is discussed further in the next chapter.

Host Management

Managing host resources (disk space, memory usage, etc.) is an important part of network management. The distinction between traditional system administration and network management has been disappearing over the last decade and is now all but gone. As Sun Microsystems puts it, "The network is the computer." If your web server or mail server is down, it doesn't matter whether your routers are running correctly—you're still going to get calls. The Host Resources MIB (RFC 2790) defines a set of objects to help manage critical aspects of Unix and Windows systems.*

Some of the objects supported by the Host Resources MIB include disk capacity, number of system users, number of running processes, and software currently installed. Today, more and more people are relying on service-oriented web sites. Making sure your backend servers are functioning properly is as important as monitoring your routers and other communications devices.

Unfortunately, some agent implementations for these platforms do not implement this MIB since it's not required.

A Brief Introduction to Remote Monitoring (RMON)

Remote Monitoring Version 1 (RMONv1, or RMON) is defined in RFC 2819; an enhanced version of the standard, called RMON Version 2 (RMONv2), is defined in RFC 2021. RMONv1 provides the NMS with packet-level statistics about an entire LAN or WAN. RMONv2 builds on RMONv1 by providing network- and application-level statistics. These statistics can be gathered in several ways. One way is to place an RMON probe on every network segment you want to monitor. Some Cisco routers have limited RMON capabilities built in, so you can use their functionality to perform minor RMON duties. Likewise, some 3Com switches implement the full RMON specification and can be used as full-blown RMON probes.

The RMON MIB was designed to allow an actual RMON probe to run in an offline mode that allows the probe to gather statistics about the network it's watching without requiring an NMS to query it constantly. At some later time, the NMS can query the probe for the statistics it has been gathering. Another feature that most probes implement is the ability to set thresholds for various error conditions and, when a threshold is crossed, alert the NMS with an SNMP trap. You can find a little more technical detail about RMON in the next chapter.

---

* Any operating system running an SNMP agent can implement Host Resources; it's not confined to agents running on Unix and Windows systems.

The Concept of Network Management

SNMP is really about network management. Network management is a discipline of its own, but before learning about the details of SNMP in Chapter 2, it's helpful to have an overview of network management itself.

What is network management? Network management is a general concept that employs the use of various tools, techniques, and systems to aid human beings in managing various devices, systems, or networks. Let's take SNMP out of the picture right now and look at a model for network management called *FCAPS*, or Fault Management, Configuration Management, Accounting Management, Performance Management, and Security Management. These conceptual areas were created by the International Organization for Standardization (ISO) to aid in the understanding of the major functions of network management systems. Let's briefly look at each of these now.

Fault Management

The goal of fault management is to detect, log, and notify users of systems or networks of problems. In many environments, downtime of any kind is not acceptable.

Fault management dictates that these steps for fault resolution be followed:

1. Isolate the problem by using tools to determine symptoms.
2. Resolve the problem.
3. Record the process that was used to detect and resolve the problem.

While step 3 is important, it is often not used. Neglecting step 3 has the unwanted effect of causing new engineers to follow steps 1 and 2 in the dark when they could have consulted a database of troubleshooting tips.

Configuration Management

The goal of configuration management is to monitor network and system configuration information so that the effects on network operation of various versions of hardware and software elements can be tracked and managed.

Any system may have a number of interesting and pertinent configuration parameters that engineers may be interested in capturing, including:

- Version of operating system, firmware, etc.
- Number of network interfaces and speeds, etc.
- Number of hard disks
- Number of CPUs
- Amount of RAM

This information generally is stored in a database of some kind. As configuration parameters change for systems, this database is updated. An added benefit to having this data store is that it can aid in problem resolution.

Accounting Management

The goal of accounting management is to ensure that computing and network resources are used fairly by all groups or individuals who access them. Through this form of regulation, network problems can be minimized since resources are divided based on capacities.

Performance Management

The goal of performance management is to measure and report on various aspects of network or system performance.

Let's look at the steps involved in performance management:

1. Performance data is gathered.
2. Baseline levels are established based on analysis of the data gathered.
3. Performance thresholds are established. When these thresholds are exceeded, it is indicative of a problem that requires attention.

One example of performance management is service monitoring. For example, an Internet service provider (ISP) may be interested in monitoring its email service response time. This includes sending emails via SMTP and getting email via POP3. See Chapter 11 for examples of how to do this.

Security Management

The goal of security management is twofold. First, we wish to control access to some resource, such as a network and its hosts. Second, we wish to help detect and prevent attacks that can compromise networks and hosts. Attacks against networks and hosts can lead to denial of service and, even worse, allow hackers to gain access to vital systems that contain accounting, payroll, and source code data.

Security management encompasses not only network security systems but also physical security. Physical security includes card access and video surveillance systems. The goal here is to ensure that only authorized individuals have physical access to vulnerable systems.

Today, network security management is accomplished through the use of various tools and systems designed specifically for this purpose. These include:

- Firewalls
- Intrusion Detection Systems (IDSs)

- Intrusion Prevention Systems (IPSs)
- Antivirus systems
- Policy management and enforcement systems

Most if not all of today's network security systems can integrate with network management systems via SNMP.

Applying the Concepts of Network Management

Being able to apply the concepts of network management is as important as learning how to use SNMP. This section of the chapter provides insights into some of the issues surrounding network management.

Business Case Requirements

The endeavor of network management involves solving a business problem through an implementation of some sort. A business case is developed to understand the impact of implementing some sort of task or function. It looks at how, for example, network administrators do their day-to-day jobs. The basic idea is to reduce costs and increase effectiveness. If the implementation doesn't save a company any money while providing more effective services, there is almost no need to implement a given solution.

Levels of Activity

Before applying management to a specific service or device, you must understand the four possible levels of activity and decide what is appropriate for that service or device:

Inactive
> No monitoring is being done, and, if you did receive an alarm in this area, you would ignore it.

Reactive
> No monitoring is being done; you react to a problem if it occurs.

Interactive
> You monitor components but must interactively troubleshoot them to eliminate side-effect alarms and isolate a root cause.

Proactive
> You monitor components, and the system provides a root-cause alarm for the problem at hand and initiates predefined automatic restoral processes where possible to minimize downtime.

Reporting of Trend Analysis

The ability to monitor a service or system proactively begins with trend analysis and reporting. Chapters 12 and 13 describe two tools that are capable of aiding in trend reporting. In general, the goal of trend analysis is to identify when systems, services, or networks are beginning to reach their maximum capacity, with enough lead time to do something about it before it becomes a real problem for end users. For example, you may discover a need to add more memory to your database server or upgrade to a newer version of some application server software that adds a performance boost. Doing so before it becomes a real problem can help your users avoid frustration and possibly keep you employed.

Response Time Reporting

If you are responsible for managing any sort of server (HTTP, SMTP, etc.), you know how frustrating it can be when users come knocking on your door to say that the web server is slow or that surfing the Internet is slow. Response time reporting measures how various aspects of your network (including systems) are performing with respect to responsiveness. Chapter 11 shows how to monitor services with SNMP.

Alarm Correlation

Alarm correlation deals with narrowing down many alerts and events into a single alert or several events that depict the real problem. Another name for this is root-cause analysis. The idea is simple, but it tends to be difficult in practice. For example, when a web server on your network goes down, and you are managing all devices between you and the server (including the switch the server is on and the router), you may get any number of alerts including ones for the server being down, the switch being down, or the router being down, depending on where the real failure is.

Let's say the router is the real issue (for example, an interface card died). You really only need to know that the router is down. Network management systems can often detect when some device or network is unreachable due to varying reasons. The key in this situation is to correlate the server, switch, and router down events into a single high-level event detailing that the router is down. This high-level event can be made up of all the entities and their alarms that are affected by the router being down, but you want to shield an operator from all of these until he is interested in looking at them. The real problem that needs to be addressed is the router's failure. Keeping this storm of alerts and alarms away from the operator helps with overall efficiency and improves the trouble resolution capabilities of the staff.

Clearing alarms is also important. For example, once the router is back up and running, presumably it's going to send an SNMP message that it has come back to life, or maybe a network management system will discover that it's back up and create an alarm to this effect. This notion of state transition, from bad to good, is common. It

---

helps operators know that something is indeed up and operational. It also helps with trending. If you see that a certain device is constantly unreliable, you may want to investigate why.

Trouble Resolution

The key to trouble resolution is knowing that what you are looking at is valuable and can help you resolve the problem. As such, alarms and alerts should aid an operator in resolving the problem. For example, when your router goes down, a cryptic message like "router down" is not helpful. If possible, alerts and alarms should provide the operator with enough detail so that she can effectively troubleshoot and resolve the problem.

Change Management

Change management deals with, well, managing change. In other words, you need to plan for both scheduled and emergency changes to your network. Not doing so can cause networks and systems to be unreliable at best and can upset the very people you work for at worst. The following sections provide a high-level overview of change management techniques. The following techniques are recommended by Cisco. See the end of this section for the URL to this paper and others on the topic of network management.

Planning for Change

Change planning is a process that identifies the risk level of a change and builds change planning requirements to ensure that the change is successful. The key steps for change planning are as follows:

- Assign all potential changes a risk level prior to scheduling the change.
- Document at least three risk levels with corresponding change planning requirements. Identify risk levels for software and hardware upgrades, topology changes, routing changes, configuration changes, and new deployments. Assign higher risk levels to nonstandard add, move, or change types of activity.
- The high-risk change process you document needs to include lab validation, vendor review, peer review, and detailed configuration and design documentation.
- Create solution templates for deployments affecting multiple sites. Include information about physical layout, logical design, configuration, software versions, acceptable hardware chassis and modules, and deployment guidelines.
- Document your network standards for configuration, software version, supported hardware, and DNS. Additionally, you may need to document things like device naming conventions, network design details, and services supported throughout the network.

Managing Change

Change management is a process that approves and schedules the change to ensure the correct level of notification with minimal user impact. The key steps for change management are as follows:

- Assign a change controller who can run change management review meetings, receive and review change requests, manage change process improvements, and act as a liaison for user groups.

- Hold periodic change review meetings with system administration, application development, network operations, and facilities groups as well as general users.

- Document change input requirements, including change owner, business impact, risk level, reason for change, success factors, backout plan, and testing requirements.

- Document change output requirements, including updates to DNS, network map, template, IP addressing, circuit management, and network management.

- Define a change approval process that verifies validation steps for higher-risk change.

- Hold postmortem meetings for unsuccessful changes to determine the root cause of change failure.

- Develop an emergency change procedure that ensures that an optimal solution is maintained or quickly restored.

High-Level Process Flow for Planned Change Management

The steps you'll need to follow during a network change are represented in Figure 1-2.* The following sections briefly discuss each box in the flow.

Scope

Scope is the who, what, where, and how for the change. In other words, you need to detail every possible impact point for the change, especially its impact on people.

Risk assessment

Everything you do to or on a network, when it comes to change, has an associated risk. The person requesting the change needs to establish the risk level for the change. It is best to experiment in a lab setting if you can before you go live with a change. This can help identify problems and aid in risk evaluation.

---

* Reprinted by permission from Cisco's "Change Management: Best Practices White Paper," Document ID 22852, *http://www.cisco.com/warp/public/126/chmgmt.shtml*.

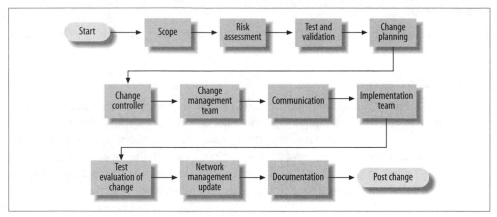

Figure 1-2. Process flow for planned change management

Test and validation

With any proposed change, you want to make sure you have all of your bases covered. Rigorous testing and validation can help with this. Depending upon the associated risk, various levels of validation may need to be performed. For example, if the change has the potential to impact a great many systems, you may wish to test the change in a lab setting. If the change doesn't work, you may also need to document backout procedures.

Change planning

For a change to be successful, you must plan for it. This includes requirements gathering, ordering software or hardware, creating documentation, and coordinating human resources.

Change controller

Basically, a change controller is a person who is responsible for coordinating all details of the change process.

Change management team

You should create a change management team that includes representation from network operations, server operations, application support, and user groups within your organization. The team should review all change requests and approve or deny each request based on completeness, readiness, business impact, business need, and any other conflicts.

 The change management team does not investigate the technical accuracy of the change; technical experts who better understand the scope and technical details should complete this phase of the change process.

Communication

Many organizations, even small ones, fail to communicate their intentions. Make sure you keep people who may be affected up-to-date on the status of the changes.

Implementation team

You should create an implementation team consisting of individuals with the technical expertise to expedite a change. The implementation team should also be involved in the planning phase to contribute to the development of the project checkpoints, testing, backout criteria, and backout time constraints. This team should guarantee adherence to organizational standards, update DNS and network management tools, and maintain and enhance the tool set used to test and validate the change.

Test evaluation of change

Once the change has been made, you should begin testing it. Hopefully you already have a set of tests documented that can be used to validate the change. Make sure you allow yourself enough time to perform the tests. If you must back out the change, make sure you test this scenario, too.

Network management update

Be sure to update any systems like network management tools, device configurations, network configurations, DNS entries, etc., to reflect the change. This may include removing devices from the management systems that no longer exist, changing the SNMP trap destination your routers use, and so forth.

Documentation

Always update documentation that becomes obsolete or incorrect when a change occurs. Documentation may end up being used by a network administrator to solve a problem. If it isn't up-to-date, he cannot be effective in his duties.

High-Level Process Flow for Emergency Change Management

In the real world, change often comes at 2 a.m. when some critical system is down. But with some effort, your on-the-fly change doesn't have to cause heartburn for you and others in the company. Documentation means a lot more during emergency changes than it does in planned changes. In the heat of the moment, things can get lost or forgotten. Accurately recording the steps and procedures taken will ensure that troubles can be resolved in the future. If you have to, take short notes while the process is unfolding. Later, write it up formally; the important thing is to remember to do it.

Figure 1-3 shows the process flow for emergency changes.[*]

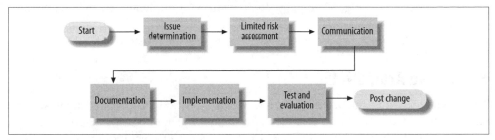

Figure 1-3. Emergency change process

Issue determination

Knowing what needs to change is generally not difficult to determine in an emergency. The key is to take one step at a time and not rush things. Yes, time is critical, but rushing can cause mistakes to be made or even bring about a resolution that doesn't fix the real issue. In some cases, the outage can be unnecessarily prolonged.

Limited risk assessment

Risk assessment is performed by the network administrator on duty, with advice from other support personnel. Her experience will guide her in how the change is classified from a risk perspective. For example, changing the version of software on a router has much greater impact than changing a device's IP address.

Communication and documentation

If at all possible, users should be notified of the change. In an emergency situation, it isn't always possible. Also, be sure to communicate any changes with the change manager. The manager will wish to add to any metrics he keeps on changes. Ensuring that documentation is up-to-date cannot be stressed enough. Having out-of-date documentation means that the staff cannot accurately troubleshoot network and systems problems in the future.

Implementation

If the process of assigning risk and documentation occurs prior to the implementation, the actual implementation should be straightforward. Beware of the potential for change coming from multiple support personnel without their knowing about each other's changes. This scenario can lead to increased potential downtime and misinterpretation of the problem.

---

[*] Reprinted by permission from Cisco's "Change Management: Best Practices White Paper," Document ID 22852, *http://www.cisco.com/warp/public/126/chmgmt.shtml*.

Test and evaluation

Be sure to test the change. Generally, the person who implemented the change also tests and evaluates it. The primary goal is to determine whether the change had the desired effect. If it did not, the emergency change process must be restarted.

Before and After SNMP

Now that you have an idea about what SNMP and network management are, we should look at the before and after pictures for implementing these concepts and technologies. Let's say that you have a network of 100 machines running various operating systems. Several machines are fileservers, a few others are print servers, another is running software that verifies credit card transactions (presumably from a web-based ordering system), and the rest are personal workstations. In addition, various switches and routers help keep the network going. A T1 circuit connects the company to the Internet, and a private connection runs to the credit card verification system.

What happens when one of the fileservers crashes? If it happens in the middle of the workweek, the people using it will notice and the appropriate administrator will be called to fix it. But what if it happens after everyone has gone home, including the administrators, or over the weekend?

What if the private connection to the credit card verification system goes down at 10 p.m. on Friday and isn't restored until Monday morning? If the problem was faulty hardware and it could have been fixed by swapping out a card or replacing a router, thousands of dollars in web site sales could have been lost for no reason. Likewise, if the T1 circuit to the Internet goes down, it could adversely affect the amount of sales generated by individuals accessing your web site and placing orders.

These are obviously serious problems—problems that can conceivably affect the survival of your business. This is where SNMP comes in. Instead of waiting for someone to notice that something is wrong and locate the person responsible for fixing the problem (which may not happen until Monday morning, if the problem occurs over the weekend), SNMP allows you to monitor your network constantly, even when you're not there. For example, it will notice if the number of bad packets coming through one of your router's interfaces is gradually increasing, suggesting that the router is about to fail. You can arrange to be notified automatically when failure seems imminent so that you can fix the router before it actually breaks. You can also arrange to be notified if the credit card processor appears to get hung—you may even be able to fix it from home. And if nothing goes wrong, you can return to the office on Monday morning knowing there won't be any surprises.

There might not be quite as much glory in fixing problems before they occur, but you and your management will rest more easily. We can't tell you how to translate that into a higher salary—sometimes it's better to be the guy who rushes in and fixes things in the middle of a crisis, rather than the guy who makes sure the crisis never occurs. But SNMP does enable you to keep logs that prove your network is running reliably and show when you took action to avert an impending crisis.

Staffing Considerations

Implementing a network management system can mean adding more staff to handle the increased load of maintaining and operating such an environment. At the same time, adding this type of monitoring should, in most cases, reduce the workload of your system administration staff. You will need:

- Staff to maintain the management station. This includes ensuring the management station is configured to properly handle events from SNMP-capable devices.
- Staff to maintain the SNMP-capable devices. This includes making sure that workstations and servers can communicate with the management station.
- Staff to watch and fix the network. This group is usually called a Network Operations Center (NOC) and is staffed 24/7. An alternative to 24/7 staffing is to implement rotating pager duty, where one person is on call at all times, but not necessarily present in the office. Pager duty works only in smaller networked environments in which a network outage can wait for someone to drive into the office and fix the problem.

There is no way to predetermine how many staff members you will need to maintain a management system. The size of the staff will vary depending on the size and complexity of the network you're managing. Some of the larger Internet backbone providers have 70 or more people in their NOCs and others have only one.

Getting More Information

Getting a handle on SNMP may seem like a daunting task. The RFCs provide the official definition of the protocol, but they were written for software developers, not network administrators, so it can be difficult to extract the information you need from them. Fortunately, many online resources are available. A good place to look is the SimpleWeb (*http://www.simpleweb.org*). SNMP Link (*http://www.SNMPLink.org*) is another good site for information. *The Simple Times*, an online publication devoted to SNMP and network management, is also useful. You can find all the issues ever published* at *http://www.simple-times.org*. SNMP Research is a commercial SNMP vendor. Aside from selling advanced SNMP solutions, its web site contains a good amount of free information about SNMP. The company's web site is *http://www.snmp.com*.

---

* At this writing, the current issue is quite old, published in December 2002.

Another great resource is Usenet news. The newsgroup most people frequent is *comp.dcom.net-management*. Another good newsgroup is *comp.protocols.snmp*. Groups such as these promote a community of information sharing, allowing seasoned professionals to interact with individuals who are not as knowledgeable about SNMP or network management. Google has a great interface for searching Usenet news group at *http://groups.google.com*.

There is an SNMP FAQ, available in two parts at *http://www.faqs.org/faqs/snmp-faq/part1/* and *http://www.faqs.org/faqs/snmp-faq/part2/*.

Cisco has some very good papers on network management, including "Network Management Basics" (*http://www.cisco.com/univercd/cc/td/doc/cisintwk/ito_doc/nmbasics.htm*) and "Change Management," from which Figure 1-2 and Figure 1-3 were drawn. Also, Douglas W. Stevenson's article, "Network Management: What It Is and What It Isn't," available at *http://www.itmweb.com/essay516.htm*, provides important background material for all students of network management.

With that background in mind, Chapter 2 delves much deeper into the details of SNMP.

## CHAPTER 2

SNMPv1 and SNMPv2

In this chapter, we start to look at SNMP in detail, specifically covering features found in SNMPv1 and SNMPv2 (we'll allude to SNMPv3 occasionally but we describe its features in detail in Chapter 3). By the time you finish this chapter, you should understand how SNMP sends and receives information, what SNMP communities are, and how to read MIB files. We'll also look in more detail at the three MIBs that were introduced in Chapter 1, namely MIB-II, Host Resources, and RMON.

SNMP and UDP

SNMP uses the User Datagram Protocol (UDP) as the transport protocol for passing data between managers and agents. UDP, defined in RFC 768, was chosen over the Transmission Control Protocol (TCP) because it is connectionless; that is, no end-to-end connection is made between the agent and the NMS when datagrams (packets) are sent back and forth. This aspect of UDP makes it unreliable since there is no acknowledgment of lost datagrams at the protocol level. It's up to the SNMP application to determine if datagrams are lost and retransmit them if it so desires. This is typically accomplished with a simple timeout. The NMS sends a UDP request to an agent and waits for a response. The length of time the NMS waits depends on how it's configured. If the timeout is reached and the NMS has not heard back from the agent, it assumes the packet was lost and retransmits the request. The number of times the NMS retransmits packets is also configurable.

At least as far as regular information requests are concerned, the unreliable nature of UDP isn't a real problem. At worst, the management station issues a request and never receives a response. For traps, the situation is somewhat different. If an agent sends a trap and the trap never arrives, the NMS has no way of knowing that it was ever sent. The agent doesn't even know that it needs to resend the trap because the NMS is not required to send a response back to the agent acknowledging receipt of the trap.

The upside to the unreliable nature of UDP is that it requires low overhead, so the impact on your network's performance is reduced. SNMP has been implemented over TCP, but this is more for special-case situations in which someone is developing an agent for a proprietary piece of equipment. In a heavily congested and managed network, SNMP over TCP is a bad idea. It's also worth realizing that TCP isn't magic and that SNMP is designed for working with networks that are in trouble—if your network never failed, you wouldn't need to monitor it. When a network is failing, a protocol that tries to get the data through but gives up if it can't is almost certainly a better design choice than a protocol that floods the network with retransmissions in its attempt to achieve reliability.

SNMP uses UDP port 161 for sending and receiving requests and port 162 for receiving traps from managed devices. Every device that implements SNMP must use these port numbers as the defaults, but some vendors allow you to change the default ports in the agent's configuration. If you change these defaults, the NMS must be made aware of the changes so that it can query the device on the correct ports.

Figure 2-1 shows the TCP/IP protocol suite, which is the basis for all TCP/IP communication. Today, any device that wishes to communicate on the Internet (e.g., Windows systems, Unix servers, Cisco routers, etc.) must use this protocol suite. This model is often referred to as a *protocol stack* since each layer uses the information from the layer directly below it and provides a service to the layer directly above it.

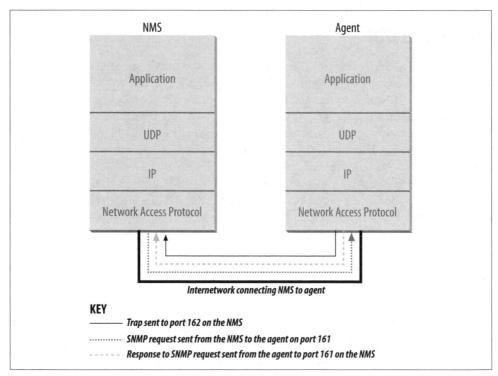

Figure 2-1. TCP/IP communication model and SNMP

When either an NMS or an agent wishes to perform an SNMP function (e.g., a request or trap), the following events occur in the protocol stack:

Application
> First, the actual SNMP application (NMS or agent) decides what it's going to do. For example, it can send an SNMP request to an agent, send a response to an SNMP request (this would be sent from the agent), or send a trap to an NMS. The application layer provides services to an end user, such as an operator requesting status information for a port on an Ethernet switch.

UDP
> The next layer, UDP, allows two hosts to communicate with one another. The UDP header contains, among other things, the destination port of the device to which it's sending the request or trap. The destination port will either be 161 (query) or 162 (trap).

IP
> The IP layer tries to deliver the SNMP packet to its intended destination, as specified by its IP address.

Media Access Control (MAC)
> The final event that must occur for an SNMP packet to reach its destination is for it to be handed off to the physical network, where it can be routed to its final destination. The MAC layer is composed of the actual hardware and device drivers that put your data onto a physical piece of wire, such as an Ethernet card. The MAC layer is also responsible for receiving packets from the physical network and sending them back up the protocol stack so that they can be processed by the application layer (SNMP, in this case).

This interaction between SNMP applications and the network is not unlike that between two pen pals. Both have messages that need to be sent back and forth to one another. Let's say you decide to write your pen pal a letter asking if she would like to visit you over the summer. By deciding to send the invitation, you've acted as the SNMP application. Filling out the envelope with your pen pal's address is equivalent to the function of the UDP layer, which records the packet's destination port in the UDP header; in this case, it's your pen pal's address. Placing a stamp on the envelope and putting it in the mailbox for the mailman to pick up is equivalent to the IP layer's function. The final act occurs when the mailman comes to your house and picks up the letter. From here, the letter will be routed to its final destination, your pen pal's mailbox. The MAC layer of a computer network is equivalent to the mail trucks and airplanes that carry your letter on its way. When your pen pal receives the letter, she will go through the same process to send you a reply.

SNMP Communities

SNMPv1 and SNMPv2 use the notion of communities to establish trust between managers and agents. An agent is configured with three community names: read-only, read-write, and trap. The community names are essentially passwords; there's no real difference between a community string and the password you use to access your account on the computer. The three community strings control different kinds of activities. As its name implies, the read-only community string lets you read data values but doesn't let you modify the data. For example, it allows you to read the number of packets that have been transferred through the ports on your router but doesn't let you reset the counters. The read-write community string is allowed to read and modify data values; with the read-write community string, you can read the counters, reset their values, and even reset the interfaces or do other things that change the router's configuration. Finally, the trap community string allows you to receive traps (asynchronous notifications) from the agent.

Most vendors ship their equipment with default community strings, typically *public* for the read-only community string and *private* for the read-write community string. It's important to change these defaults before your device goes live on the network. (You may get tired of hearing this because we say it many times, but it's absolutely essential.) When setting up an SNMP agent, you will want to configure its trap destination, which is the address to which it will send any traps it generates. In addition, since SNMP community strings are sent in clear text, you can configure an agent to send an SNMP authentication-failure trap when someone attempts to query your device with an incorrect community string. Among other things, authentication-failure traps can be very useful in determining when an intruder might be trying to gain access to your network.

Because community strings are essentially passwords, you should use the same rules for selecting them as you use for Unix or Windows user passwords: no dictionary words, spouse names, etc. An alphanumeric string with mixed upper- and lowercase letters is generally a good idea. As mentioned earlier, the problem with SNMP's authentication is that community strings are sent in plain text, which makes it easy for people to intercept them and use them against you. SNMPv3 addresses this by allowing, among other things, secure authentication and communication between SNMP devices.

There are ways to reduce your risk of attack. IP firewalls or filters minimize the chance that someone can harm any managed device on your network by attacking it through SNMP. You can configure your firewall to allow UDP traffic from only a list of known hosts. For example, you can allow UDP traffic on port 161 (SNMP requests) into your network only if it comes from one of your NMSs. The same goes for traps; you can configure your router so that it allows UDP traffic on port 162 to your NMS only if it originates from one of the hosts you are monitoring. Firewalls aren't 100% effective, but simple precautions such as these do a lot to reduce your risk.

It is important to realize that if someone has read-write access to any of your SNMP devices, he can gain control of those devices by using SNMP (for example, he can set router interfaces, switch ports down, or even modify your routing tables). One way to protect your community strings is to use a Virtual Private Network (VPN) to make sure your network traffic is encrypted. Another way is to change your community strings often. Changing community strings isn't difficult for a small network, but for a network that spans city blocks or more and has dozens (or hundreds or thousands) of managed hosts, changing community strings can be a problem. An easy solution is to write a simple Perl script that uses SNMP to change the community strings on your devices.

The Structure of Management Information

So far, we have used the term *management information* to refer to the operational parameters of SNMP-capable devices. However, we've said very little about what management information actually contains or how it is represented. The first step toward understanding what kind of information a device can provide is to understand how this data is represented within the context of SNMP. The Structure of Management Information Version 1 (SMIv1, RFC 1155) does exactly that: it defines precisely how managed objects* are named and specifies their associated datatypes. The Structure of Management Information Version 2 (SMIv2, RFC 2578) provides enhancements for SNMPv2. We'll start by discussing SMIv1, and we will discuss SMIv2 in the next section.†

The definition of managed objects can be broken down into three attributes:

Name
> The name, or object identifier (OID), uniquely defines a managed object. Names commonly appear in two forms: numeric and "human readable." In either case, the names are long and inconvenient. In SNMP applications, a lot of work goes into helping you navigate through the namespace conveniently.

Type and syntax
> A managed object's datatype is defined using a subset of Abstract Syntax Notation One (ASN.1). ASN.1 is a way of specifying how data is represented and transmitted between managers and agents, within the context of SNMP. The nice thing about ASN.1 is that the notation is machine independent. This means that a PC running Windows 2000 can communicate with a Sun SPARC machine and not have to worry about things such as byte ordering.

---

* For the remainder of this book, *management information* will be referred to as *managed objects*. Similarly, a single piece of management information (such as the operational status of a router interface) will be known as a *managed object*.

† It's worth noting that the version of SMI being used does not relate to the version of SNMP being used.

Encoding

A single instance of a managed object is encoded into a string of octets using the Basic Encoding Rules (BER). BER defines how the objects are encoded and decoded so that they can be transmitted over a transport medium such as Ethernet.

Naming OIDs

Managed objects are organized into a treelike hierarchy. This structure is the basis for SNMP's naming scheme. An object ID is made up of a series of integers based on the nodes in the tree, separated by dots (.). Although there's a human-readable form that's friendlier than a string of numbers, this form is nothing more than a series of names separated by dots, each representing a node of the tree. You can use the numbers themselves, or you can use a sequence of names that represent the numbers. Figure 2-2 shows the top few levels of this tree. (We have intentionally left out some branches of the tree that don't concern us here.)

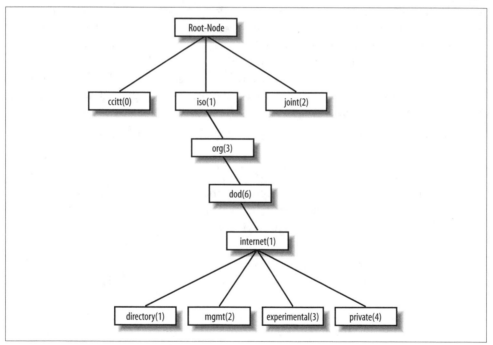

Figure 2-2. SMI object tree

In the object tree, the node at the top of the tree is called the root, anything with children is called a subtree,* and anything without children is called a leaf node. For

---

* Note that the term *branch* is sometimes used interchangeably with *subtree*.

example, Figure 2-2's root, the starting point for the tree, is called Root-Node. Its subtree is made up of *ccitt(0)*, *iso(1)*, and *joint(2)*. In this illustration, *iso(1)* is the only node that contains a subtree; the other two nodes are both leaf nodes. *ccitt(0)* and *joint(2)* do not pertain to SNMP, so they will not be discussed in this book.*

For the remainder of this book, we will focus on the *iso(1).org(3).dod(6).internet(1)* subtree, which is represented in OID form as *1.3.6.1* or as *iso.org.dod.internet*. Each managed object has a numerical OID and an associated textual name. The dotted-decimal notation is how a managed object is represented internally within an agent; the textual name, like an IP domain name, saves humans from having to remember long, tedious strings of integers.

The *directory* branch currently is not used. The *management* branch, or *mgmt*, defines a standard set of Internet management objects. The *experimental* branch is reserved for testing and research purposes. Objects under the *private* branch are defined unilaterally, which means that individuals and organizations are responsible for defining the objects under this branch. Here is the definition of the *internet* subtree, as well as all four of its subtrees:

```
internet      OBJECT IDENTIFIER ::= { iso org(3) dod(6) 1 }
directory     OBJECT IDENTIFIER ::= { internet 1 }
mgmt          OBJECT IDENTIFIER ::= { internet 2 }
experimental  OBJECT IDENTIFIER ::= { internet 3 }
private       OBJECT IDENTIFIER ::= { internet 4 }
```

The first line declares *internet* as the OID *1.3.6.1*, which is defined (the ::= is a definition operator) as a subtree of *iso.org.dod*, or *1.3.6*. The last four declarations are similar, but they define the other branches that belong to *internet*. For the *directory* branch, the notation { internet 1 } tells us that it is part of the *internet* subtree and that its OID is *1.3.6.1.1*. The OID for *mgmt* is *1.3.6.1.2*, and so on.

There is currently one branch under the *private* subtree. It's used to give hardware and software vendors the ability to define their own private objects for any type of hardware or software they want managed by SNMP. Its SMI definition is:

```
enterprises   OBJECT IDENTIFIER ::= { private 1 }
```

The Internet Assigned Numbers Authority (IANA) currently manages all the private enterprise number assignments for individuals, institutions, organizations, companies, etc.† A list of all the current private enterprise numbers can be obtained from *http://www.iana.org/assignments/enterprise-numbers*. As an example, Cisco Systems's private enterprise number is 9, so the base OID for its private object space is defined as *iso.org.dod.internet.private.enterprises.cisco*, or *1.3.6.1.4.1.9*. Cisco is free to do as

---

* The *ccitt* subtree is administered by the International Telegraph and Telephone Consultative Committee (CCITT); the *joint* subtree is administered jointly by the ISO and CCITT. As we said, neither branch has anything to do with SNMP.

† The term *private enterprise* will be used throughout this book to refer to the *enterprises* branch.

it wishes with this private branch. It's typical for companies such as Cisco that manufacture networking equipment to define their own private enterprise objects. This allows for a richer set of management information than can be gathered from the standard set of managed objects defined under the *mgmt* branch.

Companies aren't the only ones who can register their own private enterprise numbers. Anyone can do so, and it's free. The web-based form for registering private enterprise numbers can be found at *http://www.isi.edu/cgi-bin/iana/enterprise.pl*. After you fill in the form, which asks for information such as your organization's name and contact information, your request should be approved in about a week. Why would you want to register your own number? When you become more conversant in SNMP, you'll find things you want to monitor that aren't covered by any MIB, public or private. With your own enterprise number, you can create your own private MIB that allows you to monitor exactly what you want. You'll need to be somewhat clever in extending your agents so that they can look up the information you want, but it's very doable.

Defining OIDs

The SYNTAX attribute provides for definitions of managed objects through a subset of ASN.1. SMIv1 defines several datatypes that are paramount to the management of networks and network devices. It's important to keep in mind that these datatypes are simply a way to define what kind of information a managed object can hold. The types we'll be discussing are similar to those that you'd find in a computer programming language like C. Table 2-1 lists the supported datatypes for SMIv1.

Table 2-1. SMIv1 datatypes

Datatype	Description
INTEGER	A 32-bit number often used to specify enumerated types within the context of a single managed object. For example, the operational status of a router interface can be *up*, *down*, or *testing*. With enumerated types, 1 would represent up, 2 down, and 3 testing. The value zero (0) must not be used as an enumerated type, according to RFC 1155.
OCTET STRING	A string of zero or more octets (more commonly known as bytes) generally used to represent text strings, but also sometimes used to represent physical addresses.
Counter	A 32-bit number with minimum value 0 and maximum value 2^{32} - 1 (4,294,967,295). When the maximum value is reached, it wraps back to zero and starts over. It's primarily used to track information such as the number of octets sent and received on an interface or the number of errors and discards seen on an interface. A Counter is monotonically increasing, in that its values should never decrease during normal operation. When an agent is rebooted, all Counter values should be set to zero. Deltas are used to determine if anything useful can be said for successive queries of Counter values. A delta is computed by querying a Counter at least twice in a row and taking the difference between the query results over some time interval.
OBJECT IDENTIFIER	A dotted-decimal string that represents a managed object within the object tree. For example, *1.3.6.1.4.1.9* represents Cisco Systems' private enterprise OID.

Table 2-1. SMIv1 datatypes (continued)

Datatype	Description
NULL	Not currently used in SNMP.
SEQUENCE	Defines lists that contain zero or more other ASN.1 datatypes.
SEQUENCE OF	Defines a managed object that is made up of a SEQUENCE of ASN.1 types.
IpAddress	Represents a 32-bit IPv4 address. Neither SMIv1 nor SMIv2 discusses 128-bit IPv6 addresses.
NetworkAddress	Same as the IpAddress type, but can represent different network address types.
Gauge	A 32-bit number with minimum value 0 and maximum value $2^{32}-1$ (4,294,967,295). Unlike a Counter, a Gauge can increase and decrease at will, but it can never exceed its maximum value. The interface speed on a router is measured with a Gauge.
TimeTicks	A 32-bit number with minimum value 0 and maximum value $2^{32}-1$ (4,294,967,295). TimeTicks measures time in hundredths of a second. Uptime on a device is measured using this datatype.
Opaque	Allows any other ASN.1 encoding to be stuffed into an OCTET STRING.

The goal of all these object types is to define managed objects. In Chapter 1, we said that a MIB is a logical grouping of managed objects as they pertain to a specific management task, vendor, etc. The MIB can be thought of as a specification that defines the managed objects a vendor or device supports. Cisco, for instance, has literally hundreds of MIBs defined for its vast product line. For example, its Catalyst device has a separate MIB from its 7000 series router. Both devices have different characteristics that require different management capabilities. Vendor-specific MIBs are typically distributed as human-readable text files that can be inspected (or even modified) with a standard text editor such as *vi*.

 Most modern NMS products maintain a compact form of all the MIBs that define the set of managed objects for all the different types of devices they're responsible for managing. NMS administrators typically compile a vendor's MIB into a format the NMS can use. Once a MIB has been loaded or compiled, administrators can refer to managed objects using either the numeric or human-readable object ID.

It's important to know how to read and understand MIB files. The following example is a stripped-down version of MIB-II (anything preceded by -- is a comment):

```
RFC1213-MIB DEFINITIONS ::= BEGIN

    IMPORTS
            mgmt, NetworkAddress, IpAddress, Counter, Gauge,
            TimeTicks
                    FROM RFC1155-SMI
            OBJECT-TYPE
                    FROM RFC-1212;

    mib-2      OBJECT IDENTIFIER ::= { mgmt 1 }
```

```
-- groups in MIB-II

        system      OBJECT IDENTIFIER ::= { mib-2 1 }
        interfaces  OBJECT IDENTIFIER ::= { mib-2 2 }
        at          OBJECT IDENTIFIER ::= { mib-2 3 }
        ip          OBJECT IDENTIFIER ::= { mib-2 4 }
        icmp        OBJECT IDENTIFIER ::= { mib-2 5 }
        tcp         OBJECT IDENTIFIER ::= { mib-2 6 }
        udp         OBJECT IDENTIFIER ::= { mib-2 7 }
        egp         OBJECT IDENTIFIER ::= { mib-2 8 }
        transmission OBJECT IDENTIFIER ::= { mib-2 10 }
        snmp        OBJECT IDENTIFIER ::= { mib-2 11 }

    -- the Interfaces table

    -- The Interfaces table contains information on the entity's
    -- interfaces. Each interface is thought of as being
    -- attached to a 'subnetwork.' Note that this term should
    -- not be confused with 'subnet,' which refers to an
    -- addressing-partitioning scheme used in the Internet
    -- suite of protocols.

    ifTable OBJECT-TYPE
        SYNTAX  SEQUENCE OF IfEntry
        ACCESS  not-accessible
        STATUS  mandatory
        DESCRIPTION
            "A list of interface entries. The number of entries is
             given by the value of ifNumber."
        ::= { interfaces 2 }

    ifEntry OBJECT-TYPE
        SYNTAX  IfEntry
        ACCESS  not-accessible
        STATUS  mandatory
        DESCRIPTION
            "An interface entry containing objects at the subnetwork
             layer and below for a particular interface."
        INDEX   { ifIndex }
        ::= { ifTable 1 }

    IfEntry ::=
        SEQUENCE {
            ifIndex
                INTEGER,
            ifDescr
                DisplayString,
            ifType
                INTEGER,
            ifMtu
                INTEGER,
            ifSpeed
                Gauge,
```

```
            ifPhysAddress
                PhysAddress,
            ifAdminStatus
                INTEGER,
            ifOperStatus
                INTEGER,
            ifLastChange
                TimeTicks,
            ifInOctets
                Counter,
            ifInUcastPkts
                Counter,
            ifInNUcastPkts
                Counter,
            ifInDiscards
                Counter,
            ifInErrors
                Counter,
            ifInUnknownProtos
                Counter,
            ifOutOctets
                Counter,
            ifOutUcastPkts
                Counter,
            ifOutNUcastPkts
                Counter,
            ifOutDiscards
                Counter,
            ifOutErrors
                Counter,
            ifOutQLen
                Gauge,
            ifSpecific
                OBJECT IDENTIFIER
        }

    ifIndex OBJECT-TYPE
        SYNTAX  INTEGER
        ACCESS  read-only
        STATUS  mandatory
        DESCRIPTION
            "A unique value for each interface. Its value ranges
            between 1 and the value of ifNumber. The value for
            each interface must remain constant at least from one
            reinitialization of the entity's network management
            system to the next reinitialization."

        ::= { ifEntry 1 }

    ifDescr OBJECT-TYPE
        SYNTAX  DisplayString (SIZE (0..255))
        ACCESS  read-only
        STATUS  mandatory
```

```
DESCRIPTION
    "A textual string containing information about the
    interface. This string should include the name of
    the manufacturer, the product name, and the version
    of the hardware interface."
::= { ifEntry 2 }

END
```

The first line of this file defines the name of the MIB—in this case, `RFC1213-MIB`. (RFC 1213 is the RFC that defines MIB-II; many of the MIBs we refer to are defined by RFCs.) The format of this definition is always the same. The `IMPORTS` section of the MIB is sometimes referred to as the *linkage* section. It allows you to import datatypes and OIDs from other MIB files using the `IMPORTS` clause. This MIB imports the following items from `RFC1155-SMI` (RFC 1155 defines SMIv1, which we discussed earlier in this chapter):

- `mgmt`
- `NetworkAddress`
- `IpAddress`
- `Counter`
- `Gauge`
- `TimeTicks`

It also imports `OBJECT-TYPE` from RFC 1212, the *Concise MIB Definition*, which defines how MIB files are written. Each group of items imported using the `IMPORTS` clause uses a `FROM` clause to define the MIB file from which the objects are taken.

The OIDs that will be used throughout the remainder of the MIB follow the linkage section. This group of lines sets up the top level of the *mib-2* subtree. *mib-2* is defined as *mgmt* followed by *.1*. We saw earlier that *mgmt* was equivalent to *1.3.6.1.2*. Therefore, *mib-2* is equivalent to *1.3.6.1.2.1*. Likewise, the *interfaces* group under *mib-2* is defined as { `mib-2 2` }, or *1.3.6.1.2.1.2*.

After the OIDs are defined, we get to the actual object definitions. Every object definition has the following format:

```
<name> OBJECT-TYPE
    SYNTAX <datatype>
    ACCESS <either read-only, read-write, write-only, or not-accessible>
    STATUS <either mandatory, optional, or obsolete>
    DESCRIPTION
        "Textual description describing this particular managed object."
    ::= { <Unique OID that defines this object> }
```

The first managed object in our subset of the MIB-II definition is *ifTable*, which represents a table of network interfaces on a managed device (note that object names are defined using mixed case, with the first letter in lowercase). Here is its definition using ASN.1 notation:

```
ifTable OBJECT-TYPE
    SYNTAX  SEQUENCE OF IfEntry
    ACCESS  not-accessible
    STATUS  mandatory
    DESCRIPTION
        "A list of interface entries. The number of entries is given by
         the value of ifNumber."
    ::= { interfaces 2 }
```

The SYNTAX of *ifTable* is SEQUENCE OF IfEntry. This means that *ifTable* is a table containing the columns defined in *IfEntry*. The object is not-accessible, which means that there is no way to query an agent for this object's value. Its status is mandatory, which means an agent must implement this object in order to comply with the MIB-II specification. The DESCRIPTION describes exactly what this object is. The unique OID is *1.3.6.1.2.1.2.2*, or *iso.org.dod.internet.mgmt.mib-2.interfaces.2*.

Let's now look at the SEQUENCE definition from the MIB file earlier in this section, which is used with the SEQUENCE OF type in the *ifTable* definition:

```
IfEntry ::=
    SEQUENCE {
        ifIndex
            INTEGER,
        ifDescr
            DisplayString,
        ifType
            INTEGER,
        ifMtu
            INTEGER,
        .
        .
        .
        ifSpecific
            OBJECT IDENTIFIER
    }
```

Note that the name of the sequence (*IfEntry*) is mixed case, but the first letter is capitalized, unlike the object definition for *ifTable*. This is how a sequence name is defined. A sequence is simply a list of columnar objects and their SMI datatypes, which defines a conceptual table. In this case, we expect to find variables defined by *ifIndex*, *ifDescr*, *ifType*, etc. This table can contain any number of rows; it's up to the agent to manage the rows that reside in the table. It is possible for an NMS to add rows to a table. This operation is covered in "The set Operation," later in this chapter.

Now that we have *IfEntry* to specify what we'll find in any row of the table, we can look back to the definition of *ifEntry* (the actual rows of the table) itself:

```
ifEntry OBJECT-TYPE
    SYNTAX  IfEntry
    ACCESS  not-accessible
    STATUS  mandatory
```

```
DESCRIPTION
    "An interface entry containing objects at the subnetwork layer
     and below for a particular interface."
INDEX   { ifIndex }
::= { ifTable 1 }
```

ifEntry defines a particular row in the *ifTable*. Its definition is almost identical to that of *ifTable*, except we have introduced a new clause, INDEX. The index is a unique key used to define a single row in the *ifTable*. It's up to the agent to make sure the index is unique within the context of the table. If a router has six interfaces, the *ifTable* will have six rows in it. *ifEntry*'s OID is *1.3.6.1.2.1.2.2.1*, or *iso.org.dod.internet.mgmt.mib-2.interfaces.ifTable.ifEntry*. The index for *ifEntry* is *ifIndex*, which is defined as:

```
ifIndex OBJECT-TYPE
    SYNTAX   INTEGER
    ACCESS   read-only
    STATUS   mandatory
    DESCRIPTION
        "A unique value for each interface. Its value ranges between
         1 and the value of ifNumber. The value for each interface
         must remain constant at least from one reinitialization of the
         entity's network management system to the next reinitialization."
    ::= { ifEntry 1 }
```

The *ifIndex* object is read-only, which means we can see its value, but we cannot change it. The final object our MIB defines is *ifDescr*, which is a textual description for the interface represented by that particular row in the *ifTable*. Our MIB example ends with the END clause, which marks the end of the MIB. In the actual MIB-II files, each object listed in the *IfEntry* sequence has its own object definition. In this version of the MIB we list only two of them, in the interest of conserving space.

Extensions to the SMI in Version 2

SMIv2 extends the SMI object tree by adding the *snmpV2* branch to the *internet* subtree, adding several new datatypes and making a number of other changes. Figure 2-3 shows how the *snmpV2* objects fit into the bigger picture; the OID for this new branch is *1.3.6.1.6.3.1.1*, or *iso.org.dod.internet.snmpV2.snmpModules.snmpMIB.snmpMIBObjects*. SMIv2 also defines some new datatypes, which are summarized in Table 2-2.

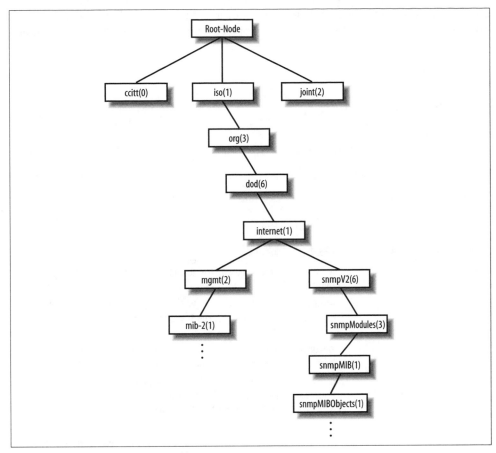

Figure 2-3. SMIv2 registration tree for SNMPv2

Table 2-2. New datatypes for SMIv2

Datatype	Description
Integer32	Same as an INTEGER.
Counter32	Same as a Counter.
Gauge32	Same as a Gauge.
Unsigned32	Represents decimal values in the range of 0 to 2^{32} - 1, inclusive.
Counter64	Similar to Counter32, but its maximum value is 18,446,744,073,709,551,615. Counter64 is ideal for situations in which a Counter32 may wrap back to 0 in a short amount of time.
BITS	An enumeration of nonnegative named bits.

The definition of an object in SMIv2 has changed slightly from SMIv1. There are some new optional fields, giving you more control over how an object is accessed, allowing you to augment a table by adding more columns, and letting you give better descriptions. Here's the syntax of an object definition for SMIv2. The changed parts are in bold:

```
<name> OBJECT-TYPE
    SYNTAX <datatype>
    UnitsParts <Optional, see below>
    MAX-ACCESS <See below>
    STATUS <See below>
    DESCRIPTION
        "Textual description describing this particular managed object."
    AUGMENTS { <name of table> }
    ::= { <Unique OID that defines this object> }
```

Table 2-3 briefly describes the object definition enhancements made in SMIv2.

Table 2-3. SMIv2 object definition enhancements

Object definition enhancement	Description
UnitsParts	A textual description of the units (i.e., seconds, milliseconds, etc.) used to represent the object.
MAX-ACCESS	An OBJECT-TYPE's ACCESS can be MAX-ACCESS in SNMPv2. The valid options for MAX-ACCESS are read-only, read-write, read-create, not-accessible, and accessible-for-notify.
STATUS	This clause has been extended to allow the current, obsolete, and deprecated keywords. current in SNMPv2 is the same as mandatory in an SNMPv1 MIB.
AUGMENTS	In some cases, it is useful to add a column to an existing table. The AUGMENTS clause allows you to extend a table by adding one or more columns, represented by some other object. This clause requires the name of the table the object will augment.

SMIv2 defines a new trap type called NOTIFICATION-TYPE, which we will discuss in "SNMP Notification" later in this chapter. SMIv2 also introduces new textual conventions that allow managed objects to be created in more abstract ways. RFC 2579 defines the textual conventions used by SNMPv2, which are listed in Table 2-4.

Table 2-4. Textual conventions for SMIv2

Textual convention	Description
DisplayString	A string of NVT ASCII characters. A DisplayString can be no more than 255 characters in length.
PhysAddress	A media- or physical-level address, represented as an OCTET STRING.
MacAddress	Defines the media-access address for IEEE 802 (the standard for LANs) in canonical[a] order. (In everyday language, this means the Ethernet address.) This address is represented as six octets.
TruthValue	Defines both true and false Boolean values.
TestAndIncr	Used to keep two management stations from modifying the same managed object at the same time.
AutonomousType	An OID used to define a subtree with additional MIB-related definitions.
VariablePointer	A pointer to a particular object instance, such as *ifDescr* for interface 3. In this case, the VariablePointer would be the OID *ifDescr.3*.

Table 2-4. Textual conventions for SMIv2 (continued)

Textual convention	Description
RowPointer	A pointer to a row in a table. For example, *ifIndex.3* points to the third row in *ifTable*.
RowStatus	Used to manage the creation and deletion of rows in a table, since SNMP has no way of doing this via the protocol itself. RowStatus can keep track of the state of a row in a table as well as receive commands for creation and deletion of rows. This textual convention is designed to promote table integrity when more than one manager is updating rows. The following enumerated types define the commands and state variables: active(1), notInService(2), notReady(3), createAndGo(4), createAndWait(5), and anddestroy(6).
TimeStamp	Measures the amount of time elapsed between the device's system uptime and some event or occurrence.
TimeInterval	Measures a period of time in hundredths of a second. TimeInterval can take any integer value from 0–2147483647.
DateAndTime	An OCTET STRING used to represent date and time information.
StorageType	Defines the type of memory an agent uses. The possible values are other(1), volatile(2), nonVolatile(3), permanent(4), and readOnly(5).
TDomain	Denotes a kind of transport service.
TAddress	Denotes the transport service address. TAddress is defined to be from 1–255 octets in length.

a *Canonical order means that the address should be represented with the least-significant bit first.*

A Closer Look at MIB-II

MIB-II is a very important management group because every device that supports SNMP must also support MIB-II. Therefore, we will use objects from MIB-II in our examples throughout this book. We won't go into detail about every object in the MIB; we'll simply define the subtrees. The section of *RFC1213-MIB* that defines the base OIDs for the *mib-2* subtree looks like this:

```
mib-2        OBJECT IDENTIFIER ::= { mgmt 1 }
system       OBJECT IDENTIFIER ::= { mib-2 1 }
interfaces   OBJECT IDENTIFIER ::= { mib-2 2 }
at           OBJECT IDENTIFIER ::= { mib-2 3 }
ip           OBJECT IDENTIFIER ::= { mib-2 4 }
icmp         OBJECT IDENTIFIER ::= { mib-2 5 }
tcp          OBJECT IDENTIFIER ::= { mib-2 6 }
udp          OBJECT IDENTIFIER ::= { mib-2 7 }
egp          OBJECT IDENTIFIER ::= { mib-2 8 }
transmission OBJECT IDENTIFIER ::= { mib-2 10 }
snmp         OBJECT IDENTIFIER ::= { mib-2 11 }
```

mib-2 is defined as *iso.org.dod.internet.mgmt.1*, or *1.3.6.1.2.1*. From here, we can see that the *system* group is mib-2.1, or *1.3.6.1.2.1.1*, and so on. Figure 2-4 shows the MIB-II subtree of the *mgmt* branch.

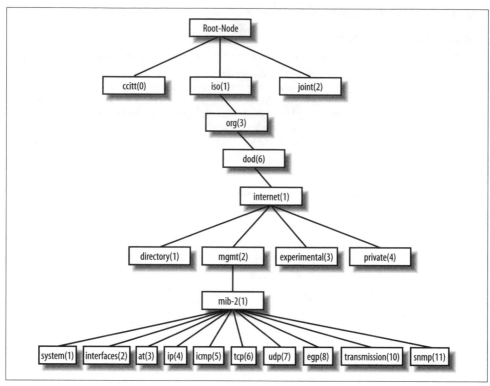

Figure 2-4. MIB-II subtree

Table 2-5 briefly describes each management group defined in MIB-II. We don't go into great detail about each group since you can pull down RFC 1213 and read the MIB yourself.

Table 2-5. Brief description of the MIB-II groups

Subtree name	OID	Description
system	*1.3.6.1.2.1.1*	Defines a list of objects that pertain to system operation, such as the system uptime, system contact, and system name.
interfaces	*1.3.6.1.2.1.2*	Keeps track of the status of each interface on a managed entity. The *interfaces* group monitors which interfaces are up or down and tracks such things as octets sent and received, errors and discards, etc.
at	*1.3.6.1.2.1.3*	The address translation (*at*) group is deprecated and is provided only for backward compatibility.
ip	*1.3.6.1.2.1.4*	Keeps track of many aspects of IP, including IP routing.
icmp	*1.3.6.1.2.1.5*	Tracks things such as ICMP errors, discards, etc.
tcp	*1.3.6.1.2.1.6*	Tracks, among other things, the state of the TCP connection (e.g., *closed*, *listen*, *synSent*, etc.).
udp	*1.3.6.1.2.1.7*	Tracks UDP statistics, datagrams in and out, etc.

Table 2-5. Brief description of the MIB-II groups (continued)

Subtree name	OID	Description
egp	1.3.6.1.2.1.8	Tracks various statistics about the Exterior Gateway Protocol (EGP) and keeps an EGP neighbor table.
transmission	1.3.6.1.2.1.10	No objects are currently defined for this group, but other media-specific MIBs are defined using this subtree.
snmp	1.3.6.1.2.1.11	Measures the performance of the underlying SNMP implementation on the managed entity and tracks things such as the number of SNMP packets sent and received.

SNMP Operations

We've discussed how SNMP organizes information, but we've left out how we actually go about gathering management information. Now we're going to take a look under the hood to see how SNMP does its thing.

The Protocol Data Unit (PDU) is the message format that managers and agents use to send and receive information. Each of the following SNMP operations has a standard PDU format:

- get
- getnext
- getbulk (SNMPv2 and SNMPv3)
- set
- getresponse
- trap
- notification (SNMPv2 and SNMPv3)
- inform (SNMPv2 and SNMPv3)
- report (SNMPv2 and SNMPv3)

In addition to running actual command-line tools, we will also provide packet dumps of the SNMP operations. For those of you who like looking at packet dumps, this will give you an inside look at what the packet structure is for each command. The packet dumps themselves were taken using the command-line version of Ethereal (*http://www.ethereal.com*). Let's take a look at each operation now. All of the get and set operations were captured with the following command:

```
$ /usr/sbin/tethereal -i lo -x -V -F libpcap -f "port 161"
```

Traps and notifications were captured with this command:

```
$ /usr/sbin/tethereal -i lo -x -V -F libpcap -f "port 162"
```

The get Operation

The get request is initiated by the NMS, which sends the request to the agent. The agent receives the request and processes it to the best of its ability. Some devices that are under heavy load, such as routers, may not be able to respond to the request and will have to drop it. If the agent is successful in gathering the requested information, it sends a getresponse back to the NMS, where it is processed. This process is illustrated in Figure 2-5.

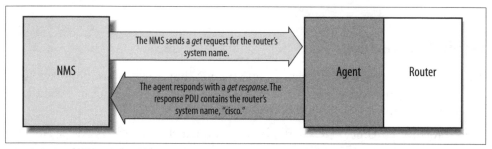

Figure 2-5. get request sequence

How did the agent know what the NMS was looking for? One of the items in the get request is a variable binding. A *variable binding*, or *varbind*, is a list of MIB objects that allows a request's recipient to see what the originator wants to know. Variable bindings can be thought of as *OID=value* pairs that make it easy for the originator (the NMS, in this case) to pick out the information it needs when the recipient fills the request and sends back a response. Let's look at this operation in action:

```
$ snmpget -v 1 -c public cisco.ora.com .1.3.6.1.2.1.1.6.0
system.sysLocation.0 = ""
```

> All the Unix commands presented in this chapter come from the Net-SNMP agent package (formerly the UCD-SNMP project), a freely available Unix and Windows agent. You can download the package from *http://net-snmp.sourceforge.net*. Appendix C summarizes the commands in this package.

Several things are going on in this example. First, we're running a command on a Unix host. The command is called snmpget. Its main job is to facilitate the gathering of management data using a get request. We've given it three arguments on the command line: the name of the device we would like to query (*cisco.ora.com*), the read-only community string (*public*), and the OID we would like gathered (*.1.3.6.1.2.1.1.6.0*). If we look back at Table 2-5, we see that *1.3.6.1.2.1.1.1* is the *system* group, but there are two more integers at the end of the OID: *.6* and *.0*. The *.6* is actually the MIB variable that we wish to query; its human-readable name is *sysLocation*. In this case, we would like to see what the system location is set to on the Cisco router. As you can see by the response (system.sysLocation.0 = ""), the system location on this router currently is not set to anything. Also note that the response from snmpget is in variable binding format, *OID=value*.

There is one more thing to look at. Why does the MIB variable have a *.0* tacked on the end? In SNMP, MIB objects are defined by the convention *x.y*, where *x* is the actual OID of the managed object (in our example, *1.3.6.1.2.1.1.6*) and *y* is the instance identifier. For *scalar objects* (that is, objects that aren't defined as a row in a table), *y* is always 0. In the case of a table, the instance identifier lets you select a specific row of the table; 1 is the first row, 2 is the second row, etc. For example, consider the *ifTable* object we looked at earlier in this chapter. When looking up values in *ifTable*, we would use a nonzero instance identifier to select a particular row in the table (in this case, a particular network interface).

 Graphical NMS applications, which include most commercial packages, do not use command-line programs to retrieve management information. We use these commands to give you a feel for how the retrieval commands work and what they typically return. The information a graphical NMS retrieves and its retrieval process are identical to these command-line programs; the NMS just lets you formulate queries and displays the results using a more convenient GUI.

The get command is useful for retrieving a single MIB object at a time. Trying to manage anything in this manner can be a waste of time, though. This is where the getnext command comes in. It allows you to retrieve more than one object from a device, over a period of time.

Now let's look at an SNMP packet as seen with Ethereal's command-line tool tethereal. Given the following command:

```
$ snmpget -v 1 -c public 127.0.0.1 sysContact.0
```

we get the following two datagram traces from tethereal:

```
Frame 1 (85 bytes on wire, 85 bytes captured)
    Arrival Time: Sep 20, 2004 13:46:15.041115000
    Time delta from previous packet: 0.000000000 seconds
    Time since reference or first frame: 0.000000000 seconds
    Frame Number: 1
    Packet Length: 85 bytes
    Capture Length: 85 bytes
Ethernet II, Src: 00:00:00:00:00:00, Dst: 00:00:00:00:00:00
    Destination: 00:00:00:00:00:00 (00:00:00_00:00:00)
    Source: 00:00:00:00:00:00 (00:00:00_00:00:00)
    Type: IP (0x0800)
Internet Protocol, Src Addr: 127.0.0.1 (127.0.0.1), Dst Addr: 127.0.0.1 (127.0.0.1)
    Version: 4
    Header length: 20 bytes
    Differentiated Services Field: 0x00 (DSCP 0x00: Default; ECN: 0x00)
        0000 00.. = Differentiated Services Codepoint: Default (0x00)
        .... ..0. = ECN-Capable Transport (ECT): 0
        .... ...0 = ECN-CE: 0
```

```
        Total Length: 71
        Identification: 0x0000 (0)
        Flags: 0x04
            .1.. = Don't fragment: Set
            ..0. = More fragments: Not set
        Fragment offset: 0
        Time to live: 0
        Protocol: UDP (0x11)
        Header checksum: 0x7ca4 (correct)
        Source: 127.0.0.1 (127.0.0.1)
        Destination: 127.0.0.1 (127.0.0.1)
    User Datagram Protocol, Src Port: 34066 (34066), Dst Port: snmp (161)
        Source port: 34066 (34066)
        Destination port: snmp (161)
        Length: 51
        Checksum: 0xfe46 (incorrect, should be 0xbbea)
    Simple Network Management Protocol
        Version: 1 (0)
        Community: public
        PDU type: GET (0)
        Request Id: 0x20a71b4c
        Error Status: NO ERROR (0)
        Error Index: 0
        Object identifier 1: 1.3.6.1.2.1.1.4.0 (SNMPv2-MIB::sysContact.0)
        Value: NULL

0000   00 00 00 00 00 00 00 00 00 00 00 00 08 00 45 00   ..............E.
0010   00 47 00 00 40 00 00 11 7c a4 7f 00 00 01 7f 00   .G..@...|.......
0020   00 01 85 12 00 a1 00 33 fe 46 30 29 02 01 00 04   .......3.F0)....
0030   06 70 75 62 6c 69 63 a0 1c 02 04 20 a7 1b 4c 02   .public.... ..L.
0040   01 00 02 01 00 30 0e 30 0c 06 08 2b 06 01 02 01   .....0.0...+....
0050   01 04 00 05 00                                    .....

Frame 2 (144 bytes on wire, 144 bytes captured)
    Arrival Time: Sep 20, 2004 13:46:15.071891000
    Time delta from previous packet: 0.030776000 seconds
    Time since reference or first frame: 0.030776000 seconds
    Frame Number: 2
    Packet Length: 144 bytes
    Capture Length: 144 bytes
Ethernet II, Src: 00:00:00:00:00:00, Dst: 00:00:00:00:00:00
    Destination: 00:00:00:00:00:00 (00:00:00_00:00:00)
    Source: 00:00:00:00:00:00 (00:00:00_00:00:00)
    Type: IP (0x0800)
Internet Protocol, Src Addr: 127.0.0.1 (127.0.0.1), Dst Addr: 127.0.0.1 (127.0.0.1)
    Version: 4
    Header length: 20 bytes
    Differentiated Services Field: 0x00 (DSCP 0x00: Default; ECN: 0x00)
        0000 00.. = Differentiated Services Codepoint: Default (0x00)
        .... ..0. = ECN-Capable Transport (ECT): 0
        .... ...0 = ECN-CE: 0
    Total Length: 130
    Identification: 0x031d (797)
    Flags: 0x04
```

```
          .1.. = Don't fragment: Set
          ..0. = More fragments: Not set
      Fragment offset: 0
      Time to live: 0
      Protocol: UDP (0x11)
      Header checksum: 0x794c (correct)
      Source: 127.0.0.1 (127.0.0.1)
      Destination: 127.0.0.1 (127.0.0.1)
  User Datagram Protocol, Src Port: snmp (161), Dst Port: 34066 (34066)
      Source port: snmp (161)
      Destination port: 34066 (34066)
      Length: 110
      Checksum: 0xfe81 (incorrect, should be 0xdf61)
  Simple Network Management Protocol
      Version: 1 (0)
      Community: public
      PDU type: RESPONSE (2)
      Request Id: 0x20a71b4c
      Error Status: NO ERROR (0)
      Error Index: 0
      Object identifier 1: 1.3.6.1.2.1.1.4.0 (SNMPv2-MIB::sysContact.0)
      Value: STRING: Root <root@localhost> (configure /etc/snmp/snmp.local.conf)

0000  00 00 00 00 00 00 00 00 00 00 00 00 08 00 45 00   .............E.
0010  00 82 03 1d 40 00 00 11 79 4c 7f 00 00 01 7f 00   ....@...yL......
0020  00 01 00 a1 85 12 00 6e fe 81 30 64 02 01 00 04   .......n..0d....
0030  06 70 75 62 6c 69 63 a2 57 02 04 20 a7 1b 4c 02   .public.W.. ..L.
0040  01 00 02 01 00 30 49 30 47 06 08 2b 06 01 02 01   .....0I0G..+....
0050  01 04 00 04 3b 52 6f 6f 74 20 3c 72 6f 6f 74 40   ....;Root <root@
0060  6c 6f 63 61 6c 68 6f 73 74 3e 20 28 63 6f 6e 66   localhost> (conf
0070  69 67 75 72 65 20 2f 65 74 63 2f 73 6e 6d 70 2f   igure /etc/snmp/
0080  73 6e 6d 70 2e 6c 6f 63 61 6c 2e 63 6f 6e 66 29   snmp.local.conf)
```

There are two frames, each labeled appropriately. Frame 1 is initiated by the client. Frame 2 is the agent's response. Ethereal is nice in that it tells us the version of SNMP in use, and the error code (defined later in this chapter in Table 2-6 and Table 2-7). Giving the following command:

```
$ snmpget -v 2c -c public 127.0.0.1 sysContact.0
```

we see the following output from tethereal:

```
Frame 1 (85 bytes on wire, 85 bytes captured)
    Arrival Time: Sep 20, 2004 13:46:26.129733000
    Time delta from previous packet: 0.000000000 seconds
    Time since reference or first frame: 0.000000000 seconds
    Frame Number: 1
    Packet Length: 85 bytes
    Capture Length: 85 bytes
Ethernet II, Src: 00:00:00:00:00:00, Dst: 00:00:00:00:00:00
    Destination: 00:00:00:00:00:00 (00:00:00_00:00:00)
    Source: 00:00:00:00:00:00 (00:00:00_00:00:00)
    Type: IP (0x0800)
Internet Protocol, Src Addr: 127.0.0.1 (127.0.0.1), Dst Addr: 127.0.0.1 (127.0.0.1)
```

```
    Version: 4
    Header length: 20 bytes
    Differentiated Services Field: 0x00 (DSCP 0x00: Default; ECN: 0x00)
        0000 00.. = Differentiated Services Codepoint: Default (0x00)
        .... ..0. = ECN-Capable Transport (ECT): 0
        .... ...0 = ECN-CE: 0
    Total Length: 71
    Identification: 0x0000 (0)
    Flags: 0x04
        .1.. = Don't fragment: Set
        ..0. = More fragments: Not set
    Fragment offset: 0
    Time to live: 0
    Protocol: UDP (0x11)
    Header checksum: 0x7ca4 (correct)
    Source: 127.0.0.1 (127.0.0.1)
    Destination: 127.0.0.1 (127.0.0.1)
User Datagram Protocol, Src Port: 34066 (34066), Dst Port: snmp (161)
    Source port: 34066 (34066)
    Destination port: snmp (161)
    Length: 51
    Checksum: 0xfe46 (incorrect, should be 0xbb8f)
Simple Network Management Protocol
    Version: 2C (1)
    Community: public
    PDU type: GET (0)
    Request Id: 0x175f7f93
    Error Status: NO ERROR (0)
    Error Index: 0
    Object identifier 1: 1.3.6.1.2.1.1.4.0 (SNMPv2-MIB::sysContact.0)
    Value: NULL


0000  00 00 00 00 00 00 00 00 00 00 00 00 08 00 45 00   ..............E.
0010  00 47 00 00 40 00 00 11 7c a4 7f 00 00 01 7f 00   .G..@...|.......
0020  00 01 85 12 00 a1 00 33 fe 46 30 29 02 01 01 04   .......3.F0)....
0030  06 70 75 62 6c 69 63 a0 1c 02 04 17 5f 7f 93 02   .public....._...
0040  01 00 02 01 00 30 0e 30 0c 06 08 2b 06 01 02 01   .....0.0...+....
0050  01 04 00 05 00                                     .....


Frame 2 (144 bytes on wire, 144 bytes captured)
    Arrival Time: Sep 20, 2004 13:46:26.129926000
    Time delta from previous packet: 0.000193000 seconds
    Time since reference or first frame: 0.000193000 seconds
    Frame Number: 2
    Packet Length: 144 bytes
    Capture Length: 144 bytes
Ethernet II, Src: 00:00:00:00:00:00, Dst: 00:00:00:00:00:00
    Destination: 00:00:00:00:00:00 (00:00:00_00:00:00)
    Source: 00:00:00:00:00:00 (00:00:00_00:00:00)
    Type: IP (0x0800)
Internet Protocol, Src Addr: 127.0.0.1 (127.0.0.1), Dst Addr: 127.0.0.1 (127.0.0.1)
    Version: 4
    Header length: 20 bytes
    Differentiated Services Field: 0x00 (DSCP 0x00: Default; ECN: 0x00)
```

```
        0000 00.. = Differentiated Services Codepoint: Default (0x00)
        .... ..0. = ECN-Capable Transport (ECT): 0
        .... ...0 = ECN-CE: 0
    Total Length: 130
    Identification: 0x031e (798)
    Flags: 0x04
        .1.. = Don't fragment: Set
        ..0. = More fragments: Not set
    Fragment offset: 0
    Time to live: 0
    Protocol: UDP (0x11)
    Header checksum: 0x794b (correct)
    Source: 127.0.0.1 (127.0.0.1)
    Destination: 127.0.0.1 (127.0.0.1)
User Datagram Protocol, Src Port: snmp (161), Dst Port: 34066 (34066)
    Source port: snmp (161)
    Destination port: 34066 (34066)
    Length: 110
    Checksum: 0xfe81 (incorrect, should be 0xdf06)
Simple Network Management Protocol
    Version: 2C (1)
    Community: public
    PDU type: RESPONSE (2)
    Request Id: 0x175f7f93
    Error Status: NO ERROR (0)
    Error Index: 0
    Object identifier 1: 1.3.6.1.2.1.1.4.0 (SNMPv2-MIB::sysContact.0)
    Value: STRING: Root <root@localhost> (configure /etc/snmp/snmp.local.conf)

0000  00 00 00 00 00 00 00 00 00 00 00 00 08 00 45 00   ..............E.
0010  00 82 03 1e 40 00 00 11 79 4b 7f 00 00 01 7f 00   ....@...yK......
0020  00 01 00 a1 85 12 00 6e fe 81 30 64 02 01 01 04   .......n..0d....
0030  06 70 75 62 6c 69 63 a2 57 02 04 17 5f 7f 93 02   .public.W..._...
0040  01 00 02 01 00 30 49 30 47 06 08 2b 06 01 02 01   .....0I0G..+....
0050  01 04 00 04 3b 52 6f 6f 74 20 3c 72 6f 6f 74 40   ....;Root <root@
0060  6c 6f 63 61 6c 68 6f 73 74 3e 20 28 63 6f 6e 66   localhost> (conf
0070  69 67 75 72 65 20 2f 65 74 63 2f 73 6e 6d 70 2f   igure /etc/snmp/
0080  73 6e 6d 70 2e 6c 6f 63 61 6c 2e 63 6f 6e 66 29   snmp.local.conf)
```

The datagram traces look similar to the SNMPv1 traces. Again, we see the version of SNMP in use, namely 2C.

The getnext Operation

The getnext operation lets you issue a sequence of commands to retrieve a group of values from a MIB. In other words, for each MIB object we want to retrieve, a separate getnext request and getresponse are generated. The getnext command traverses a subtree in lexicographic order. Since an OID is a sequence of integers, it's easy for an agent to start at the root of its SMI object tree and work its way down until it finds the OID it is looking for. This form of searching is called depth-first. When the NMS receives a response from the agent for the getnext command it just issued, it issues another getnext command. It keeps doing this until the agent returns an error, signifying that the end of the MIB has been reached and there are no more objects left to get.

If we look at another example, we can see this behavior in action. This time we'll use a command called snmpwalk. This command simply facilitates the getnext procedure for us. It's invoked just like the snmpget command, except this time we specify which branch to start at (in this case, the *system* group):

```
$ snmpwalk -v 1 -c public cisco.ora.com system
system.sysDescr.0 = "Cisco IOS Software, C2600 Software (C2600-IPBASE-M), Version 12.
3(8)T3, RELEASE SOFTWARE (fc1)
Technical Support: http://www.cisco.com/techsupport
Copyright (c) 1986-2004 by Cisco Systems, Inc.
Compiled Tue 20-Jul-04 17:03 by eaarmas"
system.sysObjectID.0 = OID: enterprises.9.1.19
system.sysUpTime.0 = Timeticks: (27210723) 3 days, 3:35:07.23
system.sysContact.0 = ""
system.sysName.0 = "cisco.ora.com"
system.sysLocation.0 = ""
system.sysServices.0 = 6
```

The getnext sequence returns seven MIB variables. Each object is part of the *system* group as it's defined in RFC 1213. We see a system object ID, the amount of time the system has been up, the contact person, etc.

Given that you've just looked up some object, how does getnext figure out which object to look up next? getnext is based on the concept of the lexicographic ordering of the MIB's object tree. This order is made much simpler because every node in the tree is assigned a number. To understand what this means, let's start at the root of the tree and walk down to the *system* node.

To get to the *system* group (OID *1.3.6.1.2.1.1*), we start at the root of the object tree and work our way down. Figure 2-6 shows the logical progression from the root of the tree all the way to the *system* group. At each node in the tree, we visit the lowest numbered branch. Thus, when we're at the root node, we start by visiting *ccitt*. This node has no nodes underneath it, so we move to the *iso* node. Since *iso* does have a child, we move to that node, *org*. The process continues until we reach the *system* node. Since each branch is made up of ascending integers (*ccitt(0) iso(1) join(2)*, for example), the agent has no problem traversing this tree structure all the way down to the *system(1)* group. If we were to continue this walk, we'd proceed to *system.1* (*system.sysLocation*), *system.2*, and the other objects in the *system* group. Next, we'd go to *interfaces(2)*, and so on.

Now let's look at what Ethereal sees. Given the following command:

```
$ snmpwalk -v 1 -c public 127.0.0.1 system
```

we get the following output from tethereal:

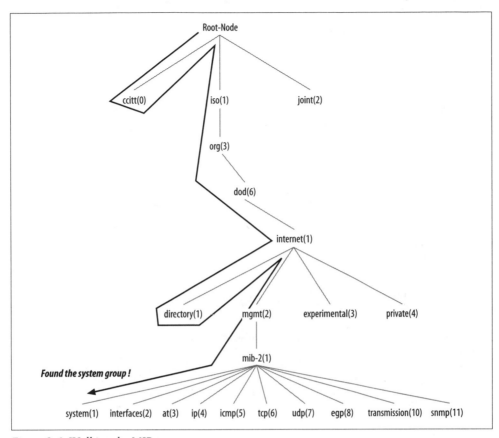

Figure 2-6. Walking the MIB tree

```
Frame 1 (82 bytes on wire, 82 bytes captured)
    Arrival Time: Sep 20, 2004 13:46:53.598461000
    Time delta from previous packet: 0.000000000 seconds
    Time since reference or first frame: 0.000000000 seconds
    Frame Number: 1
    Packet Length: 82 bytes
    Capture Length: 82 bytes
Ethernet II, Src: 00:00:00:00:00:00, Dst: 00:00:00:00:00:00
    Destination: 00:00:00:00:00:00 (00:00:00_00:00:00)
    Source: 00:00:00:00:00:00 (00:00:00_00:00:00)
    Type: IP (0x0800)
Internet Protocol, Src Addr: 10.0.1.253 (10.0.1.253), Dst Addr: 10.0.1.253 (10.0.1.
253)
    Version: 4
    Header length: 20 bytes
    Differentiated Services Field: 0x00 (DSCP 0x00: Default; ECN: 0x00)
        0000 00.. = Differentiated Services Codepoint: Default (0x00)
        .... ..0. = ECN-Capable Transport (ECT): 0
        .... ...0 = ECN-CE: 0
    Total Length: 68
    Identification: 0x0000 (0)
```

```
        Flags: 0x04
            .1.. = Don't fragment: Set
            ..0. = More fragments: Not set
        Fragment offset: 0
        Time to live: 0
        Protocol: UDP (0x11)
        Header checksum: 0x62b0 (correct)
        Source: 10.0.1.253 (10.0.1.253)
        Destination: 10.0.1.253 (10.0.1.253)
    User Datagram Protocol, Src Port: 34069 (34069), Dst Port: snmp (161)
        Source port: 34069 (34069)
        Destination port: snmp (161)
        Length: 48
        Checksum: 0x183b (incorrect, should be 0xa7f4)
    Simple Network Management Protocol
        Version: 1 (0)
        Community: public
        PDU type: GET-NEXT (1)
        Request Id: 0x00ec4809
        Error Status: NO ERROR (0)
        Error Index: 0
        Object identifier 1: 1.3.6.1.2.1 (SNMPv2-SMI::mib-2)
        Value: NULL


0000  00 00 00 00 00 00 00 00 00 00 00 00 08 00 45 00   ..............E.
0010  00 44 00 00 40 00 00 11 62 b0 0a 00 01 fd 0a 00   .D..@...b.......
0020  01 fd 85 15 00 a1 00 30 18 3b 30 26 02 01 00 04   .......0.;0&....
0030  06 70 75 62 6c 69 63 a1 19 02 04 00 ec 48 09 02   .public......H..
0040  01 00 02 01 00 30 0b 30 09 06 05 2b 06 01 02 01   .....0.0...+....
0050  05 00                                             ..


Frame 2 (160 bytes on wire, 160 bytes captured)
    Arrival Time: Sep 20, 2004 13:46:53.598662000
    Time delta from previous packet: 0.000201000 seconds
    Time since reference or first frame: 0.000201000 seconds
    Frame Number: 2
    Packet Length: 160 bytes
    Capture Length: 160 bytes
Ethernet II, Src: 00:00:00:00:00:00, Dst: 00:00:00:00:00:00
    Destination: 00:00:00:00:00:00 (00:00:00_00:00:00)
    Source: 00:00:00:00:00:00 (00:00:00_00:00:00)
    Type: IP (0x0800)
Internet Protocol, Src Addr: 10.0.1.253 (10.0.1.253), Dst Addr: 10.0.1.253 (10.0.1.
253)
    Version: 4
    Header length: 20 bytes
    Differentiated Services Field: 0x00 (DSCP 0x00: Default; ECN: 0x00)
        0000 00.. = Differentiated Services Codepoint: Default (0x00)
        .... ..0. = ECN-Capable Transport (ECT): 0
        .... ...0 = ECN-CE: 0
    Total Length: 146
    Identification: 0x031f (799)
    Flags: 0x04
        .1.. = Don't fragment: Set
```

```
            ..0. = More fragments: Not set
        Fragment offset: 0
        Time to live: 0
        Protocol: UDP (0x11)
        Header checksum: 0x5f43 (correct)
        Source: 10.0.1.253 (10.0.1.253)
        Destination: 10.0.1.253 (10.0.1.253)
    User Datagram Protocol, Src Port: snmp (161), Dst Port: 34069 (34069)
        Source port: snmp (161)
        Destination port: 34069 (34069)
        Length: 126
        Checksum: 0x1889 (incorrect, should be 0x3f0a)
    Simple Network Management Protocol
        Version: 1 (0)
        Community: public
        PDU type: RESPONSE (2)
        Request Id: 0x00ec4809
        Error Status: NO ERROR (0)
        Error Index: 0
        Object identifier 1: 1.3.6.1.2.1.1.1.0 (SNMPv2-MIB::sysDescr.0)
        Value: STRING: Linux mailworks.guarded.net 2.4.21-4.EL #1 Fri Oct 3 18:13:58 EDT
    2003 i686

    0000  00 00 00 00 00 00 00 00 00 00 00 00 08 00 45 00   ..............E.
    0010  00 92 03 1f 40 00 00 11 5f 43 0a 00 01 fd 0a 00   ....@..._C......
    0020  01 fd 00 a1 85 15 00 7e 18 89 30 74 02 01 00 04   .......~..0t....
    0030  06 70 75 62 6c 69 63 a2 67 02 04 00 ec 48 09 02   .public.g....H..
    0040  01 00 02 01 00 30 59 30 57 06 08 2b 06 01 02 01   .....0Y0W..+....
    0050  01 01 00 04 4b 4c 69 6e 75 78 20 6d 61 69 6c 77   ....KLinux mailw
    0060  6f 72 6b 73 2e 67 75 61 72 64 65 64 2e 6e 65 74   orks.guarded.net
    0070  20 32 2e 34 2e 32 31 2d 34 2e 45 4c 20 23 31 20    2.4.21-4.EL #1
    0080  46 72 69 20 4f 63 74 20 33 20 31 38 3a 31 33 3a   Fri Oct 3 18:13:
    0090  35 38 20 45 44 54 20 32 30 30 33 20 69 36 38 36   58 EDT 2003 i686

    Frame 3 (85 bytes on wire, 85 bytes captured)
        Arrival Time: Sep 20, 2004 13:46:53.682655000
        Time delta from previous packet: 0.083993000 seconds
        Time since reference or first frame: 0.084194000 seconds
        Frame Number: 3
        Packet Length: 85 bytes
        Capture Length: 85 bytes
    Ethernet II, Src: 00:00:00:00:00:00, Dst: 00:00:00:00:00:00
        Destination: 00:00:00:00:00:00 (00:00:00_00:00:00)
        Source: 00:00:00:00:00:00 (00:00:00_00:00:00)
        Type: IP (0x0800)
    Internet Protocol, Src Addr: 10.0.1.253 (10.0.1.253), Dst Addr: 10.0.1.253 (10.0.1.
    253)
        Version: 4
        Header length: 20 bytes
        Differentiated Services Field: 0x00 (DSCP 0x00: Default; ECN: 0x00)
            0000 00.. = Differentiated Services Codepoint: Default (0x00)
            .... ..0. = ECN-Capable Transport (ECT): 0
            .... ...0 = ECN-CE: 0
        Total Length: 71
```

```
        Identification: 0x0001 (1)
        Flags: 0x04
            .1.. = Don't fragment: Set
            ..0. = More fragments: Not set
        Fragment offset: 0
        Time to live: 0
        Protocol: UDP (0x11)
        Header checksum: 0x62ac (correct)
        Source: 10.0.1.253 (10.0.1.253)
        Destination: 10.0.1.253 (10.0.1.253)
User Datagram Protocol, Src Port: 34069 (34069), Dst Port: snmp (161)
        Source port: 34069 (34069)
        Destination port: snmp (161)
        Length: 51
        Checksum: 0x183e (incorrect, should be 0x9ee5)
Simple Network Management Protocol
        Version: 1 (0)
        Community: public
        PDU type: GET-NEXT (1)
        Request Id: 0x00ec480a
        Error Status: NO ERROR (0)
        Error Index: 0
        Object identifier 1: 1.3.6.1.2.1.1.1.0 (SNMPv2-MIB::sysDescr.0)
        Value: NULL


0000   00 00 00 00 00 00 00 00 00 00 00 00 08 00 45 00    ..............E.
0010   00 47 00 01 40 00 00 11 62 ac 0a 00 01 fd 0a 00    .G..@...b.......
0020   01 fd 85 15 00 a1 00 33 18 3e 30 29 02 01 00 04    .......3.>0)....
0030   06 70 75 62 6c 69 63 a1 1c 02 04 00 ec 48 0a 02    .public......H..
0040   01 00 02 01 00 30 0e 30 0c 06 08 2b 06 01 02 01    .....0.0...+....
0050   01 01 00 05 00                                      .....

Frame 4 (95 bytes on wire, 95 bytes captured)
        Arrival Time: Sep 20, 2004 13:46:53.682855000
        Time delta from previous packet: 0.000200000 seconds
        Time since reference or first frame: 0.084394000 seconds
        Frame Number: 4
        Packet Length: 95 bytes
        Capture Length: 95 bytes
Ethernet II, Src: 00:00:00:00:00:00, Dst: 00:00:00:00:00:00
        Destination: 00:00:00:00:00:00 (00:00:00_00:00:00)
        Source: 00:00:00:00:00:00 (00:00:00_00:00:00)
        Type: IP (0x0800)
Internet Protocol, Src Addr: 10.0.1.253 (10.0.1.253), Dst Addr: 10.0.1.253 (10.0.1.
253)
        Version: 4
        Header length: 20 bytes
        Differentiated Services Field: 0x00 (DSCP 0x00: Default; ECN: 0x00)
            0000 00.. = Differentiated Services Codepoint: Default (0x00)
            .... ..0. = ECN-Capable Transport (ECT): 0
            .... ...0 = ECN-CE: 0
        Total Length: 81
        Identification: 0x0320 (800)
        Flags: 0x04
```

```
              .1.. = Don't fragment: Set
              ..0. = More fragments: Not set
        Fragment offset: 0
        Time to live: 0
        Protocol: UDP (0x11)
        Header checksum: 0x5f83 (correct)
        Source: 10.0.1.253 (10.0.1.253)
        Destination: 10.0.1.253 (10.0.1.253)
    User Datagram Protocol, Src Port: snmp (161), Dst Port: 34069 (34069)
        Source port: snmp (161)
        Destination port: 34069 (34069)
        Length: 61
        Checksum: 0x1848 (incorrect, should be 0xa08c)
    Simple Network Management Protocol
        Version: 1 (0)
        Community: public
        PDU type: RESPONSE (2)
        Request Id: 0x00ec480a
        Error Status: NO ERROR (0)
        Error Index: 0
        Object identifier 1: 1.3.6.1.2.1.1.2.0 (SNMPv2-MIB::sysObjectID.0)
        Value: OID: SNMPv2-SMI::enterprises.8072.3.2.10

    0000  00 00 00 00 00 00 00 00 00 00 00 00 08 00 45 00   ..............E.
    0010  00 51 03 20 40 00 00 11 5f 83 0a 00 01 fd 0a 00   .Q. @..._.......
    0020  01 fd 00 a1 85 15 00 3d 18 48 30 33 02 01 00 04   .......=.H03....
    0030  06 70 75 62 6c 69 63 a2 26 02 04 00 ec 48 0a 02   .public.&....H..
    0040  01 00 02 01 00 30 18 30 16 06 08 2b 06 01 02 01   .....0.0...+....
    0050  01 02 00 06 0a 2b 06 01 04 01 bf 08 03 02 0a      .....+.........
```

To save space, we included only the first four frames, which are the first two getnext operations. As before, frames 1 and 3 are client requests and frames 2 and 4 are the agent's responses. Now let's look at SNMPv2's datagram traces (again we kept it short):

```
    Frame 1 (82 bytes on wire, 82 bytes captured)
        Arrival Time: Sep 20, 2004 13:47:06.413352000
        Time delta from previous packet: 0.000000000 seconds
        Time since reference or first frame: 0.000000000 seconds
        Frame Number: 1
        Packet Length: 82 bytes
        Capture Length: 82 bytes
    Ethernet II, Src: 00:00:00:00:00:00, Dst: 00:00:00:00:00:00
        Destination: 00:00:00:00:00:00 (00:00:00_00:00:00)
        Source: 00:00:00:00:00:00 (00:00:00_00:00:00)
        Type: IP (0x0800)
    Internet Protocol, Src Addr: 10.0.1.253 (10.0.1.253), Dst Addr: 10.0.1.253 (10.0.1.253)
        Version: 4
        Header length: 20 bytes
        Differentiated Services Field: 0x00 (DSCP 0x00: Default; ECN: 0x00)
            0000 00.. = Differentiated Services Codepoint: Default (0x00)
            .... ..0. = ECN-Capable Transport (ECT): 0
            .... ...0 = ECN-CE: 0
```

```
            Total Length: 68
            Identification: 0x0000 (0)
            Flags: 0x04
                .1.. = Don't fragment: Set
                ..0. = More fragments: Not set
            Fragment offset: 0
            Time to live: 0
            Protocol: UDP (0x11)
            Header checksum: 0x62b0 (correct)
            Source: 10.0.1.253 (10.0.1.253)
            Destination: 10.0.1.253 (10.0.1.253)
    User Datagram Protocol, Src Port: 34069 (34069), Dst Port: snmp (161)
            Source port: 34069 (34069)
            Destination port: snmp (161)
            Length: 48
            Checksum: 0x183b (incorrect, should be 0xa1af)
    Simple Network Management Protocol
            Version: 2C (1)
            Community: public
            PDU type: GET-NEXT (1)
            Request Id: 0x75cb182f
            Error Status: NO ERROR (0)
            Error Index: 0
            Object identifier 1: 1.3.6.1.2.1 (SNMPv2-SMI::mib-2)
            Value: NULL

    0000  00 00 00 00 00 00 00 00 00 00 00 00 08 00 45 00   ..............E.
    0010  00 44 00 00 40 00 00 11 62 b0 0a 00 01 fd 0a 00   .D..@...b.......
    0020  01 fd 85 15 00 a1 00 30 18 3b 30 26 02 01 01 04   .......0.;0&....
    0030  06 70 75 62 6c 69 63 a1 19 02 04 75 cb 18 2f 02   .public....u../.
    0040  01 00 02 01 00 30 0b 30 09 06 05 2b 06 01 02 01   .....0.0...+....
    0050  05 00                                             ..

    Frame 2 (160 bytes on wire, 160 bytes captured)
            Arrival Time: Sep 20, 2004 13:47:06.413554000
            Time delta from previous packet: 0.000202000 seconds
            Time since reference or first frame: 0.000202000 seconds
            Frame Number: 2
            Packet Length: 160 bytes
            Capture Length: 160 bytes
    Ethernet II, Src: 00:00:00:00:00:00, Dst: 00:00:00:00:00:00
            Destination: 00:00:00:00:00:00 (00:00:00_00:00:00)
            Source: 00:00:00:00:00:00 (00:00:00_00:00:00)
            Type: IP (0x0800)
    Internet Protocol, Src Addr: 10.0.1.253 (10.0.1.253), Dst Addr: 10.0.1.253 (10.0.1.
    253)
            Version: 4
            Header length: 20 bytes
            Differentiated Services Field: 0x00 (DSCP 0x00: Default; ECN: 0x00)
                0000 00.. = Differentiated Services Codepoint: Default (0x00)
                .... ..0. = ECN-Capable Transport (ECT): 0
                .... ...0 = ECN-CE: 0
            Total Length: 146
            Identification: 0x0342 (834)
```

```
    Flags: 0x04
        .1.. = Don't fragment: Set
        ..0. = More fragments: Not set
    Fragment offset: 0
    Time to live: 0
    Protocol: UDP (0x11)
    Header checksum: 0x5f20 (correct)
    Source: 10.0.1.253 (10.0.1.253)
    Destination: 10.0.1.253 (10.0.1.253)
User Datagram Protocol, Src Port: snmp (161), Dst Port: 34069 (34069)
    Source port: snmp (161)
    Destination port: 34069 (34069)
    Length: 126
    Checksum: 0x1889 (incorrect, should be 0x38c5)
Simple Network Management Protocol
    Version: 2C (1)
    Community: public
    PDU type: RESPONSE (2)
    Request Id: 0x75cb182f
    Error Status: NO ERROR (0)
    Error Index: 0
    Object identifier 1: 1.3.6.1.2.1.1.1.0 (SNMPv2-MIB::sysDescr.0)
    Value: STRING: Linux mailworks.guarded.net 2.4.21-4.EL #1 Fri Oct 3 18:13:58 EDT
2003 i686


0000  00 00 00 00 00 00 00 00 00 00 00 00 08 00 45 00   ..............E.
0010  00 92 03 42 40 00 00 11 5f 20 0a 00 01 fd 0a 00   ...B@..._ ......
0020  01 fd 00 a1 85 15 00 7e 18 89 30 74 02 01 01 04   .......~..0t....
0030  06 70 75 62 6c 69 63 a2 67 02 04 75 cb 18 2f 02   .public.g..u../.
0040  01 00 02 01 00 30 59 30 57 06 08 2b 06 01 02 01   .....0Y0W..+....
0050  01 01 00 04 4b 4c 69 6e 75 78 20 6d 61 69 6c 77   ....KLinux mailw
0060  6f 72 6b 73 2e 67 75 61 72 64 65 64 2e 6e 65 74   orks.guarded.net
0070  20 32 2e 34 2e 32 31 2d 34 2e 45 4c 20 23 31 20    2.4.21-4.EL #1
0080  46 72 69 20 4f 63 74 20 33 20 31 38 3a 31 33 3a   Fri Oct 3 18:13:
0090  35 38 20 45 44 54 20 32 30 30 33 20 69 36 38 36   58 EDT 2003 i686


Frame 3 (85 bytes on wire, 85 bytes captured)
    Arrival Time: Sep 20, 2004 13:47:06.495596000
    Time delta from previous packet: 0.082042000 seconds
    Time since reference or first frame: 0.082244000 seconds
    Frame Number: 3
    Packet Length: 85 bytes
    Capture Length: 85 bytes
Ethernet II, Src: 00:00:00:00:00:00, Dst: 00:00:00:00:00:00
    Destination: 00:00:00:00:00:00 (00:00:00_00:00:00)
    Source: 00:00:00:00:00:00 (00:00:00_00:00:00)
    Type: IP (0x0800)
Internet Protocol, Src Addr: 10.0.1.253 (10.0.1.253), Dst Addr: 10.0.1.253 (10.0.1.
253)
    Version: 4
    Header length: 20 bytes
    Differentiated Services Field: 0x00 (DSCP 0x00: Default; ECN: 0x00)
        0000 00.. = Differentiated Services Codepoint: Default (0x00)
        .... ..0. = ECN-Capable Transport (ECT): 0
```

```
        .... ...0 = ECN-CE: 0
    Total Length: 71
    Identification: 0x0001 (1)
    Flags: 0x04
        .1.. = Don't fragment: Set
        ..0. = More fragments: Not set
    Fragment offset: 0
    Time to live: 0
    Protocol: UDP (0x11)
    Header checksum: 0x62ac (correct)
    Source: 10.0.1.253 (10.0.1.253)
    Destination: 10.0.1.253 (10.0.1.253)
User Datagram Protocol, Src Port: 34069 (34069), Dst Port: snmp (161)
    Source port: 34069 (34069)
    Destination port: snmp (161)
    Length: 51
    Checksum: 0x183e (incorrect, should be 0x98a0)
Simple Network Management Protocol
    Version: 2C (1)
    Community: public
    PDU type: GET-NEXT (1)
    Request Id: 0x75cb1830
    Error Status: NO ERROR (0)
    Error Index: 0
    Object identifier 1: 1.3.6.1.2.1.1.1.0 (SNMPv2-MIB::sysDescr.0)
    Value: NULL

0000  00 00 00 00 00 00 00 00 00 00 00 00 08 00 45 00   ..............E.
0010  00 47 00 01 40 00 00 11 62 ac 0a 00 01 fd 0a 00   .G..@...b.......
0020  01 fd 85 15 00 a1 00 33 18 3e 30 29 02 01 01 04   .......3.>0)....
0030  06 70 75 62 6c 69 63 a1 1c 02 04 75 cb 18 30 02   .public....u..0.
0040  01 00 02 01 00 30 0e 30 0c 06 08 2b 06 01 02 01   .....0.0...+....
0050  01 01 00 05 00                                     .....

Frame 4 (95 bytes on wire, 95 bytes captured)
    Arrival Time: Sep 20, 2004 13:47:06.495794000
    Time delta from previous packet: 0.000198000 seconds
    Time since reference or first frame: 0.082442000 seconds
    Frame Number: 4
    Packet Length: 95 bytes
    Capture Length: 95 bytes
Ethernet II, Src: 00:00:00:00:00:00, Dst: 00:00:00:00:00:00
    Destination: 00:00:00:00:00:00 (00:00:00_00:00:00)
    Source: 00:00:00:00:00:00 (00:00:00_00:00:00)
    Type: IP (0x0800)
Internet Protocol, Src Addr: 10.0.1.253 (10.0.1.253), Dst Addr: 10.0.1.253 (10.0.1.
253)
    Version: 4
    Header length: 20 bytes
    Differentiated Services Field: 0x00 (DSCP 0x00: Default; ECN: 0x00)
        0000 00.. = Differentiated Services Codepoint: Default (0x00)
        .... ..0. = ECN-Capable Transport (ECT): 0
        .... ...0 = ECN-CE: 0
    Total Length: 81
```

```
     Identification: 0x0343 (835)
     Flags: 0x04
         .1.. = Don't fragment: Set
         ..0. = More fragments: Not set
     Fragment offset: 0
     Time to live: 0
     Protocol: UDP (0x11)
     Header checksum: 0x5f60 (correct)
     Source: 10.0.1.253 (10.0.1.253)
     Destination: 10.0.1.253 (10.0.1.253)
 User Datagram Protocol, Src Port: snmp (161), Dst Port: 34069 (34069)
     Source port: snmp (161)
     Destination port: 34069 (34069)
     Length: 61
     Checksum: 0x1848 (incorrect, should be 0x9a47)
 Simple Network Management Protocol
     Version: 2C (1)
     Community: public
     PDU type: RESPONSE (2)
     Request Id: 0x75cb1830
     Error Status: NO ERROR (0)
     Error Index: 0
     Object identifier 1: 1.3.6.1.2.1.1.2.0 (SNMPv2-MIB::sysObjectID.0)
     Value: OID: SNMPv2-SMI::enterprises.8072.3.2.10

0000  00 00 00 00 00 00 00 00 00 00 00 00 08 00 45 00   ..............E.
0010  00 51 03 43 40 00 00 11 5f 60 0a 00 01 fd 0a 00   .Q.C@..._`......
0020  01 fd 00 a1 85 15 00 3d 18 48 30 33 02 01 01 04   .......=.H03....
0030  06 70 75 62 6c 69 63 a2 26 02 04 75 cb 18 30 02   .public.&..u..0.
0040  01 00 02 01 00 30 18 30 16 06 08 2b 06 01 02 01   .....0.0...+....
0050  01 02 00 06 0a 2b 06 01 04 01 bf 08 03 02 0a      .....+.........
```

The getbulk Operation

SNMPv2 defines the getbulk operation, which allows a management application to retrieve a large section of a table at once. The standard get operation can attempt to retrieve more than one MIB object at once, but message sizes are limited by the agent's capabilities. If the agent can't return all the requested responses, it returns an error message with no data. The getbulk operation, on the other hand, tells the agent to send back as much of the response as it can. This means that incomplete responses are possible. Two fields must be set when issuing a getbulk command: nonrepeaters and max-repetitions. Nonrepeaters tell the getbulk command that the first N objects can be retrieved with a simple getnext operation. max-repetitions tells the getbulk command to attempt up to M getnext operations to retrieve the remaining objects. Figure 2-7 shows the getbulk command sequence.

In Figure 2-7, we're requesting three bindings: *sysDescr*, *ifInOctets*, and *ifOutOctets*. The total number of variable bindings that we've requested is given by the formula $N + (M * R)$, where N is the number of nonrepeaters (i.e., scalar objects in the request—in this case, 1 because *sysDescr* is the only scalar object), M is max-repetitions (in this

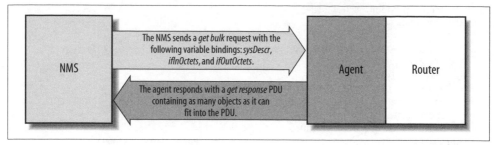

Figure 2-7. getbulk request sequence

case, we've set it arbitrarily to 3), and *R* is the number of nonscalar objects in the request (in this case, 2 because *ifInOctets* and *ifOutOctets* are both nonscalar). Plugging in the numbers from this example, we get 1 + (3 * 2) = 7, which is the total number of variable bindings that can be returned by this getbulk request.

The Net-SNMP package comes with a command for issuing getbulk queries. If we execute this command using all the parameters previously discussed, it will look like the following:

```
$ snmpbulkget -v2c -c public -Cn1 -Cr3 linux.ora.com sysDescr ifInOctets ifOutOctets
system.sysDescr.0 = " Linux snort 2.4.7-10 #1 Thu Sep 6 17:27:27 EDT 2001 i686
unknown "
interfaces.ifTable.ifEntry.ifInOctets.1 = 70840
interfaces.ifTable.ifEntry.ifOutOctets.1 = 70840
interfaces.ifTable.ifEntry.ifInOctets.2 = 143548020
interfaces.ifTable.ifEntry.ifOutOctets.2 = 111725152
interfaces.ifTable.ifEntry.ifInOctets.3 = 0
interfaces.ifTable.ifEntry.ifOutOctets.3 = 0
```

Since getbulk is an SNMPv2 command, you have to tell snmpbulkget to use an SNMPv2 PDU with the −v2c option. nonrepeaters and max-repetitions are set with the −Cn1 and −Cr3 options. This sets nonrepeaters to 1 and max-repetitions to 3. Notice that the command returned seven variable bindings: one for *sysDescr* and three each for *ifInOctets* and *ifOutOctets*.

Now let's look at a trace. If we use the following command:

```
$ snmpbulkget -v2c -Cn1 -Cr2 127.0.0.1 -c public sysDescr sysContact
```

we get the following trace:

```
Frame 1 (97 bytes on wire, 97 bytes captured)
    Arrival Time: Sep 20, 2004 20:24:19.106374000
    Time delta from previous packet: 0.000000000 seconds
    Time since reference or first frame: 0.000000000 seconds
    Frame Number: 1
    Packet Length: 97 bytes
    Capture Length: 97 bytes
Ethernet II, Src: 00:00:00:00:00:00, Dst: 00:00:00:00:00:00
    Destination: 00:00:00:00:00:00 (00:00:00_00:00:00)
    Source: 00:00:00:00:00:00 (00:00:00_00:00:00)
    Type: IP (0x0800)
```

```
Internet Protocol, Src Addr: 127.0.0.1 (127.0.0.1), Dst Addr: 127.0.0.1 (127.0.0.1)
    Version: 4
    Header length: 20 bytes
    Differentiated Services Field: 0x00 (DSCP 0x00: Default; ECN: 0x00)
        0000 00.. = Differentiated Services Codepoint: Default (0x00)
        .... ..0. = ECN-Capable Transport (ECT): 0
        .... ...0 = ECN-CE: 0
    Total Length: 83
    Identification: 0x0000 (0)
    Flags: 0x04
        .1.. = Don't fragment: Set
        ..0. = More fragments: Not set
    Fragment offset: 0
    Time to live: 0
    Protocol: UDP (0x11)
    Header checksum: 0x7c98 (correct)
    Source: 127.0.0.1 (127.0.0.1)
    Destination: 127.0.0.1 (127.0.0.1)
User Datagram Protocol, Src Port: 34193 (34193), Dst Port: snmp (161)
    Source port: 34193 (34193)
    Destination port: snmp (161)
    Length: 63
    Checksum: 0xfe52 (incorrect, should be 0x0c90)
Simple Network Management Protocol
    Version: 2C (1)
    Community: public
    PDU type: GETBULK (5)
    Request Id: 0x0f15c607
    Non-repeaters: 1
    Max repetitions: 2
    Object identifier 1: 1.3.6.1.2.1.1.1 (SNMPv2-MIB::sysDescr)
    Value: NULL
    Object identifier 2: 1.3.6.1.2.1.1.4 (SNMPv2-MIB::sysContact)
    Value: NULL


0000  00 00 00 00 00 00 00 00 00 00 00 00 08 00 45 00   ..............E.
0010  00 53 00 00 40 00 00 11 7c 98 7f 00 00 01 7f 00   .S..@...|.......
0020  00 01 85 91 00 a1 00 3f fe 52 30 35 02 01 01 04   .......?.R05....
0030  06 70 75 62 6c 69 63 a5 28 02 04 0f 15 c6 07 02   .public.(.......
0040  01 01 02 01 02 30 1a 30 0b 06 07 2b 06 01 02 01   .....0.0...+....
0050  01 01 05 00 30 0b 06 07 2b 06 01 02 01 01 04 05   ....0...+.......
0060  00                                                .


Frame 2 (211 bytes on wire, 211 bytes captured)
    Arrival Time: Sep 20, 2004 20:24:19.151924000
    Time delta from previous packet: 0.045550000 seconds
    Time since reference or first frame: 0.045550000 seconds
    Frame Number: 2
    Packet Length: 211 bytes
    Capture Length: 211 bytes
Ethernet II, Src: 00:00:00:00:00:00, Dst: 00:00:00:00:00:00
    Destination: 00:00:00:00:00:00 (00:00:00_00:00:00)
    Source: 00:00:00:00:00:00 (00:00:00_00:00:00)
    Type: IP (0x0800)
```

```
Internet Protocol, Src Addr: 127.0.0.1 (127.0.0.1), Dst Addr: 127.0.0.1 (127.0.0.1)
    Version: 4
    Header length: 20 bytes
    Differentiated Services Field: 0x00 (DSCP 0x00: Default; ECN: 0x00)
        0000 00.. = Differentiated Services Codepoint: Default (0x00)
        .... ..0. = ECN-Capable Transport (ECT): 0
        .... ...0 = ECN-CE: 0
    Total Length: 197
    Identification: 0x0052 (82)
    Flags: 0x04
        .1.. = Don't fragment: Set
        ..0. = More fragments: Not set
    Fragment offset: 0
    Time to live: 0
    Protocol: UDP (0x11)
    Header checksum: 0x7bd4 (correct)
    Source: 127.0.0.1 (127.0.0.1)
    Destination: 127.0.0.1 (127.0.0.1)
User Datagram Protocol, Src Port: snmp (161), Dst Port: 34193 (34193)
    Source port: snmp (161)
    Destination port: 34193 (34193)
    Length: 177
    Checksum: 0xfec4 (incorrect, should be 0x47bb)
Simple Network Management Protocol
    Version: 2C (1)
    Community: public
    PDU type: RESPONSE (2)
    Request Id: 0x0f15c607
    Error Status: NO ERROR (0)
    Error Index: 0
    Object identifier 1: 1.3.6.1.2.1.1.1.0 (SNMPv2-MIB::sysDescr.0)
    Value: STRING: Linux mailworks.guarded.net 2.4.21-4.EL #1 Fri Oct 3 18:13:58 EDT
2003 i686
    Object identifier 2: 1.3.6.1.2.1.1.4.0 (SNMPv2-MIB::sysContact.0)
    Value: STRING: "kjs@guarded.net"
    Object identifier 3: 1.3.6.1.2.1.1.5.0 (SNMPv2-MIB::sysName.0)
    Value: STRING: box


0000  00 00 00 00 00 00 00 00 00 00 00 00 08 00 45 00   ..............E.
0010  00 c5 00 52 40 00 00 11 7b d4 7f 00 00 01 7f 00   ...R@...{.......
0020  00 01 00 a1 85 91 00 b1 fe c4 30 81 a6 02 01 01   ..........0.....
0030  04 06 70 75 62 6c 69 63 a2 81 98 02 04 0f 15 c6   ..public........
0040  07 02 01 00 02 01 00 30 81 89 30 57 06 08 2b 06   .......0..0W..+.
0050  01 02 01 01 01 00 04 4b 4c 69 6e 75 78 20 6d 61   .......KLinux ma
0060  69 6c 77 6f 72 6b 73 2e 67 75 61 72 64 65 64 2e   ilworks.guarded.
0070  6e 65 74 20 32 2e 34 2e 32 31 2d 34 2e 45 4c 20   net 2.4.21-4.EL
0080  23 31 20 46 72 69 20 4f 63 74 20 33 20 31 38 3a   #1 Fri Oct 3 18:
0090  31 33 3a 35 38 20 45 44 54 20 32 30 30 33 20 69   13:58 EDT 2003 i
00a0  36 38 36 30 1d 06 08 2b 06 01 02 01 01 04 00 04   6860...+........
00b0  11 22 6b 6a 73 40 67 75 61 72 64 65 64 2e 6e 65   ."kjs@guarded.ne
00c0  74 22 30 0f 06 08 2b 06 01 02 01 01 05 00 04 03   t"0...+.........
00d0  62 6f 78                                          box
```

The set Operation

The set command is used to change the value of a managed object or to create a new row in a table. Objects that are defined in the MIB as read-write or read-only can be altered or created using this command. It is possible for an NMS to set more than one object at a time.

Figure 2-8 shows the set request sequence. It's similar to the other commands we've seen so far, but it actually changes something in the device's configuration as opposed to just retrieving a response to a query. Let's look at the set command in action. The following example queries the *sysLocation* variable and sets it to a value:

```
$ snmpget -v 1 -c public cisco.ora.com system.sysLocation.0
system.sysLocation.0 = ""
$ snmpset -v 1 -c private cisco.ora.com system.sysLocation.0 s "Atlanta, GA"
system.sysLocation.0 = "Atlanta, GA"
$ snmpget -v 1 -c public cisco.ora.com system.sysLocation.0
system.sysLocation.0 = "Atlanta, GA"
```

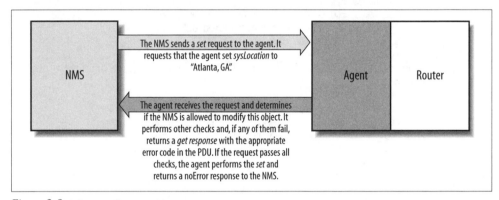

Figure 2-8. set request sequence

The first command is the familiar get command, which displays the current value of *sysLocation*. In one of the previous examples, we saw that it was undefined; this is still the case. The second command is snmpset. For this command, we supply the hostname, the read-write community string (*private*), and the variable we want to set (*system.sysLocation.0*), together with its new value (s "Atlanta, GA"). The s tells snmpset that we want to set the value of *sysLocation* to a string, and "Atlanta, GA" is the new value itself. How do we know that *sysLocation* requires a string value? The definition of *sysLocation* in RFC 1213 looks like this:

```
sysLocation OBJECT-TYPE
    SYNTAX   DisplayString (SIZE (0..255))
    ACCESS   read-write
    STATUS   mandatory
    DESCRIPTION
        "The physical location of this node (e.g., 'telephone closet,
        3rd floor')."
    ::= { system 6 }
```

The SYNTAX for *sysLocation* is DisplayString (SIZE (0..255)), which means that it's a string with a maximum length of 255 characters. The snmpset command succeeds and reports the new value of *sysLocation*. But just to confirm, we run a final snmpget, which tells us that the set actually took effect. It is possible to set more than one object at a time, but if any of the sets fail, they all fail (i.e., no values are changed). This behavior is intended.

It's time for more tethereal output. With the following set command:

```
$ snmpset -v 1 -c private 127.0.0.1 sysName.0 s box
```

we get the following output:

```
Frame 1 (89 bytes on wire, 89 bytes captured)
    Arrival Time: Sep 20, 2004 14:25:01.895097000
    Time delta from previous packet: 0.000000000 seconds
    Time since reference or first frame: 0.000000000 seconds
    Frame Number: 1
    Packet Length: 89 bytes
    Capture Length: 89 bytes
Ethernet II, Src: 00:00:00:00:00:00, Dst: 00:00:00:00:00:00
    Destination: 00:00:00:00:00:00 (00:00:00_00:00:00)
    Source: 00:00:00:00:00:00 (00:00:00_00:00:00)
    Type: IP (0x0800)
Internet Protocol, Src Addr: 127.0.0.1 (127.0.0.1), Dst Addr: 127.0.0.1 (127.0.0.1)
    Version: 4
    Header length: 20 bytes
    Differentiated Services Field: 0x00 (DSCP 0x00: Default; ECN: 0x00)
        0000 00.. = Differentiated Services Codepoint: Default (0x00)
        .... ..0. = ECN-Capable Transport (ECT): 0
        .... ...0 = ECN-CE: 0
    Total Length: 75
    Identification: 0x0000 (0)
    Flags: 0x04
        .1.. = Don't fragment: Set
        ..0. = More fragments: Not set
    Fragment offset: 0
    Time to live: 0
    Protocol: UDP (0x11)
    Header checksum: 0x7ca0 (correct)
    Source: 127.0.0.1 (127.0.0.1)
    Destination: 127.0.0.1 (127.0.0.1)
User Datagram Protocol, Src Port: 34102 (34102), Dst Port: snmp (161)
    Source port: 34102 (34102)
    Destination port: snmp (161)
    Length: 55
    Checksum: 0xfe4a (incorrect, should be 0xc029)
Simple Network Management Protocol
    Version: 1 (0)
    Community: private
    PDU type: SET (3)
    Request Id: 0x1df8e7e6
    Error Status: NO ERROR (0)
    Error Index: 0
```

```
    Object identifier 1: 1.3.6.1.2.1.1.5.0 (SNMPv2-MIB::sysName.0)
    Value: STRING: box

0000  00 00 00 00 00 00 00 00 00 00 00 00 08 00 45 00   ..............E.
0010  00 4b 00 00 40 00 00 11 7c a0 7f 00 00 01 7f 00   .K..@...|.......
0020  00 01 85 36 00 a1 00 37 fe 4a 30 2d 02 01 00 04   ...6...7.J0-....
0030  07 70 72 69 76 61 74 65 a3 1f 02 04 1d f8 e7 e6   .private........
0040  02 01 00 02 01 00 30 11 30 0f 06 08 2b 06 01 02   ......0.0...+...
0050  01 01 05 00 04 03 62 6f 78                        ......box
```

Frame 2 (89 bytes on wire, 89 bytes captured)
    Arrival Time: Sep 20, 2004 14:25:01.902787000
    Time delta from previous packet: 0.007690000 seconds
    Time since reference or first frame: 0.007690000 seconds
    Frame Number: 2
    Packet Length: 89 bytes
    Capture Length: 89 bytes
Ethernet II, Src: 00:00:00:00:00:00, Dst: 00:00:00:00:00:00
    Destination: 00:00:00:00:00:00 (00:00:00_00:00:00)
    Source: 00:00:00:00:00:00 (00:00:00_00:00:00)
    Type: IP (0x0800)
Internet Protocol, Src Addr: 127.0.0.1 (127.0.0.1), Dst Addr: 127.0.0.1 (127.0.0.1)
    Version: 4
    Header length: 20 bytes
    Differentiated Services Field: 0x00 (DSCP 0x00: Default; ECN: 0x00)
        0000 00.. = Differentiated Services Codepoint: Default (0x00)
        .... ..0. = ECN-Capable Transport (ECT): 0
        ....0 = ECN-CE: 0
    Total Length: 75
    Identification: 0x0004 (4)
    Flags: 0x04
        .1.. = Don't fragment: Set
        ..0. = More fragments: Not set
    Fragment offset: 0
    Time to live: 0
    Protocol: UDP (0x11)
    Header checksum: 0x7c9c (correct)
    Source: 127.0.0.1 (127.0.0.1)
    Destination: 127.0.0.1 (127.0.0.1)
User Datagram Protocol, Src Port: snmp (161), Dst Port: 34102 (34102)
    Source port: snmp (161)
    Destination port: 34102 (34102)
    Length: 55
    Checksum: 0xfe4a (incorrect, should be 0xc129)
Simple Network Management Protocol
    Version: 1 (0)
    Community: private
    PDU type: RESPONSE (2)
    Request Id: 0x1df8e7e6
    Error Status: NO ERROR (0)
    Error Index: 0
    Object identifier 1: 1.3.6.1.2.1.1.5.0 (SNMPv2-MIB::sysName.0)
    Value: STRING: box
```
```

```
0000   00 00 00 00 00 00 00 00 00 00 00 00 08 00 45 00    ..............E.
0010   00 4b 00 04 40 00 00 11 7c 9c 7f 00 00 01 7f 00    .K..@...|.......
0020   00 01 00 a1 85 36 00 37 fe 4a 30 2d 02 01 00 04    .....6.7.J0-....
0030   07 70 72 69 76 61 74 65 a2 1f 02 04 1d f8 e7 e6    .private........
0040   02 01 00 02 01 00 30 11 30 0f 06 08 2b 06 01 02    ......0.0...+...
0050   01 01 05 00 04 03 62 6f 78                         ......box
```

The SNMPv2 set traces are as follows:

```
Frame 1 (89 bytes on wire, 89 bytes captured)
    Arrival Time: Sep 20, 2004 14:25:12.926493000
    Time delta from previous packet: 0.000000000 seconds
    Time since reference or first frame: 0.000000000 seconds
    Frame Number: 1
    Packet Length: 89 bytes
    Capture Length: 89 bytes
Ethernet II, Src: 00:00:00:00:00:00, Dst: 00:00:00:00:00:00
    Destination: 00:00:00:00:00:00 (00:00:00_00:00:00)
    Source: 00:00:00:00:00:00 (00:00:00_00:00:00)
    Type: IP (0x0800)
Internet Protocol, Src Addr: 127.0.0.1 (127.0.0.1), Dst Addr: 127.0.0.1 (127.0.0.1)
    Version: 4
    Header length: 20 bytes
    Differentiated Services Field: 0x00 (DSCP 0x00: Default; ECN: 0x00)
        0000 00.. = Differentiated Services Codepoint: Default (0x00)
        .... ..0. = ECN-Capable Transport (ECT): 0
        .... ...0 = ECN-CE: 0
    Total Length: 75
    Identification: 0x0000 (0)
    Flags: 0x04
        .1.. = Don't fragment: Set
        ..0. = More fragments: Not set
    Fragment offset: 0
    Time to live: 0
    Protocol: UDP (0x11)
    Header checksum: 0x7ca0 (correct)
    Source: 127.0.0.1 (127.0.0.1)
    Destination: 127.0.0.1 (127.0.0.1)
User Datagram Protocol, Src Port: 34102 (34102), Dst Port: snmp (161)
    Source port: 34102 (34102)
    Destination port: snmp (161)
    Length: 55
    Checksum: 0xfe4a (incorrect, should be 0x726b)
Simple Network Management Protocol
    Version: 2C (1)
    Community: private
    PDU type: SET (3)
    Request Id: 0x34df1dbe
    Error Status: NO ERROR (0)
    Error Index: 0
    Object identifier 1: 1.3.6.1.2.1.1.5.0 (SNMPv2-MIB::sysName.0)
    Value: STRING: box


0000   00 00 00 00 00 00 00 00 00 00 00 00 08 00 45 00    ..............E.
```

```
0010  00 4b 00 00 40 00 00 11 7c a0 7f 00 00 01 7f 00    .K..@...|.......
0020  00 01 85 36 00 a1 00 37 fe 4a 30 2d 02 01 01 04    ...6...7.J0-....
0030  07 70 72 69 76 61 74 65 a3 1f 02 04 34 df 1d be    .private....4...
0040  02 01 00 02 01 00 30 11 30 0f 06 08 2b 06 01 02    ......0.0...+...
0050  01 01 05 00 04 03 62 6f 78                         ......box
```

Frame 2 (89 bytes on wire, 89 bytes captured)
    Arrival Time: Sep 20, 2004 14:25:12.989438000
    Time delta from previous packet: 0.062945000 seconds
    Time since reference or first frame: 0.062945000 seconds
    Frame Number: 2
    Packet Length: 89 bytes
    Capture Length: 89 bytes
Ethernet II, Src: 00:00:00:00:00:00, Dst: 00:00:00:00:00:00
    Destination: 00:00:00:00:00:00 (00:00:00_00:00:00)
    Source: 00:00:00:00:00:00 (00:00:00_00:00:00)
    Type: IP (0x0800)
Internet Protocol, Src Addr: 127.0.0.1 (127.0.0.1), Dst Addr: 127.0.0.1 (127.0.0.1)
    Version: 4
    Header length: 20 bytes
    Differentiated Services Field: 0x00 (DSCP 0x00: Default; ECN: 0x00)
        0000 00.. = Differentiated Services Codepoint: Default (0x00)
        .... ..0. = ECN-Capable Transport (ECT): 0
        ....0 = ECN-CE: 0
    Total Length: 75
    Identification: 0x0005 (5)
    Flags: 0x04
        .1.. = Don't fragment: Set
        ..0. = More fragments: Not set
    Fragment offset: 0
    Time to live: 0
    Protocol: UDP (0x11)
    Header checksum: 0x7c9b (correct)
    Source: 127.0.0.1 (127.0.0.1)
    Destination: 127.0.0.1 (127.0.0.1)
User Datagram Protocol, Src Port: snmp (161), Dst Port: 34102 (34102)
    Source port: snmp (161)
    Destination port: 34102 (34102)
    Length: 55
    Checksum: 0xfe4a (incorrect, should be 0x736b)
Simple Network Management Protocol
    Version: 2C (1)
    Community: private
    PDU type: RESPONSE (2)
    Request Id: 0x34df1dbe
    Error Status: NO ERROR (0)
    Error Index: 0
    Object identifier 1: 1.3.6.1.2.1.1.5.0 (SNMPv2-MIB::sysName.0)
    Value: STRING: box

```
0000  00 00 00 00 00 00 00 00 00 00 00 00 08 00 45 00    ..............E.
0010  00 4b 00 05 40 00 00 11 7c 9b 7f 00 00 01 7f 00    .K..@...|.......
0020  00 01 00 a1 85 36 00 37 fe 4a 30 2d 02 01 01 04    .....6.7.J0-....
0030  07 70 72 69 76 61 74 65 a2 1f 02 04 34 df 1d be    .private....4...
```

```
0040  02 01 00 02 01 00 30 11 30 0f 06 08 2b 06 01 02      ......0.0...+...
0050  01 01 05 00 04 03 62 6f 78                           ......box
```

get, getnext, getbulk, and set Error Responses

Error responses help you determine whether your get or set request was processed correctly by the agent. The get, getnext, getbulk, and set operations can return the error responses shown in Table 2-6. The error status for each error is shown in parentheses.

Table 2-6. SNMPv1 error messages

SNMPv1 error message	Description
noError(0)	There was no problem performing the request.
tooBig(1)	The response to your request was too big to fit into one response.
noSuchName(2)	An agent was asked to get or set an OID that it can't find; i.e., the OID doesn't exist.
badValue(3)	A read-write or write-only object was set to an inconsistent value.
readOnly(4)	This error is generally not used. The noSuchName error is equivalent to this one.
genErr(5)	This is a catchall error. If an error occurs for which none of the previous messages is appropriate, a genErr is issued.

The SNMPv1 error messages are not very robust. In an attempt to fix this problem, SNMPv2 defines additional error responses that are valid for get, set, getnext, and getbulk operations, provided that both the agent and the NMS support SNMPv2. These responses are listed in Table 2-7.

Table 2-7. SNMPv2 error messages

SNMPv2 error message	Description
noAccess(6)	A set to an inaccessible variable was attempted. This typically occurs when the variable has an ACCESS type of not-accessible.
wrongType(7)	An object was set to a type that is different from its definition. This error will occur if you try to set an object that is of type INTEGER to a string, for example.
wrongLength(8)	An object's value was set to something other than what it calls for. For instance, a string can be defined to have a maximum character size. This error occurs if you try to set a string object to a value that exceeds its maximum length.
wrongEncoding(9)	A set operation was attempted using the wrong encoding for the object being set.
wrongValue(10)	A variable was set to a value it doesn't understand. This can occur when a read-write is defined as an enumeration, and you try to set it to a value that is not one of the enumerated types.
noCreation(11)	You tried to set a nonexistent variable or create a variable that doesn't exist in the MIB.
inconsistentValue	A MIB variable is in an inconsistent state and is not accepting any set requests.
resourceUnavailable(13)	No system resources are available to perform a set.
commitFailed(14)	This error is a catchall for set failures.

Table 2-7. SNMPv2 error messages (continued)

SNMPv2 error message	Description
undoFailed(15)	A set failed and the agent was unable to roll back all the previous sets up until the point of failure.
authorizationError(16)	An SNMP command could not be authenticated; in other words, someone has supplied an incorrect community string.
notWritable(17)	A variable will not accept a set, even though it is supposed to.
inconsistentName(18)	You attempted to set a variable, but that attempt failed because the variable was in some kind of inconsistent state.

SNMP Traps

A trap is a way for an agent to tell the NMS that something bad has happened. In "Managers and Agents" in Chapter 1, we explored the notion of traps at a general level; now we'll look at them in a bit more detail. Figure 2-9 shows the trap-generation sequence.

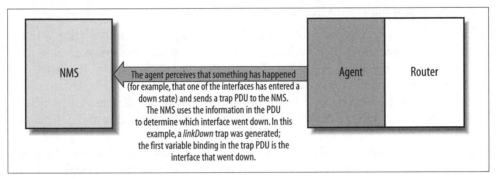

Figure 2-9. Trap-generation sequence

The trap originates from the agent and is sent to the trap destination, as configured within the agent itself. The trap destination is typically the IP address of the NMS. No acknowledgment is sent from the NMS to the agent, so the agent has no way of knowing if the trap makes it to the NMS. Since SNMP uses UDP, and since traps are designed to report problems with your network, traps are especially prone to getting lost and not making it to their destinations. However, the fact that traps can get lost doesn't make them any less useful; in a well-planned environment, they are an integral part of network management. It's better for your equipment to try to tell you that something is wrong, even if the message may never reach you, than simply to give up and let you guess what happened. Here are a few situations that a trap might report:

- A network interface on the device (where the agent is running) has gone down.
- A network interface on the device (where the agent is running) has come back up.

- An incoming call to a modem rack was unable to establish a connection to a modem.
- The fan on a switch or router has failed.

When an NMS receives a trap, it needs to know how to interpret it; that is, it needs to know what the trap means and how to interpret the information it carries. A trap is first identified by its generic trap number. There are seven generic trap numbers (0–6), shown in Table 2-8. Generic trap 6 is a special catchall category for "enterprise-specific" traps, which are traps defined by vendors or users that fall outside of the six generic trap categories. Enterprise-specific traps are further identified by an enterprise ID (i.e., an object ID somewhere in the *enterprises* branch of the MIB tree, *iso.org.dod.internet.private.enterprises*) and a specific trap number chosen by the enterprise that defined the trap. Thus, the object ID of an enterprise-specific trap is *enterprise-id.specific-trap-number*. For example, when Cisco defines special traps for its private MIBs, it places them all in its enterprise-specific MIB tree (*iso.org.dod. internet.private.enterprises.cisco*). As we'll see in Chapter 9, you are free to define your own enterprise-specific traps; the only requirement is that you register your own enterprise number with IANA.

A trap is usually packed with information. As you'd expect, this information is in the form of MIB objects and their values; as mentioned earlier, these object-value pairs are known as variable bindings. For the generic traps 0 through 5, knowledge of what the trap contains is generally built into the NMS software or trap receiver. The variable bindings contained by an enterprise-specific trap are determined by whomever defined the trap. For example, if a modem in a modem rack fails, the rack's agent may send a trap to the NMS informing it of the failure. The trap will most likely be an enterprise-specific trap defined by the rack's manufacturer; the trap's contents are up to the manufacturer, but it will probably contain enough information to let you determine exactly what failed (for example, the position of the modem card in the rack and the channel on the modem card).

Table 2-8. Generic traps

Generic trap name and number	Definition
coldStart (0)	Indicates that the agent has rebooted. All management variables will be reset; specifically, Counters and Gauges will be reset to zero (0). One nice thing about the coldStart trap is that it can be used to determine when new hardware is added to the network. When a device is powered on, it sends this trap to its trap destination. If the trap destination is set correctly (i.e., to the IP address of your NMS), the NMS can receive the trap and determine whether it needs to manage the device.
warmStart (1)	Indicates that the agent has reinitialized itself. None of the management variables will be reset.
linkDown (2)	Sent when an interface on a device goes down. The first variable binding identifies the index in the *interfaces* table for the interface that went down.

Table 2-8. Generic traps (continued)

Generic trap name and number	Definition
linkUp (3)	Sent when an interface on a device comes back up. The first variable binding identifies which interface came back up.
authenticationFailure (4)	Indicates that someone has tried to query your agent with an incorrect community string; useful in determining if someone is trying to gain unauthorized access to one of your devices.
egpNeighborLoss (5)	Indicates that an EGP neighbor has gone down.
enterpriseSpecific (6)	Indicates that the trap is enterprise-specific. SNMP vendors and users define their own traps under the *private-enterprise* branch of the SMI *object* tree. To process this trap properly, the NMS has to decode the specific trap number that is part of the SNMP message.

In Chapter 1, we mentioned that RFC 1697 is the RDBMS MIB. One of the traps defined by this MIB is *rdbmsOutOfSpace*:

```
rdbmsOutOfSpace TRAP-TYPE
    ENTERPRISE  rdbmsTraps
    VARIABLES   { rdbmsSrvInfoDiskOutOfSpaces }
    DESCRIPTION
        "An rdbmsOutOfSpace trap signifies that one of the database
        servers managed by this agent has been unable to allocate
        space for one of the databases managed by this agent. Care
        should be taken to avoid flooding the network with these traps."
    ::= 2
```

The enterprise is *rdbmsTraps* and the specific trap number is 2. This trap has one variable binding, *rdbmsSrvInfoDiskOutOfSpaces*. If we look elsewhere in the MIB, we will find that this variable is a scalar object. Its definition is:

```
rdbmsSrvInfoDiskOutOfSpaces OBJECT-TYPE
    SYNTAX  Counter
    ACCESS  read-only
    STATUS  mandatory
    DESCRIPTION
        "The total number of times the server has been unable to obtain
        disk space that it wanted, since server startup. This would be
        inspected by an agent on receipt of an rdbmsOutOfSpace trap."
    ::= { rdbmsSrvInfoEntry  9 }
```

The DESCRIPTION for this object indicates why the note about taking care to avoid flooding the network (in the DESCRIPTION text for the TRAP-TYPE) is so important. Every time the RDBMS is unable to allocate space for the database, the agent will send a trap. A busy (and full) database could end up sending this trap thousands of times a day.

Some commercial RDBMS vendors, such as Oracle, provide an SNMP agent with their database engines. Agents such as these typically have functionality above and beyond that found in the RDBMS MIB.

Now let's look at an Ethereal trace of an SNMPv1 trap. Given the following command:*

```
$ snmptrap -v 1 -c public .1.3.6.1.4.1.2789.2005 127.0.0.1 6\ 2476317 '' .1.3.6.1.4.
1.2789.2005.1 s "WWW Server Has Been\ Restarted"
```

Ethereal gives us the following trace:

```
Frame 1 (135 bytes on wire, 135 bytes captured)
    Arrival Time: Sep 20, 2004 14:38:40.191174000
    Time delta from previous packet: 0.000000000 seconds
    Time since reference or first frame: 0.000000000 seconds
    Frame Number: 1
    Packet Length: 135 bytes
    Capture Length: 135 bytes
Ethernet II, Src: 00:00:00:00:00:00, Dst: 00:00:00:00:00:00
    Destination: 00:00:00:00:00:00 (00:00:00_00:00:00)
    Source: 00:00:00:00:00:00 (00:00:00_00:00:00)
    Type: IP (0x0800)
Internet Protocol, Src Addr: 127.0.0.1 (127.0.0.1), Dst Addr: 127.0.0.1 (127.0.0.1)
    Version: 4
    Header length: 20 bytes
    Differentiated Services Field: 0x00 (DSCP 0x00: Default; ECN: 0x00)
        0000 00.. = Differentiated Services Codepoint: Default (0x00)
        .... ..0. = ECN-Capable Transport (ECT): 0
        .... ...0 = ECN-CE: 0
    Total Length: 121
    Identification: 0x0000 (0)
    Flags: 0x04
        .1.. = Don't fragment: Set
        ..0. = More fragments: Not set
    Fragment offset: 0
    Time to live: 0
    Protocol: UDP (0x11)
    Header checksum: 0x7c72 (correct)
    Source: 127.0.0.1 (127.0.0.1)
    Destination: 127.0.0.1 (127.0.0.1)
User Datagram Protocol, Src Port: 34108 (34108), Dst Port: snmptrap (162)
    Source port: 34108 (34108)
    Destination port: snmptrap (162)
    Length: 101
    Checksum: 0xfe78 (incorrect, should be 0xf82d)
Simple Network Management Protocol
    Version: 1 (0)
    Community: public
    PDU type: TRAP-V1 (4)
    Enterprise: 1.3.6.1.4.1.2789.2005 (SNMPv2-SMI::enterprises.2789.2005)
    Agent address: 127.0.0.1 (127.0.0.1)
    Trap type: ENTERPRISE SPECIFIC (6)
    Specific trap type: 2476317
    Timestamp: 181730327
```

---

* Don't worry about the details; they will be explained in Chapter 9.

```
     Object identifier 1: 1.3.6.1.4.1.2789.2005.1 (SNMPv2-SMI::enterprises.2789.2005.
1)
     Value: STRING: "WWW Server Has Been Restarted"

0000  00 00 00 00 00 00 00 00 00 00 00 00 08 00 45 00   ..............E.
0010  00 79 00 00 40 00 00 11 7c 72 7f 00 00 01 7f 00   .y..@...|r......
0020  00 01 85 3c 00 a2 00 65 fe 78 30 5b 02 01 00 04   ...<...e.x0[....
0030  06 70 75 62 6c 69 63 a4 4e 06 09 2b 06 01 04 01   .public.N..+....
0040  95 65 8f 55 40 04 7f 00 00 01 02 01 06 02 03 25   .e.U@..........%
0050  c9 1d 43 04 0a d4 fc 17 30 2d 30 2b 06 0a 2b 06   ..C.....0-0+..+.
0060  01 04 01 95 65 8f 55 01 04 1d 57 57 57 20 53 65   ....e.U...WWW Se
0070  72 76 65 72 20 48 61 73 20 42 65 65 6e 20 52 65   rver Has Been Re
0080  73 74 61 72 74 65 64                              started
```

We have only one frame since the agent initiated the trap. An SNMPv1 trap is sent from the agent and is not acknowledged by the receiver in any way, so the agent sends it and forgets about it. This is why we see just the single trace.

SNMP Notification

In an effort to standardize the PDU format of SNMPv1 traps (recall that SNMPv1 traps have a different PDU format from get and set), SNMPv2 defines a NOTIFICATION-TYPE. The PDU format for NOTIFICATION-TYPE is identical to that for get and set. RFC 2863 redefines the *linkDown* generic notification type like so:

```
linkDown NOTIFICATION-TYPE
     OBJECTS { ifIndex, ifAdminStatus, ifOperStatus }
     STATUS   current
     DESCRIPTION
          "A linkDown trap signifies that the SNMPv2 entity, acting in an
          agent role, has detected that the ifOperStatus object for one
          of its communication links left the down state and transitioned
          into some other state (but not into the notPresent state). This
          other state is indicated by the included value of ifOperStatus."
     ::= { snmpTraps 3 }
```

The list of bindings is called OBJECTS rather than VARIABLES, but little else has changed. The first object is the specific interface (*ifIndex*) that transitioned from the *linkDown* condition to some other condition. The OID for this trap is *1.3.6.1.6.3.1.1.5.3*, or *iso.org.dod.internet.snmpV2.snmpModules.snmpMIB.snmpMIBObjects.snmpTraps.linkDown*.

Let's look at how to create an SNMP notification:

```
$ snmptrap -v2c -c public 127.0.0.1 '' .1.3.6.1.6.3.1.1.5.3 ifIndex i 2 ifAdminStatus
i 1 ifOperStatus i 1
```

The datagram trace is as follows:

```
Frame 1 (162 bytes on wire, 162 bytes captured)
     Arrival Time: Sep 20, 2004 14:38:53.846768000
     Time delta from previous packet: 0.000000000 seconds
     Time since reference or first frame: 0.000000000 seconds
```

```
    Frame Number: 1
    Packet Length: 162 bytes
    Capture Length: 162 bytes
Ethernet II, Src: 00:00:00:00:00:00, Dst: 00:00:00:00:00:00
    Destination: 00:00:00:00:00:00 (00:00:00_00:00:00)
    Source: 00:00:00:00:00:00 (00:00:00_00:00:00)
    Type: IP (0x0800)
Internet Protocol, Src Addr: 127.0.0.1 (127.0.0.1), Dst Addr: 127.0.0.1 (127.0.0.1)
    Version: 4
    Header length: 20 bytes
    Differentiated Services Field: 0x00 (DSCP 0x00: Default; ECN: 0x00)
        0000 00.. = Differentiated Services Codepoint: Default (0x00)
        .... ..0. = ECN-Capable Transport (ECT): 0
        .... ...0 = ECN-CE: 0
    Total Length: 148
    Identification: 0x0000 (0)
    Flags: 0x04
        .1.. = Don't fragment: Set
        ..0. = More fragments: Not set
    Fragment offset: 0
    Time to live: 0
    Protocol: UDP (0x11)
    Header checksum: 0x7c57 (correct)
    Source: 127.0.0.1 (127.0.0.1)
    Destination: 127.0.0.1 (127.0.0.1)
User Datagram Protocol, Src Port: 34108 (34108), Dst Port: snmptrap (162)
    Source port: 34108 (34108)
    Destination port: snmptrap (162)
    Length: 128
    Checksum: 0xfe93 (incorrect, should be 0x76ba)
Simple Network Management Protocol
    Version: 2C (1)
    Community: public
    PDU type: TRAP-V2 (7)
    Request Id: 0x6737908a
    Error Status: NO ERROR (0)
    Error Index: 0
    Object identifier 1: 1.3.6.1.2.1.1.3.0 (SNMPv2-MIB::sysUpTime.0)
    Value: Timeticks: (181731693) 21 days, 0:48:36.93
    Object identifier 2: 1.3.6.1.6.3.1.1.4.1.0 (SNMPv2-MIB::snmpTrapOID.0)
    Value: OID: IF-MIB::linkDown
    Object identifier 3: 1.3.6.1.2.1.2.2.1.1 (IF-MIB::ifIndex)
    Value: INTEGER: 2
    Object identifier 4: 1.3.6.1.2.1.2.2.1.7 (IF-MIB::ifAdminStatus)
    Value: INTEGER: up(1)
    Object identifier 5: 1.3.6.1.2.1.2.2.1.8 (IF-MIB::ifOperStatus)
    Value: INTEGER: up(1)


0000  00 00 00 00 00 00 00 00 00 00 00 00 08 00 45 00   ..............E.
0010  00 94 00 00 40 00 00 11 7c 57 7f 00 00 01 7f 00   ....@...|W......
0020  00 01 85 3c 00 a2 00 80 fe 93 30 76 02 01 01 04   ...<......0v....
0030  06 70 75 62 6c 69 63 a7 69 02 04 67 37 90 8a 02   .public.i..g7...
0040  01 00 02 01 00 30 5b 30 10 06 08 2b 06 01 02 01   .....0[0...+....
0050  01 03 00 43 04 0a d5 01 6d 30 17 06 0a 2b 06 01   ...C....m0...+..
```

```
0060  06 03 01 01 04 01 00 06 09 2b 06 01 06 03 01 01   .........+......
0070  05 03 30 0e 06 09 2b 06 01 02 01 02 02 01 01 02   ..o...+.........
0080  01 02 30 0e 06 09 2b 06 01 02 01 02 02 01 07 02   ..o...+.........
0090  01 01 30 0e 06 09 2b 06 01 02 01 02 02 01 08 02   ..o...+.........
00a0  01 01                                             ..
```

SNMP inform

SNMPv2 provides an inform mechanism, which allows for acknowledged sending of traps. This operation can be useful when the need arises for more than one NMS in the network. When an inform is sent, the receiver sends a response to the sender acknowledging receipt of the event. This behavior is similar to that of the get and set requests. Note that an SNMP inform can be used to send SNMPv2 traps to an NMS. If you use an inform for this purpose, the agent will be notified when the NMS receives the trap.

SNMP report

The report operation was defined in the draft version of SNMPv2 but was never implemented. It is now part of the SNMPv3 standard and is intended to allow SNMP engines to communicate with each other (mainly to report problems with processing SNMP messages).

Host Management Revisited

Managing your hosts is an important part of network management. You would think that the Host Resources MIB would be part of every host-based SNMP agent, but this isn't the case. Some SNMP agents implement this MIB, but many don't. A few agents go further and implement proprietary extensions based upon this MIB. This is mainly due to the fact that this MIB was intended to serve as a basic, watered-down framework for host management, designed mainly to foster wide deployment.

The Host Resources MIB defines the following seven groups:

```
host            OBJECT IDENTIFIER ::= { mib-2 25 }

hrSystem        OBJECT IDENTIFIER ::= { host 1 }
hrStorage       OBJECT IDENTIFIER ::= { host 2 }
hrDevice        OBJECT IDENTIFIER ::= { host 3 }
hrSWRun         OBJECT IDENTIFIER ::= { host 4 }
hrSWRunPerf     OBJECT IDENTIFIER ::= { host 5 }
hrSWInstalled   OBJECT IDENTIFIER ::= { host 6 }
```

The *host* OID is *1.3.6.1.2.1.25* (*iso.org.dod.internet.mgmt.mib-2.host*). The remaining six groups define various objects that provide information about the system.

The *hrSystem* (*1.3.6.1.2.1.25.1*) group defines objects that pertain to the system itself. These objects include uptime, system date, system users, and system processes.

The *hrDevice* (1.3.6.1.2.1.25.3) and *hrStorage* (1.3.6.1.2.1.25.2) groups define objects pertaining to filesystems and system storage, such as total system memory, disk utilization, and CPU nonidle percentage. They are particularly helpful since they can be used to manage the disk partitions on your host. You can even use them to check for errors on a given disk device.

The *hrSWRun* (1.3.6.1.2.1.25.4), *hrSWRunPerf* (1.3.6.1.2.1.25.5), and *hrSWInstalled* (1.3.6.1.2.1.25.6) groups define objects that represent various aspects of software running or installed on the system. From these groups, you can determine what operating system is running on the host, as well as what programs the host is currently running. The *hrSWInstalled* group can be used to track which software packages are installed.

As you can see, the Host Resources MIB provides some necessary system-management objects that can be utilized by almost anyone who needs to manage critical systems.

Remote Monitoring Revisited

A thorough treatment of RMON is beyond the scope of this book, but it's worth discussing the groups that make up RMONv1. RMON probes are typically standalone devices that watch traffic on the network segments to which they are attached. Some vendors implement at least some kind of RMON probe in their routers, hubs, or switches. Chapter 8 provides an example of how to configure RMON on a Cisco router.

The RMON MIB defines the following 10 groups:

```
rmon            OBJECT IDENTIFIER ::= { mib-2 16 }
statistics      OBJECT IDENTIFIER ::= { rmon 1 }
history         OBJECT IDENTIFIER ::= { rmon 2 }
alarm           OBJECT IDENTIFIER ::= { rmon 3 }
hosts           OBJECT IDENTIFIER ::= { rmon 4 }
hostTopN        OBJECT IDENTIFIER ::= { rmon 5 }
matrix          OBJECT IDENTIFIER ::= { rmon 6 }
filter          OBJECT IDENTIFIER ::= { rmon 7 }
capture         OBJECT IDENTIFIER ::= { rmon 8 }
event           OBJECT IDENTIFIER ::= { rmon 9 }
```

RMONv1 provides packet-level statistics about an entire LAN or WAN. The *rmon* OID is *1.3.6.1.2.1.16 (iso.org.dod.internet.mgmt.mib-2.rmon)*. RMONv1 is made up of nine groups:

statistics (1.3.6.1.2.1.16.1)
Contains statistics about all the Ethernet interfaces monitored by the probe.

history (1.3.6.1.2.1.16.2)
Records periodic statistical samples from the *statistics* group.

alarm (1.3.6.1.2.1.16.3)
> Allows a user to configure a polling interval and a threshold for any object the RMON probe records.

hosts (1.3.6.1.2.1.16.4)
> Records traffic statistics for each host on the network.

hostTopN (1.3.6.1.2.1.16.5)
> Contains host statistics used to generate reports on hosts that top a list ordered by a parameter in the host table.

matrix (1.3.6.1.2.1.16.6)
> Stores error and utilization information for sets of two addresses.

filter (1.3.6.1.2.1.16.7)
> Matches packets based on a filter equation; when a packet matches the filter, it may be captured or an event may be generated.

capture (1.3.6.1.2.1.16.8)
> Allows packets to be captured if they match a filter in the filter group.

event (1.3.6.1.2.1.16.9)
> Controls the definition of RMON events.

RMONv2 enhances RMONv1 by providing network- and application-level statistical gathering. Since the only example of RMON in this book uses RMONv1, we will stop here and not go into RMONv2. However, we encourage you to read RFC 2021 to get a feel for what enhancements this version of RMON brings to network monitoring.

Reverse Engineering SNMP

You might be wondering why something like this is even a topic for SNMP. Isn't SNMP a standard, you may ask? Well, it is, but that doesn't prevent vendors from doing things in nonstandard, and downright oblique, ways. In some cases, vendors either do not publish their SNMP MIB, or they use SNMP as a means of updating a network device from a GUI. For example, the Netgear WAG302 access point comes with Windows-based management software. This software uses SNMP to gather information from the WAP. The Netgear device supports several standard SNMP MIBs, but it also has support for two additional private MIBs: Netgear's MIB and that of a third-party provider. Netgear doesn't make its private MIB available. Using Ethereal (yes, it is available for Windows, too), you can capture the traffic as you work with a management application, such as the one that comes with the Netgear device, and see what SNMP requests and responses flow over the network.

As we mentioned already, Ethereal does a nice job of telling you things like the SNMP version, error codes, OIDs, and actual data in the PDU. We even get to see the OIDs and their values. For example, the following is an excerpt from the notification trace:

```
Object identifier 3: 1.3.6.1.2.1.2.2.1.1 (IF-MIB::ifIndex)
Value: INTEGER: 2
Object identifier 4: 1.3.6.1.2.1.2.2.1.7 (IF-MIB::ifAdminStatus)
Value: INTEGER: up(1)
Object identifier 5: 1.3.6.1.2.1.2.2.1.8 (IF-MIB::ifOperStatus)
Value: INTEGER: up(1)
```

We see that *ifIndex* is set to INTEGER 2, *ifAdminStatus* is set to INTEGER 1 (which Ethereal has translated to up for us), and *ifOperStatus* is set to up as well.

We suggest that you add Ethereal to your arsenal of network tools. It can help you greatly, not only in reverse engineering SNMP, but also in terms of learning about datagram structures and the like.

## CHAPTER 3

SNMPv3

Security has been the biggest weakness of SNMP since the beginning. Authentication in SNMP versions 1 and 2 amounts to nothing more than a password (community string) sent in clear text between a manager and agent. Any security-conscious network or system administrator knows that clear-text passwords provide no real security at all. It is trivial for someone to intercept the community string, and once he has it, he can use it to retrieve information from devices on your network, modify their configuration, and even shut them down.

The Simple Network Management Protocol Version 3 (SNMPv3) addresses the security problems that have plagued both SNMPv1 and SNMPv2. For all practical purposes, security is the only issue SNMPv3 addresses; there are no other changes to the protocol. There are no new operations; SNMPv3 supports all the operations defined by versions 1 and 2. There are several new textual conventions, but these are really just more precise ways of interpreting the datatypes that were defined in earlier versions.

This chapter provides an introduction to SNMPv3. SNMPv3 agent configurations can be found in Chapter 6. Until recently, SNMPv3 was a draft standard. It is now a full standard. Vendors are notoriously slow to change, but hopefully we will see even more of them begin to support SNMPv3.

Changes in SNMPv3

Although SNMPv3 makes no changes to the protocol aside from the addition of cryptographic security, its developers have managed to make things look much different by introducing new textual conventions, concepts, and terminology. The changes to the terminology are so radical that it's hard to believe the new terms essentially describe the same software as the old ones, but they do. However, they do differ in how they relate to each other, and they specify much more precisely the pieces that an SNMP implementation needs.

The most important change is that Version 3 abandons the notion of managers and agents. Both managers and agents are now called SNMP entities. Each entity consists of an SNMP engine and one or more SNMP applications, which are discussed in the following sections. These new concepts are important because they define an architecture rather than simply a set of messages; the architecture helps to separate different pieces of the SNMP system in a way that makes a secure implementation possible. Let's look at what these concepts mean, starting with the RFCs that define them (Table 3-1).

Table 3-1. RFCs for SNMPv3

Number	Name
RFC 3411	Architecture for SNMP Frameworks
RFC 3412	Message Processing and Dispatching
RFC 3413	SNMP Applications
RFC 3414	User-based Security Model (USM)
RFC 3415	View-based Access Control Model (VACM)
RFC 3416	Protocol Operations for SNMPv2
RFC 3417	Transport Mappings for SNMPv2
RFC 3418	MIB for SNMPv2
RFC 2576	Coexistence Between SNMP Versions
RFC 2570	Introduction to SNMPv3
RFC 2786	Diffie-Hellman USM Key Management

Note that USM and VACM are discussed in a little more detail later in this chapter.

The SNMPv3 Engine

The engine is composed of four pieces: the Dispatcher, the Message Processing Subsystem, the Security Subsystem, and the Access Control Subsystem. The Dispatcher's job is to send and receive messages. It tries to determine the version of each received message (i.e., v1, v2, or v3) and, if the version is supported, hands the message off to the Message Processing Subsystem. The Dispatcher also sends SNMP messages to other entities.

The Message Processing Subsystem prepares messages to be sent and extracts data from received messages. A Message Processing Subsystem can contain multiple message processing modules. For example, a subsystem can have modules for processing SNMPv1, SNMPv2, and SNMPv3 requests. It may also contain a module for other processing models that are yet to be defined.

The Security Subsystem provides authentication and privacy services. Authentication uses either community strings (SNMP v1 and v2) or SNMPv3 user-based authentication. User-based authentication uses the MD5 or SHA algorithms to authenticate users without sending a password in the clear. The privacy service uses the DES algorithm to encrypt and decrypt SNMP messages. Currently, DES is the only algorithm used, though others may be added in the future.

The Access Control Subsystem is responsible for controlling access to MIB objects. You can control what objects a user can access as well what operations she is allowed to perform on those objects. For example, you might want to limit a user's read-write access to certain parts of the *mib-2* tree while allowing read-only access to the entire tree.

SNMPv3 Applications

Version 3 divides most of what we have come to think of as SNMP into a number of applications:

Command generator
> Generates get, getnext, getbulk, and set requests and processes the responses. This application is implemented by an NMS, so it can issue queries and set requests against entities on routers, switches, Unix hosts, etc.

Command responder
> Responds to get, getnext, getbulk, and set requests. This application is implemented by an entity on a Cisco router or Unix host. (For versions 1 and 2, the command responder is implemented by the SNMP agent.)

Notification originator
> Generates SNMP traps and notifications. This application is implemented by an entity on a router or Unix host. (For versions 1 and 2, the notification originator is part of an SNMP agent. Freestanding utilities for generating traps are also available.)

Notification receiver
> Receives traps and inform messages. This application is implemented by an NMS.

Proxy forwarder
> Facilitates message passing between entities.

RFC 3411 allows additional applications to be defined over time. This ability to extend the SNMPv3 framework is a significant advantage over the older SNMP versions.

What Does an Entity Look Like?

Thus far, we've talked about the SNMPv3 entity in terms of abstract definitions. Figure 3-1 (taken from RFC 3411) shows how the components that make up an entity fit together.

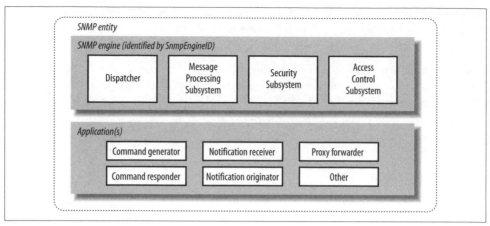

Figure 3-1. SNMPv3 entity

SNMPv3 Textual Conventions

SNMPv3 defines a number of additional textual conventions, outlined in Table 3-2.

Table 3-2. SNMPv3 textual conventions

Textual convention	Description
snmpEngineID	An administratively unique identifier for an SNMP engine. Objects of this type are for identification, not for addressing, even though an address can be used in the generation of a specific value. RFC 3411 provides a detailed discussion of how snmpEngineIDs are created.
snmpSecurityModel	An SNMP securityModel (SNMPv1, SNMPv2, or USM). USM stands for User-based Security Model, which is the security method used in SNMPv3.
snmpMessageProcessingModel	A message processing model used by the Message Processing Subsystem.
snmpSecurityLevel	The level of security at which SNMP messages can be sent, or the level of security at which operations are being processed. Possible values are noAuthNoPriv (without authentication and without privacy), authNoPriv (with authentication but without privacy), and authPriv (with authentication and with privacy). These three values are ordered such that noAuthNoPriv is less than authNoPriv and authNoPriv is less than authPriv.
snmpAdminString	An octet string containing administrative information, preferably in human-readable form. The string can be up to 255 bytes long.
snmpTagValue	An octet string containing a tag value. Tag values are preferably in human-readable form. According to RFC 3413, valid example tags include acme, router, and host.
snmpTagList	An octet string containing a list of tag values. Tag values are preferably in human-readable form. According to RFC 3413, valid examples of a tag list are the empty string, acme router, and host managerStation.
KeyChange	An object used to change authentication and privacy keys.

The next two sections will look at the USM and VACM in a little more detail.

USM

The User-based Security Model (USM) and the View Access Control Model (VACM) together detail the security enhancements added with SNMPv3. Let's start with the USM.

The Basics

We need to get some terminology out of the way before we can look at the USM in any detail:

snmpEngineID
> This is an unambiguous identifier for an SNMP engine as well as the SNMP entity that corresponds to the engine. The syntax for this identifier is OctetString and it cannot be zero length. Most SNMPv3 applications allow for the user to input a value for snmpEngineID. If one is not specified, the value is computed using a combination of enterprise ID and IP or MAC address.

snmpEngineBoots
> A count of the number of times an SNMP engine has rebooted.

snmpEngineTime
> The number of seconds since the snmpEngineBoots counter was last incremented.

snmpSecurityLevel
> There are three security levels. The first is no authentication or privacy (noAuth-NoPriv). Note that if this mode is used, a securityName is still required. The second is authentication and no privacy (authNoPriv). The third and final one is authentication and privacy (authPriv). While you can have authentication without privacy, you cannot have privacy without authentication.

Authoritative SNMP engine
> A nonauthoritative engine must discover the snmpEngineId of the authoritative engine with which it communicates. The rules for designating the authoritative engine are as follows: if the SNMP message requires a response (get, getnext, get-bulk, set, or inform), the receiver of these messages is authoritative. If the message does not require a response (trap or report), the sender of the message is authoritative. Generally, an SNMP agent is authoritative and an NMS is nonauthoritative.

An SNMPv3 message (packet) format has the following fields:

msgVersion
> The SNMP version of the message, set to 3.

msgID
> The msgID is used between a manager and agent to coordinate request and response messages.

msgMaxSize

> The msgMaxSize is the maximum message size supported by a sender of an SNMP message.

msgFlags

> msgFlags is an 8-bit value that specifies whether a report PDU is to be generated, whether privacy is used, and whether authentication is used.

msgSecurityModel

> Specifies which security model was used by the sender of the message. Current values are 1, 2, and 3 for SNMPv1, SNMPv2c, and SNMPv3, respectively.

msgSecurityParameters

> msgSecurityParameters contains security-specific information.

contextEngineID

> Uniquely identifies an SNMP entity. An SNMP entity is the combination of an SNMP engine and SNMP applications. This is discussed in the section on VACM.

contextName

> contextName identifies a particular context within an SNMP engine.

scopedPDU

> A block of data made up of a contextEngineID, contextName, and SNMP PDU.

The msgSecurityParameters in an SNMPv3 message are as follows:

msgAuthoritativeEngineID

> The snmpEngineID of the authoritative engine.

msgAuthoritativeEngineBoots

> The snmpEngineBoots of the authoritative engine.

msgAuthoritativeEngineTime

> The snmpEngineTime of the authoritative engine.

msgUserName

> The user who may be authenticating and encrypting the message.

msgAuthenticationParameters

> This value is null if no authentication is used. Otherwise, the field contains the computer HMAC message digest for the message. Currently the RFC specifies that MD5 and SHA must be used.

msgPrivacyParameters

> This value is null if no encryption is used. Otherwise, this field is used to form the initial value of the Cipher Block Chaining mode of the Data Encryption Standard (CBC-DES) algorithm.

Figure 3-2[*] shows the entire SNMPv3 message.

---

[*] This image is reprinted from the paper "SNMPv3: A Security Enhancement for SNMP" by William Stallings, which can be found online at *http://www.comsoc.org/livepubs/surveys/public/4q98issue/stallings.html*.

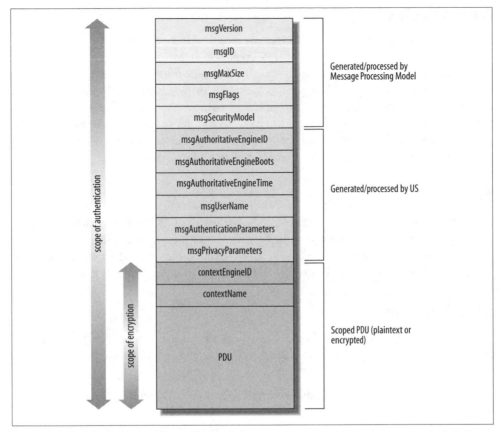

Figure 3-2. SNMPv3 message format

Discovery

The USM requires that the msgSecurityParameters contain the snmpEngineID, snmpEngineBoots, and snmpEngineTime of the authoritative engine. Before any get, get-next, or set operation can be used, the nonauthoritative engine must obtain these values from the authoritative engine. A discovery process is used to obtain this information.

USM Timeliness

Once a nonauthoritative engine has learned the value of snmpEngineBoots and snmpEngineTime, it must maintain its own local notion of what these values are supposed to be. The nonauthoritative engine increments the learned snmpEngineTime every second so that it stays up-to-date with the authoritative engine's own notion of snmpEngineTime. If snmpEngineTime rolls over, snmpEngineBoots must be incremented. The USM Timeliness Module is intended to help thwart message delay or replay.

Authentication

MD5, or Message Digest 5, and SHA1, or Secure Hash Algorithm 1, are used for authenticating SNMPv3 messages. MD5 creates a digest of 128 bits and SHA1 creates a digest of 160 bits. Both digests are fixed in size and cannot be used solely for authentication. The keyed Hashing for Message Authentication (HMAC) algorithm is used in conjunction with MD5 and SHA1 to compute message digests. An authentication passphrase or secret key is appended to the data before the digests are computed. The secret key must be known by both the sender and the receiver. The RFCs specify that this passphrase must be at least eight characters long.

Privacy

Encryption of SNMP data is accomplished by using the CBC-DES algorithm. As with authentication, a secret key or passphrase must be known by the sender and receiver and used in the encryption process. A USM User Table is used to store the passphrase and other details transmitted with the packet in the `msgPrivacyParameters`.

USM User Table

Every entity maintains a User Table that stores all the users who have access to the system via SNMP. The User Table includes the following elements:

Username
> A textual username. Sometimes referred to as a security name.

Authentication protocol
> Details what, if any, authentication protocol is to be used. Valid values include `usmNoAuthProtocol`, `usmHMACMD5AuthProtocol`, and `usmHMACSHAAuthProtocol`.

Authentication key
> The passphrase used for authentication. Must be at least eight characters long.

Privacy protocol
> Details what, if any, privacy protocol is to be used. Valid values include `usmNoPrivProtocol` and `usmDESPrivProtocol`.

Privacy key
> The passphrase used for privacy. Must be at least eight characters long.

`usmUserSpinLock`
> The `usmUserSpinLock` is an advisory lock that allows for the coordination of multiple attempts to modify the User Table.

Localized Keys and Changing Keys

A localized key allows for the same passphrase to be used by a single user on many different engines. It keeps an operator from having to remember a different passphrase for each SNMP engine he must interact with. The `KeyChange` type allows for users to change their keys securely.

VACM

VACM is used to control access to managed objects in a MIB or MIBs. This is where the Access Control Subsystem comes into play.

The Basics

The `msgFlags`, `msgSecurityModel`, and `scopedPDU` fields are used by VACM for message access. Each parameter is used to determine access to managed objects. An error is returned to the sender if access is not allowed for the request type. VACM makes use of four tables for different aspects of access control. We will discuss these tables next.

Context Table

The `vacmContextTable` is a collection of managed objects that have access constraints which are associated with a context name. The `vacmContextTable` stores all available contexts. The table is indexed by a `contextName`, and each row in this table contains:

vacmContextName
> A textual name for the context

Security to Group Table

The `vacmSecurityToGroupTable` is used to store group information. A group is made up of zero or more `securityModel` and `securityName` combinations. This combination defines what managed objects can be accessed. The table itself is indexed by a `securityModel` and `securityName`. The table contains rows made up of the following columns:

vacmSecurityModel
> The security model in use—e.g., USM.

vacmSecurityName
> In the case of the USM, `securityName` and `userName` are identical.

vacmGroupName
> A textual name for the group to which this table entry belongs.

Access Table

The `vacmAccessTable` is used to store the access rights defined for groups. This table is indexed by a `groupName`, `contextPrefix`, `securityModel`, and `securityLevel`. Each row in this table contains:

vacmGroupName
> A name of a group with access rights.

vacmAccessContextMatch
> A simple form of wildcarding. A value of *exact* dictates that the index contextName must exactly match the value in vacmAccessContextPrefix. If set to *prefix*, the index contextName can simply match the first few characters of the value in vacmAccessContextPrefix.

vacmAccessContextPrefix
> An index contextName must match either exactly or partially the value of vacmAccessContextPrefix.

vacmAccessSecurityModel
> The securityModel that must be used to gain access.

vacmAccessSecurityLevel
> Defines the minimum securityLevel that must be used to gain access.

vacmAccessReadViewName
> The authorized MIB viewName used for read access.

vacmAccessWriteViewName
> The authorized MIB viewName used for write access.

vacmAccessNotifyViewName
> The authorized MIB viewName used for notify access.

View Tree Family Table

The vacmViewTreeFamilyTable is used to store MIB views. A MIB view is defined as a family of view subtrees that pair an OID subtree value with a mask value. The mask indicates which subidentifiers of the associated subtree OID are significant to the MIB view's definition.

All the MIB views are stored in the vacmViewTreeFamilyTable. It is indexed by a viewName and an OID of a MIB subtree. The VACM MIB defines the vacmViewSpinLock advisory lock that is used to allow several SNMP engines to coordinate modifications to this table. Each row in the vacmViewTreeFamilyTable contains:

vacmViewTreeFamilyViewName
> A textual name for the MIB view.

vacmViewTreeFamilySubtree
> The OID subtree that, when combined with the mask, defines one or more MIB view subtrees.

vacmViewTreeFamilyMask
> A bit mask that, in combination with the corresponding OID subtree, defines one or more MIB view subtrees.

`vacmViewTreeFamilyType`
> Indicates whether the corresponding MIB view subtrees defined by the OID subtree and mask are included or excluded from the MIB view.

Figure 3-3 shows the logic flow for VACM.

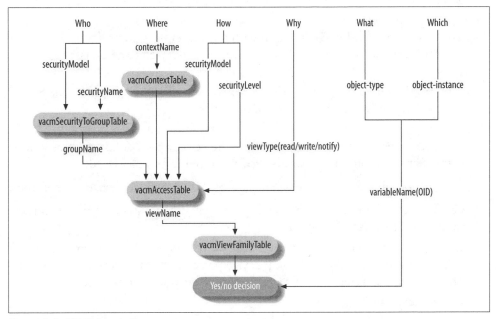

Figure 3-3. VACM logic flow

SNMPv3 in the Real World

Let's briefly outline the common configuration options you should expect when you have to configure an SNMPv3 device or network management platform:

Username
> This is the textual description of the person responsible for the SNMP entity that is to be managed. Sometimes referred to as security name.

Security level
> Some applications require you to explicitly set the security level and others determine it based on the combination of authentication and privacy protocol in use. The specified values are `noAuthNoPriv`, which is no authentication and no privacy, `authNoPriv`, which is authentication and no privacy, and `authPriv`, which is authentication and privacy. Note that you cannot have privacy without authentication, but you can have authentication without privacy.

which is authentication and privacy. Note that you cannot have privacy without authentication, but you can have authentication without privacy.

Authentication protocol

The protocol used for authentication—that is, to prove that you are who you say you are. Currently, MD5 and SHA1 are specified in the RFCs.

Authentication passphrase

The passphrase used in conjunction with the authentication protocol. It must be at least eight characters long. You may also see it referred to as a password.

Privacy protocol

The protocol used for privacy, that is, to encrypt the data portion of the SNMP packet. Currently, DES is specified in the RFCs.

Privacy passphrase

The passphrase used in conjunction with the privacy protocol. It must be at least eight characters long. You may also see it referred to as a password.

Here are the logical steps you take when using SNMPv3-enabled devices and entities:

1. Create a USM entry on a device with proper USM attributes: username, authentication protocol, etc.

2. Configure the management station (if it supports SNMPv3) with the proper USM attributes for the managed device. Note that the username and passphrases created in step 1 will need to be entered manually in this step.

3. Begin managing the device.

After all the gory technical details, isn't it nice to see that the basics of SNMPv3 really aren't all that scary?

SNMPv3 provides some much-needed security for SNMP. Many vendors already support SNMPv3, but many others, of course, do not. Vendors are often slow to change, mainly because SNMP support is generally an afterthought during the development life cycle of a switch, router, or software system. In fact, SNMP is often a bolt-on feature that isn't heavily tested and is rarely updated. But we in the network management field can only hope that more vendors embrace not only SNMP but also SNMPv3.

## CHAPTER 4

NMS Architectures

Now that you understand the basic concepts behind how network management stations (NMSs) and agents communicate, it's time to introduce the concept of a network management architecture. Before rushing out to deploy SNMP management, you owe it to yourself to put some effort into developing a coherent plan. If you simply drop NMS software on a few of your favorite desktop machines, you're likely to end up with something that doesn't work very well. By NMS architecture, we mean a plan that helps you use NMSs effectively to manage your network. A key component of network management is selecting the proper hardware (i.e., an appropriate platform on which to run your NMS) and making sure that your management stations are located in such a way that they can observe the devices on your network effectively.

Hardware Considerations

Managing a reasonably large network requires an NMS with substantial computing power. In today's complex networked environments, networks can range in size from a few nodes to thousands of nodes. The process of polling and receiving traps from hundreds or thousands of managed entities can be taxing on the best of hardware. Your NMS vendor will be able to help you determine what kind of hardware is appropriate for managing your network. Most vendors have formulas for determining how much RAM you will need to achieve the level of performance you want, given the requirements of your network. It usually boils down to the number of devices you want to poll, the amount of information you will request from each device, and the interval at which you want to poll them. The software you want to run is also a consideration. NMS products such as OpenView are large, heavyweight applications; if you want to run your own scripts with Perl, you can get away with a much smaller management platform.

Is it possible to say something more helpful than "ask your vendor"? Yes. First, although we've become accustomed to thinking of NMS software as requiring a midrange workstation or high-end PC, desktop hardware has advanced so much in the past year or two that running this software is within the range of any modern PC.

Specifically, surveying the recommendations of a number of vendors, we have found that they suggest a PC with at least a 2 or 3 GHz CPU, 512 MB to 1 GB of memory, and 1-2 GB of disk space. Requirements for Sun SPARC and HP workstations are similar.

Let's look at each of these requirements:

2 or 3 GHz CPU
> This is well within the range of any modern desktop system, but you probably can't bring your older equipment out of retirement to use as a management station.

512 MB to 1 GB of memory
> You'll probably have to add memory to any off-the-shelf PC; Sun and HP workstations come with more generous memory configurations. Frankly, vendors tend to underestimate memory requirements anyway, so it won't hurt to upgrade to 2 GB. Fortunately, RAM is usually cheap these days, though memory prices fluctuate from day to day.

1-2 GB of disk space
> This recommendation is probably based on the amount of space you'll need to store the software, and not on the space you'll need for logfiles, long-term trend data, etc. But again, disk space is cheap these days, and skimping is counterproductive.

Let's think a bit more about how long-term data collection affects your disk requirements. First, you should recognize that some products have only minimal data-collection facilities, while others exist purely for the purpose of collecting data (for example, MRTG). Whether you can do data collection effectively depends to some extent on the NMS product you've selected. Therefore, before deciding on a software product, you should think about your data-collection requirements. Do you want to do long-term trend analysis? If so, that will affect both the software you choose and the hardware on which you run it.

For a starting point, let's say that you have 1,000 nodes, you want to collect data every minute, and you're collecting 1 KB of data per node. That's 1 MB per minute, 1.4 GB per day—you'll fill a 40GB disk in about a month. That's bordering on extravagant. But let's look at the assumptions:

- Collecting data every minute is certainly excessive; every 10 minutes should do. Now your 40GB disk will store almost a year's worth of data.

- A network with 1,000 nodes isn't that big. But do you really want to store trend data for all your users' PCs? Much of this book is devoted to showing you how to control the amount of data you collect. Instead of 1,000 nodes, let's first count interfaces. And let's forget about desktop systems—we really care about trend data for our network backbone: key servers, routers, switches, etc. Even on a midsize network, we're probably talking about 100 or 200 interfaces.

- The amount of data you collect per interface depends on many factors, not the least of which is the format of the data. An interface's status may be up or down—that's a single bit. If it's being stored in a binary data structure, it may be represented by a single bit. But if you're using *syslog* to store your log data and writing Perl scripts to do trend analysis, your *syslog* records are going to be 80 bytes or so, even if you are storing only 1 bit of information. Data-storage mechanisms range from *syslog* to fancy database schemes—you obviously need to understand what you're using, and how it will affect your storage requirements. Furthermore, you need to understand how much information you really want to keep per interface. If you want to track only the number of octets going in and out of each interface and you're storing this data efficiently, your 40GB disk could easily last the better part of a century.

Seriously, it's hard to estimate your storage requirements when they vary over two or three orders of magnitude. But the lesson is that no vendor can tell you what your storage requirements will be. A gigabyte should be plenty for log data on a moderately large network, if you're storing data only for a reasonable subset of that network, not polling too often, and not saving too much data. But that's a lot of variables, and you're the only one in control of them. Keep in mind, though, that the more data you collect, the more time and CPU power will be required to grind through all that data and produce meaningful results. It doesn't matter whether you're using expensive trend-analysis software or some homegrown scripts—processing lots of data is expensive. At least in terms of long-term data collection, it's probably better to err by keeping too little data around than by keeping too much.

NMS Architectures

Before going out and buying all your equipment, it's worth spending some time coming up with an architecture for your network that will make it more manageable. The simplest architecture has a single management station that is responsible for the entire network, as shown in Figure 4-1.

The network depicted in Figure 4-1 has three sites: New York, Atlanta, and San Jose. The NMS in New York is responsible for managing not only the portion of the network in New York, but also those in Atlanta and San Jose. Traps sent from any device in Atlanta or San Jose must travel over the Internet to get to the NMS in New York. The same thing goes for polling devices in San Jose and Atlanta: the NMS in New York must send its requests over the Internet to reach these remote sites. For small networks, an architecture like this can work well. However, when the network grows to the point that a single NMS can no longer manage everything, this architecture becomes a real problem. The NMS in New York can get behind in its polling of the remote sites, mainly because it has so much to manage. The result is that when problems arise at a remote site, they may not get noticed for some time. In the worst case, they might not get noticed at all.

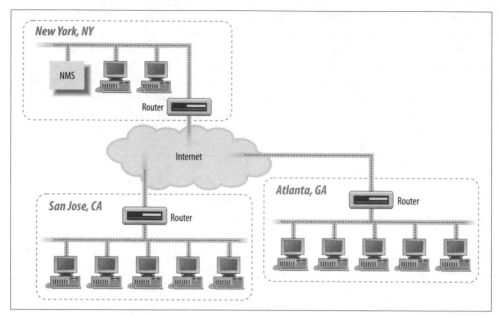

Figure 4-1. Single NMS architecture

It's also worth thinking about staffing. With a single NMS, your primary operations staff would be in New York, watching the health of the network. But problems frequently require somebody on-site to intervene. This requires someone in Atlanta and San Jose, plus the coordination that entails. You may not need a full-time network administrator, but you will need someone who knows what to do when a router fails.

When your network grows to a point where one NMS can no longer manage everything, it's time to move to a distributed NMS architecture. The idea behind this architecture is simple: use two or more management stations and locate them as close as possible to the nodes they are managing. In the case of our three-site network, we would have an NMS at each site. Figure 4-2 shows the addition of two NMSs to the network.

This architecture has several advantages, not the least of which is flexibility. With the new architecture, the NMSs in Atlanta and San Jose can act as standalone management stations, each with a fully self-sufficient staff, or they can forward events to the NMS in New York. If the remote NMSs forward all events to the NMS in New York, there is no need to put additional operations staff in Atlanta and San Jose. At first glance, this looks like we've returned to the situation of Figure 4-1, but that isn't quite true. Most NMS products provide some kind of client interface for viewing the events currently in the NMS (traps received, responses to polls, etc.). Since the NMS that forwards events to New York has already discovered the problem, we're simply letting the NMS in New York know about it so that it can be dealt with appropri-

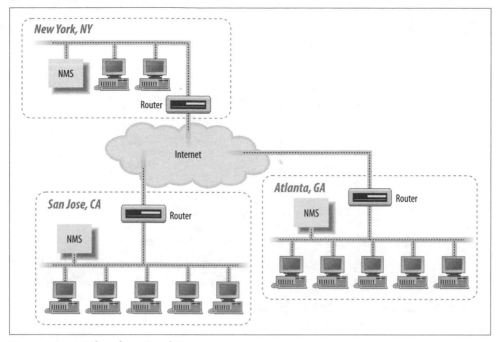

Figure 4-2. Distributed NMS architecture

ately. The New York NMS didn't have to use valuable resources to poll the remote network to discover that there was a problem.

The other advantage is that, if the need arises, you can put operations staff in Atlanta and San Jose to manage each of these remote locations. If New York loses connectivity to the Internet, events forwarded from Atlanta or San Jose will not make it to New York. With operations staff in Atlanta and San Jose, and the NMSs at these locations acting in standalone mode, a network outage in New York won't matter. The remote-location staff will continue as if nothing has happened.

Another possibility with this architecture is a hybrid mode: you staff the operations center in New York 24 hours a day, 7 days a week, but you staff Atlanta and San Jose only during business hours. During off-hours, they rely on the NMS and operations staff in New York to notice and handle problems that arise. But during the critical (and busiest) hours of the day, Atlanta and San Jose don't have to burden the New York operators.

Both of the architectures we have discussed use the Internet to send and receive management traffic. This poses several problems, mainly dealing with security and overall reliability. A better solution is to use private links to perform all your network management functions. Figure 4-3 shows how the distributed NMS architecture can be extended to make use of such links.

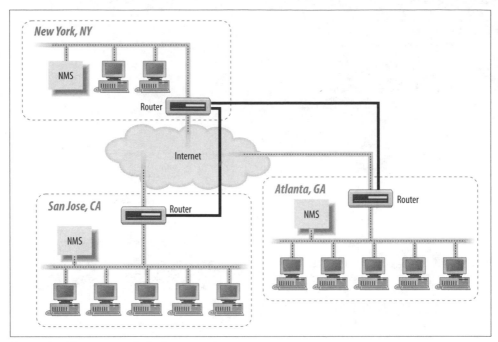

Figure 4-3. Using private links for network management

Let's say that New York's router is the core router for the network. We establish private (but not necessarily high-speed) links between San Jose and New York, and between New York and Atlanta. This means that San Jose will not only be able to reach New York, but it will also be able to reach Atlanta via New York. Atlanta will use New York to reach San Jose, too. The private links (denoted by thicker router-to-router connections) are primarily devoted to management traffic, though we could put them to other uses. Using private links has the added benefit that our community strings are never sent out over the Internet. The use of private network links for network management works equally well with the single NMS architecture, too. Of course, if your corporate network consists entirely of private links and your Internet connections are devoted to external traffic only, using private links for your management traffic is the proverbial "no-brainer."

One final item worth mentioning is the notion of trap-directed polling. This doesn't really have anything to do with NMS architecture, but it can help to alleviate an NMS's management strain. The idea behind trap-directed polling is simple: the NMS receives a trap and initiates a poll to the device that generated the trap. The goal of this scenario is to determine whether there is indeed a problem with the device while allowing the NMS to ignore (or devote few resources to) the device in normal operation. If an organization relies on this form of management, it should implement it in such a way that non-trap-directed polling is almost done away with. That is, it should avoid polling devices at regular intervals for status information. Instead, the management stations should simply wait to receive a trap before polling a device. This form of management can significantly reduce the resources needed by an NMS to manage a network. However, it has an important disadvantage: traps can get lost in the network and never make it to the NMS. This is a reality of the connectionless nature of UDP and the imperfect nature of networks.

A Look Ahead

Web-based network management entails the use of the HyperText Transfer Protocol (HTTP) and the Common Gateway Interface (CGI) to manage networked entities. It works by embedding a web server in an SNMP-compatible device, along with a CGI engine to convert SNMP-like requests (from a web-based NMS) to actual SNMP operations, and vice versa. Web servers can be embedded into such devices at very low monetary and operating cost.

Figure 4-4 is a simplified diagram of the interaction between a web-based NMS and a managed device. The CGI application bridges the gap between the management application and the SNMP engine. In some cases, the management application can be a collection of Java applets that are downloaded to the web browser and executed on the web-based manager. Current versions of OpenView ship with a web-based GUI. SNMPc also has web-based capabilities. They have a Java client for the network management console and the recently released SNMPc Online, which is a web-based reporting frontend.

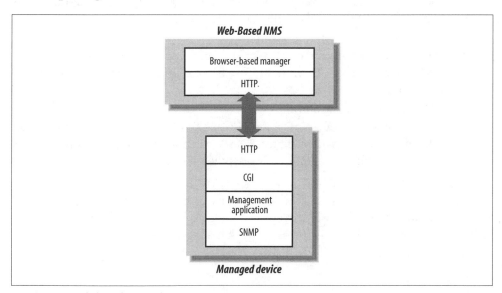

Figure 4-4. Web-based network management

Web-based network management could eliminate, or at least reduce, the need for traditional NMS software. NMS software can be expensive to purchase, set up, and maintain. Most of today's major NMS vendors support only a few popular versions of Unix and have only recently begun to support Windows, thus limiting your operating-system choices. With a web-based NMS, however, these two concerns are moot. For the most part, web browsers are free, and Unix, Windows, and Apple platforms all run the popular browsers.

Web-based network management should not be viewed as a panacea, though. It is a good idea, but it will take some time for vendors to embrace this technology and move toward web integration of their existing products. There is also the issue of standardization, or the lack of it. The Web-Based Enterprise Management (WBEM) Initiative addresses this by defining a standard for web-based management. Industry leaders such as Cisco and BMC Software are among the original founders of WBEM. You can learn more about this initiative at the Distributed Management Task Force's web page, *http://www.dmtf.org/standards/wbem*.

Another important standard in this area is XML (eXtensible Markup Language). XML is a markup language used for the interchange of structured data. XML makes use of DTDs (Document Type Definitions) or schemas to specify a document's structure and, in the case of schemas, to validate data. A DTD or schema is similar to an SNMP MIB. XML may be used for network management purposes in the following scenarios:

Using XML in place of standard SNMP over UDP
> In environments where UDP traffic isn't permissible, XML can be used as an intermediary application-level protocol. Of course, this requires a mapping layer to translate from XML to SNMP and vice versa.

Converting SNMP MIBs to XML for portability
> This has the distinct advantage of allowing languages and systems that support XML parsing to access MIB information. Java is a language that can easily interact with XML.

Using XML for command and control
> While this may seem like a perversion of what XML was originally intended for, applications are being written that use XML as an application-level protocol for not only exchanging messages, but also sending control messages.

As new technology comes to the forefront, SNMP researchers, vendors, and users will embrace it whenever it makes sense. This is evidenced by the adoption of SNMPv3 as well as by the use of web technologies for tackling the problems presented by the ever-expanding scope of network management.

## CHAPTER 5

Configuring Your NMS

Now that you have picked out some software to use in your environment, it's time to talk about installing and running it. In this chapter, we will look at a few NMS packages in detail. While we list several packages in Appendix F, we will dig into only a few packages here, and we'll use these packages in examples throughout the rest of the book. These examples should allow you to get most other SNMP-based network management packages up and running with very little effort.

HP's OpenView Network Node Manager

Network Node Manager (NNM) is a licensed software product. The package includes a feature called Instant-On that allows you to use the product for a limited time (60 days) while you are waiting for your real license to arrive. During this period, you are restricted to a 250-managed-node license, but the product's capabilities aren't limited in any other way. When you install the product, the Instant-On license is enabled by default.

Check out the OpenView scripts located in OpenView's *bin* directory (normally */opt/OV/bin*). One particularly important group of scripts sets environment variables that allow you to traverse OpenView's directory structure much more easily. These scripts are named *ov.env-vars.csh*, *ov.envvars.sh*, etc. (that is, *ov.envvars* followed by the name of the shell you're using). When you run the appropriate script for your shell, it defines environment variables such as $OV_BIN, $OV_MAN, and $OV_TMP, which point to the OpenView *bin*, *man*, and *tmp* directories, respectively. Thus, you can easily go to the directory containing OpenView's manual pages with the command *cd $OV_MAN*. These environment variables are used throughout this book and in all of OpenView's documentation.

Running NNM

To start the OpenView GUI on a Unix machine, define your DISPLAY environment variable and run the command $OV_BIN/ovw. This starts OpenView's NNM. If your NNM has performed any discovery, the nodes it has found should appear under your Internet (top-level) icon. If you have problems starting NNM, run the command $OV_BIN/ovstatus -c and then $OV_BIN/ovstart or $OV_BIN/ovstop, respectively, to start or stop it. By default, NNM installs the necessary scripts to start its daemons when the machine boots. OpenView will perform all of its functions in the background, even when you aren't running any maps. This means that you do not have to keep a copy of NNM running on your console at all times and you don't have to start it explicitly when your machine reboots.

When the GUI starts, it presents you with a clickable high-level map. This map, called the Root map, provides a top-level view of your network. The map gives you the ability to see your network without having to see every detail at once. If you want more information about any item in the display, whether it's a subnet or an individual node, click on it. You can drill down to see any level of detail you want—for example, you can look at an interface card on a particular node. The more detail you want, the more you click. Figure 5-1 shows a typical NNM map.

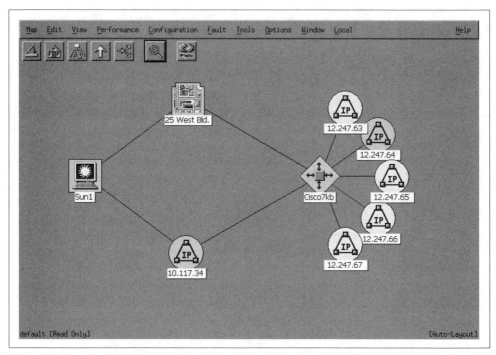

Figure 5-1. A typical NNM map

The menu bar (see Figure 5-2) allows you to traverse the map with a bit more ease. You have options such as closing NNM (the leftmost button, which resembles a closing door), going straight to the Home map (the second button from the left, which is, not surprisingly, a house),* the Root map (the third-left, a hierarchical diagram), the parent or previous map (the fourth-left button, an up arrow), or the quick navigator (the fifth-left button, a right arrow with two diverging arrows).† There is also a magnifying glass button that lets you pan through the map or zoom in on a portion of it.

Figure 5-2. OpenView NNM menu bar

 Before you get sick of looking at your newly discovered network, keep in mind that you can add some quick and easy customizations that will transform your hodgepodge of names, numbers, and icons into a coordinated picture of your network.

The netmon Process

NNM's daemon process (*netmon*) starts automatically when the system boots and is responsible for discovering nodes on your network, in addition to a few other tasks. In NNM's menu, go to Options → Network Polling Configurations: IP. A window should appear that looks similar to Figure 5-3.

Figure 5-3 shows the General area of the configuration wizard. The other areas are IP Discovery, Status Polling, and Secondary Failures. The General area allows us to specify a filter (in this example, NOUSERS) that controls the discovery process—we might not want to see every device on the network. We discuss the creation of filters in "Using OpenView Filters," later in this chapter. We elected to discover beyond the license limit, which means that NNM will discover more objects on our network than our license allows us to manage. "Excess" objects (objects past the license's limit) are placed in an unmanaged state so that you can see them on your maps but can't control them through NNM. This option is useful when your license limits you to a specific number of managed nodes.

The IP Discovery area (Figure 5-4) lets us enable or disable the discovery of IP nodes. Using the "auto adjust" discovery feature allows NNM to figure out how often to probe the network for new devices. The more new devices it finds, the more often it

* You can set any map as your Home map. When you've found the map you'd like to use, go to Map → Submap → Set This Submap as Home.

† This is a special map in which you can place objects that you need to watch frequently. It allows you to access them quickly, without having to find them by searching through the network map.

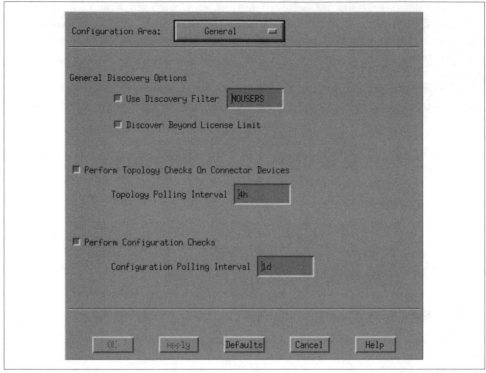

Figure 5-3. OpenView's General network polling configuration options

polls; if it doesn't find any new devices, it slows down, eventually waiting one day (1d) before checking for any new devices. If you don't like the idea that the discovery interval varies (or perhaps more realistically, if you think that probing the network to find new devices will consume more resources than you like, either on your network management station or on the network itself), you can specify a fixed discovery interval. Finally, the Discover Level-2 Objects button tells NNM to discover and report devices that are at the second layer of the OSI network model. This category includes things such as unmanaged hubs and switches, many AppleTalk devices, and so on.

Figure 5-5 shows the Status Polling configuration area. Here you can turn status polling on or off and delete nodes that have been down or unreachable for a specified length of time. The example in Figure 5-5 is configured to delete nodes after they've been down for one week (1w).

The DHCP polling options are, obviously, especially useful in environments that use DHCP. They allow you to establish a relationship between polling behavior and IP addresses. You can specify a filter that selects addresses that are assigned by DHCP. Then you can specify a time after which *netmon* will delete nonresponding DHCP addresses from its map of your network. If a device is down for the given amount of time, *netmon* disassociates the node and IP address. The rationale for this behavior is

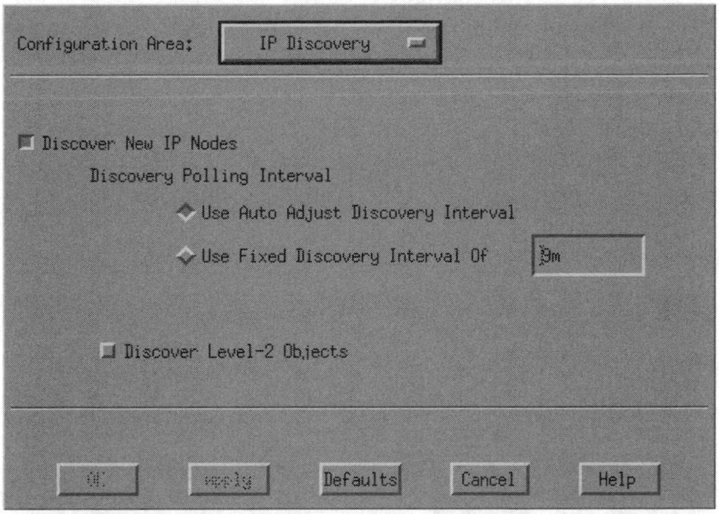

Figure 5-4. OpenView's IP Discovery network polling configuration options

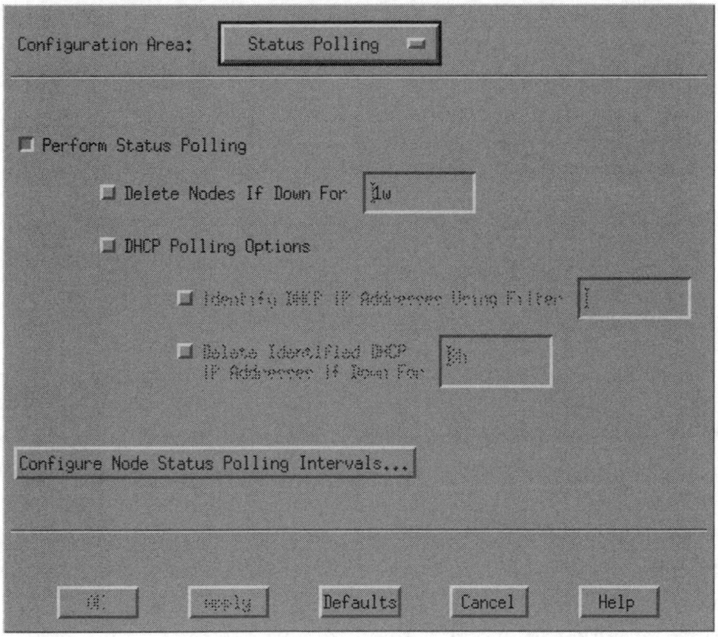

Figure 5-5. OpenView's Status Polling network polling configuration options

simple: in a DHCP environment, the disappearance of an IP address often means that the node has received a new IP address from a DHCP server. In that case, continuing to poll the old address is a waste of effort and is possibly even misleading, since the address may be reassigned to a different host.

Finally, the Secondary Failures configuration area shown in Figure 5-6 allows you to tell the poller how to react when it sees a secondary failure. This occurs when a node beyond a failed device is unreachable—for example, when a router goes down, making the file server that is connected via one of the router's interfaces unreachable. In this configuration area, you can state whether to show alarms for secondary failures or suppress them. If you choose to suppress them, you can set up a filter that identifies important nodes in your network that should not be suppressed even if they are deemed secondary failures.

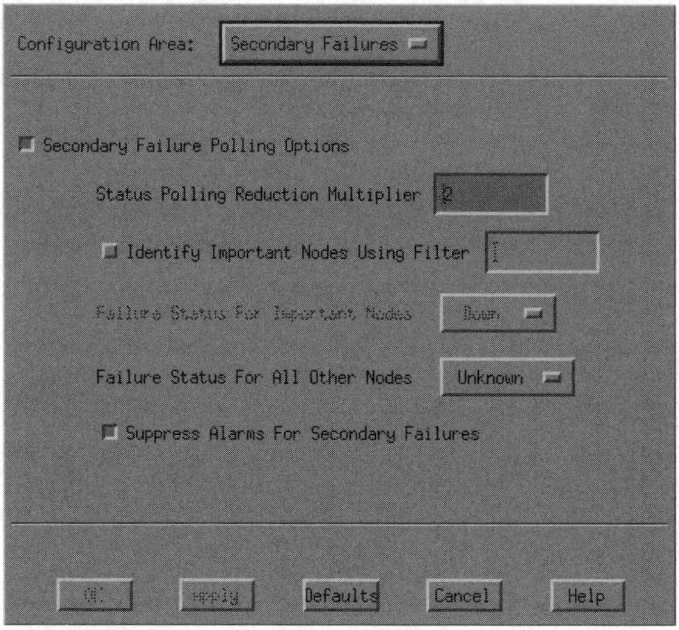

Figure 5-6. OpenView's Secondary Failures network polling configuration options

Once your map is up, you may notice that nothing is getting discovered. Initially, *netmon* won't discover anything beyond the network segment to which your NMS is attached. If your NMS has an IP address of 24.92.32.12, you will not discover your devices on 123.67.34.0. NNM finds adjacent routers and their segments, as long as they are SNMP compatible, and places them in an unmanaged (tan colored) state on the map.* This means that anything in and under that icon will not be polled or discovered. Selecting the icon and going to Edit → Manage Objects tells NNM to begin managing this network and allows *netmon* to start discovering nodes within it. You can quit managing nodes at any time by clicking on UnManage instead of Manage.

---

* In NNM, go to Help → Display Legend for a list of icons and their colors.

If your routers do not show any adjacent networks, you should try testing them with Fault → Test IP/TCP/SNMP. Add the name of your router, click Restart, and see what kind of results you get back. If you get a message that says "OK except for SNMP," read Chapter 6 as well as the next section in this chapter, which discusses setting up the default community names within OpenView.

netmon also allows you to specify a seed file that helps it to discover objects faster. The seed file contains individual IP addresses, IP address ranges, or domain names that narrow the scope of hosts that are discovered. You can create the seed file with any text editor—just put one address or hostname on each line. Placing the addresses of your gateways in the seed file sometimes makes the most sense since gateways maintain ARP tables for your network. *netmon* will subsequently discover all the other nodes on your network, thus freeing you from having to add all your hosts to the seed file. For more useful information, see the documentation for the -s switch to *netmon* and the Local Registration Files (LRFs).

NNM has another utility, called *loadhosts*, that lets you add nodes to the map one at a time. Here is an example of how you can add hosts, in a sort of freeform mode, to the OpenView map. Note the use of the -m option, which sets the subnet to 255.255. 255.0:

```
$ loadhosts -m 255.255.255.0
10.1.1.12 gwrouter1
```

Once you have finished adding as many nodes as you'd like, press Ctrl-D to exit the command.

Configuring Polling Intervals

The SNMP Configuration page is located off the main screen under Options → SNMP Configuration. A window similar to the one in Figure 5-7 should appear. This window has four sections: Specific Nodes, IP Address Wildcards, Default, and the entry area (cropped in this example). Each section contains the same general areas: Node or IP Address, Get Community, Set Community, Proxy (if any), Timeout, Retry, Port, and Polling. The Default area, which is unfortunately at the bottom of the screen, sets up the default behavior for SNMP on your network—that is, the behavior (community strings, etc.) for all hosts that aren't listed as "specific nodes" or that match one of the wildcards. The Specific Nodes section allows you to specify exceptions on a per-node basis. IP Wildcard allows you to configure properties for a range of addresses. This is especially useful if you have networks that have different get and set community names.* All areas allow you to specify a Timeout in seconds

---

* These community names are used in different places throughout NNM. For example, when polling an object with *xnmbrowser*, you won't need to enter (or remember) the community string if it (or its network) is defined in the SNMP configurations.

and a Retry value. The Port field gives you the option of inserting a different port number (the default port is 161). Polling is the frequency at which you would like to poll your nodes.

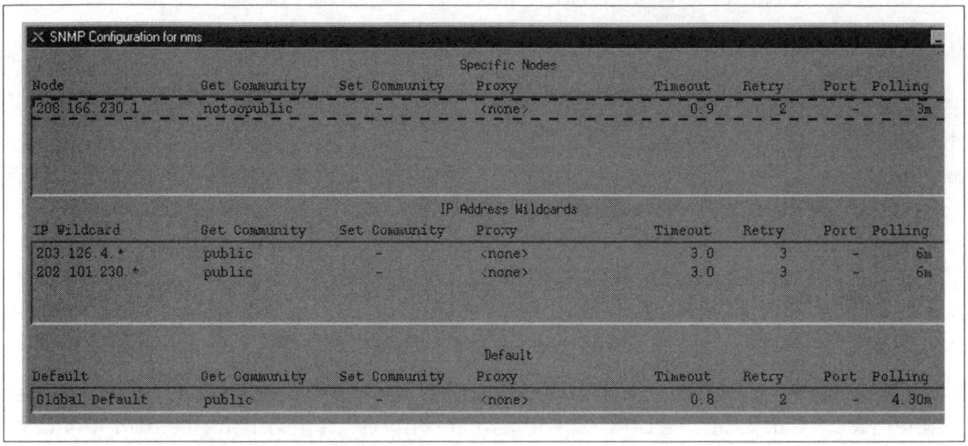

Figure 5-7. OpenView's SNMP Configuration page

It's important to understand how timeouts and retries work. If we look at Specific Nodes, we see a Timeout of .9 seconds and a Retry of 2 for 208.166.230.1. If Open-View doesn't get a response within .9 seconds, it tries again (the first retry) and waits 1.8 seconds. If it still doesn't get anything back, it doubles the timeout period again to 3.6 seconds (the second retry); if it still doesn't get anything back, it declares the node unreachable and paints it red on NNM's map. With these Timeout and Retry values, it takes about 6 seconds to identify an unreachable node.

Imagine what would happen if we had a Timeout of 4 seconds and a Retry of 5. By the fifth try, we would be waiting 128 seconds, and the total process would take 252 seconds. That's more than four minutes! For a mission-critical device, four minutes can be a long time for a failure to go unnoticed.

This example shows that you must be very careful about your Timeout and Retry settings—particularly in the Default area, because these settings apply to most of your network. Setting your Timeout and Retry too high and your Polling periods too low will make *netmon* fall behind; it will be time to start over before the poller has worked through all your devices.* This is a frequent problem when you have many nodes, slow networks, small polling times, and high numbers for Timeout and Retry.† Once a system falls behind, it will take a long time to discover problems with the devices it is currently monitoring, as well as to discover new devices. In some cases, NNM may

---

* Keep in mind that most of NNM's map is polled using regular *ping*s and not SNMP.

† Check the manpage for *netmon* for the -a switch, especially around -a12. You can try to execute *netmon* with an -a \ ?, which lists all the valid -a options. If you see any negative numbers in *netmon.trace* after running netmon -a12, your system is running behind.

not discover problems with downed devices at all! If your Timeout and Retry values are set inappropriately, you won't be able to find problems and you will be unable to respond to outages.

Falling behind can be very frustrating. We recommend starting your Polling period very high and working your way down until you feel comfortable. Ten to twenty minutes is a good starting point for the Polling period. During your initial testing phase, you can always set a wildcard range for your test servers, etc.

A Few Words About NNM Map Colors

By now, discovery should be taking place, and you should be starting to see some new objects appear on your map. You should see a correlation between the colors of these objects and the colors in NNM's Event Categories (see Chapter 9 for more about Event Categories). If a device is reachable via ping, its color will be green. If the device cannot be reached, it will turn red. If something "underneath" the device fails, the device will become off-green, indicating that the device itself is OK, but something underneath it has a nonnormal status. For example, a router may be working, but a web server on the LAN behind it may have failed. The status source for an object like this is Compound or Propagated. (The other types of status source are Symbol and Object.) The Compound status source is a great way to see if there is a problem at a lower level while still keeping an eye on the big picture. It alerts you to the problem and allows you to start drilling down until you reach the object that is under duress.

It's always fun to shut off or unplug a machine and watch its icon turn red on the map. This can be a great way to demonstrate the value of the new management system to your boss. You can also learn how to cheat and make OpenView miss a device, even though it was unplugged. With a relatively long polling interval, it's easy to unplug a device and plug it back in before OpenView has a chance to notice that the device isn't there. By the time OpenView gets around to it, the node is back up and looks fine. Long polling intervals make it easy to miss such temporary failures. Lower polling intervals make it less likely that OpenView will miss something, but more likely that *netmon* will fall behind, and in turn miss other failures. Take small steps so as not to crash or overload *netmon* or your network.

Using OpenView Filters

Your map may include some devices you don't need, want, or care about. For example, you may not want to poll or manage users' PCs, particularly if you have many users and a limited license. It may be worthwhile for you to ignore these user devices to open more slots for managing servers, routers, switches, and other more important devices. *netmon* has a filtering mechanism that allows you to control precisely which devices you manage. It lets you filter out unwanted devices, cleans up your maps, and can reduce the amount of management traffic on your network.

In this book, we warn you repeatedly that polling your network the wrong way can generate huge amounts of management traffic. This happens when people or programs use default polling intervals that are too fast for the network or the devices on the network to handle. For example, a management system might poll every node in your 10.1.0.0 network—conceivably thousands of them—every two minutes. The poll may consist of SNMP get or set requests, simple pings, or both. OpenView's NNM uses a combination of these to determine if a node is up and running. Filtering saves you (and your management) the trouble of having to pick through a lot of useless nodes and reduces the load on your network. Using a filter allows you to keep the critical nodes on your network in view. It allows you to poll the devices you care about and ignore the devices you don't care about. The last thing you want is to receive notification each time a user turns off his PC when he leaves for the night.

Filters also streamline network management by letting you exclude DHCP users from network discovery and polling. DHCP and BOOTP are used in many environments to manage large IP address pools. While these protocols are useful, they can make network management a nightmare, since it's often hard to figure out what's going on when addresses are being assigned, deallocated, and recycled.

In our environment, we use DHCP only for our users. All servers and printers have hardcoded IP addresses. With our setup, we can specify all the DHCP clients and then state that we want everything *but* these clients in our discovery, maps, etc. The following example should get most users up and running with some pretty good filtering. Take some time to review OpenView's "A Guide to Scalability and Distribution for HP OpenView Network Node Manager" manual for more in-depth information on filtering.*

The default filter file, which is located in *$OV_CONF/C*, is broken up into three sections:

- Sets
- Filters
- FilterExpressions

In addition, lines that begin with // are comments. // comments can appear anywhere; some of the other statements have their own comment fields built in.

Sets allow you to place individual nodes into a group. This can be useful if you want to separate users based on their geographic locations, for example. You can then use these groups or any combination of IP addresses to specify your Filters, which are also grouped by name. You then can take all of these groupings and combine them into FilterExpressions. If this seems a bit confusing, it is! Filters can be very confusing,

---

* This manual is available at *http://ovweb.external.hp.com/ovnsmdps/pdf/j1240-90001.pdf*.

especially when you add complex syntax and not-so-logical logic (&&, ||, etc.). The basic syntax for defining Sets, Filters, and FilterExpressions looks like this:

```
name "comments or description" { contents }
```

Every definition contains a name, followed by comments that appear in double quotes and then the command surrounded by brackets. Our default filter,[*] named filters, is located in *$OV_CONF/C* and looks like this:

```
// lines that begin with // are considered COMMENTS and are ignored!
// Beginning of MyCompanyName Filters

Sets {

    dialupusers "DialUp Users" { "dialup100", " dialup101", \
                " dialup102" }
}

Filters {

    ALLIPRouters "All IP Routers" { isRouter }

    SinatraUsers "All Users in the Sinatra Plant" { \
        ("IP Address" ~ 199.127.4.50-254) || \
        ("IP Address" ~ 199.127.5.50-254) || \
        ("IP Address" ~ 199.127.6.50-254) }

    MarkelUsers "All Users in the Markel Plant" { \
        ("IP Address" ~ 172.247.63.17-42) }

    DialAccess "All DialAccess Users" { "IP Hostname" in dialupusers }
}

FilterExpressions
{
    ALLUSERS "All Users" { SinatraUsers || MarkelUsers || DialAccess }

    NOUSERS "No Users " { !ALLUSERS }
}
```

Now let's break down this file into pieces to see what it does.

Sets

First, we defined a Set[†] called dialupusers containing the hostnames (from DNS) that our dial-up users will receive when they dial into our facility. These are perfect examples of things we don't want to manage or monitor in our OpenView environment.

---

[*] Your filter, if right out of the box, will look much different. The one shown here is trimmed to ease the pains of writing a filter.

[†] These Sets have nothing to do with the *snmpset* operation with which we have become familiar.

Filters

The Filters section is the only required section. We defined four filters: `ALLIPRouters`, `SinatraUsers`, `MarkelUsers`, and `DialAccess`. The first filter says to discover nodes that have the field value `isRouter`. OpenView can set the object attribute for a managed device to values such as `isRouter`, `isHub`, `isNode`, etc.* These attributes can be used in Filter expressions to make it easier to filter on groups of managed objects, as opposed to IP address ranges, for example.

The next two filters specify IP address ranges. The `SinatraUsers` filter is the more complex of the two. In it, we specify three IP address ranges, each separated by logical OR symbols (`||`). The first range (`("IP Address" ~ 199.127.6.50-254`)) says that if the IP address is in the range 199.127.6.50–199.127.6.254, filter it and ignore it. If it's not in this range, the filter looks at the next range to see if it's in that one. If it's not, the filter looks at the final IP range. If the IP address isn't in any of the three ranges, the filter allows it to be discovered and subsequently managed by NNM. Other logical operators should be familiar to most programmers: `&&` represents a logical AND, and `!` represents a logical NOT.

The final filter, `DialAccess`, allows us to exclude all systems that have a hostname listed in the `dialupusers` Set, which was defined at the beginning of the file.

FilterExpressions

The next section, FilterExpressions, allows us to combine the filters we have previously defined with additional logic. You can use a FilterExpression anywhere you would use a Filter. Think of it like this: you create complex expressions using Filters, which in turn can use Sets in the `contents` parts of their expressions. You can then use FilterExpressions to create simpler yet more robust expressions. In our case, we take all the filters from above and place them into a FilterExpression called `ALLUSERS`. Since we want our NNM map to contain nonuser devices, we then define a group called `NOUSERS` and tell it to ignore all user-type devices with the command `!ALLUSERS`. As you can see, FilterExpressions can also aid in making things more readable. When you have finished setting up your filter file, use the $OV_BIN/ ovfiltercheck program to check your new filters' syntax. If there are any problems, it will let you know so that you can fix them.

Now that we have our filters defined, we can apply them by using the ovtopofix command.

If you want to remove nodes from your map, use $OV_BIN/ovtopofix -f FILTER_ NAME. Let's say that someone created a new DHCP scope without telling you and suddenly all the new users are now on the map. You can edit the *filters* file, create a new group with the IP address range of the new DHCP scope, add it to the `ALLUSERS`

---

* Check out the *$OV_FIELDS* folder for a list of fields.

FilterExpression, and run ovfiltercheck. If there are no errors, run $OV_BIN/ovtopofix -f NOUSERS to update the map on the fly. Then stop and restart *netmon*—otherwise, it will keep discovering these unwanted nodes using the old filter. We run ovtopofix every month or so to take out some random nodes.

Loading MIBs into OpenView

Before you continue exploring OpenView's NNM, take time to load some vendor-specific MIBs.* This will help you later on when you start interacting (polling, graphing, etc.) more with SNMP-compatible devices. Go to Options → Load/Unload MIBs: SNMP. This presents you with a window in which you can add vendor-specific MIBs to your database. Alternatively, you can run the command $OV_BIN/ xnmloadmib and bypass having to go through NNM directly.

That's the end of our brief tour of OpenView configuration. It's impossible to provide a complete introduction to configuring OpenView in this chapter, so we tried to provide a survey of the most important aspects of getting it running. There can be no substitute for the documentation and manual pages that come with the product itself.

Castle Rock's SNMPc Enterprise Edition

We'll end the chapter with a brief discussion of Castle Rock's SNMPc, Version 7.0, which runs on Microsoft Windows.† SNMPc is a simpler product than OpenView in many respects. However, even though it's simpler, it's far from featureless. It's also cheaper than OpenView, which makes it ideal for shops that don't have a lot of money to spend on an NMS platform but need the support and backing that a commercial product provides.

Installation of SNMPc is straightforward. The installer asks for the license number and a discovery seed device. The seed device is similar to a seed file for OpenView's *netmon*. In the case of SNMPc, we recommend giving it the IP address (or hostname) of your gateway since this device can be used to discover other segments of your network. The installer gives you the option (checkbox) of turning on or off the discovery during the initial start. Bigger networks might opt to deactivate the initial discovery to prevent a flood of requests (and maybe auth failures).

---

* Some platforms and environments refer to loading a MIB as *compiling* it.

† SNMPc runs on Windows Server 2003, Windows 2000, Windows XP, and Windows NT. The WorkGroup edition and console also run on Windows ME and Windows 98.

SNMPc's Map

Once SNMPc is up and running, you will see any devices it has discovered in the Root map view. Figure 5-8 shows the main button bar. The far-right button (the house) gets you to the highest level on the map. The zooming tools allow you to pan in and out of the map, increasing or decreasing the amount of detail it shows. You can also reach the Root submap by selecting View → Map View → Root Submap.

Figure 5-8. SNMPc main button bar

Discovery and Filters

Once you are done playing around with your maps, it's time to start tuning your polling parameters. Go to Config → Discovery/Polling. This should bring up a menu that looks like Figure 5-9. Looking at the menu tabs, it's easy to tell that you will be able to configure your Seeds, Communities, Filters, and TCP service polling (Proto) here. SNMPc filters are equivalent to OpenView filters, but they are much simpler.

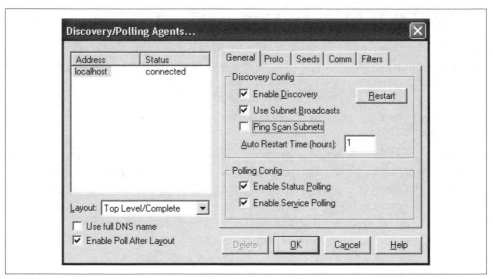

Figure 5-9. SNMPc Discovery/Polling Agents menu

The General tab lets you control SNMPc's polling and discovery behavior. The checkbox for enabling and disabling discovery is self-explanatory. The Enable Status Polling checkbox determines whether SNMPc will ping the nodes on your network periodically to determine whether they are responding. By default, all nodes are polled every 10 to 30 seconds. To change these default values, you can either edit the properties of each device (one by one), select and highlight multiple devices (using your Ctrl key), or use the object selection tool. You can bring up this tool by going to View → Selection Tool. The Discover Ping Nodes checkbox (under the Proto tab) lets you specify if you want to discover devices that have an IP or IPX entity but do not have an SNMP agent. SNMPc will also check whether a device supports various protocols such as SMTP, HTTP, etc. This feature allows you to set up custom menu items based on what services the device is running. The Find TCP Ports section of the Proto tab lets you specify the protocols for which SNMPc will test.

The Seeds tab allows you to specify SNMP devices that will help the discovery process along. This tab allows you to specify more than one seed IP address. (Remember that you're asked for a seed address device when you install the product.)

The Comm tab lets you specify the community strings for your network. You can specify multiple community names; SNMPc will try the different community names when discovering your nodes. Once SNMPc figures out which community is correct for a given device, it inserts the community string in the Get Community attribute for that particular device. This simply means the newly discovered device will be saved with its community string.

The final tab, Filters, allows you to exclude certain IP addresses from being discovered. You can specify individual addresses or use an asterisk (*) as a wildcard to specify entire networks.

Discovery Run-Through

Let's have SNMPc discover a small home network. First, I configure the discovery engine to find non-SNMP devices.

Figure 5-10 shows that the Find Non-SNMP (Ping) Nodes checkbox is selected. This setting will find devices on your network that are up but are not running an SNMP agent and can be helpful in getting a general map of your entire network. When you click OK, SNMPc does its thing. After a few moments, SNMPc creates a map that looks like Figure 5-11.

In this example, SNMPc has found my small home network, 192.168.1. If I double-click on the icon on the map, I see the actual devices on my home network, as shown in Figure 5-12.

I have two machines: a Linux server and a laptop. Figure 5-13 shows a closer view of these discovered devices.

Notice that the LinuxServer icon has the word *snmp* as part of the icon. This means it responded to SNMP polls. The loanera22p icon, however, is not running an SNMP agent, yet the discovery engine found it and placed the word *icmp* to denote that the machine is up and running but is not responding to SNMP polls.

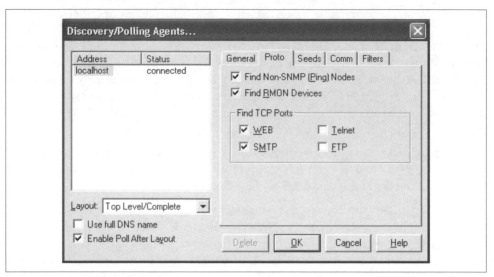

Figure 5-10. Finding non-SNMP devices

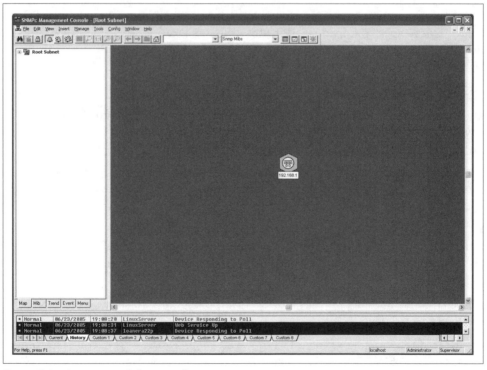

Figure 5-11. Root network discovered

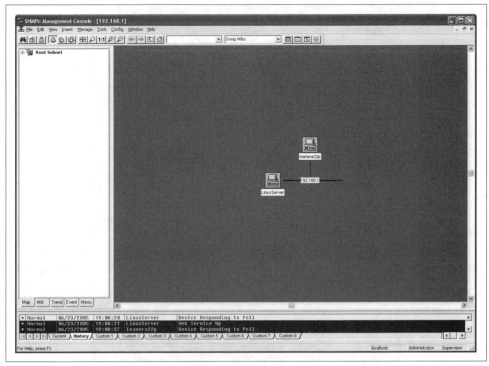

Figure 5-12. The devices on the 192.168.1 network

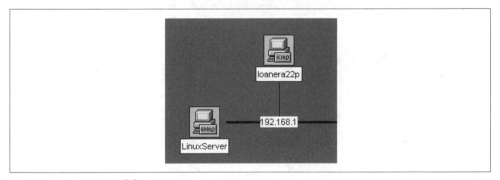

Figure 5-13. Discovered devices

Configuring SNMPv3

Not only can SNMPc poll SNMPv1 and SNMPv2 devices, but it can also poll SNMPv3 devices. This is a very nice feature and further shows that Castle Rock is committed to producing a full-featured network management platform. Let's briefly look at how you would configure SNMPv3-specific parameters.

Right-click on a device and select Properties to display a window like that shown in Figure 5-14.

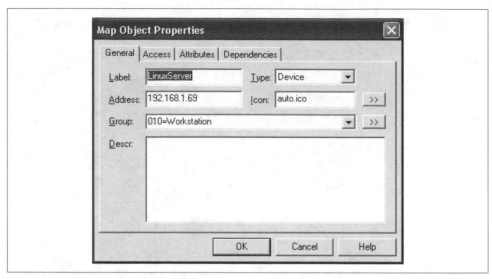

Figure 5-14. Map Object Properties

Select the Access tab to see the SNMP configuration parameters, in Figure 5-15.

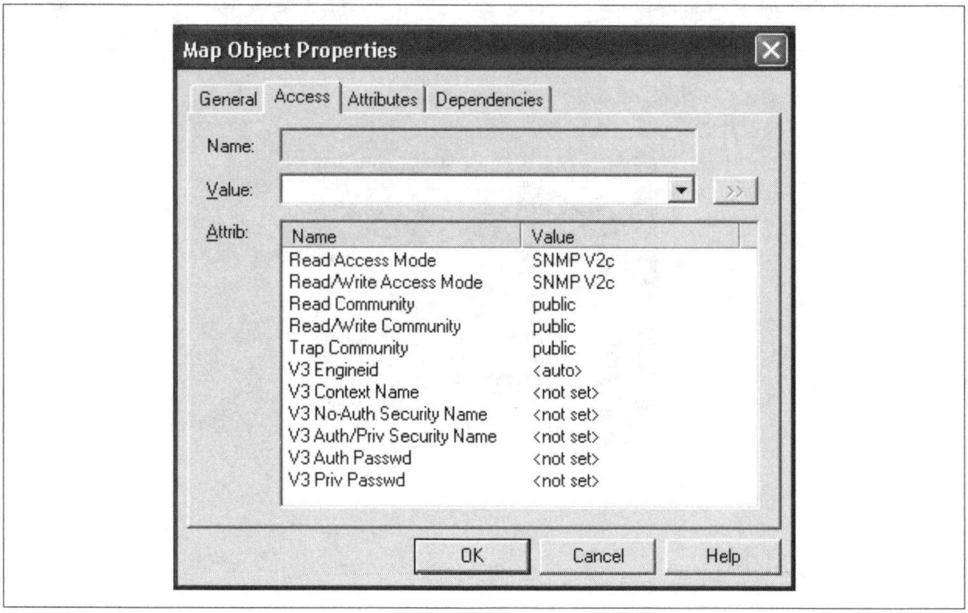

Figure 5-15. SNMP parameters

As you can see, there are several attributes to choose from. If you select either Read/ Access Mode or Read/Write Access Mode and expand the Value drop-down box, you will see the different modes available to you, as in Figure 5-16.

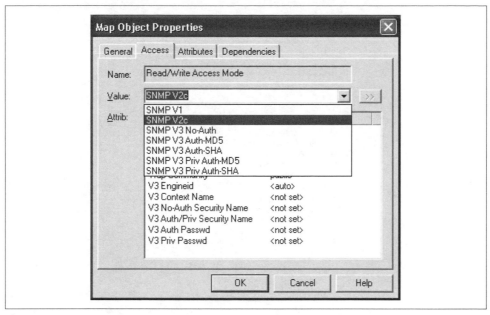

Figure 5-16. Access modes

Figure 5-16 shows the various SNMPv1, SNMPv2, and SNMPv3 access modes available to you. SNMPc supports only DES for privacy. If my SNMP agent used MD5 for authentication and DES for privacy, I would configure the map object as shown in Figure 5-17.

Note that Read Access Mode and Read/Write Access Mode are both SNMP V3 Priv Auth-MD5. This means SNMPc will use MD5 for authentication. Since SNMPc supports only DES for privacy, it is implied that it will use this protocol for encrypting the data. My SNMPv3 username is kjs, the authentication password is mypassword, and the privacy password is myotherpassword.*

Loading MIBs into SNMPc

Like any reasonably comprehensive network management product, SNMPc can load new MIBs. According to the SNMPc documentation, you place new MIB source files in the *\snmpcnt\mibfiles* directory on the server computer. Note that on my system, the full path for the MIB files is *C:\Program Files\SNMPc Network Manager\mibfiles*, so check both locations.

---

* Of course, these are just passwords for this example. In real life, one would never use such lame passwords.

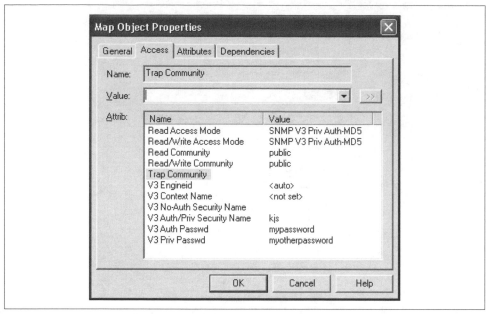

Figure 5-17. SNMPv3 configuration

Once you have copied your MIB file to this directory (make sure it has a *.mib* extension), select Config → Mib Database from the menu bar to display the Compile Mibs window shown in Figure 5-18.

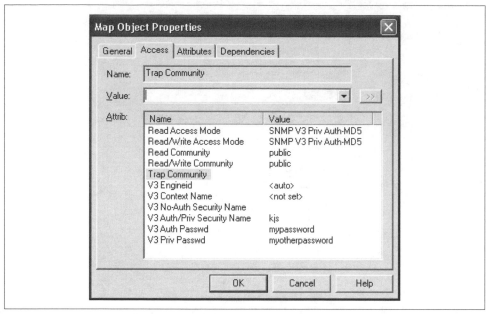

Figure 5-18. Compile Mibs window

Click Add to find the MIB file you want to add. This brings up another window where you can find the MIB you want to add in the list and click OK. You will now be back at the Compile Mibs window. Click Compile to compile all the MIBs, including the one you just added. This may take a little bit of time. Once it's done and there are no errors, you should see a window similar to Figure 5-19.

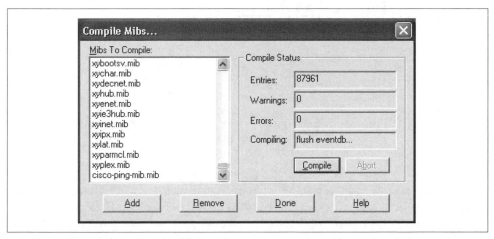

Figure 5-19. Completion of MIB compile

If you want to learn more about adding MIBs, click on the Help button.

SNMPc is a compact NMS that provides some added features, such as trend reporting. A thorough treatment of its installation is beyond the scope of this book. The online help system that comes with SNMPc is very good, and we recommend that you take full advantage of it.

CHAPTER 6
Configuring SNMP Agents

By this time, you should understand what an SNMP agent is: it's nothing more than software that lives on the device you want to monitor. It responds to requests from the NMS and generates traps. This chapter discusses how to configure agents. It starts by defining some standard configuration parameters that are common to all SNMP agents, and then goes into some advanced parameters you might run into when configuring your equipment. The bulk of this chapter walks through the configuration for a number of common devices, paying attention to security issues.

Parameter Settings

All SNMP devices share the following common configurable parameters:

- *sysLocation*
- *sysContact*
- *sysName*
- Read-write and read-only access community strings (and frequently, a trap community string)
- Trap destination

sysLocation is the physical location for the device being monitored. Its definition in RFC 1213 is:

```
sysLocation OBJECT-TYPE
    SYNTAX  DisplayString (SIZE (0..255))
    ACCESS  read-write
    STATUS  mandatory
    DESCRIPTION
        "The physical location of this node (e.g., 'telephone closet,
        3rd floor')."
    ::= { system 6 }
```

As you can see, its SYNTAX is DisplayString, which means it can be an ASCII string of characters; its size is declared to be, at most, 255 characters. This particular object is useful for determining where a device is located. This kind of practical information is essential in a large network, particularly if it's spread over a wide area. If you have a misbehaving switch, it's very convenient to be able to look up the switch's physical location. Unfortunately, *sysLocation* frequently isn't set when the device is installed and even more often isn't changed when the device is moved. Unreliable information is worse than no information, so use some discipline and keep your devices up-to-date.

RFC 1213's definition of *sysContact* is similar to that of *sysLocation*:

```
sysContact OBJECT-TYPE
    SYNTAX  DisplayString (SIZE (0..255))
    ACCESS  read-write
    STATUS  mandatory
    DESCRIPTION
        "The textual identification of the contact person for this managed
         node, together with information on how to contact this person."
    ::= { system 4 }
```

sysContact is a `DisplayString`. It's fairly obvious what it's used for: it identifies the primary contact for the device in question. It is important to set this object with an appropriate value, as it can help your operations staff determine who needs to be contacted in the event of some catastrophic failure. You can also use it to make sure you're notified, if you're responsible for a given device, when someone needs to take your device down for maintenance or repairs. As with *sysLocation*, make sure to keep this information up-to-date as your staff changes. It's not uncommon to find devices for which the *sysContact* is someone who left the company several years ago.

*sysName*s hould be set to the fully qualified domain name (FQDN) for the managed device. In other words, it's the hostname associated with the managed device's IP address. The RFC 1213 definition follows:

```
sysName OBJECT-TYPE
    SYNTAX  DisplayString (SIZE (0..255))
    ACCESS  read-write
    STATUS  mandatory
    DESCRIPTION
        "An administratively-assigned name for this managed node. By
         convention, this is the node's fully-qualified domain name."
    ::= { system 5 }
```

The read-only and read-write parameters are the community strings for read-only and read-write access. Notice that *sysLocation*, *sysContact*, and *sysName* all have ACCESS values of `read-write`. With the appropriate read-write community string, anyone can change the definition of these objects and many more objects of significantly greater importance. Ultimately, it's not a huge problem if somebody maliciously makes your router lie about its location—you probably already know that it isn't located in Antarctica. But someone who can do this can also fiddle with your routing tables and do other kinds of much more serious damage. Someone who has only the read-only community string can certainly find out more information about your network than you would like to reveal to an outsider. Setting the community strings is extremely important to maintaining a secure environment. Most devices are shipped with default community strings that are well known. Don't assume that you can put off setting your community strings until later.

The trap destination parameters specify the addresses to which traps are sent. There's nothing really magical here—since traps are asynchronous notifications generated by your devices, the agent needs to know who should receive notification. Many devices support authentication-failure traps, which are generated if someone attempts to access them using incorrect community strings. This feature is extremely useful, as it allows you to detect attempts to break into your devices. Many devices also support the ability to include a community string with traps; you can configure the NMS to respond only to traps that contain the proper community string.

Many devices have additional twists on the access and trap parameters. For example, Cisco devices allow you to create different community strings for different parts of the MIB—you can use this to allow people to set some variables, but not others. Many vendors allow you to place restrictions on the hosts that are allowed to make SNMP requests. That is, the device will respond only to requests from certain IP addresses, regardless of the community string.

The range of configuration options you're likely to run into is limited only by the imagination of the vendors, so it's obviously impossible for us to describe everything you might encounter. "Agent Configuration Walkthroughs," later in this chapter, will give you an idea of how some agents implement the standard configuration parameters, and a little insight into what other features might be available.

Security Concerns

Chapter 2 discussed the security issues with SNMPv1 and SNMPv2. The biggest problem, of course, is that the read-only and read-write community strings are sent as clear-text strings; the agent or the NMS performs no encryption. Therefore, the community strings are available to anyone with access to a packet sniffer. That certainly means almost anyone on your network with a PC and the ability to download widely available software. Does that make you uncomfortable? It should.

Obviously, you need to take the same precautions with the community strings that you would with your superuser or administrator passwords. Choose community strings that are hard to guess. Mixed-case alphanumeric strings are good choices for community strings; don't use dictionary words. Although someone with the read-only community string can't do as much damage as someone with the read-write string, you might as well take the same precautions for both. Don't forget to change your community strings—most devices ship with preconfigured community strings that are extremely easy to guess.

That doesn't solve the problems with packet sniffers. When you're configuring an agent, it's a good idea to limit the devices that can make SNMP requests (assuming that your agent allows you to make this restriction). That way, even if someone gets the community strings, he'll have to spoof the IP address of one of your management stations to do any damage.

Of course, many people know how to spoof IP addresses these days, and it's not a really good idea to assume that you can trust your employees. A better solution to the problem is to prevent the SNMP packets from being visible on your external network connections and parts of your network where you don't want them to appear. This requires configuring your routers and firewalls with access lists that block SNMP packets from the outside world (which may include parts of your own network). If you don't trust the users of your network, you may want to set up a separate administrative network to be used for SNMP queries and other management operations. This is expensive and inflexible—it's hard to imagine extending such a network beyond your core routers and servers—but it may be what your situation requires.

If you want to use SNMP to monitor your network from home, be extremely careful. You do not want your community strings traveling over the public Internet in an unencrypted form. If you plan to use SNMP tools directly from home, make sure to install VPN software, or some form of tunneling, to keep your SNMP traffic private. A better approach to home monitoring is to use a web interface; by using SSL, you can prevent others from seeing your usage graphs. (No network management products that we're aware of support SSL out of the box, but they do allow you to integrate with external servers, such as Apache, which do support SSL.)

SNMPv3 fixes most of the security problems; in particular, it makes sure that the community strings are always encrypted.

Agent Configuration Walkthroughs

In the following sections, we will walk through the configurations of some typical SNMP agents. We have chosen devices that are found on almost every modern network (PCs, Unix servers, routers, UPSs, etc.). The point of this discussion isn't to show you how your particular agent is configured—that would not be practical, given the hundreds of devices and vendors out there. Our intent is to give you a feel for what the common options are, and what steps you'll typically go through to configure an agent.

Windows Agents (Net-SNMP)

Microsoft makes an SNMP agent for its operating systems. Unfortunately, it's not exactly the most feature-rich agent in the world. In this section, we'll install the Net-

SNMP agent on Windows. The nice thing about this agent is that it's free. For those of you who need the support of a commercial product, take a look at Concord's SNMP agent; it's covered later in this chapter.

The Net-SNMP agent is available from *http://net-snmp.sourceforge.net*. We discuss the Net-SNMP agent for Windows in this section, and the nice thing about this is that both environments share the same configuration settings. Review the section about the Unix agent later in this chapter for details on advanced configurations.

We should point out some differences between the Windows version and the Unix version of the agent. If we wait until the end of this section, they might not catch your attention as easily:

- The version that you download from the Internet is a precompiled binary. It doesn't have support for SNMPv3 built in. You can build this support in, but you will need the Microsoft Visual C++ compiler. Download the source distribution from the Net-SNMP URL listed earlier, unpack it, and read the section in the *README.win32* file called "Microsoft Visual C++ - Workspace – Building" if you want to compile a version with SNMPv3 support.

- The configuration file takes all the same options as the Unix version of the agent. The one difference is that on Windows, paths use forward slashes. For example, a normal Windows path looks like this: *C:\somepath\where\data\lives*. In the Net-SNMP configuration files for Windows, this same path would be *C:/some-path/where/data/lives*. Just be aware of this difference.

Go to the Net-SNMP site and download the prebuilt binary for Windows. Once it's downloaded, double-click the icon to display a setup screen as in Figure 6-1.

Click Next, which brings up a window like the one in Figure 6-2.

Select "I accept the terms in the License Agreement" (after you have actually read it) and click Next to display Figure 6-3.

The Base Components option will install command-line tools and other things. This is actually a good idea, because then you can use the same Net-SNMP command-line tools we use throughout the book; the options are the same. The next two options install the SNMP agent and a trap receiver. The fourth option installs the Net-SNMP Perl modules. If you are interested in using Perl, you will need to install a Perl interpreter. You can get a very good Windows interpreter from *http://www.activestate.com*.

Figure 6-4 appears when you click Next. You are selecting the location where you want to install the package. The default, *C:\usr*, is a bit odd for Windows, but we suggest leaving it as is mainly because all the Unix examples in this book use that base directory.

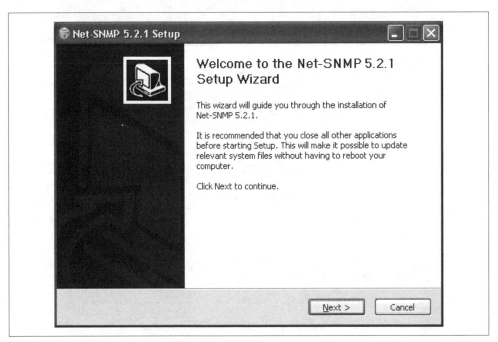

Figure 6-1. Net-SNMP initial install screen

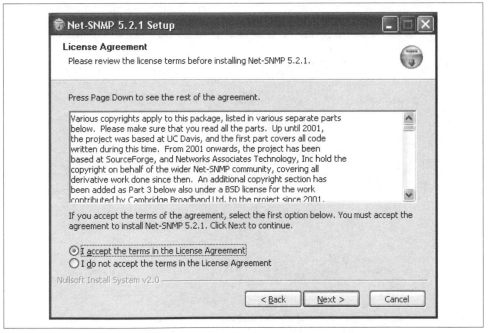

Figure 6-2. Net-SNMP license agreement

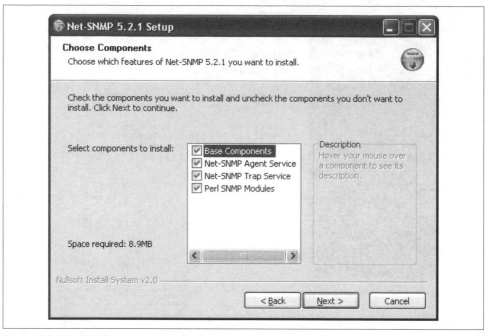

Figure 6-3. Net-SNMP component selection

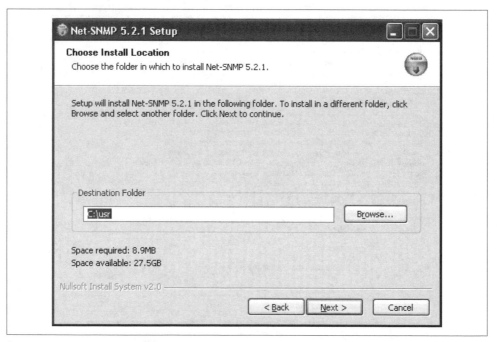

Figure 6-4. Net-SNMP install location

Once the package is installed, you need to register the agent as a service so that it will start upon reboot. This also gives you greater control over the agent. Here is the command sequence, assuming you installed the package in *C:\usr*.

```
C:\Documents and Settings\kschmidt\Desktop>cd c:\usr

C:\usr>registeragent.bat
Registering snmpd as a service using the following additional options:
.
 -Lf "C:/usr/log/snmpd.log"
.
.
For information on running snmpd.exe and snmptrapd.exe as a Windows
service, see 'How to Register the Net-SNMP Agent and Trap Daemon as
Windows services' in README.win32.
.
Press any key to continue . . .

C:\usr>
```

Once this is done, you need to start the agent. Go to the Control Panel and bring up the Administrative Tools. Once this loads, double-click the Services icon. Scroll through the list of services until you find the Net-SNMP service. It should not be running, as shown in the status column in Figure 6-5.

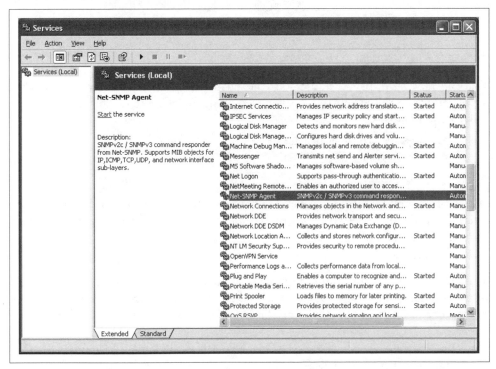

Figure 6-5. Windows Services

Click on "Start the service" and it should start running, as shown in Figure 6-6.

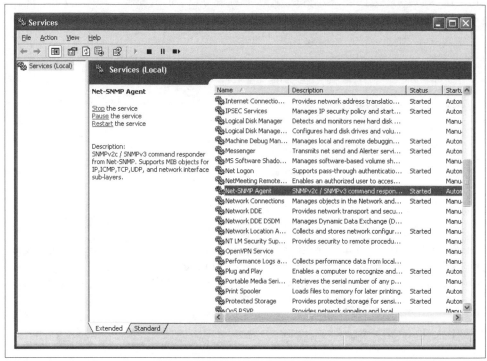

Figure 6-6. The running Net-SNMP agent

You can now stop, pause, and restart the agent. Start it and then try to access the agent. You can use the SNMP tools installed on the machine to do this, using the following commands:

```
C:\usr>snmpwalk -v2c -c public localhost
Timeout: No Response from localhost

C:\usr>
```

We get a timeout because we haven't configured the agent to respond to any SNMP queries. To do this, use your favorite editor to create a file called *c:\usr\etc\snmp\snmpd.conf* and add this line to it:

```
rwcommunity public
```

This sets up a read-write community string of public. Please note that this example is just for demonstration purposes. You should choose a more robust community string. For the changes to take effect, you need to go to the Services panel and click Restart.

 When you make changes to Net-SNMP files, to have them take effect you must go to the Services panel and restart the agent service.

Once you have done that, try the same command again, and the agent responds to our SNMP query:

```
C:\usr>snmpwalk -v2c -c public localhost
SNMPv2-MIB::sysDescr.0 = STRING: Windows loanera22p 5.1.2600 Service Pack 1 XP P
rofessional x86 Family 6 Model 8 Stepping 10
SNMPv2-MIB::sysObjectID.0 = OID: NET-SNMP-MIB::netSnmpAgentOIDs.13
DISMAN-EVENT-MIB::sysUpTimeInstance = Timeticks: (4540) 0:00:45.40
SNMPv2-MIB::sysContact.0 = STRING: USER
SNMPv2-MIB::sysName.0 = STRING: loanera22p
SNMPv2-MIB::sysLocation.0 = STRING: unknown
SNMPv2-MIB::sysORLastChange.0 = Timeticks: (5) 0:00:00.05
SNMPv2-MIB::sysORID.1 = OID: IF-MIB::ifMIB
SNMPv2-MIB::sysORID.2 = OID: TCP-MIB::tcpMIB
SNMPv2-MIB::sysORID.3 = OID: IP-MIB::ip
SNMPv2-MIB::sysORID.4 = OID: UDP-MIB::udpMIB
SNMPv2-MIB::sysORID.5 = OID: SNMPv2-MIB::snmpMIB
SNMPv2-MIB::sysORID.6 = OID: SNMP-VIEW-BASED-ACM-MIB::vacmBasicGroup
SNMPv2-MIB::sysORID.7 = OID: SNMP-FRAMEWORK-MIB::snmpFrameworkMIBCompliance
SNMPv2-MIB::sysORID.8 = OID: SNMP-MPD-MIB::snmpMPDCompliance
SNMPv2-MIB::sysORID.9 = OID: SNMP-USER-BASED-SM-MIB::usmMIBCompliance
```

Now, if you don't want to run the agent as a service, you can run it from the command line. The command is simply *snmpd*:

```
C:\usr>snmpd
No log handling enabled - turning on stderr logging
NET-SNMP version 5.2.1
```

The Net-SNMP folks have done a really nice job of putting the Windows distribution together. It may seem like quite a few steps are involved, but believe me you would not even be done installing the Microsoft agent at this point. If you want to know more about configuring the agent, read the section about the Unix version later in this chapter. The *snmpconf* Perl script that comes with the Unix version also comes with the Windows version, so you can use it to create configuration files.

HP OpenView Agent for HP-UX and Solaris

One text configuration file controls the parameters for the OpenView agent; the file is typically named */etc/SnmpAgent.d/snmpd.conf*, or */etc/snmpd.conf* on older systems. You don't need to edit this file for the agent to function normally. If you do edit it, you must stop and restart the master agent by executing the *SnmpMaster* script, first with a stop and then a start :

```
$ /sbin/init.d/SnmpMaster stop
$ /sbin/init.d/SnmpMaster start
```

Simple configuration

The following configuration file configures the agent to respond to get requests using the community name *public* and set requests using the community name *private*.

There are no restrictions on which MIBs can be queried, or which hosts can make the queries. This configuration has no security, since the community strings are set to commonly used defaults and are widely known. The OpenView agent sends authentication-failure traps by default, so you don't have to enable these traps in the configuration file.

```
get-community-name:     public
set-community-name:     private
trap-dest:              127.0.0.1
contact:                B.Gates
location:               12 Pyramid - Egypt
```

The simplest configuration is to edit the file and place more reasonable community names in the first two lines. We can't say it too much: community names are essentially passwords. Use the same rules for picking community names that you would for choosing the root password. You should always set the destination trap host (trap-dest) to the IP address of the host that will receive the trap.

The next example configures several different community names:

```
get-community-name:     public
get-community-name:     media
set-community-name:     hushed
set-community-name:     veryprivate
set-community-name:     shhhh
```

We have created two get (read-only) communities and three set (read-write) communities. These communities can be used as you see fit. (In real life, we would have chosen more obscure names.) For example, you might give your operations group in New York *public* community access and your operations group in Atlanta *media* community access. The remaining set communities can further be subdivided among various administrators and other staff who need read-write access.

Advanced configuration

Setting up multiple community strings doesn't sound very useful, and by itself, it isn't. But you can take the concept a step further and create different communities, each consisting of a few particular hosts and able to access only some of the objects SNMP manages. The next example allows the host 10.123.56.25 to issue gets using the community name *comname* and sets using the community name *private*. The host 10.123.46.101 can issue gets using only the community name *comname*. You cannot use hostnames after the IP: directive; you must use IP addresses.

```
get-community-name      comname IP: 10.123.56.25 10.123.46.101
set-community-name      private IP: 10.123.56.25
```

You can also configure the agent to restrict access to MIB subtrees based on IP addresses. The next example allows any host to get any object under *iso.org.dod. internet.mgmt.mib-2*, except for objects in the *interfaces* subtree. The minus sign (-) in front of *interfaces* instructs the agent to disallow access to this subtree.

```
get-community-name      public VIEW: mib-2 -interfaces
```

The final example sets up multiple community names for both sets and gets. An administrator who is located at host 10.123.46.25 and knows the *admin* community string has read access to the entire MIB tree; with the *adminset* community string, he has write access to the entire tree. Someone with the *operator* community string can sit anywhere and access everything in *mib-2* except for the *interfaces* subtree, but must be sitting at his desk (10.123.56.101) to issue sets and is not allowed to set anything in the *mib-2* subtree.

```
get-community-name    operator VIEW: mib-2 -interfaces
get-community-name    admin    IP: 10.123.56.25
set-community-name    operset  IP: 10.123.46.101 VIEW: -mib-2
set-community-name    adminset IP: 10.123.56.25
```

Net-SNMP for Unix

Net-SNMP is an open source agent that is freely available from *http://net-snmp. sourceforge.net*. We will focus on Net-SNMP Version 5.2.1, which is the most recent as of this publication. Once you have downloaded and unpacked the distribution, cd into the directory in which you unpacked Net-SNMP and read the *README* and *INSTALL* files. These files provide general information on installing the agent and don't require much explanation here.

Net-SNMP uses a *configure* script to make sure your environment has some key utilities and libraries installed, so it can be compiled successfully. Many configuration options are settable when you run this script. To see a list of them, run the following command:

```
net-snmp-5.2.1/> ./configure --help
```

One common option is - -prefix=PATH. This specifies an alternate installation directory. By default, Net-SNMP will install in */usr/local/bin*, */usr/local/man*, etc.

We'll be running *configure* without any options, which means our Net-SNMP build will have default values assigned for various options. For example, the agent binary will be placed in */usr/local/sbin*. Run the following command to begin the configuration process:

```
net-snmp-5.2.1/> ./configure
```

Note that by default, Net-SNMP does not compile in the Host Resources MIB. You will want to add this to the configure line if you want to access things like CPU statistics, memory and disk information, etc. Run configure like so:

```
net-snmp-5.2.1/> ./configure –with-mib-modules=host
```

You will see various messages about what features *configure* is looking for and whether they're found.

After running for a while, *configure* will ask for some basic SNMP information:

```
************* Configuration Section *************

You are about to be prompted by a series of questions. Answer
```

```
them carefully, as they determine how the snmp agent and related
applications are to function.

     After the configure script finishes, you can browse the newly
created config.h file for further - less important - parameters to
modify. Be careful if you re-run configure though since config.h will
be over written.

-Press return to continue-
```

When you press Return, you'll be prompted for the particular version of SNMP you wish to use:

```
disabling above prompt for future runs...  yes
checking System Contact Information...

*** Default SNMP Version:

        Starting with Net-SNMP 5.0, you can choose the default version of
the SNMP protocol to use when no version is given explicitly on the
command line, or via an 'snmp.conf' file.  In the past this was set to
SNMPv1, but you can use this to switch to SNMPv3 if desired.  SNMPv3
will provide a more secure management environment (and thus you're
encouraged to switch to SNMPv3), but may break existing scripts that
rely on the old behaviour.  (Though such scripts will probably need to
be changed to use the '-c' community flag anyway, as the SNMPv1
command line usage has changed as well.).
   At this prompt you can select "1", "2" (for SNMPv2c), or "3" as
the default version for the command tools (snmpget, ...) to use.  This
can always be overridden at runtime using the -v flag to the tools, or
by using the "defVersion" token in your snmp.conf file.
   Providing the --with-default-snmp-version="x" parameter to ./configure
will avoid this prompt.

Default version of SNMP to use (3): 3
setting Default version of SNMP to use to...  3
```

We've decided to select version 3 as our default. Since it's now a full IETF standard, there is no reason to not use it. As noted in the text before the prompt, you can always override the version for the command-line tools with the –v switch.

Next we are asked to configure the system contact:

```
checking System Contact Information...


*** System Contact Information:

        Describes who should be contacted about the host the agent is
running on.  This information is available in the MIB-II tree.  This
can also be over-ridden using the "syscontact" syntax in the agent's
configuration files.
   Providing the --with-sys-contact="contact" parameter to ./configure
will avoid this prompt.
```

```
System Contact Information (kjs@): snmpadmin@oreilly.com
setting System Contact Information to...  snmpadmin@ora.com
```

We've decided to set our contact information to something useful, but we could have left it blank. The next item you're asked to configure is system location. We've chosen an informative value, but again we could have left it blank:

```
checking System Location...


*** System Location:

        Describes the location of the system.  This information is
available in the MIB-II tree.  this can also be over-ridden using the
"syslocation" syntax in the agent's configuration files.
   Providing the --with-sys-location="location" parameter to ./configure
will avoid this prompt.

System Location (Unknown): FTP Server #1, O'Reilly Data Center
setting System Location to...  FTP Server #1, O'Reilly Data Center
```

The final options you need to configure are the locations of *snmpd*'s logfile and its persistent storage. In both cases, you simply press Enter to accept the default locations.

```
checking Location to write logfile...


*** Logfile location:

        Enter the default location for the snmpd agent to dump
information & errors to.  If not defined (enter the keyword "none"
at the prompt below) the agent will use stdout and stderr instead.
(Note: This value can be over-ridden using command line options.)
   Providing the --with-logfile="path" parameter to ./configure
will avoid this prompt.

Location to write logfile (/var/log/snmpd.log): <Enter>
setting Location to write logfile to...  /var/log/snmpd.log
checking Location to write persistent information...


*** snmpd persistent storage location:

        Enter a directory for the SNMP library to store persistent
data in the form of a configuration file.  This default location is
different than the old default location (which was for ucd-snmp).  If
you stay with the new path, I'll ask you in a second if you wish to
copy your files over to the new location (once only).  If you pick
some other path than the default, you'll have to copy them yourself.
There is nothing wrong with picking the old path (/var/ucd-snmp) if
you'd rather.
   Providing the --with-persistent-directory="path" parameter to
./configure will avoid this prompt.
```

```
Location to write persistent information (/var/net-snmp): <Enter>
setting Location to write persistent information to... /var/net-snmp
configure: creating ./config.status
config.status: creating Makefile
config.status: creating snmplib/Makefile
config.status: creating apps/Makefile
config.status: creating apps/snmpnetstat/Makefile
config.status: creating agent/Makefile
config.status: creating agent/helpers/Makefile
config.status: creating agent/mibgroup/Makefile
config.status: creating local/Makefile
config.status: creating testing/Makefile
config.status: creating man/Makefile
config.status: creating mibs/Makefile
config.status: creating net-snmp-config
config.status: creating include/net-snmp/net-snmp-config.h
config.status: executing default commands


---------------------------------------------------------
               Net-SNMP configuration summary:
---------------------------------------------------------

    SNMP Versions Supported:    1 2c 3
    Net-SNMP Version:           5.2.1
    Building for:               linux
    Network transport support:  Callback Unix TCP UDP
    SNMPv3 Security Modules:    usm
    Agent MIB code:             mibII ucd_snmp snmpv3mibs notification target agent_
mibs agentx utilities host
    SNMP Perl modules:          disabled
    Embedded perl support:      disabled
    Authentication support:     MD5 SHA1
    Encryption support:         DES AES


---------------------------------------------------------
```

You can now compile your new package with the make command. The compilation process displays many messages, most of which you can ignore. In short, if it completes, you've succeeded and can proceed to installation. If not, you will see errors and should investigate what went wrong. Install your new package with the command make install. By default, this command installs various executables in */usr/local/bin* and other important information in */usr/local/share/snmp*.

At this point, you can configure the agent further by using one of two approaches:

- Run the program */usr/local/bin/snmpconf*, which asks you a lot of questions and creates a configuration file. The configuration script is surprisingly confusing, though, so it's hard to recommend this approach.

- Craft a configuration by hand. If you're not interested in SNMPv3, this is fairly easy.

Running the configuration script

The configuration script is rather long and complex. Here are a few pointers:

- It starts by asking whether you want to create *snmp.conf* or *snmpd.conf*. To configure the agent, select *snmpd.conf*. *snmp.conf* sets up some defaults for command-line tools such as *snmpget*. Strictly speaking, creating *snmp.conf* isn't necessary.

- Most of the configurable options have to do with SNMPv3.

- When you're finished configuring, the script leaves the configuration file in your current directory. You can place the files in *~/.snmp*, if they're for your own use, or in */usr/local/share/snmp*, if you want this configuration to be used by everyone on the system.

Creating a configuration by hand

If you don't want to use SNMPv3, creating your own configuration file is easy. Here's a very simple configuration file:

```
syslocation     "O'Reilly Data Center"
syscontact      snmpadmin@oreilly.com
rwcommunity     private
rocommunity     public
authtrapenable  1
trapcommunity   trapsRus
trapsink        nmshost.oreilly.com
trap2sink       nmshost.oreilly.com
```

The configuration items should be familiar: we're setting up the system location; the system contact; the read-write, read-only, and trap community strings; and the destination to which traps should be sent. We're also enabling authentication traps. Note that we configured destinations for both SNMP Version 1 and Version 2 traps. The trap destination lines (`trapsink` and `trap2sink`) can also have a trap community string, if the NMS at the given host requires a different community name.

The `rwcommunity` and `rocommunity` lines allow us to be a bit more sophisticated than the example indicates. We're allowed to specify the network or subnet to which the community strings apply, and an object ID that restricts queries to MIB objects that are underneath that OID. For example, if you want to restrict read-write access to management stations on the subnetwork 10.0.15.0/24, you could use the line:

```
rwcommunity     private 10.0.15.0
```

If you take this route, you should certainly look at the *EXAMPLE.conf* file in the directory in which you built Net-SNMP. You can modify this file and install it in the appropriate location (either *~/.snmp/snmpd.conf* or */usr/local/share/snmp/snmpd.conf*), or you can take ideas from it and use them in your own configuration. It includes some particularly clever tricks that we'll discuss in Chapter 10 (they are well beyond the simple configuration we're discussing here).

Finally, let's look at configuring Net-SNMP to use SNMPv3. We'll also discuss a few utility commands that can help make managing the various security options much easier. Keep in mind that because of its security features, SNMPv3 is user based. Even though you may not want to use authentication or privacy, you may still need to provide a username, even if it is blank.

 To use SHA and DES encrytion, you will need to install the OpenSSL libraries on the machine where you built (or plan to build) Net-SNMP. Go to *http://www.openssl.org* to get these.

To create a user named *kschmidt* who has read-write access to the *system* subtree, add the following line to your *snmpd.conf* file:

```
rwuser  kschmidt auth system
```

To create a user with read-only access, use the command rouser instead of rwuser. The auth keyword requests secure authentication, but not privacy: the SNMP packets themselves aren't encrypted. The other possibilities are noauth (no authentication and no privacy) and priv (authentication and privacy). Now add the following line to */usr/local/share/snmp/snmpd.conf*:

```
createUser kschmidt MD5 mysecretpass
```

This creates an MD5 password for the user *kschmidt*. The password assigned to *kschmidt* is mysecretpass. To create a user with a DES passphrase in addition to an MD5 password, add the following line to */usr/local/share/snmp/snmpd.conf*:

```
createUser kschmidt MD5 mysecretpass DES mypassphrase
```

If you omit mypassphrase, Net-SNMP sets the DES passphrase to be the same as the MD5 password. The RFCs for SNMPv3 recommend that passwords and passphrases be at least eight characters long; Net-SNMP enforces this recommendation and won't accept shorter passwords.

When the agent is started, it reads the configuration file and computes secret keys for the users you have added.

Now we can perform an snmpwalk using Version 3 authentication. The following command specifies Version 3, with the username kschmidt, requesting authentication without privacy using the MD5 algorithm. The password is mysecretpass:

```
$ snmpwalk -v 3 -u kschmidt -l authNoPriv -a MD5 -A mysecretpass \
server.ora.com
system.sysDescr.0 = Linux server 2.2.14-VA.2.1 #1 Mon Jul 31 21:58:22 PDT 2000 i686
system.sysObjectID.0 = OID: enterprises.ucdavis.ucdSnmpAgent.linux
system.sysUpTime.0 = Timeticks: (1360) 0:00:13.60
system.sysContact.0 = "Ora Network Admin"
system.sysName.0 = server
system.sysLocation.0 = "Atlanta, Ga"
system.sysServices.0 = 0
system.sysORLastChange.0 = Timeticks: (0) 0:00:00.00
system.sysORTable.sysOREntry.sysORID.1 = OID: ifMIB
```

```
...
UDP-MIB::udpOutDatagrams.0 = No more variables left in this MIB View (It is past the
end of the MIB tree)
```

Note that we see only objects from the *system* subtree, even though the command tries to walk the entire tree. This limitation occurs because we have given *kschmidt* access only to the *system* subtree. If *kschmidt* tries to query a subtree he is not allowed to access, he gets the following result:

```
$ snmpwalk -v 3 -u kschmidt -l authNoPriv -a MD5 -A mysecretpass \
server.ora.com interfaces
IF-MIB::interfaces = No Such Object available on this agent at this OID
```

If you want privacy in addition to authentication, use a command like this:

```
$ snmpwalk -v 3 -u kschmidt -l authPriv -a MD5 -A mysecretpass -x DES -X \
mypassphrase server.ora.com
```

Using snmpusm to manage users

The Net-SNMP utility *snmpusm* is used to maintain SNMPv3 users. This utility can be very useful when it comes to managing and creating users on the fly.

 Note that to use this command, your SNMPv3 user must have write access to the usmUserTable in the agent. With user *kschmidt*, we restricted his access to the *system* subtree by adding this line to the *snmpd.conf* file: rwuser kschmidt auth system. This can be remedied by simply removing the system attribute: rwuser kschmidt auth.

The following command creates the user *kjs* by cloning the *kschmidt* user:

```
$ snmpusm -v 3 -u kschmidt -l authNoPriv -a MD5 -A mysecretpass localhost create \
kjs kschmidt
```

Since *kjs* was cloned from *kschmidt*, the two users now have the same authorization, password, and passphrase. It's obviously essential to change *kjs*'s password. To do so, use snmpusm with the –Ca option. Similarly, to change the privacy passphrase, use –Cx. The following two commands change the password and passphrase for the new user *kjs*:

```
$ snmpusm -v 3 -l authNoPriv -u kschmidt -a MD5 -A mysecretpass localhost -Ca passwd
mysecretpass mynewpass kjs
$ snmpusm -v 3 -l authPriv -u kschmidt -a MD5 -A mysecretpass localhost -Cx passwd
mypassphrase mynewphrase kjs
```

There are many things to note about this seemingly simple operation:

- You must know both the password and passphrase for *kschmidt* to set up a new password and passphrase for *kjs*. Presumably this is the case since you are the admin who is allowed to write to the usmUserTable.

- According to the documentation, Net-SNMP allows you to clone on to the same user only once. Attempts to reclone a previously cloned user appear to succeed but are silently ignored. The SNMPv3 USM specification (RFC 3414) mandates this particular behavior.

- *snmpusm* can only clone users; it can't create them from scratch. Therefore, you must create the initial user by hand, using the process described earlier. (This isn't quite true. *snmpusm* can create a user, but once you've done so you have to assign it a password by changing its previous password. So, you're in a Catch-22: the new user doesn't have a password, but you can't change his password. The only way to do this is by cloning the last user you created, and changing the password as we described here.)

For the user to be written to the persistent *snmpd.conf* file, you must either stop and restart the agent or send a HUP signal to the *snmpd* process. This forces the agent to write the current state of the user table to disk, so the agent can reread it upon startup. Note that using kill –9 does not produce the desired result.

The snmpusm command exists primarily to allow end users to manage their own passwords and passphrases. As the administrator, you may want to change your users' passwords and passphrases periodically. This is possible only if you keep a master list of users and their passwords and passphrases.

If the engine ID changes, you will have to regenerate all the usernames, passwords, and passphrases. (Remember that the engine ID depends in part on the host's IP address and therefore changes if you have to change the address.) To do this, stop the agent and edit the */var/net-snmp/snmpd.conf* file. Remove all the persistent usmUser entries and add new createUser commands (as described previously) for your users. A usmUser entry looks something like this:

```
usmUser 1 3 0x80001f8880389a8f7c2f5ba342 0x6b6a7300 0x6b6a7300 NULL .1.3.6.1.6.3.10.
1.1.2 0x0ecdaf0c88993c416bd8f0a555a11a3a .1.3.6.1.6.3.10.1.2.2
0xf64fee1207d9a959e53c47398e05e872 ""
```

Concord SystemEDGE Agent for Unix and Windows

Concord SystemEDGE is a commercial product that can be used as a subagent to the standard Windows agent. On Unix systems, this agent can be used either as a stand-alone agent or side by side with an existing agent. It runs on Linux, Solaris, and other operating systems. The CD on which the product is shipped includes agents for all the platforms SystemEDGE supports. Whenever possible, SystemEDGE uses the platform's native package manager to make installation easier. Each architecture-dependent version of the agent comes with an easy-to-follow *README* file for installation. See Chapter 10 for a discussion of this agent's capabilities.

Simple configuration

The SystemEDGE configuration file is located in */etc/sysedge.cf*. Use your editor of choice to make changes to this file. You must stop and restart SystemEDGE for your changes to take effect. The configuration file format is the same for all the versions of SystemEDGE.

For a typical SNMP configuration, *sysedge.cf* looks like this:

```
community public read-only
community veryprivate read-write 127.0.0.1 10.123.56.25
community traps 127.0.0.1
```

Comment lines begin with a # character. The first parameter sets the read-only community to public. The read-write community is defined to be veryprivate. The two IP addresses following the read-write community string are an access list that tells the agent to allow set operations from *localhost* (127.0.0.1) and 10.123.56.25 only. Always use an access list if possible; without this security feature, any host can execute set operations. Note that there is a space between the two addresses, not a Tab character. The third option tells the agent where to send traps; in this case, to *localhost* (127.0.0.1).

The agent sends authentication-failure traps by default, and we strongly recommend using them. If you don't want authentication-failure traps, include the following line in your configuration file:

```
no_authen_traps
```

Advanced configuration

SystemEDGE provides some powerful self-monitoring capabilities. These extensions (found only in Concord's Empire private enterprise MIB) are similar to the RMON MIB, which is discussed in Chapter 8. Empire's extensions can reduce network load by allowing the agent, rather than an NMS, to perform monitoring (polling) of important system objects. For example, the agent can be instructed to make sure the free space available in the root filesystem stays above some predefined threshold. When this threshold is crossed, the agent sends a trap to the NMS so that the condition can be dealt with appropriately.

The following line shows how you can monitor and restart sendmail if it dies:

```
watch process procAlive 'sendmail' 1 0x100 60 'Watch Sendmail' '/etc/init.d/sendmail
start'
```

This monitor sends a trap to the NMS, defined earlier as community traps 127.0.0.1, when the sendmail process dies. The agent then executes */etc/init.d/sendmail start* to restart the process. The general form of this command is:

```
watch process procAlive 'procname' index flags interv 'description' 'action'
```

The *procname* parameter is a regular expression that SystemEDGE uses to select the processes that it is monitoring; in this case, we're watching processes with the name *sendmail*. Each entry in the process-monitoring table must have a unique *index*; in this example, we used the value 1. We could have picked any integer, as long as that integer was not already in use in the table. The *flag* parameter is a hexadecimal* flag that changes the behavior of the monitor. We specified a flag of 0x100, which tells the monitor that the process it's watching spawns child processes; this flag ensures that SystemEDGE will take action only when the parent sendmail process dies, not when any of the children die. The use of process-monitor flags is beyond the scope of this chapter; see the manual that comes with SystemEDGE for more information. The *interv* parameter specifies how often (in seconds) the agent checks the process's status. We have set the interval to 60 seconds. The *description* parameter contains information about the process being monitored; it can be up to 128 characters in length. It is a good idea to use a description that indicates what is being monitored, since the agent stores this value in the monitor table for retrieval by an NMS and includes it in the variable bindings when a trap is sent. The final parameter is the action the monitor will take when the process dies; we chose to restart the daemon.

SystemEDGE can be extended by using plug-ins. These plug-ins manage and monitor applications such as Apache (web server), Exchange (Microsoft mail), and Oracle (database), to name a few. A "top processes" plug-in named *topprocs* comes with every distribution. The following statement tells SystemEDGE to load this plug-in for 64-bit Solaris (this statement is similar for other Unix platforms, and for Windows):

```
sysedge_plugin /opt/EMPsysedge/plugins/topprocs/topprocs-sol64bit.so
```

The folks at Concord have taken great care to add useful comments to the *sysedge.cf* file. The comments are often all you need to configure the agent.

Cisco Devices

Cisco Systems produces a wide range of routers, switches, and other networking equipment. The configuration process is virtually the same on all Cisco devices, because they share the IOS operating system.† There are some minor differences in the parameters that can be configured on every device; these generally have to do with the capabilities of the device, rather than the SNMP implementation.

To configure the SNMP parameters, you must be in *enable* mode. You can use the following commands to see what traps are available:

```
router> enable
Password: mypassword
router# config terminal
router(config)# snmp-server enable traps ?
  bgp          Enable BGP state change traps
  envmon       Enable SNMP environmental monitor traps
```

---

* Generally speaking, there are several ways to represent hexadecimal numbers. SystemEDGE uses the notion of a number prefixed with *0x*, which should be familiar to C and Perl programmers.

† There are some exceptions to this rule, such as the PIX firewalls. These exceptions usually mean that the product is made by a company that Cisco acquired.

```
frame-relay  Enable SNMP frame-relay traps
isdn         Enable SNMP isdn traps
<cr>
```

The question mark tells the router to respond with the possible completions for the command you're typing. You can use this feature throughout the entire command-line interface. If the part of the command you have already typed has a syntax error, the router will give you the "Unrecognized command" message when you type the question mark. <cr> tells you that you can exit without configuring the command (snmp-server enable traps in this case) by pressing Return.

Simple configuration

Here's a simple configuration that lets you start using the SNMP agent:

```
router(config)# snmp-server community private RW
router(config)# snmp-server community public RO
router(config)# snmp-server trap-authentication
router(config)# snmp-server location Delta Building - 1st Floor
router(config)# snmp-server contact J Jones
router(config)# snmp-server host 10.123.135.25 public
```

Most of these commands set parameters with which you should be familiar by now. We define two communities, public and private, with read-only (RO) and read-write (RW) permissions, respectively. snmp-server trap-authentication turns on authentication-failure traps. The command snmp-server host 10.123.135.25 public configures the destination to which traps should be sent. The IP address is set to the address of our NMS. The community string public will be included in the traps.

Advanced configuration

The following configuration item tells the device what interface it should use when sending out SNMP traps:

```
router(config)# snmp-server trap-source VLAN1
```

Configuring the trap source is useful because routers, by definition, have multiple interfaces. This command allows you to send all your traps out through a particular interface.

There may be times when you want to send only certain traps to your NMS. The next item sends only environmental monitor traps to the specified host, 172.16.52.25 (the *envmon* option is not available on all Cisco devices):

```
router(config)# snmp-server host 172.16.52.25 public envmon
```

One of the most frightening SNMP sets is the Cisco shutdown, which lets you shut down the router from the NMS. The good news is that you have to include a switch in the configuration before the router will respond to shutdown commands. Issuing the following command disables shutdowns:

```
router(config)# no snmp-server system-shutdown
```

To receive traps about authentication failures (something trying to poll your device with the wrong community name), add the following line:

```
router(config)# snmp-server trap-authentication
```

The final advanced configuration parameter is an access list. The first line sets up access list 15. It states that the IP address 10.123.56.25 is permitted to access the agent. The second line says that anyone that passes access list 15 (i.e., a host with IP address 10.123.56.25) and gives the community name *notsopublic* has read-only (RO) access to the agent. Access lists are a very powerful tool for controlling access to your network. They're beyond the scope of this book, but if you're not familiar with them, you should be.

```
router(config)# access-list 15 permit 10.123.56.25
router(config)# snmp-server community notsopublic RO 15
```

Configuring SNMPv3

The first task in configuring SNMPv3 is to define a view. To simplify things, we'll create a view that allows access to the entire *internet* subtree:

```
router(config)# snmp-server view readview internet included
```

This command creates a view called *readview*. If you want to limit the view to the *system* tree, for example, replace internet with system. The included keyword states that the specified tree should be included in the view; use excluded if you want to exclude a certain subtree.

Next, create a group that uses the new view. The following command creates a group called *readonly*; v3 means that SNMPv3 should be used. The auth keyword specifies that the entity should authenticate packets without encrypting them; read readview says that the view named *readview* should be used whenever members of the *readonly* group access the router.

```
router(config)# snmp-server group readonly v3 auth read readview
```

Now let's create a user. The following command creates a user called *kschmidt*, who belongs to the *readonly* group. auth md5 specifies that the router should use MD5 to authenticate the user (the other possibility is sha). The final item on the command line is the user's password or passphrase, which cannot exceed 64 characters.

```
router(config)# snmp-server user kschmidt readonly v3 auth md5 mysecretpass
```

This configuration uses encryption only to prevent passwords from being transferred in the clear. The SNMP packets themselves, which may contain information that you don't want available to the public, are sent without encryption and can therefore be read by anyone who has a packet sniffer and access to your network. If you want to go a step further and encrypt the packets themselves, use a command like this:

```
router(config)# snmp-server user kschmidt readonly v3 auth md5 mysecretpass \
priv des56 passphrase
```

The additional keywords on this command specify privacy (i.e., encryption for all SNMP packets), use of DES 56-bit encryption, and a passphrase to use when encrypting packets.

The encrypted passwords and passphrases depend on the engine ID, so if the engine ID changes, you'll need to delete any users you have defined (with the familiar IOS no command), and re-create them (with snmp-server user commands). Why would the engine ID change? It's possible to set the engine ID on the IOS command line. You should never need to set the engine ID explicitly, but if you do, you'll have to delete and re-create your users.

This has been the briefest of introductions to configuring SNMPv3 on a Cisco router. For more details, see Cisco's documentation, which is available at *http://www.cisco. com/univercd/cc/td/doc/product/software/ios120/120newft/120t/120t3/snmp3.htm*.

That's it! You now have a working SNMP configuration for your Cisco router.

APC Symetra

APC's uninterruptible power supplies (UPSs) are typical of a large class of products that aren't usually considered network devices, but that have incorporated a network interface for the purpose of management.

To configure an APC UPS, you can use its management port (a familiar serial port to which you can connect a console terminal) or, assuming that you've performed basic network configuration, telnet to the UPS's IP address. SNMP configuration is the same regardless of the method you use. Either way, you get a Text User Interface (TUI) that presents you with rather old-fashioned menus—you type your menu selection (usually a number) followed by Enter to navigate through the menus.

We'll assume that you've already performed basic network configuration, such as assigning an IP address for the UPS. To configure SNMP, go to the Network menu and select 5 to go into the SNMP submenu. You should get a menu like this:

```
------- SNMP -------------------------------------------------------

    1- Access Control 1
    2- Access Control 2
    3- Access Control 3
    4- Access Control 4
    5- Trap Receiver 1
    6- Trap Receiver 2
    7- Trap Receiver 3
    8- Trap Receiver 4
    9- System
    10- Summary

    ?- Help
<ENTER> Redisplay Menu
```

```
<ESC> Return To Previous Menu

>
```

You need to configure three distinct sections: Access Control, Trap Receiver, and System. To see a summary of the current SNMP settings, use the Summary submenu.

This particular device allows us to specify four IP addresses for access control and four IP addresses to receive traps. The access control items allow you to configure the IP addresses of your management stations—this is similar to the access lists we've seen in other devices, and is obviously basic to security. The UPS will reply only to queries from the IP addresses you have listed. Configuration is a bit awkward—you need to go to a separate menu to configure each IP address. Here's what you'll see when configuring the Access Control 1 submenu:

```
------- Access Control 1 -----------------------------------------

        Access Control Summary
        #  Community  Access      NMS IP
        -----------------------------------------------------------
        1  public     Read        10.123.56.25
        2  private    Write       10.123.56.25
        3  public2    Disabled    0.0.0.0
        4  private2   Disabled    0.0.0.0

    1- Community      : public
    2- Access Type    : Read
    3- NMS IP Address : 10.123.56.25
    4- Accept Changes :

    ?- Help
<ENTER> Redisplay Menu
  <ESC> Return To Previous Menu


>
```

The first part of the menu summarizes the state of access control. On this menu, we can change only the first item on the list. The special address 0.0.0.0 is a wildcard—it means that the UPS will respond to queries from any IP address. Although addresses 3 and 4 are set to 0.0.0.0, these addresses are currently disabled, and that's how we want to keep them. We want the UPS to respond only to the management stations we explicitly list.

On this menu, we've configured items 1 (the community string), 2 (the access type), and 3 (the IP address). We've set the community string to public (not a choice you'd want in a real configuration), the access type to Read (allowing various SNMP get operations, but no set operations), and the NMS IP address to 10.123.56.25. The net effect is that the UPS's SNMP agent will accept get requests from IP address 10.123. 56.25 with the community name *public*. When you are satisfied with the configuration, enter a 4 to accept your changes.

To configure the second access control item, press Esc to return to the previous menu; then select 2. As you can see, we allow 10.123.56.25 to perform set operations. We don't have any other management stations, so we've left items 3 and 4 disabled.

Once the Access Control section is complete, you can start configuring traps. The Trap Receivers section is simply a list of NMSs that receive traps. As with Access Control, four trap receivers can be configured. To get to the first trap receiver, return to the SNMP menu and select menu 5. A typical trap receiver setup looks like this:

```
------- Trap Receiver 1 --------------------------------------------

        Trap Receiver Summary
        #  Community  Generation  Authentication  Receiver NMS IP
        ---------------------------------------------------------------
        1  public     Enabled     Enabled         10.123.56.25
        2  public     Enabled     Enabled         0.0.0.0
        3  public     Enabled     Enabled         0.0.0.0
        4  public     Enabled     Enabled         0.0.0.0

    1- Trap Community Name : public
    2- Trap Generation     : Enabled
    3- Authentication Traps: Enabled
    4- Receiver NMS IP     : 10.123.56.25
    5- Accept Changes      :

    ?- Help
<ENTER> Redisplay Menu
  <ESC> Return To Previous Menu


 >
```

Once again, the first part of the menu is a summary of the trap receiver configuration. We've already set the first trap receiver to the address of our NMS, enabled trap generation, and enabled the generation of authentication traps—as always, a good idea. The traps we generate will include the community string *public*. Note that trap receivers 2, 3, and 4 are set to 0.0.0.0. On this menu, 0.0.0.0 is not a wildcard; it's just an invalid address that means you haven't yet configured the trap receiver's IP address. It's basically the same as leaving the entry disabled.

The final configuration items that should be set are on the System submenu, found under the SNMP main menu:

```
------- System --------------------------------------------------

    1- sysName      : ups1.ora.com
    2- sysContact   : Douglas Mauro
    3- sysLocation  : Apache Hilo Deck
    4- Accept Changes :

    ?- Help
<ENTER> Redisplay Menu
  <ESC> Return To Previous Menu


 >
```

After you have finished configuring all your SNMP parameters, use the Summary submenu for a quick look at what you have done. A typical setup will look something like this:

```
-------------------------------------------------------------------------
        SNMP Configuration Summary

        sysName          : ups1.ora.com
        sysLocation      : Apache Hilo Deck
        sysContact       : Douglas Mauro

        Access Control Summary
        #  Community  Access     NMS IP
        -------------------------------------------------------------------
        1  public     Read       10.123.56.25
        2  private    Write      10.123.56.25
        3  public2    Disabled   0.0.0.0
        4  private2   Disabled   0.0.0.0

        Trap Receiver Summary
        #  Community  Generation  Authentication  Receiver NMS IP
        -----------------------------------------------------------
        1  public     Enabled     Enabled         10.123.56.25
        2  public     Enabled     Enabled         0.0.0.0
        3  public     Enabled     Enabled         0.0.0.0
        4  public     Enabled     Enabled         0.0.0.0

        Press <ENTER> to continue...
```

Upon completion and verification, use the Esc key to take you all the way out to the Logout menu.

## CHAPTER 7

Polling and Setting

We've put a lot of work into getting things set up so that we can use SNMP effectively. But now that we've installed a fancy node manager and configured agents on all our devices, what can we do? How can we interact with the devices that are out there?

The three basic SNMP operations are snmpget, snmpset, and snmpwalk. They are fairly self-explanatory: snmpget reads a value from a managed device, snmpset sets a value on a device, and snmpwalk reads a portion of the MIB tree from a device. For example, you can use snmpget to query a router and find out its administrative contact (i.e., the person to call if the router appears to be broken), snmpset to change this contact information, and snmpwalk to traverse a MIB to get an idea of which objects the router has implemented or to retrieve status information on all the router's interfaces.

This chapter shows you how to use these operations in day-to-day network management. First, we will use Perl to demonstrate how you can set, get, and walk objects in a script (the nice thing about using Perl is that you can easily extend the simple scripts in this chapter to fit your needs and environment). We will then use HP OpenView and Net-SNMP to perform the same operations, but from the command line. Finally, as an alternative to the command line, we will demonstrate OpenView's graphical MIB Browser, which has a nice interface for getting, setting, and walking MIB data.

Retrieving a Single MIB Value

Let's start by querying a router for the name of its administrative contact. This operation, called polling, is accomplished with the SNMP get command. The following Perl script, *snmpget.pl*, uses an SNMP Perl module to retrieve the information we want:

```
#!/usr/local/bin/perl
#filename: /opt/local/perl_scripts/snmpget.pl
```

```
use BER;
use SNMP_util;
use SNMP_Session;
$MIB1 = ".1.3.6.1.2.1.1.4.0";
$HOST = "orarouter1";
($value) = &snmpget("public\@$HOST","$MIB1");
if ($value) { print "Results :$MIB1: :$value:\n"; }
else { warn "No response from host :$HOST:\n"; }
```

This script is obviously very primitive, but it is also easy to understand, even if you're not an experienced Perl user. Its importance isn't in what it does, which is very little, but as a template you can use to insert SNMP operations into other programs. (If you are not used to writing quick Perl programs, or you are unfamiliar with the language, a good starting point is the official Perl web site, *http://www.perl.com*.) The script starts with three use statements, which are similar to #include statements in C. The use statements load Perl modules containing functions and definitions for working with SNMP. The three modules we use are:

BER

> Describes how to encode management data into bit patterns for transmission. Basic Encoding Rules (BER) is an ISO standard.

SNMP_util

> Defines a set of functions that use the SNMP_Session module to make it much more programmer friendly. SNMP_util itself uses BER and SNMP_Session, but in this first script, we chose to reference these other modules explicitly. In future programs, we'll just use SNMP_util.

SNMP_Session

> Provides Perl with core SNMP functionality.

The next two lines specify the data we want to get. We have hardcoded the object ID of a particular piece of data defined by the MIB and the hostname from which we want to retrieve this MIB data. In a more flexible program, you might want to get these values from the command line, or build a user interface to help users specify exactly what they are interested in retrieving. For the time being, however, this will get us started. It is easy enough to replace orarouter1 with the hostname or IP address of the device you want to poll. The OID we are requesting is stored in the variable $MIB1. The value .1.3.6.1.2.1.1.4.0 requests the device's administrative contact. Again, you can replace this with any OID of your choice. We used the numeric form of this object, but you can also use the textual form for the OID, which is *.org.dod.internet.mgmt.mib-2.system.sysContact.0*. You can abbreviate this further to *sysContact* because SNMP_util defines some parts of the OID string for us (for example, SNMP_util defines *sysContact* as *1.3.6.1.2.1.1.4.0*), but it's often safer to be explicit and use the entire OID. Don't forget to include the *.0* at the end of your OID. The *.0* states that we want the first (0) and only instance of *iso.org.dod.internet. mgmt.mib-2.system.sysContact.0*.

The next line polls the device. The snmpget function retrieves the data from the device specified by the variable $HOST. Notice the two arguments to the function. The first is the device we want to poll, preceded by the community name public. (If you need to use another community name—you did change the community names when you configured the device, didn't you?—you'll have to modify this line and insert your community name in place of it.) The second argument to snmpget is the OID in which we are interested. If you type the code in yourself, do not forget the parentheses around $value. If you omit the parentheses, $value will be set to the number of items in the array snmpget returns.

Once we have polled the device, we print either the output or an error message. We put a colon before and after any output that we print; this makes it easy to see if there are any hidden characters in the output. The decimal integer "16" is *very* different from "16\n", which is the decimal integer 16 followed by a newline character.

Now let's run the program:

```
$ /opt/local/perl_scripts/snmpget.pl
Results :.1.3.6.1.2.1.1.4.0: :ORA IT Group:
```

snmpget.pl prints the OID we requested, followed by the actual value of that object, which is ORA IT Group. Don't worry if the return value for sysContact is wrong or blank. (The trick of putting colons before and after the output will make it clear if sysContact is blank or empty.) This probably means that no one has configured an administrative contact or that it was configured incorrectly. We'll show you how to fix that when we discuss the set operation. If you get an error, skip to the end of this chapter to see a list of some errors and their appropriate fixes.

We will now modify *snmpget.pl* to poll any host and any OID we want. This is accomplished by passing the host and OID as command-line arguments to the Perl script:

```
#!/usr/local/bin/perl
#filename: /opt/local/perl_scripts/snmpget.pl
use SNMP_util;
$MIB1 = shift;
$HOST = shift;
($MIB1) && ($HOST) || die "Usage: $0 MIB_OID HOSTNAME";
($value) = &snmpget("$HOST","$MIB1");
if ($value) { print "Results :$MIB1: :$value:\n"; }
else { warn "No response from host :$HOST:\n"; }
```

Now that this program is a little more flexible, it is possible to look up different kinds of information on different hosts. We even left out the community string, which allows us to poll hosts with different community names. Here's how to run the new version of *snmpget.pl*:

```
$ /opt/local/perl_scripts/snmpget.pl .1.3.6.1.2.1.1.1.0 public@orarouter1
Results :.1.3.6.1.2.1.1.1.0: : Cisco IOS Software, C2600 Software (C2600-IPBASE-M),
Version 12.3(8)T3, RELEASE SOFTWARE (fc1)
Technical Support: http://www.cisco.com/techsupport
```

```
Copyright (c) 1986-2004 by Cisco Systems, Inc.
Compiled Tue 20-Jul-04 17:03 by eaarmas:
```

In this example, we asked the router to describe itself by looking up the OID .1.3.6. 1.2.1.1.1.0 (*system.sysDesc.0*). The result tells us that orarouter1 is a Cisco router running Version 12.3(8)T3 of the IOS operating system, along with some other useful information.

Using HP OpenView to Retrieve Values

Let's start by looking up our router's administrative contact (*system.sysContact.0*) and see if we get the same result as we did with our previous Perl script. The arguments to OpenView's snmpget* are the community name, the hostname of the device we want to poll, and the OID of the data we are requesting; we gave the OID in numeric form, but again, we could have given it as a text string:

```
$ /opt/OV/bin/snmpget -c public orarouter1 .1.3.6.1.2.1.1.4.0
system.sysContact.0 : DISPLAY STRING- (ascii):  ORA IT Group
```

Although this looks a little different from the output of the Perl script, it tells us the same thing. snmpget prints the OID we requested on the command line, making it easy to verify that we polled the right object. Again, note that the trailing .0 is important. The output also tells us the object's datatype: DISPLAY STRING- (ascii). Back in Chapter 2, we discussed the datatypes that SNMP uses; some of the common types are INTEGER, OCTET STRING, Counter, and IpAddress. Finally, the output gives us the information we asked for: the router is administered by the ORA IT Group, which is the value returned from the SNMP get request.

Now let's do the same thing using OpenView's GUI interface. From the Network Node Manager's display, select Misc → SNMP MIB Browser.† If you don't have NNM running, you can start the MIB Browser from the command line using this command: /opt/OV/bin/xnmbrowser. Figure 7-1 shows the GUI. Its input fields are similar to the variables we have been setting in our Perl scripts: Name or IP Address, Community Name, MIB Object ID, MIB Instance, SNMP Set Value, and MIB Values.

Let's use this browser to run an snmpget. Start by inserting a Name or IP Address and Community Name in the input boxes provided. To enter the object you want to retrieve, use the MIB Object ID field and the text box below it. MIB Object ID shows us that we are currently in the subtree *.iso.org.dod.internet*. The text area shows the objects at the next level of the tree: *directory*, *mgmt*, etc. (To see the numeric OIDs for these objects, click on their names and then on the Describe button.) Then browse down through the MIB by double-clicking mgmt, then mib-2, system, and

---

* Most OpenView executable files are located in *opt/OV/bin*.

† If you find that the SNMP MIB Browser menu item is grayed out and cannot be clicked on, click on an SNMP object on your NNM map. You should then be able to click on the menu item to start your GUI.

finally sysContact. Click on sysContact and then on Start Query. The result that appears in the MIB Values field (as shown in Figure 7-2) should look very similar to the value that was returned in the command-line example.

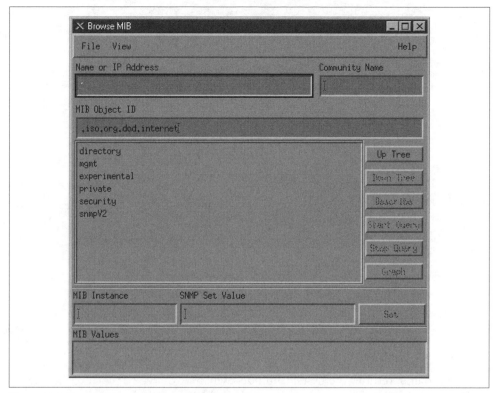

Figure 7-1. OpenView xnmbrowser default

Let's go back to the command line and poll for sysDesc again:

```
$ /opt/OV/bin/snmpget orarouter1 .1.3.6.1.2.1.1.1.0
system.sysDescr.0 : DISPLAY STRING- (ascii):  Cisco IOS Software, C2600 Software
(C2600-IPBASE-M), Version 12.3(8)T3, RELEASE SOFTWARE (fc1)
Technical Support: http://www.cisco.com/techsupport
Copyright (c) 1986-2004 by Cisco Systems, Inc.
Compiled Tue 20-Jul-04 17:03 by eaarmas
```

Looks the same, right? Notice that we left out the community string. We can do this because the default *get* community string is *public*, which is the correct community string for the target host, orarouter1. You can change your default community strings in OpenView's global settings. Let's see if we can get an object with a different datatype:

```
$ /opt/OV/bin/snmpget  orarouter1 .1.3.6.1.2.1.1.3.0
system.sysUpTime.0 : Timeticks: (159857288) 18 days, 12:02:52.88
```

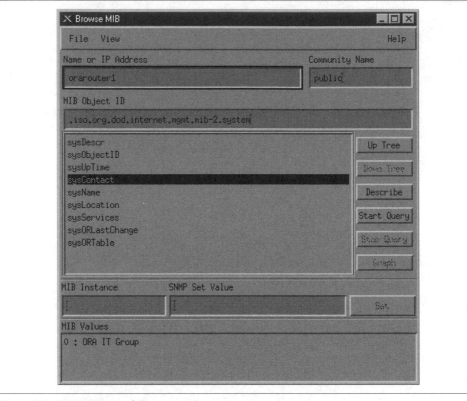

Figure 7-2. OpenView xnmbrowser response

This command returns the system uptime, which is of type TimeTicks. TimeTicks (RFC 1155) represents a nonnegative integer, which counts the time in hundredths of a second since some epoch. Ignoring the number in parentheses, this shows us that our router has been up and operational for 18 days, 12 hours, 02 minutes, and so on. The big number in parentheses is the exact amount of time the machine has been up, in hundredths of a second. If you do the math, you will see this adds up to 18.501 days, or 18 days, 12 hours, and a little bit: exactly what we expect.

Using Net-SNMP

The Net-SNMP tools provide an excellent command-line interface to SNMP operations. These tools are also commonly known as UCD-SNMP—you'll still find this older name in many references and even in the code itself.

Chapter 6 discussed how to compile, install, and configure the Net-SNMP agent. If you've done that, you've already compiled and installed the SNMP tools. They're shipped in the same package as the SNMP agent, and no real configuration is necessary for them. There is a configuration program, called *snmpconf*, which can be used to generate an *snmp.conf* file that provides default values for some of the options to the commands.* Unless you're using SNMPv3, though, it isn't really necessary. It might be handy to set up a default community string, but in practice, this is of only limited use: you probably have different community strings on different devices anyway. If you decide to use *snmpconf* to create the tool configuration file, make sure that you place *snmp.conf* in the *.snmp* subdirectory of your home directory or (if you want the options to apply to all users) in */usr/local/share/snmp*.

We'll assume that you won't do any configuration and will simply use the tools "out of the box." Here's a simple poll that asks a router for its location:

```
$ snmpget -v1 -c public orarouter1 .1.3.6.1.2.1.1.6.0
SNMPv2-MIB::sysLocation.0 = STRING: Sebastopol CA
```

It's fairly simple: we provided the hostname of the router we wanted to poll, a community string, and the OID of the object we wanted to retrieve. Instead of using the numeric OID, you can use the lengthy human-readable form. To save typing, *snmpget* assumes everything up to the object name and instance ID. Therefore, the following command is exactly equivalent to the previous one:

```
$ snmpget -v1 -c public orarouter1 sysLocation.0
SNMPv2-MIB::sysLocation.0 = STRING: Sebastopol CA
```

We'll take a look at the *snmpwalk* and *snmpset* commands that come with the Net-SNMP package later in this chapter, but the package contains many tools and is well worth a more detailed explanation. One tool that's particularly useful is *snmptranslate*, which converts between the numeric and textual names of MIB objects and can do things such as look up the definition of an object in a MIB file. The software distribution comes with a number of standard MIBs; you can place additional MIB files in */usr/local/share/snmp/mibs*. Appendix C gives an overview of the Net-SNMP package.

Retrieving Multiple MIB Values

The syntax for snmpwalk is similar to the syntax for its cousin, snmpget. As discussed in Chapter 2, snmpwalk traverses a MIB starting with some object, continuously returning values until it gets to the end of that object's branch. For example, the upcoming Perl script begins walking the *.iso.org.dod.internet.mgmt.mib-2.interfaces.ifTable.ifEntry.ifDescr* object and provides a description of each Ethernet interface on the device it polls.

This new script is a minor modification of *snmpget.pl*. We turned the scalar $value into the array @values;† we need an array because we expect to get multiple values

---

* This is the same command used to create *snmpd.conf*, which configures the Net-SNMP agent. The *snmp.conf* configuration file is similar in form to *snmpd.conf*.

† The Perl program we used earlier could have used the array instead of the scalar as well. This is possible because Perl's version of *snmpget* allows for multiple OIDs, not just one. To specify multiple OIDs, place a comma (,) between each OID. Remember to enclose each OID within its own double quotes.

back. We also called the function *snmpwalk* instead of *snmpget* (syntactically, the two functions are the same):

```perl
#!/usr/local/bin/perl
#filename: /opt/local/perl_scripts/snmpwalk.pl
use SNMP_util;
$MIB1 = shift;
$HOST = shift;
($MIB1) && ($HOST) || die "Usage: $0 MIB_OID HOSTNAME";
(@values) = &snmpwalk("$HOST","$MIB1");
if (@values) { print "Results :$MIB1: :@values:\n"; }
else { warn "No response from host :$HOST:\n"; }
```

Here's how to run the script:

$ **/opt/local/perl_scripts/snmpwalk.pl .1.3.6.1.2.1.2.2.1.2 orarouter1**

This command walks down the *.iso.org.dod.internet.mgmt.mib-2.interfaces.ifTable. ifEntry.ifDescr* object, returning information about the interfaces that are on the router. The results look something like this:

```
Results :.1.3.6.1.2.1.2.2.1.2: :1:Ethernet0 2:Serial0 3:Serial1:
```

The output depends on the interfaces on the host or router you are polling. To give some examples, we've run this script against some of the machines on our network. Here are the results.

Cisco 7000 router:

```
Results :.1.3.6.1.2.1.2.2.1.2: :1:Ethernet0/0 2:Ethernet0/1 3:TokenRing1/0
4:TokenRing1/1 5:TokenRing1/2 6:TokenRing1/3 7:Serial2/0 8:Serial2/1
9:Serial2/2 10:Serial2/3 11:Serial2/4 12:Serial2/5 13:Serial2/6 14:Serial2/7
15:FastEthernet3/0 16:FastEthernet3/1 17:TokenRing4/0 18:TokenRing4/1:
```

Linux workstation:

```
Results :.1.3.6.1.2.1.2.2.1.2: :1:lo 2:eth0 3:sit0:
```

Sun workstation:

```
Results :.1.3.6.1.2.1.2.2.1.2: :1:lo0 2:hme0:
```

Windows XP Pro PC:

```
Results :.1.3.6.1.2.1.2.2.1.2: :1:MS TCP Loopback interface
2: NETGEAR WG511 54 Mbps Wireless PC Card:
```

APC uninterruptible power supply:

```
Results :.1.3.6.1.2.1.2.2.1.2: :1:peda:
```

For each device, we see at least one interface. As you'd expect, the router has many interfaces. The first interface on the router is listed as 1:Ethernet0/0, the second is listed as 2:Ethernet0/1, and so on, up through interface 18. SNMP keeps track of interfaces as a table, which can have many entries. Even single-homed devices usually have two entries in the table: one for the network interface and one for the loopback interface. The only device in the previous example that really has a single interface is the APC UPS—but even in this case, SNMP keeps track of the interface through a table that is indexed by an instance number.

This feature allows you to append an instance number to an OID to look up a particular table element. For example, we would use the OID *.1.3.6.1.2.1.2.2.1.2.1* to look at the first interface of the Cisco router, *.1.3.6.1.2.1.2.2.1.2.2* to look at the second, and so on. In a more human-readable form, *ifDescr.1* is the first device in the interface description table, *ifDescr.2* is the second device, and so on.

Walking the MIB Tree with OpenView

Switching over to OpenView's *snmpwalk*, let's try to get every object in the *.iso.org. dod.internet.mgmt.mib-2.system* subtree:

```
$ /opt/OV/bin/snmpwalk oraswitch2 .1.3.6.1.2.1.1
system.sysDescr.0 : DISPLAY STRING- (ascii):  Cisco IOS Software, C2600 Software
(C2600-IPBASE-M), Version 12.3(8)T3, RELEASE SOFTWARE (fc1)
Technical Support: http://www.cisco.com/techsupport
Copyright (c) 1986-2004 by Cisco Systems, Inc.
Compiled Tue 20-Jul-04 17:03 by eaarmas
system.sysObjectID.0: OBJECT IDENTIFIER:
.iso.org.dod.internet.private.enterprises.cisco.ciscoProducts.cisco2509
system.sysUpTime.0 : Timeticks: (168113316) 19 days, 10:58:53.16
system.sysContact.0 : DISPLAY STRING- (ascii):  J.C.M. Pager 555-1212
system.sysName.0 : DISPLAY STRING- (ascii):  oraswitch2.ora.com
system.sysLocation.0 : DISPLAY STRING- (ascii): Sebastopol CA
system.sysServices.0 : INTEGER: 6
```

Let's go to the GUI MIB Browser and try that same walk. Repeat the steps you took for *snmpget* using the GUI. This time insert the OID *.1.3.6.1.2.1.1* and click the Start Query button. Check out the results.

> The GUI figures out whether it needs to perform an *snmpwalk* or *snmpget*. If you give an instance value (being specific), the browser performs an *snmpget*. Otherwise, it does an *snmpwalk*. If you are looking for more speed and less cost to your network, include the instance value.

What will happen if you walk the entire *.iso* subtree? It may hurt or even crash your machine, because in most cases, the device can return several thousand values. Each interface on a router can add thousands of values to its MIB tables. If each object takes .0001 seconds to compute and return, and there are 60,000 values to return, it will take your device 6 seconds to return all the values—not counting the load on the network or on the monitoring station. If possible, it is always a good idea to perform an *snmpwalk* starting at the MIB subtree that will provide you with the specific information you are looking for, as opposed to walking the entire MIB.

It might be useful to get a feel for how many MIB objects a given device has implemented. One way to do this is to count the number of objects each *snmpwalk* returns. This can be accomplished with the Unix grep command. The -c switch to grep tells it to return the number of lines that matched. The period (.) tells grep to match everything. Starting from the *.system* object (*.1.3.6.1.2.1.1*), let's go back one and see how many objects are implemented in the *mib-2* subtree. Take the last *.1* off the object ID and run the snmpwalk command again, this time piping the results into grep -c:

```
$ /opt/OV/bin/snmpwalk oraswitch2 .1.3.6.1.2.1 |  grep -c .
```

The number of objects you see will depend on the type of device and the software running on it. When we tried several different devices, we got results ranging from 164 to 5,193.

This command is great when you want to walk a MIB to see all the types of values that a device is capable of returning. When we are trying out a new device or MIB, we often walk some decent-sized portion of the MIB and read through all the returned values, looking for any info that may be of interest. When something catches our eye, we go to the MIB definition and read its description. Many GUI MIB Browsers allow you to check the description with the click of a button. In Open-View's GUI, click on the OID and then on Describe.

Walking the Tree with Net-SNMP

Net-SNMP's snmpwalk is very similar in form and function to OpenView's. Here's how you use it:

```
$ snmpwalk -v1 -c public orarouter1 .1.3.6.1.2.1.1
SNMPv2-MIB::system.sysDescr.0 = STRING: Cisco IOS Software, C2600 Software (C2600-
IPBASE-M), Version 12.3(8)T3, RELEASE SOFTWARE (fc1)
Technical Support: http://www.cisco.com/techsupport
Copyright (c) 1986-2004 by Cisco Systems, Inc.
Compiled Tue 20-Jul-04 17:03 by eaarmas
SNMPv2-MIB::system.sysObjectID.0 = OID: enterprises.9.1.284
SNMPv2-MIB::system.sysUpTime.0 = Timeticks: (100946413) 11 days, 16:24:24.13
SNMPv2-MIB::system.sysContact.0 = STRING: thenetworkadministrator@oreilly.com
SNMPv2-MIB::system.sysName.0 = STRING: orarouter1@oreilly.com
SNMPv2-MIB::system.sysLocation.0 = STRING: Sebastopol CA
SNMPv2-MIB::system.sysServices.0 = STRING: 6
SNMPv2-MIB::system.sysORLastChange.0 = Timeticks: (0) 0:00:00.00
```

There aren't any real surprises. Again, you can use an object name rather than a numerical ID; because you're walking a tree, you don't need to specify an instance number.

Setting a MIB Value

With snmpget and snmpwalk, we have retrieved management information only from devices. The next logical step is to change the value of a MIB object via SNMP. This operation is known as snmpset, or set. In this section, we'll read the value of an object, use snmpset to change its value, and read the value again to prove that it's been changed.

There's obviously some danger here: what happens if you change a variable that's critical to the state of the system you're monitoring? In this chapter, we'll deal only with some simple objects, such as the administrative contact, that won't damage anything if they're changed incorrectly. Therefore, if you keep the OIDs correct, you shouldn't worry about hurting any of your devices. All the objects we set in this chapter have an ACCESS of read-write. It's a good idea to get a feel for which objects are writable by reading the MIB in which the object is defined—either one of the RFCs, or a MIB file provided by your vendor.

Let's get started. Run the following OpenView command (or use one of the other programs we've discussed) to find out the *sysContact* for your chosen device:

```
$ /opt/OV/bin/snmpget -c public orarouter1 .1.3.6.1.2.1.1.4.0
system.sysContact.0 : DISPLAY STRING- (ascii):  ORA IT Group
```

The -c public switch passes the community string *public* to the snmpget command.

 Keep in mind that your devices shouldn't use the same (default) community strings that are used in this book. In addition, using the same string for the read-only (snmpget) and read-write (snmpset) communities is a poor idea.

Now let's run the OpenView snmpset command. This command takes the value specified in quotes on the command line and uses it to set the object indicated by the given OID. Use the same OID (*system.sysContact.0*). Since the new value for *sysContact* contains words and possibly numbers, we must also specify the variable type octetstring.* Run the OpenView snmpset command with the following parameters:

```
$ /opt/OV/bin/snmpset -c private orarouter1 .1.3.6.1.2.1.1.4.0 \
octetstring "Meg A. Byte  555-1212"
system.sysContact.0 : DISPLAY STRING- (ascii):  Meg A. Byte  555-1212
```

The result shows that snmpset successfully changed the router's contact person to Meg A. Byte 555-1212. If you don't see this result, the set was not successful. Table 7-2 shows some of the common error messages you might receive and steps you can take to correct the problems. To confirm the value the device has stored in *sysContact*, we can repeat the snmpget command.

If we use OpenView's GUI, things start to get a bit easier to see, set, and confirm. Use the GUI to get the value of *sysContact*. Once you have confirmed that a value is there, type a description in the SNMP Set Value text box. Since there is only one instance for *sysContact*, you have to insert a 0 (zero) for the MIB Instance. After you

---

* If you read RFC 1213 (MIB-II), you will note that *sysLocation* has a SYNTAX of DisplayString. This is really a textual convention of type OCTET STRING with a size of 0.255 octets.

have completed all the required input items, click on the Set button located to the right of the SNMP Set Value text box. You should see a pop-up window that reads "Set has completed successfully." To verify that the set actually occurred, click on Start Query. (It should be apparent to you by now that using a GUI such as Open-View's MIB Browser program makes getting and setting MIB objects much easier.)

To show how this can be done programmatically, we will write another small Perl script, named *snmpset.pl*:

```perl
#!/usr/local/bin/perl
#filename: /opt/local/perl_scripts/snmpset.pl
use SNMP_util;
$MIB1 = ".1.3.6.1.2.1.1.6.0";
$HOST = "oraswitch2";
$LOC  = "@ARGV";
($value) = &snmpset("private\@$HOST","$MIB1",'string',"$LOC");
if ($value) { print "Results :$MIB1: :$value:\n"; }
else { warn "No response from host :$HOST:\n"; }
```

Let's run this script:

```
$ /opt/local/perl_scripts/snmpset.pl A bld JM-10119 floor 7
Results :.1.3.6.1.2.1.1.6.0: :A bld JM-10119 floor 7:
```

Using the *snmpget.pl* script, we can verify that the set took place:

```
$ /opt/local/perl_scripts/snmpget.pl .1.3.6.1.2.1.1.6.0 public@oraswitch2
Results :.1.3.6.1.2.1.1.1.0: :A bld JM-10119 floor 7:
```

Now we'll use the Net-SNMP snmpset utility to change the system contact:

```
$ snmpset -v1 -c private oraswitch2 sysContact.0 s myself
SNMPv2-MIB::system.sysContact.0 = myself
$ snmpget -v1 -c public oraswitch2 sysContact.0
SNMPv2-MIB::system.sysContact.0 = myself
```

There's nothing really confusing here. We supplied a community string, a host-name, and an object ID, followed by a datatype (s for String) and the new value of *sysContact*. Just to convince ourselves that the set actually took place, we followed it with an snmpget. The only additional thing you need to know is the mechanism for specifying datatypes. Net-SNMP uses the single-character abbreviations shown in Table 7-1.

Table 7-1. Net-SNMP datatype abbreviations

Abbreviation	Meaning
a	IP address
b	Bits
d	Decimal string
D	Double
F	Float
i	Integer

Table 7-1. Net-SNMP datatype abbreviations (continued)

Abbreviation	Meaning
I	Signed int64
o	Object ID
s	String
t	Time ticks
u	Unsigned integer
U	Unsigned int64
x	Hexadecimal string

Error Responses

Table 7-2 shows the error responses that a device might return while executing the commands presented in this chapter. Consult your local documentation if these explanations do not cover your exact problem.

Table 7-2. Error responses

Server responded with	Explanation
Contained under subtree	snmpwalk returns this error if you have tried going down a MIB tree and are already at the end, or if the tree doesn't exist on the client.
No response arrived before timeout	Possible causes include an invalid community name, an agent that is not running, or an inaccessible node.
Agent reported error with variable	You are trying to set to an object with a datatype that is not the same as (or close to) the variable's specified type. For example, if the variable wants a DisplayString, you'll get this error if you send it an INTEGER. Read through the MIB to see what SYNTAX type the variable needs.
Missing instance value for...	When you are setting a value, you must supply the entire OID and instance. A scalar object will end with zero (0) and a tabular object will end with the instance number of the object in a table. Verify that the instance number you're using with snmpget is correct and retry your set.
Access is denied for variable	This may happen if you are trying to set a value on a read-only object. Review the MIB to see what the object's ACCESS setting is.

CHAPTER 8
Polling and Thresholds

SNMP gives you the ability to poll your devices regularly, collecting their management information. Furthermore, you can tell the NMS that there are certain thresholds that, if crossed, require some sort of action. For example, you might want to be notified if the traffic at an interface jumps to an extremely high (or low) value; that event might signal a problem with the interface, or insufficient capacity, or even a hostile attack on your network. When such a condition occurs, the NMS can forward an alarm to an event-correlation engine or have an icon on an OpenView map flash. To make this more concrete, let's say that the NMS is polling the status of an interface on a router. If the interface goes down, the NMS reports what has happened so that the problem can be resolved quickly.

SNMP can perform either internal or external polling. Internal polling is typically used in conjunction with an application that runs as a daemon or a facility such as cron that periodically runs a local application. External polling is done by the NMS. The OpenView NMS provides a great implementation of external polling; it can graph and save your data for later retrieval or notify you if it looks like something has gone wrong. Many software packages make good NMSs, and if you're clever about scripting, you can throw together an NMS that's fine-tuned to your needs. In this chapter, we will look at a few of the available packages.

Polling is like checking the oil in a car; this analogy may help you to think about appropriate polling strategies. Three distinct items concern us when checking the oil: the physical process (opening the hood, pulling out the dipstick, and putting it back in); the preset gauge that tells us if we have a problem (is the level too high, too low, or just right?); and the frequency with which we check it (once an hour, week, month, or year).

Let's assume that you ask your mechanic to go to the car and check the oil level. This is like an NMS sending a packet to a router to perform an snmpget on some piece of information. When the mechanic is finished, you pay him $30 and go on your way. Because a low oil level may result in real engine damage, you want to check the oil regularly. So, how long should you wait until you send the mechanic out to the car again? Checking the oil has a cost: in this scenario, you paid $30. In networks, you pay with bandwidth. Like money, you have only so much bandwidth, and you can't spend it frivolously. So, the real question is, how long can you wait before checking the oil again without killing your budget?

The answer lies within the car itself. A finely tuned race car needs to have its fluids at perfect levels. A VW Beetle,[*] unlike a race car, can have plus or minus a quart at any time without seriously hindering its performance. You're probably not driving a Beetle, but you're probably not driving a race car either. So, you decide that you can check the oil level about every three weeks. But how will you know what is low, high, or just right?

The car's dipstick tells you. Your mechanic doesn't need to know the car model, engine type, or even the amount of oil in the car; he only needs to know what value he gets when he reads the dipstick. On a network, a device's dipstick is called an agent, and the dipstick reading is the SNMP response packet. All SNMP-compatible devices contain standardized agents (dipsticks) that can be read by any mechanic (NMS). It is important to keep in mind that the data gathered is only as good as the agent, or mechanic, that generated it.

In both cases, some predefined threshold determines the appropriate action. In the oil example, the threshold is "low oil," which triggers an automatic response: add oil. (Crossing the "high oil" threshold might trigger a different kind of response.) If we're talking about a router interface, the possible values we might receive are "up" and "down." Imagine that your company's gateway to the Internet, a port on a router, must stay up 24 hours a day, 7 days a week. If that port goes down, you could lose $10,000 for each second it stays down. Would you check that port often? Most organizations won't pay someone to check router interfaces every hour, let alone every second. Even if you had the time, that wouldn't be fun, right? This is where SNMP polling comes in. It allows network managers to guarantee that mission-critical devices are up and functioning properly, without having to pay someone to constantly monitor routers, servers, etc.

Once you determine your monitoring needs, you can specify at what interval you would like to poll a device or set of devices. This is typically referred to as the poll interval and can be as granular as you like (e.g., every second, every hour, etc.). The threshold value at which you take action doesn't need to be binary: you might decide that something's obviously wrong if the number of packets leaving your Internet connection falls below a certain level.

[*] The old ones from the 1960s, not the fancy modern ones.

Whenever you are figuring out how often to poll a device, remember to keep three things in mind: the device's agent/CPU, bandwidth consumption, and the types of values you are requesting. Some values you receive may be 10-minute averages. If this is the case, it is a waste to poll every few seconds. Review the MIBs surrounding the data for which you are polling. Our preference is to start polling fairly often. Once we see the trends and peak values, we back off. This can add congestion to the network but ensures that we don't miss any important information.

Whatever the frequency at which you poll, keep in mind other things that may be happening on the network. Be sure to stagger your polling times to avoid other events if possible. Keep in mind backups, data loads, routing updates, and other events that can cause stress on your networks or CPUs.

Internal Polling

It may seem like a waste of bandwidth to poll a device just to find out that everything is OK. On a typical day, you may poll dozens of devices hundreds or thousands of times without discovering any failures or outages. Of course, that's really what you want to find out—and you'll probably conclude that SNMP has served its purpose the first time you discover a failed device and get the device back online before users have had a chance to start complaining. However, in the best of all possible worlds, you'd get the benefits of polling without the cost: that is, without devoting a significant chunk of your network's bandwidth to monitoring its health.

This is where internal polling comes in. As its name implies, internal polling is performed by an agent that is internal, or built in, to the device you want to manage. Since polling is internal to the device, it doesn't require traffic between the agent and your NMS. Furthermore, the agent doing the polling does not have to be an actual SNMP agent, which can allow you to monitor systems (either machines or software) that do not support SNMP. For example, some industrial-strength air-conditioning equipment vendors provide operational status information via a serial port. If the air-conditioning unit is attached to a terminal server or similar device, it becomes easy to use scripting languages to monitor the unit and generate traps if the temperature exceeds a certain threshold. This internal program can be written in your favorite scripting language, and it can check any status information to which you can get access. All you need is a way to get data from the script to the management station.

One strategy for writing a polling program is to use "hooks" within a program to extract information that can then be fed into an SNMP trap and sent to the NMS. We will cover traps more in Chapter 9. Another way to do internal polling is to use a program (e.g., *sh*, Perl, or C) that is run at set intervals. (On Unix, you would use cron to run a program at fixed intervals; there are similar services on other operating systems.) Hooks and cron-driven scripts both allow you to check internal variables and report errors as they are found. Here is a Perl script that checks for the existence of a file and sends a trap if the file is not found:

```
#!/usr/local/bin/perl
# Filename: /opt/local/perl_scripts/check4file.pl

use SNMP_util "0.54";  # This will load the BER and SNMP_Session modules for us

$FILENAME = "/etc/passwd";

#
# if the /etc/passwd file does not exist, send a trap!
#
if(!(-e $FILENAME)) {
    snmptrap("public\@nms:162", ".1.3.6.1.4.1.2789", "sunserver1", 6, 1547, \
             ".1.3.6.1.4.1.2789.1547.1", "string", "File \:$FILENAME\: Could\
             NOT Be Found");
}
```

Here is what the Sun-style *crontab* looks like:

```
$ crontab -l

# Check for this file every 15 minutes and report trap if not found
4,19,34,49 * * * * /opt/local/perl_scripts/check4file.pl
```

Notice that we poll four minutes after each quarter hour rather than on the quarter hour. The next poll we insert into the *crontab* file may run five minutes after the quarter hour (5,20,35,50). This practice prevents us from starting a huge number of programs at the same time. It's a particularly good idea to avoid polling on the hour—that's a popular time for random programs and cron jobs to start up. Consult the cron manpage if you are unfamiliar with its operation.

Remote Monitoring (RMON)

RMON is a supplement to the MIB-II group. This group, if supported by the device's SNMP agent, allows us to do both internal and external polling. We can poll devices through a remote NMS (external polling) or have the local RMON agent check itself periodically and report any errors (internal polling). The RMON agent will send traps when error conditions are found.

Many devices support RMON, making it an effective mechanism for internal polling. For example, Cisco supports the Events and Alarms RMON categories. You can configure the Alarms category to poll MIBs internally and react in different ways when a rising or falling threshold occurs. Each threshold has the option of calling an internal event. Figure 8-1 shows the flow that these two RMON categories take.

The distinction between alarms and events is important. Each alarm is tied to a specific event that defines what action to perform when the alarm goes off. Once a threshold is met, triggering an alarm, the alarm calls the event, which can perform

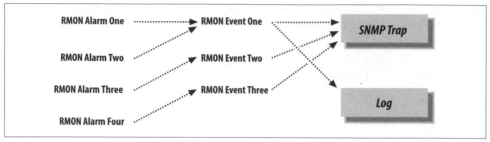

Figure 8-1. RMON process flow

additional functions, including sending traps to the NMS and writing a record in a log. Standard SNMP traps are preconfigured by the agent's vendor, which gives network managers no control over setting any kind of thresholds; however, RMON allows a network manager to set rising and falling thresholds. Figure 8-2 represents the interaction between a router's RMON agent and an NMS.

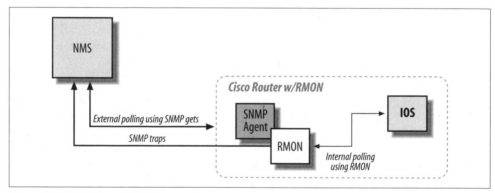

Figure 8-2. RMON and NMS interaction

In Figure 8-2, the Cisco router's SNMP agent forwards a trap to the NMS. Notice the direction of communication: RMON trap transmission is unidirectional. The NMS receives the trap from the Cisco router and decides what action to take, if any.

In addition to sending traps, we can also log events; if we so choose, we can even log the event without generating a trap. Logging can be particularly useful when you are initially configuring RMON alarms and events. If you make your alarm conditions too sensitive, you can clog your NMS with trigger-happy RMON events. Logging can help you fine-tune your RMON alarms before they are released into production.

RMON configuration

As a practical example of how to configure RMON, we will use Cisco's RMON implementation, starting with events. The following IOS command defines an RMON event:

```
rmon event number [log] [trap community] [description string] [owner string]
```

If you're familiar with IOS, you should be expecting a corresponding no command that discards an RMON event:

```
no rmon event number
```

The parameters to these IOS commands are:

number

> Specifies the unique identification number for the event. This value must be greater than 0; a value of 0 is not allowed.

log

> Tells the agent to log the entry when triggered. This argument is optional.

trap community

> Specifies the trap community string, i.e., a community string to be included with the trap. Many network management programs can be configured to respond only to traps with a particular community string.

description string

> Describes the event.

owner string

> Ties the event or item to a particular person.

Here are two examples of how to create Cisco RMON events. The first line creates a rising alarm, which facilitates sending a trap to the NMS. The second creates a falling alarm that might indicate that traffic has returned to an acceptable level (this alarm is logged but doesn't generate a trap):

```
(config)#rmon event 1 log trap public description "High ifInOctets" owner dmauro
(config)#rmon event 2 log description "Low ifInOctets" owner dmauro
```

You can also use logging to keep track of when the events were called. Though you can configure traps without logging, what happens if the line to your NMS goes down? Logging ensures that you don't lose information when the NMS is disabled. We suggest using both log and trap on all your events. You can view the logs of your RMON events by issuing the following command on the router:

```
orarouter1# show rmon event

Event 1 is active, owned by dmauro
 Description is High ifInOctets
 Event firing causes log and trap to community public, last fired 00:00:00
Event 2 is active, owned by dmauro
 Description is Low ifInOctets
 Event firing causes log, last fired 00:00:00
```

The following Net-SNMP command walks the *rmon* event table, which displays the values we just set:

```
$ snmpwalk -v1 -c public -m orarouter1 .iso.org.dod.internet.mgmt.mib-2.rmon
RMON-MIB::eventIndex.1 = INTEGER: 1
RMON-MIB::eventIndex.2 = INTEGER: 2
```

```
RMON-MIB::eventDescription.1 = STRING: High ifInOctets
RMON-MIB::eventDescription.2 = STRING: Low ifInOctets
RMON-MIB::eventType.1 = INTEGER: logandtrap(4)
RMON-MIB::eventType.2 = INTEGER: log(2)
RMON-MIB::eventCommunity.1 = STRING: "public"
RMON-MIB::eventCommunity.2 = ""
RMON-MIB::eventLastTimeSent.1 = Timeticks: (0) 0:00:00.00
RMON-MIB::eventLastTimeSent.2 = Timeticks: (0) 0:00:00.00
RMON-MIB::eventOwner.1 = STRING: "dmauro"
RMON-MIB::eventOwner.2 = STRING: "dmauro"
RMON-MIB::eventStatus.1 = INTEGER: valid(1)
RMON-MIB::eventStatus.2 = INTEGER: valid(1)
```

Most of the information we set on the command line is available through SNMP. We see two events, with indexes 1 and 2. The first event has the description High ifInOctets; it is logged and a trap is generated; the community string for the event is public; the event's owner is dmauro; the event is valid, which essentially means that it is enabled; and we also see that the event has not yet occurred because the value of *eventLastTimeSent* is *0:00:00.00*.[*] Instead of using the command line to define these events, we could have used snmpset either to create new events or to modify events we already have. If you take this route, keep in mind that you must set the *eventEntry.eventStatus* to 1, for "valid," for the event to work properly.

 You can poll the objects *ifDescr* and *ifType* in the *mgmt.interfaces.ifEntry* subtree to help you identify which instance number you should use for your devices. If you are using a device with multiple ports, you may need to search the *ifType*, *ifAdminStatus*, and *ifOperStatus* objects to help you identify what's what. In the next section, "External Polling," we will see that it is not necessary to keep track of these MIB variables (the external polling software takes care of this for us).

Now that we have our events configured, let's start configuring alarms to do some internal polling. We need to know what we are going to poll, what type of data is returned, and how often we should poll. Assume that the router is our default gateway to the Internet. We want to poll the router's second interface, which is a serial interface. Therefore, we want to poll *mgmt.interfaces.ifEntry.ifInOctets.2* to get the number of outbound octets on that interface, which is an INTEGER type.[†] To be precise, the *ifInOctets* MIB object is defined as "the total number of octets received on the interface, including framing characters." (The *.2* at the end of the OID indicates the second entry in the *ifEntry* table. On our router, this denotes the second inter-

---

[*] Timeticks: (0) shows that no event occurred. This value is useful if you plan to write your own script to query the RMON objects on your router.

[†] From RFC 2819, *alarmVariable* (the object/MIB we are going to poll) needs to resolve to an ASN.1 primitive type of INTEGER, Counter, Gauge, or TimeTicks.

face, which is the one we want to poll.) We want to be notified if the traffic on this interface exceeds 90,000 octets/second; we'll assume things are back to normal when the traffic falls back under 85,000 octets/second. This gives us the rising and falling thresholds for our alarm. Next, we need to figure out the interval at which we are going to poll this object. Let's start by polling every 60 seconds.

Now we need to put all this information into a Cisco RMON alarm command. Here is the command to create an alarm:

```
rmon alarm number variable interval {delta | absolute}
    rising-threshold value [event-number]
    falling-threshold value [event-number]
    [owner string]
```

The following command discards the alarm:

```
no rmon alarm number
```

The parameters to these commands are:

number
Specifies the unique identification number assigned to the alarm.

variable
Specifies which MIB object to monitor.

interval
Specifies the frequency (in seconds) at which the alarm monitors the MIB variable.

delta
Indicates that the threshold values given in the command should be interpreted in terms of the difference between successive readings.

absolute
Indicates that the threshold values given in the command should be interpreted as absolute values; i.e., the difference between the current value and preceding values is irrelevant.

rising-threshold *value [event-number]*
Specifies the *value* at which the alarm should be triggered, calling the event, when the value is rising. *event-number* is the event that should be called when the alarm occurs. The event number is optional because the threshold doesn't have to be assigned an event. If either of the two thresholds is left blank, the event number will be set to 0, which does nothing.

falling-threshold *value [event-number]*
Specifies the *value* at which the alarm should be triggered, calling the event, when the value is falling. *event-number* is the event that should be called when the alarm occurs. The event number is optional because the threshold doesn't have to be assigned an event. If either of the two thresholds is left blank, the event number will be set to 0, which does nothing.

owner *string*

Ties this alarm to a particular person.

To configure the alarm settings we just described, enter the following command, in *configuration* mode, on a Cisco console:

```
orarouter1(config)#rmon alarm 25 ifEntry.10.2 60 absolute \
rising-threshold 90000 1 falling-threshold 85000 2 owner dmauro
```

This command configures alarm number 25, which monitors the object in *ifEntry.10.2* (instance 2 of *ifEntry.ifInOctets*, or the input octets on interface 2) every 60 seconds. It has a rising threshold of 90,000 octets, which has event number 1 tied to it: event 1 is called when traffic on this interface exceeds 90,000 octets/second. The falling threshold is set to 85,000 octets and has event number 2 tied to it. Here's how the alarm looks in the router's internal tables:

```
orarouter1#show rmon alarm

Alarm 1 is active, owned by dmauro
 Monitors ifEntry.10.2 every 60 second(s)
 Taking absolute samples, last value was 87051
 Rising threshold is 90000, assigned to event 1
 Falling threshold is 85000, assigned to event 2
 On startup enable rising or falling alarm
```

The last line of output says that the router will enable the alarm upon reboot. As you'd expect, you can also look at the alarm settings through the RMON MIB, beginning with the subtree *1.3.6.1.2.1.16*. As with the events themselves, we can create, change, edit, and delete entries using snmpset.

One problem with internal polling is that getting trends and seeing the data in a graph or table is difficult. Even if you develop the backend systems to gather MIB objects and display them graphically, retrieving data is sometimes painful. The Multi Router Traffic Grapher (MRTG) is a great program that allows you to do both internal and external polling. Furthermore, it is designed to generate graphs of your data in HTML format. MRTG is covered in Chapter 12.

External Polling

It is often impossible to poll a device internally, for technical, security, or political reasons. For example, the System Administration group may not be in the habit of giving out the root password, making it difficult for you to install and maintain internal polling scripts. However, they may have no problem with installing and maintaining an SNMP agent such as Concord's SystemEDGE or Net-SNMP. It's also possible that you will find yourself in an environment in which you lack the knowledge to build the tools necessary to poll internally. Despite the situation, if an SNMP agent is present on a machine that has objects worth polling, you can use an external device to poll the machine and read the objects' values.* This external device can be one or more NMSs or other machines or devices. For instance, when you have a decent-size network, it is sometimes convenient, and possibly necessary, to distribute polling among several NMSs.

Each of the external polling engines we will look at uses the same polling methods, although some NMSs implement external polling differently. We'll start with the OpenView xnmgraph program, which can be used to collect and display data graphically. You can even use OpenView to save the data for later retrieval and analysis. We'll include some examples that show how you can collect data and store it automatically and how you can retrieve that data for display. Castle Rock's SNMPc also has an excellent data-collection facility that we will use to collect and graph data.

Collecting and Displaying Data with OpenView

One of the easiest ways to get some interesting graphs with OpenView is to use the xnmgraph program. You can run xnmgraph from the command line and from some of NNM's menus. One practical way to graph is to use OpenView's xnmbrowser to collect some data and then click Graph. It's as easy as that. If the node you are polling has more than one instance (say, multiple interfaces), OpenView will graph all known instances. When an NMS queries a device such as a router, it determines how many instances are in the *ifTable* and retrieves management data for each entry in the table.

OpenView Graphing

Figure 8-3 shows the sort of graph you can create with NNM. To create this graph, we started the browser (Figure 8-2) and clicked down through the MIB tree until we found the *.iso.org.dod.internet.mgmt.mib-2.interfaces.ifTable.ifEntry* list. Once there, we clicked on *ifInOctets*; then, while holding down the Ctrl key, we clicked on *ifOutOctets*. After both were selected and we verified that the Name or IP Address field displayed the node we wanted to poll, we clicked on the Graph button.

Once the graph has started, you can change the polling interval and the colors used to display different objects. You can also turn off the display of some or all of the object instances. The menu item View → Line Configuration lets you specify which objects you would like to display; it can also set multipliers for different items. For example, to display everything in K, multiply the data by .001. There is also an

---

* Many devices say they are SNMP compatible but support only a few MIBs. This makes polling nearly impossible. If you don't have the object(s) to poll, there is nothing you can do, unless there are hooks for an extensible agent. Even with extensible agents, unless you know how to program, the *Simple* in *SNMP* goes away fast.

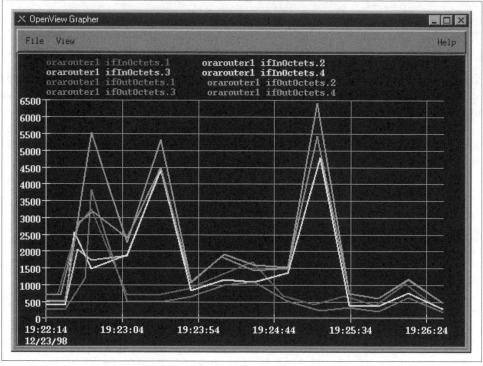

Figure 8-3. OpenView xnmgraph of octets in/out

option (View → Statistics) that shows a statistical summary of your graph. Figure 8-4 shows some statistics from the graph in Figure 8-3. While the statistics menu is up, you can left-click on the graph, and the statistics window will display the values for the specific date and time to which you are pointing with the mouse.

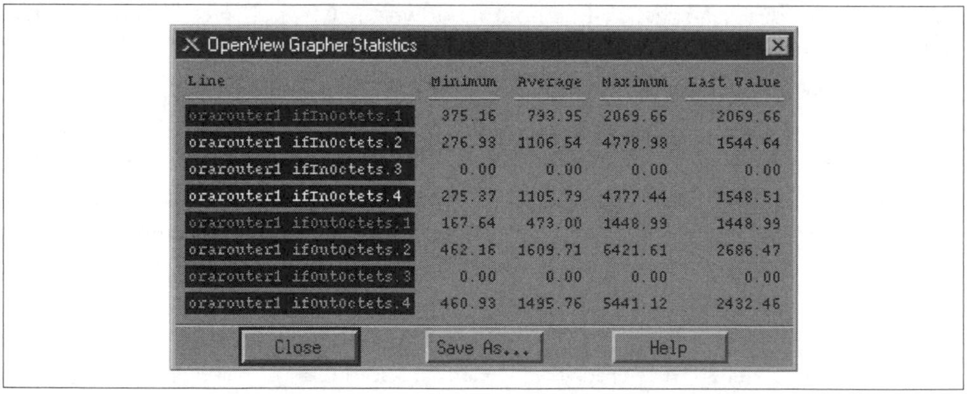

Line	Minimum	Average	Maximum	Last Value
orarouter1 ifInOctets.1	375.16	793.95	2069.66	2069.66
orarouter1 ifInOctets.2	276.93	1106.54	4778.98	1544.64
orarouter1 ifInOctets.3	0.00	0.00	0.00	0.00
orarouter1 ifInOctets.4	275.37	1105.79	4777.44	1548.51
orarouter1 ifOutOctets.1	167.64	473.00	1448.99	1448.99
orarouter1 ifOutOctets.2	462.16	1609.71	6421.61	2686.47
orarouter1 ifOutOctets.3	0.00	0.00	0.00	0.00
orarouter1 ifOutOctets.4	460.93	1495.76	5441.12	2432.46

Figure 8-4. xnmgraph statistics

Starting xnmgraph from the command line allows you to start the grapher at a specific polling period and gives you several other options. By default, OpenView polls at 10-second intervals. In most cases, this is fine, but if you are polling a multiport router to check if some ports are congested, a 10-second polling interval may be too quick and could cause operational problems. For example, if the CPU is busy answering SNMP queries every 10 seconds, the router might get bogged down and become very slow, especially if the router is responsible for OSPF or other CPU-intensive tasks. You may also see messages from OpenView complaining that another poll has come along while it is still waiting for the previous poll to return. Increasing the polling interval usually gets rid of these messages.

Some of NNM's default menus let you use the grapher to poll devices depending on their type. For example, you can select the object type "router" on the NNM and generate a graph that includes all your routers. Whether you start from the command line or from the menu, sometimes you will get a message back that reads "Requesting more lines than number of colors (25). Reducing number of lines." This message means that there aren't enough colors available to display the objects you are trying to graph. The only good ways to avoid this problem are to break up your graphs so that they poll fewer objects, or eliminate object instances you don't want. For example, you probably don't want to graph router interfaces that are down (for whatever reason) and other "dead" objects. We will soon see how you can use a regular expression as one of the arguments to the xnmgraph command to graph only those interfaces that are up and running.

Although the graphical interface is very convenient, the command-line interface gives you much more flexibility. The following shell script displays the graph in Figure 8-3 (i.e., the graph we generated through the browser):

```
#!/bin/sh
# filename: /opt/OV/local/scripts/graphOctets
# syntax: graphOctets <hostname>
/opt/OV/bin/xnmgraph -c public -mib \
".iso.org.dod.internet.mgmt.mib-2.interfaces.ifTable.ifEntry.ifInOctets:::::::::,\
.iso.org.dod.internet.mgmt.mib-2.interfaces.ifTable.ifEntry.ifOutOctets:::::::::" \
$1
```

You can run this script with the command:

```
$ /opt/OV/local/scripts/graphOctets orarouter1
```

The worst part of writing the script is figuring out what command-line options you want—particularly the long strings of nine colon-separated options. All these options give you the ability to refine what you want to graph, how often you want to poll the objects, and how you want to display the data. (We'll discuss the syntax of these options as we go along, but for the complete story, see the xnmgraph(1) manpage.) In this script, we're graphing the values of two MIB objects, *ifInOctets* and *ifOutOctets*. Each OID we want to graph is the first (and in this case, the only) option in the string of colon-separated options. On our network, this command produces eight traces: input and output octets for each of our four interfaces. You can add other OIDs to the graph by adding sets of options, but at some point, the graph will become too confusing to be useful. It will take some experimenting to use the xnmgraph command efficiently, but once you learn how to generate useful graphs you'll wonder how you ever got along without it.

 Keeping your scripts neat is not only good practice but also aesthetically pleasing. Using a \ at the end of a line indicates that the next line is a continuation of the current line. Breaking your lines intelligently makes your scripts more readable. Be warned that the Unix shells do *not* like extra whitespace after the \. The only character after each \ should be one carriage return.

Now, let's modify the script to include more reasonable labels—in particular, we'd like the graph to show which interface is which, instead of just showing the index number. In our modified script, we've used numerical object IDs, mostly for formatting convenience, and we've added a sixth option to the ugly sequence of colon-separated options: *.1.3.6.1.2.1.2.2.1.2* (this is the *ifDescr*, or interface description, object in the interface table). This option says to poll each instance and use the return value of snmpget .1.3.6.1.2.1.2.2.1.2.INSTANCE as the label. This should give us meaningful labels. Here's the new script:

```
#!/bin/sh
# filename: /opt/OV/local/scripts/graphOctets
# syntax: graphOctets <hostname>
/opt/OV/bin/xnmgraph -c public -title Bits_In_n_Out -mib \
".1.3.6.1.4.1.9.2.2.1.1.6::::::.1.3.6.1.2.1.2.2.1.2:::,\
.1.3.6.1.4.1.9.2.2.1.1.8::::::.1.3.6.1.2.1.2.2.1.2:::" $1
```

To see what we'll get for labels, here's the result of walking *.1.3.6.1.2.1.2.2.1.2*:

```
$ snmpwalk orarouter1 .1.3.6.1.2.1.2.2.1.2
interfaces.ifTable.ifEntry.ifDescr.1 : DISPLAY STRING- (ascii):  Ethernet0
interfaces.ifTable.ifEntry.ifDescr.2 : DISPLAY STRING- (ascii):  Serial0
interfaces.ifTable.ifEntry.ifDescr.3 : DISPLAY STRING- (ascii):  Serial1
```

Figure 8-5 shows our new graph. With the addition of this sixth option, the names and labels are much easier to read.

Meaningful labels and titles are important, especially if management is interested in seeing the graphs. A label that contains an OID and not a textual description is of no use. Some objects that are useful in building labels are *ifType* (*.1.3.6.1.2.1.2.2.1.3*) and *ifOperStatus* (*.1.3.6.1.2.1.2.2.1.8*). Be careful when using *ifOperStatus*; if the status of the interface changes during a poll, the label does not change. The label is evaluated only once.

One of the most wasteful things you can do is poll a useless object. This often happens when an interface is administratively down or not configured. Imagine that you

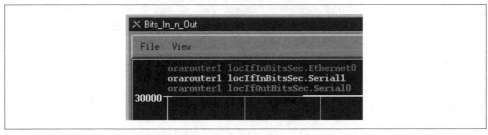

Figure 8-5. OpenView xnmgraph with new labels

have 20 serial interfaces, but only one is actually in use. If you are looking for octets in and out of your serial interfaces, you'll be polling 40 times and 38 of the polls will always read 0. OpenView's xnmgraph allows you to specify an OID and regular expression to select what should be graphed. To put this feature to use, let's walk the MIB to see what information is available:

```
$ snmpwalk orarouter1 .1.3.6.1.2.1.2.2.1.8
interfaces.ifTable.ifEntry.ifOperStatus.1 : INTEGER: up
interfaces.ifTable.ifEntry.ifOperStatus.2 : INTEGER: up
interfaces.ifTable.ifEntry.ifOperStatus.3 : INTEGER: down
```

This tells us that only two interfaces are currently up. By looking at *ifDescr*, we see that the live interfaces are *Ethernet0* and *Serial0*; *Serial1* is down. Notice that the type of *ifOperStatus* is INTEGER, but the return value looks like a string. How is this? RFC 1213 defines string values for each possible return value:

```
ifOperStatus OBJECT-TYPE
    SYNTAX  INTEGER {
                up(1),       —ready to pass packets
                down(2),
                testing(3)   —in some test mode
            }
    ACCESS  read-only
    STATUS  mandatory
    DESCRIPTION
        "The current operational state of the interface. The testing(3)
         state indicates that no operational packets can be passed."
    ::= { ifEntry 8 }
```

It's fairly obvious how to read this: the integer value 1 is converted to the string up. We can therefore use the value 1 in a regular expression that tests *ifOperStatus*. For every instance we will check the value of *ifOperStatus*; we will poll that instance and graph the result only if the status returns 1. In pseudocode, the operation would look something like this:

```
if (ifOperStatus == 1) {
    pollForMIBData;
    graphOctets;
}
```

Here's the next version of our graphing script. To put this logic into a graph, we use the OID for *ifOperStatus* as the fourth colon option and the regular expression (1) as the fifth option:

```
#!/bin/sh
# filename: /opt/OV/local/scripts/graphOctets
# syntax: graphOctets <hostname>
/opt/OV/bin/xnmgraph -c public \
-title Octets_In_and_Out_For_All_Up_Interfaces \
-mib ".1.3.6.1.2.1.2.2.1.10:::.1.3.6.1.2.1.2.2.1.8:1::::, \
.1.3.6.1.2.1.2.2.1.16:::.1.3.6.1.2.1.2.2.1.8:1::::" $1
```

This command graphs the *ifInOctets* and *ifOutOctets* of any interface that has a current operational state equal to 1, or up. It therefore polls and graphs only the ports that are important, saving on network bandwidth and simplifying the graph. Furthermore, we're less likely to run out of colors while making the graph because we won't assign them to useless objects. Note, however, that this selection happens only during the first poll and stays effective throughout the entire life of the graphing process. If the status of any interface changes after the graph has been started, nothing in the graph will change. The only way to discover any changes in interface status is to restart xnmgraph.

Finally, let's look at:

- How to add a label to each OID we graph
- How to multiply each value by a constant
- How to specify the polling interval

The cropped graph in Figure 8-6 shows how the labels change when we run the following script:

```
#!/bin/sh
# filename: /opt/OV/local/scripts/graphOctets
# syntax: graphOctets <hostname>
/opt/OV/bin/xnmgraph -c public -title Internet_Traffic_In_K -poll 68 -mib \
".1.3.6.1.4.1.9.2.2.1.1.6:Incoming_Traffic:::.1.3.6.1.2.1.2.2.1.2::.001:,\
.1.3.6.1.4.1.9.2.2.1.1.8:Outgoing_Traffic:::.1.3.6.1.2.1.2.2.1.2::.001:" \
$1
```

The labels are given by the second and sixth fields in the colon-separated options (the second field provides a textual label to identify the objects we're graphing and the sixth uses the *ifDescr* field to identify the particular interface); the constant multiplier (.001) is given by the eighth field; and the polling interval (in seconds) is given by the -poll option.

By now it should be apparent how flexible OpenView's xnmgraph program really is. These graphs can be important tools for troubleshooting your network. When a network manager receives complaints from customers regarding slow connections, he can look at the graph of *ifInOctets* generated by xnmgraph to see if any router interfaces have unusually high traffic spikes.

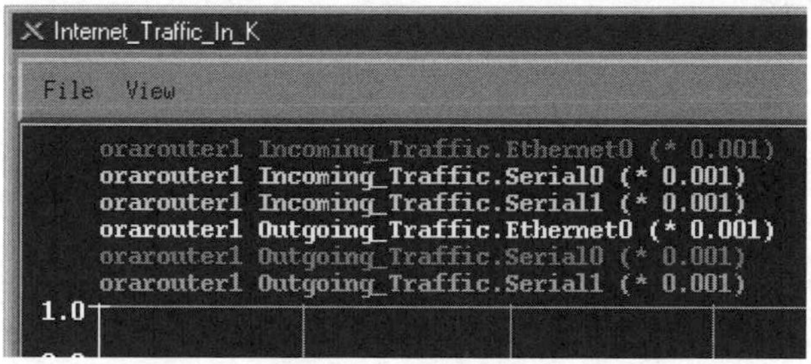

Figure 8-6. xnmgraph with labels and multipliers

Graphs like these are also useful when you're setting thresholds for alarms and other kinds of traps. The last thing you want is a threshold that is too "triggery" (one that goes off too many times) or a threshold that won't go off until the entire building burns to the ground. It's often useful to look at a few graphs to get a feel for your network's behavior before you start setting any thresholds. These graphs will give you a baseline from which to work. For example, say you want to be notified when the battery on your UPS is low (which means it is being used) and when it is back to normal (fully charged). The obvious way to implement this is to generate an alarm when the battery falls below some percentage of full charge, and another alarm when it returns to full charge. So the question is: what value can we set for the threshold? Should we use 10% to indicate that the battery is being used and 100% to indicate that it's back to normal? We can find the baseline by graphing the device's MIBs.[*] For example, with a few days' worth of graphs, we can see that our UPS's battery stays right around 94–97% when it is not in use. There was a brief period where the battery dropped down to 89% when it was performing a self-test. Based on these numbers, we may want to set the "in use" threshold at 85% and the "back to normal" threshold at 94%. This pair of thresholds gives us plenty of notification when the battery's in use but won't generate useless alarms when the device is in self-test mode. The appropriate thresholds depend on the type of devices you are polling, as well as the MIB data that is gathered. Doing some initial testing and polling to get a baseline (normal numbers) will help you set thresholds that are meaningful and useful.

Before leaving xnmgraph, we'll take a final look at the nastiest aspect of this program: the sequence of nine colon-separated options. In the examples, we've demonstrated the most useful combinations of options. In more detail, here's the syntax of the graph specification:

```
object:label:instances:match:expression:instance-label:truncator:multiplier:nodes
```

---

[*] Different vendors have different UPS MIBs. Refer to your particular vendor's MIB to find out which object represents low battery power.

The parameters are:

object

    The OID of the object whose values you want to graph. This can be in either numeric or human-readable form, but it should *not* have an instance number at the end. It can also be the name of an expression (expressions are discussed in Appendix A).

label

    A string to use in making the label for all instances of this object. This can be a literal string or the OID of some object with a string value. The label used on the graph is made by combining this label (for all instances of the object) with *instance-label*, which identifies individual instances of an object in a table. For example, in Figure 8-6, the labels are *Incoming_Traffic* and *Outgoing_Traffic*; *instance-label* is *1.3.6.1.2.1.2.2.1.2*, or the *ifDescr* field for each object being graphed.

instances

    A regular expression that specifies which instances of *object* to graph. If this is omitted, all instances are graphed. For example, the regular expression 1 limits the graph to instance 1 of *object*; the regular expression [4-7] limits the graph to instances 4 through 7. You can use the *match* and *expression* fields to further specify which objects to match.

match

    The OID of an object (not including the instance ID) to match against a regular expression (the match expression) to determine which instances of the object to display in the graph.

expression

    A regular expression; for each instance, the object given by *match* is compared to this regular expression. If the two match, the instance is graphed.

instance-label

    A label to use to identify particular instances of the object you are graphing. This is used in combination with the *label* and *truncator* fields to create a label for each instance of each object being graphed.

truncator

    A string that will be removed from the initial portion of the instance label to make it shorter.

multiplier

    A number that's used to scale the values being graphed.

nodes

    The nodes to poll to create the graph. You can list any number of nodes, separated by spaces. The wildcard * polls all the nodes in OpenView's database. If you omit this field, xnmgraph takes the list of nodes from the final argument on the command line.

The only required field is *object*; however, as we've seen, you must have all eight colons even if you leave some (or most) of the fields empty.

OpenView Data Collection and Thresholds

Once you close the OpenView graphs, the data in them is lost forever. OpenView provides a way to fix this problem with data collection. Data collection allows the user to poll and record data continuously. It can also look at these results and trigger events. One benefit of data collection is that it can watch the network for you while you're not there; you can start collecting data on Friday and then leave for the weekend, knowing that any important events will be recorded in your absence.

You can start OpenView's Data Collection and Thresholds function from the command line, using the command $OV_BIN/xnmcollect, or from NNM under the Options menu. This brings you to the Data Collection and Thresholds window, shown in Figure 8-7, which displays a list of all the collections you have configured and a summary of the collection parameters.

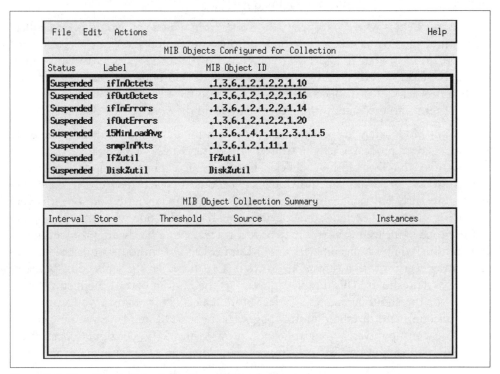

Figure 8-7. OpenView's Data Collection and Thresholds window

Configured collections that are in Suspended mode appear in a dark or bold font. This indicates that OpenView is not collecting any data for these objects. A Collecting status indicates that OpenView is polling the selected nodes for the given object and saving the data. To change the status of a collection, select the object, click on Actions, and then click on either Suspend Collection or Resume Collection. (Note that you must save your changes before they will take effect.)

Designing collections

To design a new collection, select Edit → Add MIB Object. This takes you to a new screen. At the top, click on MIB Object* and click down through the tree until you find the object you would like to poll. To look at the status of our printer's paper tray, for example, we need to navigate down to:

.iso.org.dod.internet.private.enterprises.hp.nm.system.net-peripheral.net-printer.generalDeviceStatus.gdStatusEntry.gdStatusPaperOut (.1.3.6.1.4.1.11.2.3.9.1.1.2.8).†

The object's description suggests that this is the item we want: it reads "This indicates that the peripheral is out of paper." (If you already know what you're looking for, you can enter the name or OID directly.) Once there, you can change the name of the collection to something that is easier to read. Click OK to move forward. This brings you to the menu shown in Figure 8-8.

The Source field is where you specify the nodes from which you would like to collect data. Enter the hostnames or IP addresses you want to poll. You can use wildcards like *198.27.6.** in your IP addresses; you can also click Add Map to add any nodes currently selected. We suggest that you start with one node for testing purposes. Adding more nodes to a collection is easy once you have everything set up correctly; you just return to the window in Figure 8-8 and add the nodes to the Source list.

Collection Mode lets you specify what to do with the data NNM collects. There are four collection modes: Exclude Collection; Store, Check Thresholds; Store, No Thresholds; and Don't Store, Check Thresholds. Except for Exclude Collection, which allows us to turn off individual collections for each device, the collection modes are fairly self-explanatory. (Exclude Collection may sound odd, but it is very useful if you want to exclude some devices from data collection without stopping the entire process; for example, you may have a router with a hardware problem that is bombarding you with meaningless data.) Data collection without a threshold is easier than collection with a threshold, so we'll start there. Set the Collection Mode to Store, No Thresholds. This disables (grays out) the bottom part of the menu, which is used for threshold parameters. (Select Store, Check Thresholds if you want both data collection and threshold monitoring.) Then click OK and save the new collection. You can now watch your collection grow in the *$OV_DB/snmpCollect* directory. Each collection consists of a binary datafile, plus a file with the same name

---

* You can collect the value of an expression instead of a single MIB object.

† This object is in HP's private MIB, so it won't be available unless you have HP printers and have installed the appropriate MIBs. Note that there is a standard printer MIB, RFC 1759, but HP's MIB has more useful information.

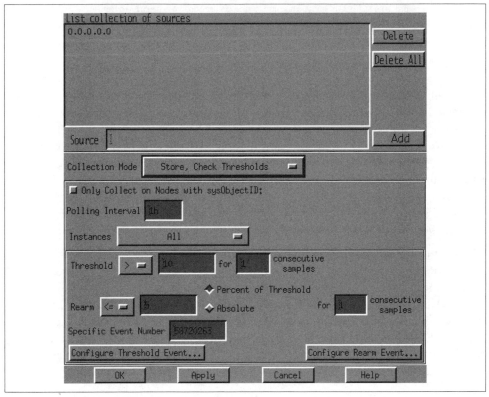

Figure 8-8. OpenView poll configuration menu

preceded by an exclamation mark (!); this file stores the collection information. The data collection files will grow without bounds. To trim these files without disturbing the collector, delete all files that do not contain an ! mark.

Clicking on Only Collect on Nodes with sysObjectID allows you to enter a value for *sysObjectID*. *sysObjectID* (*iso.org.dod.internet.mgmt.mib-2.system.sysObjectID*) lets you limit polling to devices made by a specific manufacturer. Its value is the enterprise number the device's manufacturer has registered with IANA. For example, Cisco's enterprise number is 9, and HP's is 11 (the complete list is available at *http://www.iana.org/assignments/enterprise-numbers*); therefore, to restrict polling to devices manufactured by HP, set the *sysObjectID* to 11. RFC 1213 formally defines *sysObjectID* (*1.3.6.1.2.1.1.2*) as follows:

```
sysObjectID OBJECT-TYPE
    SYNTAX  OBJECT IDENTIFIER
    ACCESS  read-only
    STATUS  mandatory
    DESCRIPTION
        "The vendor's authoritative identification of the network
        management subsystem contained in the entity. This value
        is allocated within the SMI enterprises subtree (1.3.6.1.4.1)
```

```
and provides an easy and unambiguous means for determining
what kind of box' is being managed. For example, if vendor
'Flintstones, Inc.' was assigned the subtree 1.3.6.1.4.1.4242,
it could assign the identifier 1.3.6.1.4.1.4242.1.1 to its
'Fred Router'."
::= { system 2 }
```

The polling interval is the period at which polling occurs. You can use one-letter abbreviations to specify units: s for seconds, m for minutes, h for hours, and d for days. For example, 32s indicates 32 seconds; 1.5d indicates one and a half days. When we're designing a data collection, we usually start with a very short polling interval—typically 7s (7 seconds between each poll). You probably wouldn't want to use a polling interval this short in practice (all the data you collect is going to have to be stored somewhere), but when you're setting up a collection, it's often convenient to use a short polling interval. You don't want to wait a long time to find out whether you're collecting the right data.

The next option is a drop-down menu that specifies what instances should be polled. The options are All, From List, and From Regular Expression. In this case, we're polling a scalar item, so we don't have to worry about instances; we can leave the setting to All or select From List and specify instance 0 (the instance number for all scalar objects). If you're polling a tabular object, you can either specify a comma-separated list of instances or choose the From Regular Expression option and write a regular expression that selects the instances you want. Save your changes (File → Save), and you're done.

Creating a threshold

Once you've set all this up, you've configured NNM to periodically collect the status of your printer's paper tray. Now for something more interesting: let's use thresholds to generate some sort of notification when the traffic coming in through one of our network interfaces exceeds a certain level. To do this, we'll look at a Cisco-specific object, *locIfInBitsSec* (more formally *iso.org.dod.internet.private.enterprises.cisco.local. linterfaces.lifTable.lifEntry.locIfInBitsSec*), whose value is the five-minute average of the rate at which data arrives at the interface, in bits per second. (There's a corresponding object called *locIfOutBitsSec*, which measures the data leaving the interface.) The first part of the process should be familiar: start Data Collection and Thresholds by going to the Options menu of NNM, then select Edit → Add MIB Object. Navigate through the object tree until you get to *locIfInBitsSec*; click OK to get back to the screen shown in Figure 8-8. Specify the IP addresses of the interfaces you want to monitor and set the collection mode to Store, Check Thresholds; this allows you to retrieve and view the data at a later time. (We typically turn on the Store function so that we can verify that the collector is actually working and view any data that has accumulated.) Pick a reasonable polling interval—again, when you're testing it's reasonable to use a short interval—then choose which instances you'd like to poll, and you're ready to set thresholds.

The Threshold field lets you specify the point at which the value you're monitoring becomes interesting. What "interesting" means is up to you. In this case, let's assume that we're monitoring a T1 connection, with a capacity of 1.544 Mbits/second. Let's say somewhat arbitrarily that we'll start worrying when the incoming traffic exceeds 75% of our capacity. So, after multiplying 1.544 by .75, we set the threshold to > 1158000. Of course, network traffic is fundamentally bursty, so we won't worry about a single peak—but if we have two or three consecutive readings that exceed the threshold, we want to be notified. So let's set "consecutive samples" to 3: that shields us from getting unwanted notifications, while providing ample notification if something goes wrong.

Setting an appropriate consecutive samples value will make your life much more pleasant, though picking the right value is something of an art. Another example is monitoring the /tmp partition of a Unix system. In this case, you may want to set the threshold to >= 85, the number of consecutive samples to 2, and the poll interval to 5m. This will generate an event when the usage on /tmp exceeds 85% for two consecutive polls. This choice of settings means that you won't get a false alarm if a user copies a large file to /tmp and then deletes the file a few minutes later. If you set consecutive samples to 1, NNM generates a Threshold event as soon as it notices that /tmp is filling up, even if the condition is only temporary and nothing to be concerned about. It then generates a Rearm event after the user deletes the file. Since we are really only worried about /tmp filling up and staying full, setting the consecutive threshold to 2 can help reduce the number of false alarms. This is generally a good starting value for consecutive samples, unless your polling interval is very high.

The rearm parameters let us specify when everything is back to normal or is, at the very least, starting to return to normal. This state must occur before another threshold is met. You can specify either an absolute value or a percentage. When monitoring the packets arriving at an interface, you might want to set the rearm threshold to something like 926,400 bits per second (an absolute value that happens to be 60% of the total capacity) or 80% of the threshold (also 60% of capacity). Likewise, if you're generating an alarm when /tmp exceeds 85% of capacity, you might want to rearm when the free space returns to 80% of your 85% threshold (68% of capacity). You can also specify the number of consecutive samples that need to fall below the rearm point before NNM considers the rearm condition met.

The final option, Configure Threshold Event, asks what OpenView events you would like to execute for each state. You can leave the default event, or you can refer to Chapter 9 for more on how to configure events. The Threshold state needs a specific event number that must reside in the HP enterprise. The default Threshold event is *OV_DataCollectThresh - 58720263*. Note that the Threshold event is always an odd number. The Rearm event is the next number after the Threshold event: in this case, 58720264. To configure events other than the default, click on Configure Threshold Event and, when the new menu comes up, add one event (with an odd number) to the HP section and a second event for the corresponding Rearm. After making the additions, save and return to the Collection window to enter the new number.

When you finish configuring the data collection, click OK. This brings you back to the Data Collection and Thresholds menu. Select File → Save to make your current additions active. On the bottom half of the MIB Object Collection Summary window, click on your new object and then select Actions → Test SNMP. This brings up a window showing the results of an SNMP test on that collection. After the test, wait long enough for your polling interval to have expired once or twice. Then click on the object collection again, but this time select Actions → Show Data. This window shows the data that has been gathered so far. Try blasting data through the interface to see if you can trigger a Threshold event. If the Threshold events are not occurring, verify that your threshold and polling intervals are set correctly. After you've seen a Threshold event occur, watch how the Rearm event gets executed. When you're finished testing, go back and set up realistic polling periods, add any additional nodes you would like to poll, and turn off storing if you don't want to collect data for trend analysis. Refer to the *$OV_LOG/snmpCol.trace* file if you are having any problems getting your data collection rolling. Your HP OpenView manual should describe how to use this trace file to troubleshoot most problems.

Once you have collected some data, you can use xnmgraph to display it. The xnmgraph command to use is similar to the ones we saw earlier; it's an awkward command that you'll want to save in a script. In the following script, the –browse option points the grapher at the stored data:

```
#!/bin/sh
# filename: /opt/OV/local/scripts/graphSavedData
# syntax: graphSavedData <hostname>
/opt/OV/bin/xnmgraph -c public -title Bits_In_n_Out_For_All_Up_Interfaces \
-browse -mib \
 ".1.3.6.1.4.1.9.2.2.1.1.6:::.1.3.6.1.2.1.2.2.1.8:1:.1.3.6.1.2.1.2.2.1.2:::,\
.1.3.6.1.4.1.9.2.2.1.1.8:::.1.3.6.1.2.1.2.2.1.8:1:.1.3.6.1.2.1.2.2.1.2:::" \
$1
```

Once the graph has started, no real (live) data is graphed; the display is limited to the data that has been collected. You can select File → Update Data to check for and insert any data that has been gathered since the start of the graph. Another option is to leave off –browse, which allows the graph to continue collecting and displaying the live data along with the collected data.

Finally, to graph all the data that has been collected for a specific node, go to NNM and select the node you would like to investigate. Then select Performance → Graph SNMP Data → Select Nodes from the menus. You will get a graph of all the data that has been collected for the node you selected. Alternately, select the All option in Performance → Graph SNMP Data. With the number of colors limited to 25, you will usually find that you can't fit everything into one graph.

Castle Rock's SNMPc

The workgroup edition of Castle Rock's SNMPc program has similar capabilities to the OpenView package. It uses the term *trend reporting* for its data collection and threshold facilities. The enterprise edition of SNMPc even allows you to export data to a web page.

To see how SNMPc works, let's graph the *snmpOutPkts* object. This object's OID is *1.3.6.1.2.1.11.2* (*iso.org.dod.internet.mgmt.mib-2.snmp.snmpOutPkts*). It is defined in RFC 1213 as follows:

```
snmpOutPkts OBJECT-TYPE
    SYNTAX  Counter
    ACCESS  read-only
    STATUS  mandatory
    DESCRIPTION
        "The total number of SNMP messages which were passed from
         the SNMP protocol entity to the transport service."
    ::= { snmp 2 }
```

We'll use the *orahub* device for this example. Start by clicking on the MIB Database selection tab shown in Figure 8-9; this is the tab at the bottom of the screen that looks something like a spreadsheet—it's the second from the left. Click down the tree until you come to *iso.org.dod.internet.mgmt.mib-2.snmp*. Click on the object you would like to graph (for this example, *snmpOutPkts*). You can select multiple objects with the Ctrl key.

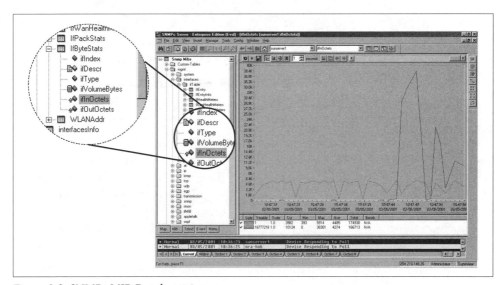

Figure 8-9. SNMPc MIB Database view

 SNMPc has a nonstandard way of organizing MIB information. To get to the *snmpOutPkts* object, you need to click down through the following: Snmp Mibs → mgmt → snmp → snmpInfo. Though this is quicker than the RFC-based organization used by most products, it does get a little confusing, particularly if you work with several products.

Once you have selected the appropriate MIB object, return to the top level of your map by either selecting the house icon or clicking on the Root Subnet tab (at the far left) to select the device you would like to poll. Instead of finding and clicking on the device, you can enter the device's name by hand. If you have previously polled the device, you can select it from the drop-down box. Figure 8-10 shows what a completed menu bar should look like.

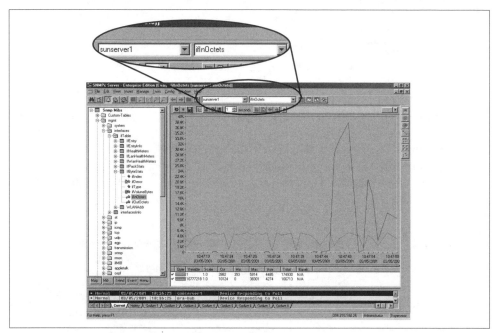

Figure 8-10. SNMPc menu bar graph section

To begin graphing, click the button with the small jagged graph (the third from the right). Another window will appear displaying the graph (Figure 8-11). The controls at the top change the type of graph (line, bar, pie, distribution, etc.) and the polling interval and allow you to view historical data (the horizontal slider bar). Review the documentation on how each of these work or, better yet, play around to learn these menus even faster.

Once you have a collection of frequently used graphs, you can insert them into the custom menus. Let's insert a menu item in the Tools menu that displays all the information in the *snmpInfo* table as a pie chart. Click on the Custom Menus tab (the last one), right-click on the *Tools* folder, and then left-click on Insert Menu. This gets you to the Add Custom Menu window (Figure 8-12). Enter a menu name and select Pie for the display type. Use the browse button (>>) to click down the tree of MIB objects until you reach the *snmpInfo* table and click OK. Back at Add Custom Menu, use the checkboxes in the Use Selected Object section to specify the types of nodes that will be able to respond to this custom menu item. For example, to chart *snmp-*

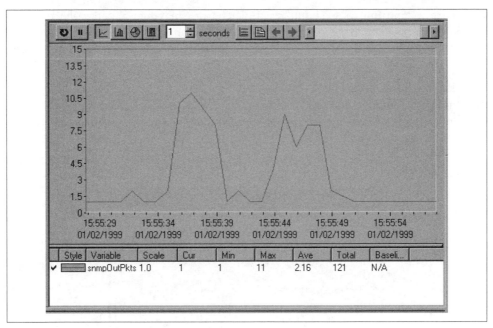

Figure 8-11. SNMPc snmpOutPkts graph section

Info, a device obviously needs to support SNMP, so we've checked the Has SNMP box. This information is used when you (or some other user) try to generate this chart for a given device. If the device doesn't support the necessary protocols, the menu entry for the pie chart will be disabled.

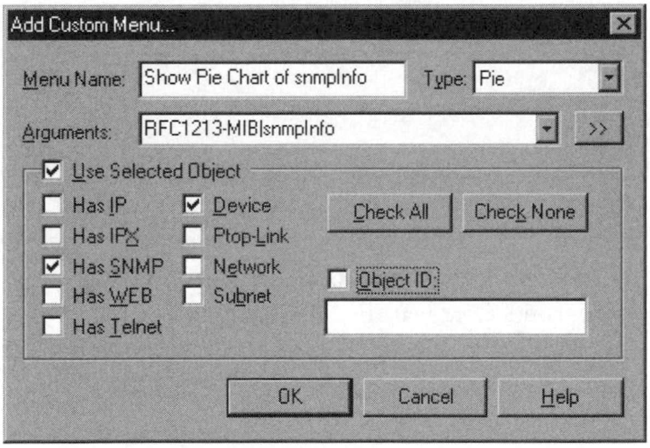

Figure 8-12. SNMPc Add Custom Menu window

Click OK and proceed to your map to find a device to test. Any SNMP-compatible device should suffice. Once you have selected a device, click on Tools and then Show

Pie Chart of snmpInfo. You should see a pie chart displaying the data collected from the MIB objects you have configured. (If the device doesn't support SNMP, this option will be disabled.) Alternately, you could have double-clicked your new menu item in the Custom Menu tab.

SNMPc has a threshold system called Automatic Alarms that can track the value of an object over time to determine its highs and lows (peaks and troughs) and get a baseline. After it obtains the baseline, it alerts you if something strays out of bounds. In the main menu, selecting Config → Trend Reports brings up the menu shown in Figure 8-13.

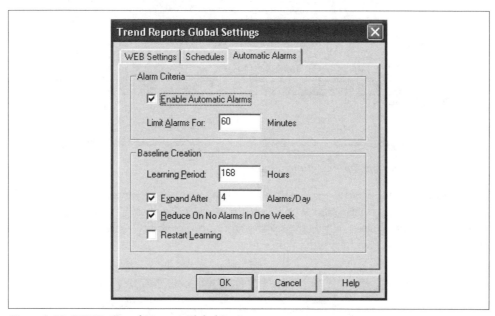

Figure 8-13. SNMPc Trend Reports Global Settings menu

Check the Enable Automatic Alarms box to enable this feature. The Limit Alarms For box lets you specify how much time must pass before you can receive another alarm of the same nature. This prevents you from being flooded by the same message over and over again. The next section, Baseline Creation, lets you configure how the baseline will be learned. The learning period is how long SNMPc should take to figure out what the baseline really is. The Expand After option, if checked, states how many alarms you can get in one day before SNMPc increases the baseline parameters. In Figure 8-13, if we were to get four alarms in one day, SNMPc would increase the threshold to prevent these messages from being generated so frequently. Checking the Reduce On No Alarms In One Week box tells SNMPc to reduce the baseline if we don't receive any alarms in one week. This option prevents the baseline from being set so high that we never receive any alarms. If you check the last option and click OK, SNMPc will restart the learning process. This gives you a way to wipe the slate clean and start over.

Open Source Tools for Data Collection and Graphing

One of the most powerful tools for data collection and graphing is MRTG, familiar to many in the open source community. It collects statistics and generates graphical reports in the form of web pages. In many respects, it's a different kind of animal than the tools discussed in this chapter. RRDtool is the successor to MRTG. Cricket is a popular frontend for RRDtool. We cover MRTG in Chapter 12 and Cricket and RRDtool in Chapter 13.

CHAPTER 9

Traps

Traps provide a way for an agent to send a monitoring station asynchronous notification about conditions that the monitor should know about. The traps that an agent can generate are defined by the MIBs it supports; the number of traps can range from zero to hundreds. To see what traps are defined in any MIB file, search for the term *TRAP-TYPE* (SMIv1) or *NOTIFICATION-TYPE* (SMIv2) in the MIB file. This search will quickly get you a list of possible traps.

Of course, just having asynchronous traps arrive at your NMS isn't terribly useful. You can configure the NMS's response to different traps; the response can be anything from discarding the trap to running a script that sends a message to your pager (or even takes some drastic action, such as shutting down your power supplies). In this chapter, we'll show you how to handle incoming traps using OpenView and other tools such as Perl. Then we'll discuss how to read and configure different aspects of trap events. Finally, we'll show you how to define your own traps to report special conditions of particular interest for your network.

Understanding Traps

Before discussing the tools for receiving and generating traps, it's worth reviewing what a trap is. Traps were introduced in Chapter 2. A trap is basically an asynchronous notification sent from an SNMP agent to a network management station. Like everything else in SNMP, traps are sent using UDP (port 162) and are therefore unreliable. This means that the sender cannot assume that the trap actually arrives nor can the destination assume that it's getting all the traps being sent its way. Of course, on a healthy network, most traps should reach their destinations. But if networks were always healthy, we wouldn't need SNMP.

In somewhat more detail, a trap is a bundle of data that's defined by a MIB. Traps fall into two categories: generic and enterprise specific. There are seven generic trap numbers (0–6), defined in Chapter 2 in Table 2-8, for conditions ranging from system reboots (*coldStart*) and interface state changes (*linkUp* and *linkDown*) to generic trap 6 (*enterpriseSpecific*). Enterprise-specific traps are the loophole that makes the trap mechanism so powerful. Anyone with an enterprise number can define enterprise-specific traps for whatever conditions she considers worth monitoring. An enterprise-specific trap is identified by two pieces of information: the enterprise ID of the organization that defined the trap and the specific trap number assigned by that organization. The notion of an enterprise-specific trap is extremely flexible because organizations are allowed to subdivide their enterprises as much as they like. For example, if your enterprise number is 2789, your enterprise ID is *.1.3.6.1.4.1.2789*. But you can further subdivide this, defining traps with enterprise IDs such as *.1.3.6.1.4.1.2789.5000*, *.1.3.6.1.4.1.2789.5001*, and so on.

The fact that you've received a trap and therefore know its generic trap number, enterprise ID, and specific trap number is often all you need to diagnose a problem. But traps also carry additional information. In the case of generic traps 0–5, the specific information is predefined and hardwired into the NMS. When you receive a generic trap, the NMS knows how to interpret the information it contains and will be able to display it appropriately, whether it's the time of the reboot or the identity of the interface that just changed state. In contrast, the information carried by an enterprise-specific trap is entirely up to the person who defined the trap. An enterprise-specific trap can contain any number of variable bindings, or MIB object-value pairs. When you define your own traps, you can decide what information is appropriate for them to carry. The objects contained in a trap can be standard MIB objects, vendor-specific objects, or objects of your own devising. It's common to define objects purely for the purpose of including them within a trap.

SNMPv2 Traps

SNMPv2 defines traps in a slightly different way. In a MIB, SNMPv1 traps are defined as TRAP-TYPE, SNMPv2 traps are defined as NOTIFICATION-TYPE. SNMPv2 also does away with the notion of generic traps—instead, it defines many specific traps (properly speaking, notifications) in public MIBs. SNMPv3 traps, which are discussed briefly in Chapter 3, are simply SNMPv2 traps with added authentication and privacy capabilities. Most SNMP implementations support only Version 1.

Receiving Traps

Let's start by discussing how to deal with incoming traps. Handling incoming traps is the responsibility of the NMS. Some NMSs do as little as display the incoming traps to standard output (*stdout*). However, an NMS server typically has the ability to react to SNMP traps it receives. For example, when an NMS receives a *linkDown* trap from a router, it might respond to the event by paging the contact person, displaying a pop-up message on a management console, or forwarding the event to another NMS. This procedure is streamlined in commercial packages but still can be achieved with freely available open source programs.

HP OpenView

OpenView uses three pieces of software to receive and interpret traps:

- ovtrapd (1M)
- xnmtrap
- xnmevents

OpenView's main trap-handling daemon is called ovtrapd. This program listens for traps generated by devices on the network and hands them off to the Postmaster daemon (pmd). In turn, pmd triggers what OpenView calls an event. Events can be configured to perform actions ranging from sending a pop-up window to NNM users, forwarding the event to other NMSs, or doing nothing at all. The configuration process uses xnmtrap, the Event Configurations GUI. The xnmevents program displays the events that have arrived, sorting them into user-configurable categories.

OpenView keeps a history of all the traps it has received; to retrieve that history, use the command $OV_BIN/ovdumpevents. In older versions of OpenView, traps are kept in an event logging file in *$OV_LOG/trapd.log*. By default, this file rolls over after it grows to 4 MB. It is then renamed *trapd.log.old* and a new *trapd.log* file is started. If you are having problems with traps, either because you don't know whether they are reaching the NMS or because your NMS is being bombarded by too many events, you can use tail –f to watch *trapd.log* so that you can see the traps as they arrive. (You can also use *ovdumpevents* to create a new file.) To learn more about the format of this file, refer to OpenView's manual pages for trapd.conf (4) and ovdumpevents (1M).

Recent releases of OpenView instead put traps into the OpenView Event Database. Many admins prefer the old logfile format, however. If you are running a recent release of OpenView and want to see a *trapd.log* file of all your traps, run ovdumpevents to create this file.

It might be helpful to define exactly what an OpenView event is. Think of it as a small record, similar to a database record. This record defines which trap OpenView should watch out for. It further defines what sort of action (send an email, page someone, etc.), if any, should be performed.

Using NNM's Event Configurations

OpenView uses an internal definition file to determine how to react to particular situations. This definition file is maintained by the xnmtrap program. We can start xnmtrap by selecting Options → Event Configurations (in the NNM GUI) or by giving the command $OV_BIN/xnmtrap. In the Enterprise Identification window, scroll down and click on the enterprise name OpenView .1.3.6.1.4.1.11.2.17.1. This displays a list in the Event Identification window. Scroll down in this list until you reach

OV_Node_Down. Double-click on this event to bring up the Event Configurator (Figure 9-1).

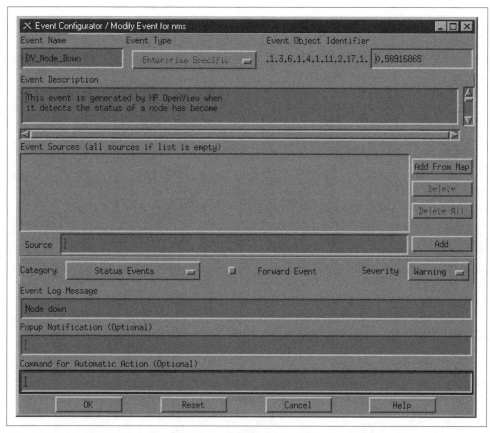

Figure 9-1. OpenView Event Configurator—OV_Node_Down

Figure 9-1 shows the *OV_Node_Down* event in the Event Configurator. When this event is triggered, it inserts an entry containing the message "Node down," with a severity level of Warning, into the Status Events category. OpenView likes to have a leading 0 (zero) in the Event Object Identifier, which indicates whether this is an event or trap—there is no way to change this value yourself. The number before the 0 is the enterprise OID; the number after the 0 is the specific trap number—in this case, 58916865.* Later we will use these numbers as parameters when generating our own traps.

---

* This is the default number that OpenView uses for this *OV_Node_Down* trap.

Selecting event sources

The Source option is useful when you want to receive traps from certain nodes and ignore traps from other nodes. For example, if you have a development router that people are taking up and down all day, you probably would rather not receive all the events generated by the router's activity. In this case, you could use the Source field to list all the nodes from which you would like to receive traps and leave out the development router. To do this, you can either type each hostname by hand and click Add after each one, or select each node (using the Ctrl and mouse-click sequence) on your OpenView Network Node Map and click Add From Map. Unfortunately, the resulting list isn't easy to manage. Even if you take the time to add all the current routers to the Event Sources, you'll eventually add a new router (or some other hardware you want to manage). You then have to go back to *all* your events and add your new devices as sources. OpenView allows you to use pattern matching and source files, making it easier to tailor and maintain the source list.

Setting event categories

When NNM receives an event, it sorts the event into an event category. The Categories drop-down box lets you assign the event you're configuring to a category. The list of available categories will probably include the following predefined categories (you can customize this list by adding categories specific to your network and deleting categories, as we'll see later in this section):

- Error events
- Threshold events
- Status events
- Configuration events
- Application alert events
- Don't log or display
- Log only

The last two categories really aren't event categories in the true sense of the word. If you select "Don't log or display," OpenView will not save the event in its database and will not display the Event Log Message in any Event Categories. OpenView will display the Popup Notification in a pop-up window and run the Command for Automatic Action. The "Log only" option tells OpenView not to display the event but to keep a log of the event in its database.[*]

---

[*] As mentioned earlier, you can convert the database into a logfile using the ovdumpevents command.

"Log only" is useful if you have some events that are primarily informational; you don't want to see them when they arrive, but you would like to record them for future reference. The Cisco event *frDLCIStatusChange - .1.3.6.1.2.1.10.32.0.1* is a good example of such an event. It tells us when a Virtual Circuit has changed its operational state. If displayed, we will see notifications whenever a node goes down and whenever a circuit changes its operational state to down. This information is redundant because we have already gotten a status event of "node down" and a DLCI change.* With this event set to "Log only" we can go to the logfile only when we think things are fishy.

Forwarding events and event severities

The Forward Event radio button, once checked, allows you to forward an event to other NMSs. This feature is useful if you have multiple NMSs or a distributed network management architecture. Say that you are based in Atlanta, but your network has a management station in New York in addition to the one on your desk. You don't want to receive all of New York's events, but you would like the *node_down* information forwarded to you. On New York's NMS, you could click Forward Event and insert the IP address of your NMS in Atlanta. When New York receives a *node_down* event, it will forward the event to Atlanta.

The Severity drop-down list assigns a severity level to the event. OpenView supports six severity levels: Unknown, Normal, Warning, Minor, Major, and Critical. The severity levels are color-coded to make identification easier; Table 9-1 shows the color associated with each severity level. The levels are listed in order of increasing severity. For example, an event with a severity level of Warning has a higher precedence than an event with a severity level of Minor.

Table 9-1. OpenView severity levels

Severity	Color
Unknown	Blue
Normal	Green
Warning	Cyan
Minor	Yellow
Major	Orange
Critical	Red

The colors are used both on OpenView's maps and in the Event Categories. Parent objects, which represent the starting point for a network, are displayed in the color

---

* OpenView has a feature called Event Correlation that groups certain events together to avoid flooding the user with redundant information. You can customize these settings with a developer's kit.

of the highest severity level associated with any object underneath them.* For example, if an object represents a network with 250 nodes and one of those nodes is down (a Critical severity), the object will be colored red, regardless of how many nodes are up and functioning normally. The term for how OpenView displays colors in relation to objects is *status source*; it is explained in more detail in Chapter 5.

Log messages, notifications, and automatic actions

Returning to Figure 9-1, the Event Log Message and Popup Notification fields are similar but serve different purposes. The Event Log Message is displayed when you view the Event Categories and select a category from the drop-down list. The Popup Notification, which is optional, displays its message in a window that appears on any server running OpenView's NNM. Figure 9-2 shows a typical pop-up message. The event name, delme in this case, appears in the titlebar. The time and date at which the event occurred are followed by the event message, "Popup Message Here." To create a pop-up message like this, insert "Popup Message Here" in the Popup Notification section of the Event Configurator. Every time the event is called, a pop-up will appear.

Figure 9-2. OpenView pop-up message

The last section of the Event Configurator is the Command for Automatic Action. The automatic action allows you to specify a Unix command or script to execute when OpenView receives an event. You can run multiple commands by separating them with a semicolon, much as you would in a Unix shell. When configuring an automatic action, remember that rsh can be very useful. We like to use rsh sunserver1 audioplay -v50 /opt/local/sounds/siren.au, which causes a siren audio file to play. The automatic action can range from touching a file to opening a trouble ticket.

In each Event Log Message, Popup Notification, and Command for Automatic Action, special variables can help you identify the values from your traps or events. These variables provide the user with additional information about the event. Here are some of the variables you can use (the online help has a complete list):

* Parent objects can show status (colors) in four ways: Symbol, Object, Compound, or Propagated.

$1

Print the first passed attribute (i.e., the value of the first variable binding) from the trap.

$2

Print the second passed attribute.

$n

Print the *n*th attribute as a value string. Must be in the range of 1–99.

$*

Print all the attributes as [seq] name (type).

Before you start running scripts for an event, find out the average number of traps you are likely to receive for that event. This is especially true for *OV_Node_Down*. If you write a script that opens a trouble ticket whenever a node goes down, you could end up with hundreds of tickets by the end of the day. Monitoring your network will make you painfully aware of how much your network "flaps," or goes up and down. Even if the network goes down for a second, for whatever reason, you'll get a trap, which will in turn generate an event, which might register a new ticket, send you a page, etc. The last thing you want is "The Network That Cried Down!" You and other people on your staff will start ignoring all the false warnings and may miss any serious problems that arise. One way to estimate how frequently you will receive events is to log events in a file ("Log only"). After a week or so, inspect the logfile to see how many events accumulated (i.e., the number of traps received). This is by no means scientific, but it will give you an idea of what you can expect.

Custom Event Categories

OpenView uses the default categories for all its default events. Look through the *$OV_CONF/C/trapd.conf* file to see how the default events are assigned to categories. You can add categories by going to Event Configuration → Edit → Configure → Event Categories. Figure 9-3 shows this menu, with some custom categories added.

It's worth your while to spend time thinking about what categories are appropriate for your environment. If you plow everything into the default categories, you will be bothered by the Critical "Printer Needs Paper" event when you really want to be notified of the Critical "Production Server on Fire" event. Either event will turn Status Events red. The categories in Figure 9-3 are a good start, but think about the types of events and activities that will be useful for your network. The Scheduled and Unscheduled (S/U) Downtime category is a great example of a category that is more for human intervention than for reporting network errors. Printer Events is a nice destination for your "Printer Needs Paper" and "Printer Jammed" messages.

Even though none of the default categories is required (except for Error), we recommend that you don't delete them, precisely because they are used for all of the default events. Deleting the default categories without first reconfiguring all the

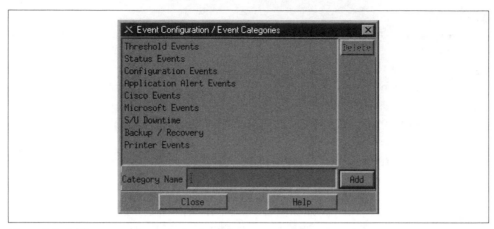

Figure 9-3. Adding event categories in OpenView

default events will cause problems. Any event that does not have an event category available will be put into the default Error category. To edit the categories, copy the *trapd.conf* file into */tmp* and modify */tmp/trapd.conf* with your favorite editor. The file has some large warnings telling you never to edit it by hand, but sometimes a few simple edits are the best way to reassign events. An entry in the portion of the file that defines event behavior looks like this:

```
EVENT RMON_Rise_Alarm .1.3.6.1.2.1.16.0.1 "Threshold Events" Warning
FORMAT RMON Rising Alarm: $2 exceeded threshold $5; value = $4. (Sample type = \
$3; alarm index = $1)
SDESC
This event is sent when an RMON device exceeds a preconfigured threshold.
EDESC
```

It's fairly obvious what these lines do: they map a particular RMON event into the Threshold Events category with a severity of Warning; they also specify what should happen when the event occurs. To map this event into another category, change Threshold Events to the appropriate category. Once you've edited the file, use the following command to merge in your updates:

```
$ $OV_BIN/xnmevents -l load /tmp/trapd.conf
```

The Event Categories Display

The Event Categories window (Figure 9-4) is displayed on the user's screen when NNM is started. It provides a very brief summary of what's happening on your network; if it is set up appropriately, you can tell at a glance whether there are any problems you should be worrying about.

If the window gets closed during an OpenView session, you can restart it using the Fault → Events menu item or by issuing the command $OV_BIN/xnmevents. The menu displays all the event categories, including any categories you have created.

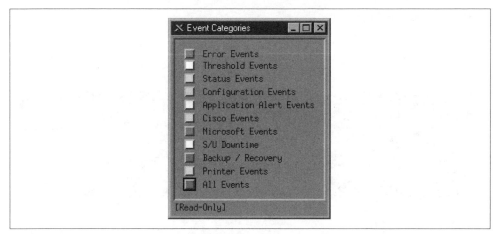

Figure 9-4. OpenView Event Categories

Two categories are special: the Error category is the default category used when an event is associated with a category that cannot be found; the All category is a placeholder for all events and cannot be configured by the Event Configurator. The window shows you the highest severity level of any event in each event category.

The box to the left of Status Events is cyan (a light blue), showing that the highest unacknowledged severity in the Status Events category is Warning. Clicking on that box displays an alarm browser that lists all the events received in the category. A nice feature of the Event Categories display is the ability to restore a browser's state or reload events from the *trapd.log* and *trapd.log.old* files. Reloading events is useful if you find that you need to restore messages you deleted in the past.

 OpenView extends the abilities of Event Categories by keeping a common database of acknowledged and unacknowledged events. Thus, when a user acknowledges an event, all other users see this event updated.

At the bottom of Figure 9-4, the phrase "[Read-Only]" means that you don't have write access to Event Categories. If this phrase isn't present, you have write access. OpenView keeps track of events in a single database, though older versions stored events on a per-user basis, using a special database located in *$OV_LOG/xnmevents. <username>*. With write access, you have the ability to update this file whenever you exit. By default, you have write access to your own event category database, unless someone has already started the database by starting a session with your username. There may be only one write-access Event Categories per user, with the first one getting write access and all others getting read-only privileges.

The Alarms Browser

Figure 9-5 shows the alarms browser for the Status Events category. In it we see a single Warning event, which is causing the Status Events category to show cyan.

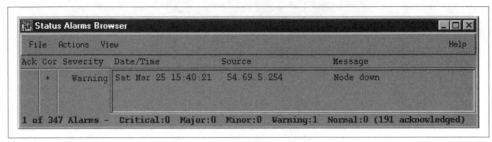

Figure 9-5. OpenView alarms browser

The color of the Status Events box is determined by the highest precedence event in the category. Therefore, the color won't change until either you acknowledge the highest precedence event or an event arrives with an even higher precedence. Clicking in the far-left column (Ack)* acknowledges the message and sets the severity to 0.

The Actions menu in the alarms browser allows you to acknowledge, deacknowledge, or delete some or all events. You can even change the severity of an event. Keep in mind that this does *not* change the severity of the event on other Event Categories sessions that are running. For example, if one user changes the severity of an event from Critical to Normal, the event will remain Critical for other users. The View menu lets you define filters, which allow you to include or discard messages that match the filter.

When configuring events, keep in mind that you may receive more traps than you want. When this happens, you have two choices. First, you can go to the agent and turn off trap generation, if the agent supports this. Second, you can configure your trap view to ignore these traps. We saw how to do this earlier: you can set the event to "Log only" or try excluding the device from the Event Sources list. If bandwidth is a concern, you should investigate why the agent is sending out so many traps before trying to mask the problem.

Creating Events Within OpenView

OpenView gives you the option of creating additional (private) events. Private events are just like regular events, except that they belong to your private enterprise subtree rather than to a public MIB. To create your own events, launch the Event Configuration window from the Options menu of NNM. You will see a list of all currently loaded events (Figure 9-6).

---

* OpenView also supports Event Correlation, which has a column in this window as well.

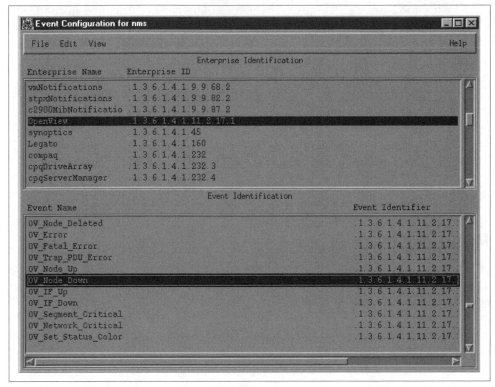

Figure 9-6. OpenView's Event Configuration window

The window is divided into two panes. The top pane displays the Enterprise Identification, which is the leftmost part of an OID. Clicking on an enterprise ID displays all the events belonging to that enterprise in the lower pane. To add your own enterprise ID, select Edit → Add → Enterprise Identification and insert your enterprise name and a registered enterprise ID.[*] Now you're ready to create private events. Click on the enterprise name you just created; the enterprise ID you've associated with this name will be used to form the OID for the new event. Click Edit → Add → Event, and then type the Event Name for your new event, making sure to use Enterprise Specific (the default) for the event type. Insert an Event Object Identifier. This identifier can be any number that hasn't already been assigned to an event in the currently selected enterprise. Finally, click OK and save the event configuration (using File → Save).

To copy an existing event, click on the event you wish to copy and select Edit → Copy Event; you'll see a new window with the event you selected. From this point on, the process is the same.

---

[*] Refer to Chapter 2 for information about obtaining your own enterprise ID.

Traps with "no format" are traps for which nothing has been defined in the Event Configuration window. There are two ways to solve this problem: you can either create the necessary events on your own, or load a MIB that contains the necessary trap definitions, as discussed in Chapter 5. "No format" traps are frequently traps defined in a vendor-specific MIB that hasn't been loaded. Loading the appropriate MIB often fixes the problem by defining the vendor's traps and their associated names, IDs, comments, severity levels, etc.

 Before loading a MIB, review the types of traps the MIB supports. You will find that most traps you load come, by default, in LOGONLY mode. This means that you will *not* be notified when the traps come in. After you load the MIB, you may want to edit the events it defines, specifying the local configuration that best fits your site.

Monitoring Traps with Perl

If you can't afford an expensive package like OpenView, you can use the Perl language to write your own monitoring and logging utility. You get what you pay for since you will have to write almost everything from scratch. On the other hand, you'll learn a lot and probably have a better appreciation for the finer points of network management. One of the most elementary, but effective, programs to receive traps is in a distribution of SNMP Support for Perl 5, written by Simon Leinen. Here's a modified version of Simon's program:

```perl
#!/usr/bin/perl

use SNMP_Session;
use BER;
use Socket;

$session = SNMPv1_Session->open_trap_session (  );
while (($trap, $sender, $sender_port) = $session->receive_trap ()) {
    chomp ($DATE=`/bin/date \'+%a %b %e %T\'`);
    print STDERR "\n$DATE - " . inet_ntoa($sender)
        . " - port: $sender_port\n";
    print_trap ($session, $trap);
}

sub print_trap{
    ($this, $trap) = @_;
    my($community, $ent, $agent, $gen, $spec, $dt, $bindings)
        = $this->decode_trap_request ($trap);
    print "   Community:\t".$community."\n";
    print "   Enterprise:\t".BER::pretty_oid ($ent)."\n";
    print "   Agent addr:\t".inet_ntoa ($agent)."\n";
    print "   Generic ID:\t$gen\n";
    print "   Specific ID:\t$spec\n";
    print "   Uptime:\t".BER::pretty_uptime_value ($dt)."\n";
    $prefix = "   bindings:\t";
    my ($binding, $oid, $value);
    while ($bindings ne '') {
```

```
        ($binding,$bindings) = &decode_sequence ($bindings);
        ($oid, $value) = decode_by_template ($binding, "%0%@");
        print $prefix.BER::pretty_oid ($oid).
              " => ".pretty_print ($value)."\n";
        $prefix = "\t\t";
    }
}
```

This program displays traps as they are received from different devices in the network. Here's some output, showing two traps:

```
Mon Apr 28 22:07:44 - 10.123.46.26 - port: 63968
    community:   public
    enterprise:  1.3.6.1.4.1.2789.2500
    agent addr:  10.123.46.26
    generic ID:  6
    specific ID: 5247
    uptime:      0:00:00
    bindings:    1.3.6.1.4.1.2789.2500.1234 => 14264026886

Mon Apr 28 22:09:46 - 172.16.51.25 - port: 63970
    community:   public
    enterprise:  1.3.6.1.4.1.2789.2500
    agent addr:  172.16.253.2
    generic ID:  6
    specific ID: 5247
    uptime:      0:00:00
    bindings:    1.3.6.1.4.1.2789.2500.2468 => Hot Swap Now In Sync
```

The output format is the same for both traps. The first line shows the date and time at which the trap occurred, together with the IP address of the device that sent the trap. Most of the remaining output items should be familiar to you. The bindings output item lists the variable bindings that were sent in the trap PDU. In the preceding example above, each trap contained one variable binding. The object ID is in numeric form, which isn't particularly friendly. If a trap has more than one variable binding, this program displays each binding, one after another.

An ad hoc monitoring system can be fashioned by using this Perl script to collect traps and some other program to inspect the traps as they are received. Once the traps are parsed, the possibilities are endless. You can write user-defined rules that watch for significant traps and, when triggered, send an email alert, update an event database, send a message to a pager, etc. These kinds of solutions work well if you're in a business with little or no budget for commercially available NMS software or if you're on a small network and don't need a heavyweight management tool.

Using the Network Computing Technologies Trap Receiver

The Trap Receiver by Network Computing Technologies is a freely available program that's worth trying.* This program, which currently runs only on Windows-

---

* This software can be found at *http://www.ncomtech.com/download.htm*.

based systems, displays trap information as it's received. It has a standard interface but can be configured to execute certain actions against traps, like OpenView's Command for Automatic Action function. Figure 9-7 shows Trap Receiver's user interface.

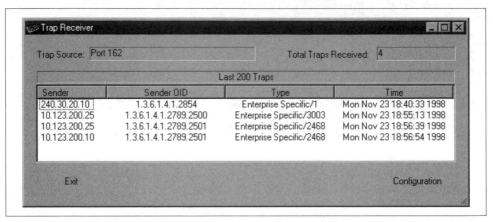

Figure 9-7. Trap Receiver

You can log and forward messages and traps, send email or a page in response to a trap, as well as execute commands. By writing some code in C or C++, you can gain access to an internal trap stream. This program can be a great starting place for Windows administrators who want to use SNMP but lack the resources to implement something like OpenView. It's simple to use, extensible, and free.

Receiving Traps Using Net-SNMP

The last trap receiver we'll discuss is part of the Net-SNMP package, which is also freely available. snmptrapd allows you to send SNMP trap messages to facilities such as Unix *syslog* or *stdout*. For most applications the program works in the background, shipping messages to *syslog*(8). There are some configuration parameters for the *syslog* side of snmptrapd; these tell snmptrapd what facility level it should use for the *syslog* messages. The following command forwards traps to standard output (–Lo) rather than to *syslog* and does not fork off into the background (–f):

```
$ ./snmptrapd -f -Lo
2005-05-05 08:00:24 NET-SNMP version 5.2.1 Started.
2005-05-05 08:03:05 sunserver2.ora.com [12.1.45.26] (via UDP: [12.1.45.26]:37223)
TRAP, SNMP v1, community public
        SNMPv2-SMI::enterprises.2789.2500.1224 Enterprise Specific Trap (1224)
Uptime: 60 days, 14:41:38.72
        SNMPv2-SMI::enterprises.2789.2500.1224 = INTEGER: 123123

2005-05-05 08:10:16 sunserver2.ora.com [12.1.45.26] (via UDP: [12.1.45.26]:37223)
TRAP, SNMP v1, community public
    SNMPv2-SMI::enterprises.2789.2500.1445 Enterprise Specific Trap (1445) Uptime:
60 days, 14:41:38.72
        SNMPv2-SMI::enterprises.2789.2500.1445 = STRING: "Fail Over Complete"
```

By now the output should look familiar; it's similar to the reports generated by the other programs we've seen in this chapter. The Net-SNMP trap daemon is another great tool for scriptwriters. A simple Perl script can watch the file in which snmptrapd logs its traps, looking for important events and reacting accordingly. It's easy to build a powerful and flexible monitoring system at little or no expense.

The Net-SNMP trap daemon can also handle SNMPv2/SNMPv3 traps and informs. Recall that inform was introduced in SNMPv2. It allows a sender to receive an acknowledgment when the receiver gets the trap. To configure snmptrapd to receive both SNMPv3 traps and informs, care must be taken. You must add a `createUser` command to the *snmpd.conf* file. For example, to receive informs, I have the following in my *snmpd.conf* file:

```
createUser kschmidt MD5 mysecretpass DES mypassphrase
```

When snmptrapd starts up, it will discover the remote engine ID of the sender of the inform. To understand the role of the engine ID, let's look at a `createUser` entry that can be used to handle SNMPv3 traps:

```
createUser -e 0x012345 kschmidt MD5 mysecretpass DES mypassphrase
```

The difference is the inclusion of the –e switch. This configures the engine ID of the remote machine that will send us traps. In other words, we need to know it ahead of time. Refer to RFC 3411 for a specific algorithm for creating the engine ID. The next section shows how to send SNMPv3 traps from Net-SNMP.

In this section, we have looked at several packages that can receive traps and act on them, based on the traps' content. Keep in mind that all of these programs, whether they're free or cost tens of thousands of dollars, are basically doing the same thing: listening on some port (usually UDP port 162) and waiting for SNMP messages to arrive. What sets the various packages apart is their ability to do something constructive with the traps. Some let you program hooks that execute some other program when a certain trap is received. The simpler trap monitors just send a message logging the trap to one or more files or facilities. These packages are generally less expensive than the commercial trap monitors but can be made to operate like full-fledged systems with some additional programming effort. Languages such as Perl give you the ability to extend these simpler packages.

Sending Traps

By now you should have a mechanism in place for receiving traps. In this section, we'll look at some different utilities that send traps and allow you to develop traps that are appropriate for your environment. You'll notice that almost all trap utilities are command-line based. This allows you to execute the command from within a script, which is almost always what you want to do. For example, you can write a shell script that checks disk space every five minutes and sends a trap to the NMS if you're running low. You can also use these trap generators within existing programs and scripts. If you have a Perl script that accesses a database, you can use the Perl SNMP module to send a trap from within the script if a database insert fails. The possibilities are almost endless.

Although there are many different snmptrap programs, they are all fundamentally similar. In particular, though their command-line syntax may vary, they all expect roughly the same arguments:

Port

The UDP port to which to send the trap. The default port is 162.

SNMP version

The SNMP version appropriate for the trap you want to send. Many traps are defined only for Version 2. Note that many SNMP tools support only Version 1.

Hostname or IP address of NMS

The hostname or IP address of your NMS—i.e., the trap's destination. It is better to use an IP address than a hostname in case you are sending traps during a DNS outage. Remember that SNMP is most valuable when your network is failing; therefore, try to avoid assuming that you have a fully functional network when you design traps.

Community name

The community name to be sent with the trap. Most management stations can be configured to ignore traps that don't have an appropriate community string.

Enterprise OID

The full enterprise OID for the trap you want to send: everything in the trap's OID from the initial *.1* up to the enterprise number, including any subtrees within the enterprise but not the specific trap number. For example, if your enterprise number is 2789, you've further subdivided your enterprise to include a group of traps numbered 5000, and you want to send specific trap 1234, the enterprise OID would be *.1.3.6.1.4.1.2789.5000*.

If you have some reason to send a generic trap, you can set the enterprise ID to anything you want—but it's probably best to set the enterprise ID to your own enterprise number, if you have one.

Now for the most confusing case. A few specific traps are defined in various public MIBs. How do you send them? Basically, you construct something that looks like an enterprise OID. One such trap is *rdbmsOutOfSpace*, which is defined in the RDBMS MIB. Its complete OID is *.1.3.6.1.2.1.39.2.2* (*.iso.org.dod.internet. mgmt.mib-2.rdbmsMIB.rdbmsTraps.rdbmsOutOfSpace*). To send this trap, which is really an SNMPv2 notification, you would use everything up to *rdbmsTraps* as the enterprise OID, and the entire object ID as the specific trap number.

Hostname or IP address of sender

The IP address of the agent that is sending the trap. Although this may appear to be superfluous, it can be important if there is a proxy server between the agent and the NMS. This parameter allows you to record the actual address of the agent within the SNMP packet; in turn, the NMS will read the agent's address from the trap and ignore the packet's sender address. If you don't specify this parameter, it will almost always default to the address of the machine sending the trap.

Generic trap number
A number in the range 0–6. The true generic traps have numbers 0–5; if you're sending an enterprise-specific trap, set this number to 6. Table 2-8 in Chapter 2 lists the generic traps.

Specific trap number
A number indicating the specific trap you want to send. If you're sending a generic trap, this parameter is ignored—you're probably better off setting it to zero. If you're sending a specific trap, the trap number is up to you. For example, if you send a trap with the OID *.1.3.6.1.4.1.2500.3003.0*, 3003 is the specific trap number.

Timestamp
The time elapsed between the last initialization of the network entity and the generation of the trap.

OID_1, type_1, value_1
Data bindings to be included in the trap. Each data binding consists of an OID together with a datatype, followed by the value you want to send. Most programs let you include any number of data bindings in a trap. Note that the OIDs for these variable bindings are often specific to the trap and therefore "underneath" the specific OID for the trap. But this isn't a requirement, and it's often useful to send bindings that aren't defined as part of the trap.

Before we start to tackle this section, let's take a moment to review what we learned in Chapter 2 about the various datatypes:

- Each variable that we send has a particular datatype.
- Different datatypes are supported by different versions of SNMP.
- Some common datatypes are `INTEGER`, `OctetString`, `Null`, `Counter`, `Gauge`, and `TimeTicks`.

Be aware that not all programs support all datatypes. For example, the Perl SNMP module supports only the `OctetString`, `INTEGER`, and `OID` types, while the OpenView and Net-SNMP snmptrap commands support these three and many more. For each package we use, we will list, if applicable, the datatypes the program supports.

In the next sections, we'll discuss snmptrap programs from HP, Network Computing Technologies, and Net-SNMP. We'll also include a script that uses a Perl module to send traps. If you are not using these particular programs in your environment, don't worry. You should still be able to relate these examples to your in-house programs.

Sending Traps with OpenView

OpenView has a command-line program for generating arbitrary traps, called snmptrap. snmptrap supports the counter, counter32, counter64,[*] gauge, gauge32, integer, integer32, ipaddress, null, objectidentifier, octetstring, octetstringascii, octetstringhex, octetstringoctal, opaque, opaqueascii, opaquehex, opaqueoctal, timeticks, and unsigned32 datatypes. Its command-line structure looks like this:

```
snmptrap -c community [-p port] node_addr enterprise_id agent-addr generic \
specific timestamp [OID type value] ...
```

Here's a typical snmptrap command. It sends one trap, with three ASCII-string variable bindings for values:

```
$ /opt/OV/bin/snmptrap -c public nms \
.1.3.6.1.4.1.2789.2500 "" 6 3003 "" \
.1.3.6.1.4.1.2789.2500.3003.1 octetstringascii "Oracle" \
.1.3.6.1.4.1.2789.2500.3003.2 octetstringascii "Backup Not Running" \
.1.3.6.1.4.1.2789.2500.3003.3 octetstringascii "Call the DBA Now for Help"
```

It's a complicated command, and it's hard to imagine that you would ever type it on the command line. Let's break it up into pieces. The first line specifies the community string (public) and the address to which the trap should be sent (nms, though in practice it would be better to use an IP address rather than a node name). The next line is in many respects the most complicated. It specifies the enterprise ID for the trap we're going to send (.1.3.5.1.6.1.2789.2500, which is a subtree of the enterprise-specific tree we've devoted to traps); the address of the agent sending the trap (in this case, the null string "", which defaults to the agent's address; if you're using a proxy server, it is useful to specify the agent's address explicitly); the generic trap number (6, which is used for all enterprise-specific traps); the specific trap number (3003, which we've assigned); and a timestamp ("", which defaults to the current time).

The remaining three lines specify three variable bindings to be included with the trap. For each binding, we have the variable's object ID, its datatype, and its value. The variables we're sending are defined in our private (enterprise-specific) MIB, so their OIDs all begin with *.1.3.6.1.4.1.2789.2500*. All the variables are strings, so their datatype is octetstringascii. The trap PDU will be packed with these three strings, among other things. The program that receives the trap will decode the trap PDU and realize that there are three variable bindings in the trap. These variable bindings, like the one that reads "Call the DBA Now for Help," can be used to alert the operator that something bad has happened.

---

[*] This type works only on agents that support SNMPv2.

Sending Traps with Perl

In Chapter 7, we learned how to use the get and set pieces of the SNMP Perl module. In this section, we'll see how to use the snmptrap() routine to generate traps. Currently, SNMP_util supports only three types for traps: string, int, and oid. This can seem limiting, but it covers most needs. Here's how snmptrap is called:

```
snmptrap(communityname@host:port_number, enterpriseOID, host_name_from, \
generic_ID, specific_ID, OID, type, value, [OID, type, value ...])
```

One call to snmptrap can include any number of values; for each value, you must specify the object ID, the datatype, and the value you're reporting. The next script generates a trap with only one value:

```
#!/usr/local/bin/perl
# Filename: /opt/local/perl_scripts/snmptrap.pl

use SNMP_util "0.54";  # This will load the BER and SNMP_Session for us

snmptrap("public\@nms:162", ".1.3.6.1.4.1.2789", "sunserver1", 6, 1247, \
        ".1.3.6.1.4.1.2789.1247.1", "int", "2448816");
```

The call to snmptrap() sends a trap to port 162 on host nms. The trap is sent from host sunserver1; it contains a single variable binding, for the object .1.3.6.1.4.1. 2789.1247.1. The OID's type is int and its value is 2448816.

Now let's try sending a trap with multiple values (multiple variable bindings). The first object we'll report is an integer, to which we give the arbitrary value 4278475. The second object has a string value and is a warning that our database has stopped. Because we're using OIDs that belong to our own enterprise, we can define these objects to be anything we want:

```
snmptrap("public\@nms:162", ".1.3.6.1.4.1.2789", "sunserver2", 6, 3301, \
        ".1.3.6.1.4.1.2789.3301.1", "int",    "4278475", \
        ".1.3.6.1.4.1.2789.3301.2", "string", "Sybase DB Stopped");
```

We can use the Net-SNMP snmptrapd program to monitor the traps coming in. We executed the preceding Perl code while running snmptrapd in *stdout* mode and received:

```
$ ./snmptrapd -f -Lo
2005-05-05 08:00:24 NET-SNMP version 5.2.1 Started.
2005-05-05 08:03:05 sunserver2.ora.com [12.1.45.26] (via UDP: [12.1.45.26]:37223)
TRAP, SNMP v1, community public
        SNMPv2-SMI::enterprises.2789.3301 Enterprise Specific Trap (3301) Uptime: 60
days, 14:41:38.72
        SNMPv2-SMI::enterprises.2789.3301.1 = INTEGER: 4278475
        SNMPv2-SMI::enterprises.2789.3301.2 = STRING: "Sybase DB Stopped"
```

snmptrapd reported both of the values we sent in the trap: we see the integer value 4278475 and the notification that Sybase has stopped. Although this example is highly artificial, it's not all that different from what you would do when writing your own monitoring software. You would write whatever code is necessary to monitor vital systems such as your database and use the Perl SNMP module to send traps when significant events occur. You can then use any program capable of receiving traps to inform you when the traps arrive. If you want, you can add logic that analyzes the values sent in the trap or takes other actions, such as notifying an operator via a pager.

Sending Traps with Network Computing Technologies' Trap Generator

This command-line utility runs on Windows and, more recently, on Unix (to be specific, Solaris 2.6, Linux, Irix 6.2, and HP-UX). It understands the String, Counter, Gauge, Integer, Address, OID, TimeTicks, and Octet datatypes. You specify each of these types to the tool with S, C, G, I, A, O, T, and H, respectively. The command line for trapgen looks like this:

```
trapgen -d DestinationIpAddress:port -c CommunityName
            -o senderOID -i senderIP -g GenericTrapType
            -s SpecificTrapType -t timestamp -v OID TYPE VALUE
```

Here's how to use trapgen to send a trap notifying us that the UPS battery is running low. We use the String datatype to send an informative message, and we use trap 4025.1 from our private enterprise ID, 2789:

```
C:\tools> trapgen -d nms:162 -c public -o ^
1.3.6.1.4.1.2789.4025 -i 10.123.456.4 -g 6 -s 4025 -t 124501 ^
-v 1.3.6.1.4.1.2789.4025.1 S 5 Minutes Left On UPS Battery
```

This trap will be sent to our network management station (which has the hostname nms) on port 162, which is the standard port for SNMP traps. Any management station should be able to receive the trap and act on it appropriately. You can use this command in Windows batch scripts and in Unix shell scripts. Therefore, you can use trapgen to generate traps as you need them: you can write scripts that monitor key processes and generate traps when any interesting events take place. As with the earlier Perl example, you can use this simple trap generator in your environment if you don't need a heavy-duty management system.

Sending Traps with Net-SNMP

This snmptrap program looks very similar to OpenView's snmptrap. This program uses a single letter to refer to datatypes, as shown in Table 9-2.

Table 9-2. Net-SNMP snmptrap datatypes

Abbreviation	Datatype
a	IP address
C	Counter32
D	Decimal string

Table 9-2. Net-SNMP snmptrap datatypes (continued)

Abbreviation	Datatype
I	Integer
N	Null
O	Object ID
S	String
T	Time ticks
U	Unsigned integer
X	Hexadecimal string
b	Bits

Here's how the Net-SNMP snmptrap program is invoked:

```
snmptrap hostname community enterprise-oid agent \
generic-trap specific-trap uptime [OID type value]...
```

If you use two single quotes ('') in place of the time, snmptrap inserts the current time into the trap. The following command generates a trap with a single value. The object ID is 2005.1, within our private enterprise; the value is a string that tells us that the web server has been restarted:

```
$ snmptrap nms public .1.3.6.1.4.1.2789.2005 ntserver1 6 2476317 '' \
.1.3.6.1.4.1.2789.2005.1 s "WWW Server Has Been Restarted"
```

Here's how to send a Version 2 notification with Net-SNMP:

```
$ snmptrap -v2c nms public '' .1.3.6.1.6.3.1.1.5.3 \
ifIndex i 2 ifAdminStatus i 1 ifOperStatus i 1
```

The command is actually simpler than its Version 1 equivalent. It has no generic numbers, specific numbers, or vendor IDs. The '' argument defaults to the current system uptime. The OID specifies the *linkDown* notification, with three data bindings specifying the link's status. The definition of *linkDown* in the IF-MIB states that the *linkDown* notification must include the *ifIndex*, *ifAdminStatus*, and *ifOperStatus* objects, which report the index of the interface that went down, its administrative status, and its operational status, respectively. For *ifAdminStatus* and *ifOperStatus*, a value of 1 indicates that the link is up. So, this notification reports that interface 2 has changed its state from "down" to "up."

Finally, here's how to send an SNMPv3 trap:

```
$ snmptrap -e 0x012345 -v3 -l authPriv -u kschmidt -a MD5 \ -A mysecretpass -x DES -X
mypassphrase localhost '' \ .1.3.6.1.4.1.2789.2005 .1.3.6.1.4.1.2789.2005.1 s \
"WWW Server Has Been Restarted"
```

Notice the –e command-line flag; it specifies this application's engine ID. The corresponding trap receiver should be configured with this value.

The snmptrap command-line tool is great for integrating SNMP monitoring into shell scripts and other programs.

Forcing Your Hardware to Generate Traps

When you install a new piece of equipment, you should verify that it generates traps correctly. Testing your equipment's ability to generate traps has the added benefit of testing the behavior of your NMS; you can ensure that it handles traps in the way you want. The best way to test new hardware is to read your vendor's MIB and look for all the TRAP-TYPEs it has defined. This will give you a good feel for the sort of traps your vendor has implemented. For example, I read through the APC MIB and noticed that the unit sends a trap when it goes onto battery power if the AC power goes out. To test this feature, I secured the area in our datacenter and switched off the circuit breaker to simulate a power failure. The trap was generated, but it showed up in the Error event category because I did not have the correct MIB loaded in OpenView. I took the OID from the Error events and searched the APC MIBs for a match. When I found one, I loaded the MIB file into OpenView and repeated the test. This time, when the trap was received, OpenView put an informative message in the Event Categories.

Most SNMP-compatible routers, switches, and network devices can generate *linkDown* traps. From RFC 1157, a *linkDown* trap is a "failure in one of the communication links represented in the agent's configuration." This means that if you start unplugging ports on your router, you should receive traps, right? Yes, but first make sure you don't start disconnecting production database servers. Furthermore, make sure you don't disconnect the port by which your device would send the trap back to the NMS. Remember, SNMP is designed with the assumption that the network is unreliable—if something sends a trap but there's no way for the trap to reach its destination, no one will find out. By default, a *linkDown* trap won't appear in Open-View's Event Categories because the default setting for *linkDown* is "Log only"; watch the log file *$OV_LOG/trapd.log* to see these traps arrive. Once you have a mechanism for receiving traps, bringing the link up and down on your device should send some traps your way.

Receiving Traps with SNMPc

SNMPc has support for a great many trap types out of the box. Let's first look at what SNMPc does when it gets a *coldStart* trap from an SNMP agent. Figure 9-8 shows a pop-up window from SNMPc when our agent is restarted.

Figure 9-9 also shows the events in the active event window with the appropriate color status—in this case, the color is magenta.

And of course, the icon for my LinuxServer changed to the color of the next most severe event, which is the *coldStart* event (see Figure 9-10).

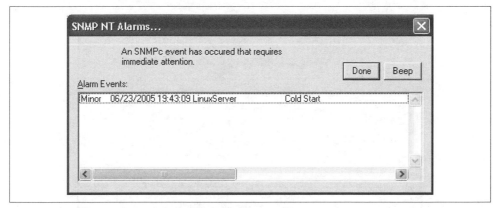

Figure 9-8. SNMPc trap pop-up window

Figure 9-9. SNMPc event viewer

Figure 9-10. SNMPc map object's color status

If you right-click on the Cold Start event and select Edit Event Actions, you can change the properties for this trap. Figure 9-11 shows this window.

The Message input box allows you to change the text of the event as seen in the event window. If you click on the Actions tab, you can change the actions for this event filter (Figure 9-12).

The priority is currently magenta, but you can change it to whatever you see fit. The checkboxes on the right near the top control how SNMPc reacts to this event. Checking Log causes the event to show up in the event window. Alarm causes a pop-up window to appear like the one in Figure 9-8. You have other options at your disposal including running a program, playing a sound, or sending an email. The Clear Events checkbox allows you to dictate what, if any, other events will cause this event to be automatically cleared. If you select authenticationFailure, for example, and click Yes, if an *authenticationFailure* is received after the *coldStart* event, the *coldStart* event will be cleared.

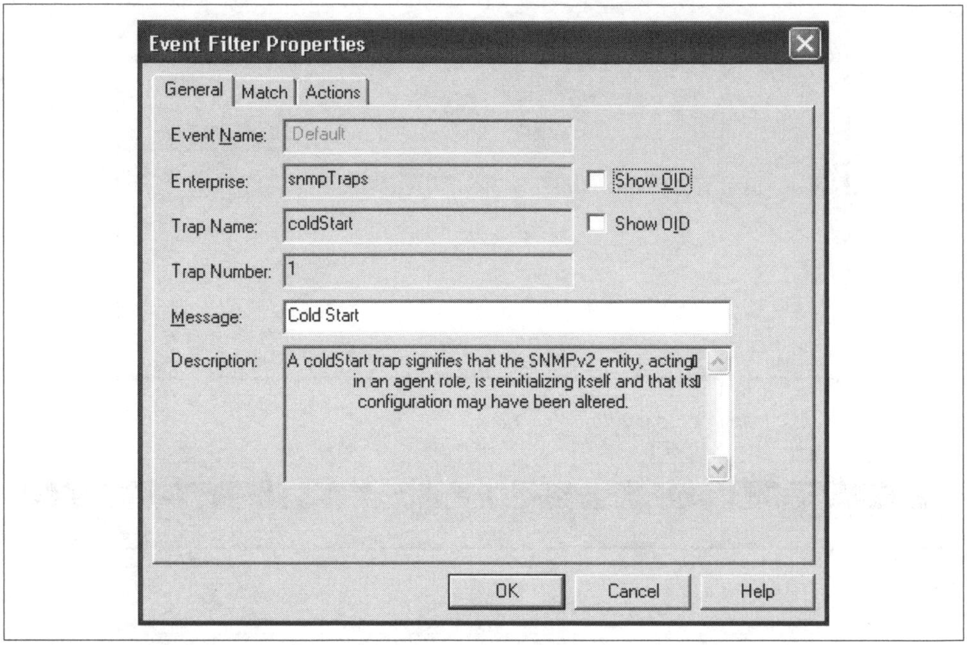

Figure 9-11. SNMPc event actions editor

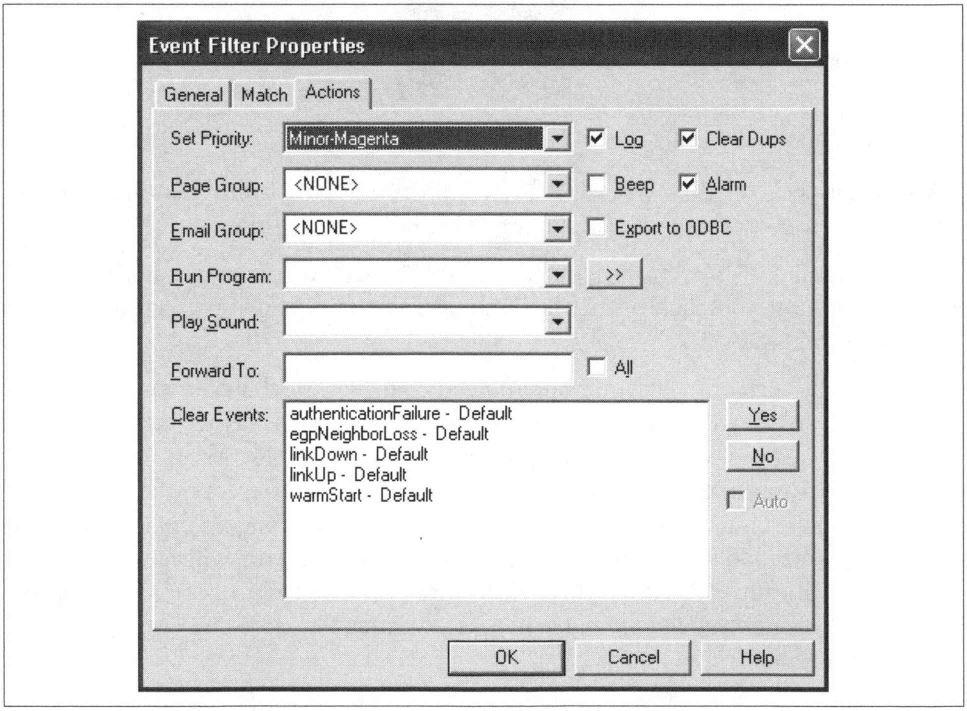

Figure 9-12. SNMPc event actions

To see the actual trap details, right-click the event and select Event Properties to display the screen shown in Figure 9-13.

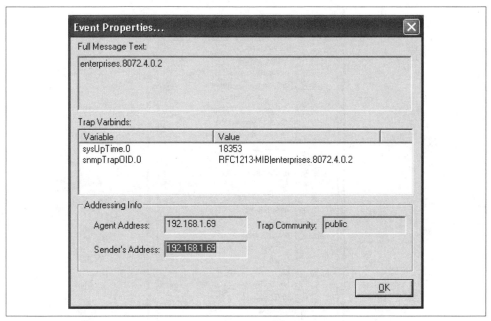

Figure 9-13. SNMPc trap details

Figure 9-13 shows the full text for the event and the variable bindings.

Finally, go back to the event window, right-click on the event, and select Acknowledge so that the event can move from the Current event tab to the History event tab. Figure 9-9 shows these tabs.

Custom trap actions

Let's say you want to add a custom action to an SNMP trap. First see Chapter 5 for a discussion on how to add your MIBs to SNMPc. Once you have done this, you are ready to customize an action. We have already loaded the Cisco Ping MIB in our SNMPc system. This MIB allows you to configure Cisco routers to send out ICMP messages to one or more remote hosts. As an optional setting for this feature, the Cisco device can send you a trap when it is done sending these messages.

The first thing to do is to find the entry in the Event Selection tab of the Selection tool. If you don't see this, go to View → Select Tool. Then select the Event tab at the bottom of the tool. You should see a window similar to Figure 9-14.

Since the events are in alphabetical order, it is easy to find the *ciscoPingMIBTrapPrefix* action. When you expand it, it has two actions: *Default* and *ciscoPingCompletion*. Right-click on the *ciscoPingCompletion* action and select Insert Event Filter. This will bring up a window like Figure 9-15.

Figure 9-14. SNMPc event action selection

Here you change the Event Name to suit your taste. You can also change the Message input as well, which is what will be displayed in the Event log window. The

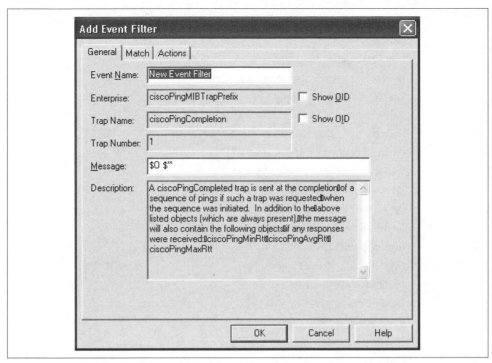

Figure 9-15. SNMPc event filter details

Message input can be free-form text and/or contain special characters. These characters are summarized in Table 9-3.

Table 9-3. Summary of arguments for SNMPc message box

Argument	Displays
$$	The dollar ($) symbol
$V	Expanded event message (use this argument when adding a *Run Program* setting in the Actions dialog)
$W	Console frame window number
$M	Server IP Address
$R	Address of sending entity (could be the same as the target device, or could be a Polling Agent address)
$F	Event Action Filter name
$f	Event Action Filter database record number
$O	Trap Name as a textual string
$o	Trap Object Identifier in dot format
$P	Device parent submap name
$A	Address of target device (device that the event is about)
$T	Trap Community Name
$x	Date the event occurred, in local format at server

Table 9-3. Summary of arguments for SNMPc message box (continued)

Argument	Displays
$X	Time the event occurred, in time zone of server
$@	Time the event occurred, in seconds since Jan. 1, 1970
$U	Value of sysUpTime in the event trap
$N	The map object name of the target device
$i	The map database record number of the target device
$G	The Get Community name of the target device
$S	The Set Community name of the target device
$E	The timeout attribute, in seconds, of the target device
$Y	The max retries for the target device
$P	The name of the map parent subnet object
$C	The number of variables in the event trap
$*	All variables as "[seq] name (type): value"
$-*n*	The *n*th variable as "name (type): value"
$+*n*	The *n*th variable as "name: value"
$*n*	The *n*th variable as "value"
$>*n*	All variables from the *n*th as "value"
$>-*n*	All variables from the *n*th as "[seq] name (type): value"
$>+*n*	All variables from the *n*th as "name: value"

Next you have to associate a device, or set of devices, with this trap. Select the Match tab at the top of the window. You have two choices. You can associate a group of nodes with this trap, which means all traps received from any device in this group will have this action applied to it. Figure 9-16 shows this option.

The second option is to specify individual devices to apply this trap to. Click the Add button, which will bring up the Browse Map Tree in Figure 9-17.

Here you can select as many individual devices as you want. In Figure 9-18, Linux-Server shows up under Sources.

The next step would be to click on the Actions tab and configure the Priority and color and any other options you want. We discussed this in the previous section, so there is no need to reexamine it here.

Click on the OK button to save your Event filter. It will be updated in the Event Selection tree, as shown in Figure 9-19.

That's all there is to creating custom filters and actions.

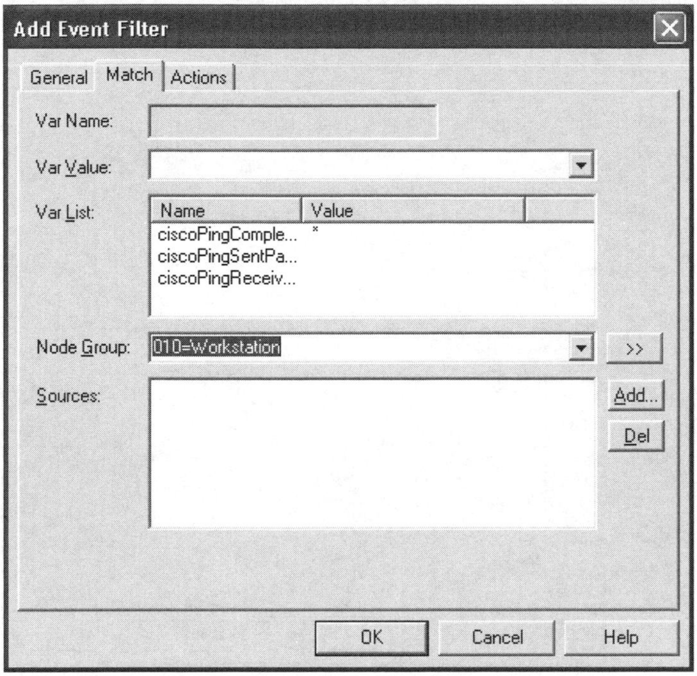

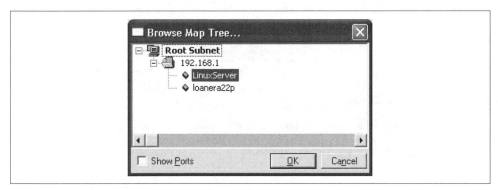

Figure 9-16. SNMPc: apply actions to devices

Figure 9-17. Browsing the map in SNMPc

Using Hooks with Your Programs

A hook is a convenient interface that lets you integrate your own code into some other product. The Emacs text editor is a good example of a program that uses hooks, almost entirely, to allow its users to extend how it operates. Let's look at the following simple program to explain this concept further:

```
# Logical Sample Program NH1
# PROGRAM COMMENTS
# PROGRAM BEGINS
```

Figure 9-18. LinuxServer added to Sources

Figure 9-19. Custom filter added

```
PROGRAM ADDS          $VAR1 + $VAR2 = $VAR3
PROGRAM SUBTRACTS     $VAR5 - $VAR6 = $VAR7
PROGRAM PRINTS RESULTS $VAR3 $VAR7

# PROGRAM ENDS
```

This program simply ADDS, SUBTRACTS, and PRINTS RESULTS; it does not have any hooks. To add a feature, you have to modify the code. For a small program like this, that is a trivial exercise, but it would be difficult in a longer program. The next program contains some hooks that let you add extensions:

```
# Logical Sample Program H1
# PROGRAM COMMENTS
# PROGRAM BEGINS
   PROGRAM RUNS $PATH/start.sh

   PROGRAM ADDS          $VAR1 + $VAR2 = $VAR3
   PROGRAM SUBTRACTS     $VAR5 - $VAR6 = $VAR7
```

```
    PROGRAM PRINTS RESULTS $VAR3 $VAR7

    PROGRAM RUNS $PATH/end.sh
# PROGRAM ENDS
```

Notice the two additional RUNS statements. These hooks allow you to run anything you want at the start or end of the program. The first program, *start.sh*, might be as simple as the command echo "I am starting," which sends a simple message to the system or management console. This script could also call one of the trap-generation programs to send a trap to the NMS stating that some program is starting. It would be even more useful to send a message when the program terminates, possibly including information about the program's status. Here's a slightly more complicated program that runs a script, providing a number of arguments so that the script can send useful information back to the NMS when it generates a trap:

```
# Logical Sample Program H2
# PROGRAM COMMENTS
# PROGRAM BEGINS
    PROGRAM RUNS $PATH/start.sh $PROGRAM_NAME

    PROGRAM ADDS          $VAR1 + $VAR2 = $VAR3
    PROGRAM SUBTRACTS     $VAR5 - $VAR6 = $VAR7
    PROGRAM PRINTS RESULTS $VAR3 $VAR7

    PROGRAM RUNS $PATH/end.sh $PROGRAM_NAME $VAR1 $VAR2 $VAR3 $VAR5 $VAR6 $VAR7
# PROGRAM ENDS
```

With the additional arguments available to the hook programs, we can generate messages like "The Program Widget has ended with sales at $4 and YTD at $7." If your hook programs are shell scripts, you can simply add snmptrap commands using a text editor. Once you finish adding the snmptrap code, you can test your hook program by running it on the command line.

Many scripts can benefit from snmptrap hooks. On Solaris or Linux machines, for example, some of your */etc/init.d* scripts can be retrofitted to make use of snmptrap commands. It might be useful to have some kind of notification when important processes such as your web server or DNS server start and stop. Having such information on hand might make life much easier for your help desk. (The Concord SystemEDGE SNMP agent provides more rigorous process-monitoring capabilities. See Chapter 10 for more information on this product.)

It's harder to add hooks to programs written in languages like C because you need access to the source code as well as the ability to figure out where to place the hooks. Once you have identified where your hooks go and you have added them, you must recompile the source code. Some programs have hooks built in, allowing you to run external programs or RPCs. Check your program's documentation for the locations of these hooks. This is much more convenient than trying to build your own hooks into another program. Once you have established what these external programs are called, you can start writing your own traps or adding to existing ones.

CHAPTER 10
Extensible SNMP Agents

There will come a time when you want to extend an agent's functionality. Extending an agent usually means adding or changing the MIBs the agent supports. Many agents that claim to support SNMP cover only a minimal number of somewhat useless MIBs—obviously a frustrating situation for someone who is planning on doing lots of automated network management. Upgrading your software to a newer version of SNMP—say, Version 2 or 3—won't help; you won't get any more information out of a device than if you were using SNMPv1. The newer versions of SNMP add features to the protocol (such as additional security or more sophisticated options for retrieving and setting values), but the information that's available from any device is defined in the agent's MIBs, which are independent of the protocol itself.

When you are faced with an agent's limitations, you can turn to extensible agents.* These programs, or extensions to existing programs, allow you to extend a particular agent's MIB and retrieve values from an external source (a script, program, or file). In some cases, data can be returned as if it were coming from the agent itself. Most of the time you will not see a difference between the agent's native MIBs and your extensible ones. Many extensible agents give you the ability to read files, run programs, and return their results; they can even return tables of information. Some agents have configurable options that allow you to run external programs, and have preset functions, such as disk-space checkers, built in.

The OpenView, Net-SNMP, and SystemEDGE agents are all examples of extensible agents. OpenView provides a separate extensible agent that allows you to extend the master agent (*snmpdm*); requests for the extensible agent won't work unless the master agent is running. You can start and stop the extensible agent without disturbing the master agent. To customize the extensible agent, you define new objects using the ASN.1 format, as specified by the SMI. The Net-SNMP agent takes an alternate approach. It doesn't make a distinction between the master agent and the extensible

---

* We don't make a distinction between existing agents that can be extended and agents that exist purely to support extensions. We'll call them both "extensible agents."

agent; there's only one agent to worry about. You can use ASN.1 to define new objects (as with the OpenView extensible agent), but there's also a facility for adding extensions without writing any ASN.1, making this agent significantly more accessible for the novice administrator. SystemEDGE is similar to Net-SNMP in that there is only one agent to worry about. Of the three agents discussed in this chapter, it is the easiest to extend. Figure 10-1 compares the design strategies of the OpenView, Net-SNMP, and SystemEDGE agents.

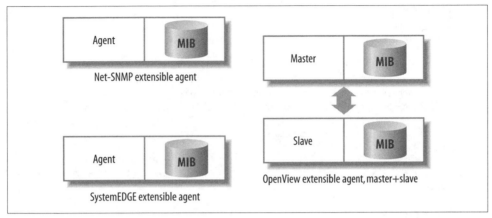

Figure 10-1. Architecture of extensible agents

All three agents have fairly comprehensive configuration options and all allow you to extend the local agent without heavy programming. You may need to write some scripts or a few short C programs, but with the sample programs here and the thousands more that are on the Internet,* nonprogrammers can still get a lot done.

We'll start with the Net-SNMP agent, since it is the simplest, and then move to SystemEDGE. We'll round out the discussion with OpenView's extensible agent. Be sure to see Chapter 6 for information on where to obtain these agents.

Net-SNMP

When you install the Net-SNMP package,† it creates a sample *snmpd.conf* configuration file called *EXAMPLE.conf* in the source directory. This file contains some great examples that demonstrate how to extend your agent. Read through it to see the types of things you can and can't do. We will touch on only a few of Net-SNMP's features: checking for any number of running processes (proc), executing a com-

---

* See *SNMPLinks.org (http://www.snmplink.org/Tools.html)* for links to commercial and free SNMP software.

† Net-SNMP was formerly called UCD-SNMP and as a result, you'll see references to the University of California at Davis in the code.

mand that returns a single line or multiple lines of output (exec), and checking disk-space utilization (disk).

The main Net-SNMP configuration file can be found at *$NET_SNMP_HOME/share/ snmp/snmpd.conf*, where *$NET_SNMP_HOME* is the directory in which you installed Net-SNMP. Here is the configuration file that we will use for the remainder of this section:

```
# Filename: $NET_SNMP_HOME/share/snmp/snmpd.conf
# Check for processes running
# Items in here will appear in the ucdavis.procTable
proc sendmail 10 1
proc httpd

# Return the value from the executed program with a passed parm.
# Items in here will appear in the ucdavis.extTable
exec FileCheck /opt/local/shell_scripts/filecheck.sh /tmp/vxprint.error

# Multiline return from the command
# This needs its own OID
# I have used a subset of my registered enterprise ID (2789) within the OID
exec .1.3.6.1.4.1.2021.2789.51 FancyCheck /opt/local/shell_scripts/fancycheck.sh \
    /core

# Check disks for their mins
disk / 100000
```

 Note that the system-monitoring OIDs presented in this section can be found in the UCD-SNMP-MIB.

Whenever you make changes to the Net-SNMP agent's configuration file, you can have it reread the configuration by sending the process an HUP signal:

```
$ ps -ef | grep snmpd
    root   12345     1  0   Nov 16 ?          2:35 /usr/local/bin/snmpd
$ kill -HUP 12345
```

Now let's look at the file itself. The first proc command says to check for the process sendmail. The numbers 10 and 1 define how many sendmail processes we want running at any given time (a maximum of 10 and a minimum of 1). The second proc command says that we want at least one httpd process running. To see what effect these commands have on our agent, let's look at an snmpwalk of the *ucdavis.proc-Table (.1.3.6.1.4.1.2021.2)*:

```
$ snmpwalk sunserver2 public .1.3.6.1.4.1.2021.2
enterprises.ucdavis.procTable.prEntry.prIndex.1 = 1
enterprises.ucdavis.procTable.prEntry.prIndex.2 = 2
enterprises.ucdavis.procTable.prEntry.prNames.1 = "sendmail"
enterprises.ucdavis.procTable.prEntry.prNames.2 = "httpd"
enterprises.ucdavis.procTable.prEntry.prMin.1 = 1
enterprises.ucdavis.procTable.prEntry.prMin.2 = 0
enterprises.ucdavis.procTable.prEntry.prMax.1 = 10
```

```
enterprises.ucdavis.procTable.prEntry.prMax.2 = 0
enterprises.ucdavis.procTable.prEntry.prCount.1 = 1
enterprises.ucdavis.procTable.prEntry.prCount.2 = 6
enterprises.ucdavis.procTable.prEntry.prErrorFlag.1 = 0
enterprises.ucdavis.procTable.prEntry.prErrorFlag.2 = 0
enterprises.ucdavis.procTable.prEntry.prErrMessage.1 = ""
enterprises.ucdavis.procTable.prEntry.prErrMessage.2 = ""
enterprises.ucdavis.procTable.prEntry.prErrFix.1 = 0
enterprises.ucdavis.procTable.prEntry.prErrFix.2 = 0
```

The agent returns the contents of the *procTable*. In this table, the sendmail and httpd process entries occupy instances 1 and 2. prMin and prMax are the minimum and maximum numbers we set for the sendmail and httpd processes.[*] The prCount value gives us the number of processes currently running: it looks like we have one sendmail process and six httpd processes. To see what happens when the number of processes falls outside the range we specified, let's kill all six httpd processes and look at the *procTable* again (instead of listing the whole table, we'll walk only instance 2, which describes the httpd process):

```
$ snmpwalk sunserver2 public .1.3.6.1.4.1.2021.2
enterprises.ucdavis.procTable.prEntry.prIndex.1 = 1
enterprises.ucdavis.procTable.prEntry.prNames.1 = "httpd"
enterprises.ucdavis.procTable.prEntry.prMin.1 = 0
enterprises.ucdavis.procTable.prEntry.prMax.1 = 0
enterprises.ucdavis.procTable.prEntry.prCount.1 = 0
enterprises.ucdavis.procTable.prEntry.prErrorFlag.1 = 1
enterprises.ucdavis.procTable.prEntry.prErrMessage.1 = "No httpd
process running."
enterprises.ucdavis.procTable.prEntry.prErrFix.1 = 0
```

We had six httpd processes running and now, per prCount, we have none. The prErrMessage reports the problem, and the prErrorFlag has changed from 0 to 1, indicating that something is wrong. This flag makes it easy to poll the agent, using the techniques discussed in Chapter 8, and see that the httpd processes have stopped. Let's try a variation on this theme. If we set prMin to indicate that we want more than six httpd processes running, and then restart httpd, our prErrMessage is:

```
enterprises.ucdavis.procTable.prEntry.prErrMessage.1 = "Too few
httpd running (# = 0)"
```

The next command in the configuration file is exec; this command allows us to execute any program and return the program's results and exit value to the agent. This is helpful when you already have a program you would like to use in conjunction with the agent. We've written a simple shell script called *filecheck.sh* that checks whether the file that's passed to it on the command line exists. If the file exists, it returns a 0 (zero); otherwise, it returns a 1 (one):

---

[*] When prMin and prMax are both 0, it says that we want at least one and a maximum of infinity processes running.

```
#!/bin/sh
# FileName: /opt/local/shell_scripts/filecheck.sh

if [ -f $1 ]; then
    exit 0
fi
exit 1
```

Our configuration file uses *filecheck.sh* to check for the existence of the file */tmp/vxprint.error*. Once you have the *filecheck.sh* script in place, you can see the results it returns by walking *ucdavis.extTable* (.1.3.6.1.4.1.2021.8):

```
$ snmpwalk sunserver2 public .1.3.6.1.4.1.2021.8
enterprises.ucdavis.extTable.extEntry.extIndex.1 = 1
enterprises.ucdavis.extTable.extEntry.extNames.1 = "FileCheck"
enterprises.ucdavis.extTable.extEntry.extCommand.1 =
"/opt/local/shell_scripts/filecheck.sh /tmp/vxprint.error"
enterprises.ucdavis.extTable.extEntry.extResult.1 = 0
enterprises.ucdavis.extTable.extEntry.extOutput.1 = ""
enterprises.ucdavis.extTable.extEntry.extErrFix.1 = 0
```

The first argument to the exec command[*] in the configuration file is a label that identifies the command so that we can easily recognize it in the *extTable*. In our case, we used FileCheck—that's not a particularly good name, because we might want to check the existence of several files, but could have named it anything we deemed useful. Whatever name you choose is returned as the value of the *extTable.extEntry.extNames.1* object. Because the file */tmp/vxprint.error* exists, *filecheck.sh* returns a 0, which appears in the table as the value of *extTable.extEntry.extResult.1*. You can also have the agent return a line of output from the program. Change *filecheck.sh* to perform an ls -la on the file if it exists:

```
#!/bin/sh
# FileName: /opt/local/shell_scripts/filecheck.sh

if [ -f $1 ]; then
    ls -la $1
    exit 0
fi

exit 1
```

When we poll the agent, we see the output from the script in the *extOutput* value the agent returns:

```
enterprises.ucdavis.extTable.extEntry.extOutput.1 = \
"  16 -rw-r--r--   1 root     other       2476 Feb 3 17:13 /tmp/vxprint.error."
```

---

[*] See the *EXAMPLE.conf* configuration file introduced at the beginning of this chapter.

This simple trick works only if the script returns a single line of output. If your script returns more than one line of output, insert an OID in front of the string name in the exec command.

Here's the next command from our *snmpd.conf* file:

```
exec .1.3.6.1.4.1.2021.2789.51 FancyCheck /opt/local/shell_scripts/fancycheck.sh \
/core
```

This command runs the program *fancycheck.sh*, with the identifying string FancyCheck. We won't bother to list *fancycheck.sh*; it's just like *filecheck.sh*, except that it adds a check to determine the file type. The OID identifies where in the MIB tree the agent will place the result of running the command. It needs to be in the *ucdavis* enterprise *(.1.3.6.1.4.1.2021)*. We recommend that you follow the *ucdavis* enterprise ID with your own enterprise number, to prevent collisions with objects defined by other sources and avoid overwriting one of *ucdavis*'s subtrees. Follow your enterprise number with another number to identify this particular command. In this case, our enterprise ID is 2789 and we assign the arbitrary number 51 to this command. Thus, the complete OID is *.1.3.6.1.4.1.2021.2789.51*.

Here are the results from walking the *.1.3.6.1.4.1.2021.2789.51* subtree:

```
$ snmpwalk sunserver2 public .1.3.6.1.4.1.2021.2789.51
enterprises.ucdavis.2789.51.1.1 = 1
enterprises.ucdavis.2789.51.2.1 = "FancyCheck"
enterprises.ucdavis.2789.51.3.1 =
"/opt/local/shell_scripts/fancycheck.sh /core"
ucdavis.2789.51.100.1 = 0
ucdavis.2789.51.101.1 = "-rw-r--r--   1 root      other
346708 Feb 14 16:30 /core."
ucdavis.2789.51.101.2 = "/core:..ELF 32-bit MSB core file SPARC
Version 1, from 'httpd'."
ucdavis.2789.51.102.1 = 0
```

Notice that we have a few additional lines in our output. *2789.51.100.1* is the exit number, *2789.51.101.1* and *2789.51.101.2* are the output from the command, and *2789.51.102.1* is the *errorFix* value. These values can be useful when you are trying to debug your new extension. (Unfortunately, snmpwalk can give you only the numeric OID, not the human-readable name, because snmpwalk doesn't know what *2789.51.x* is.)

The last task for Net-SNMP's extensible agent is to perform some disk-space monitoring. This is a great option that lets you check the availability of disk space and return multiple (useful) values. The disk option takes a filesystem mount point followed by a number. Here is what our entry looks like in *snmpd.conf*:

```
# Check disks for their mins
disk / 100000
```

The definition of the disk option from *UCD-SNMP-MIB.txt* is "Minimum space required on the disk (in kBytes) before the errors are triggered." Let's first take a look on *sunserver2* to see what the common df program returns:

```
$ df -k /
Filesystem              kbytes    used   avail capacity  Mounted on
/dev/dsk/c0t0d0s0       432839   93449  296110    24%    /
```

To see what SNMP has to say about the disk space on our server, run snmpwalk against the *ucdavis.diskTable* object (*.1.3.6.1.4.1.2021.9*). This returns virtually the same information as the df command:

```
$ snmpwalk sunserver2 public .1.3.6.1.4.1.2021.9
enterprises.ucdavis.diskTable.dskEntry.dskIndex.1 = 1
enterprises.ucdavis.diskTable.dskEntry.dskPath.1 = "/" Hex: 2F
enterprises.ucdavis.diskTable.dskEntry.dskDevice.1 =
"/dev/dsk/c0t0d0s0"
enterprises.ucdavis.diskTable.dskEntry.dskMinimum.1 = 100000
enterprises.ucdavis.diskTable.dskEntry.dskMinPercent.1 = -1
enterprises.ucdavis.diskTable.dskEntry.dskTotal.1 = 432839
enterprises.ucdavis.diskTable.dskEntry.dskAvail.1 = 296110
enterprises.ucdavis.diskTable.dskEntry.dskUsed.1 = 93449
enterprises.ucdavis.diskTable.dskEntry.dskPercent.1 = 24
enterprises.ucdavis.diskTable.dskEntry.dskErrorFlag.1 = 0
enterprises.ucdavis.diskTable.dskEntry.dskErrorMsg.1 = ""
```

As you can see, the Net-SNMP agent has many customizable features that allow you to tailor your monitoring without having to write your own object definitions. Be sure to review *$NET_SNMP_HOME/share/snmp/mibs/UCD-SNMP-MIB.txt* for complete definitions of all of Net-SNMP's variables. While we touched on only a few customizable options here, you will find many other useful options in the *EXAMPLE.conf* file that comes with the Net-SNMP package.

SystemEDGE

The SystemEDGE agent is also extensible. No other system processes need to be run to extend this agent. It comes with three predefined extended objects: DNS for Unix, Network Information System (NIS) for Unix, and Remote Pinger for Unix and Windows XP, 2000, and NT. The first object returns the domain name of the underlying operating system, the second returns the NIS domain name of the underlying operating system, and the third sends Internet Control Message Protocol (ICMP) requests to a remote host from the system on which the agent is running. While these are nice scripts to have, what we want to focus on is how to add your own OIDs to the agent.

Extensibility for Unix and Windows

The SystemEDGE agent has a private MIB that defines a table called the *extensionGroup*. Its full OID is *1.3.6.1.4.1.546.14* (*iso.org.dod.internet.private.enterprises. empire.extensionGroup*). This is where you define your own objects. The first object

---

you define has the OID *extensionGroup.1.0* (*1.3.6.1.4.1.546.14.1.0*), where the *.0* indicates that the object is scalar; the next has the OID *extensionGroup.2.0*, and so on. Note that all the objects defined this way must be scalar. For advanced users, Concord has developed a plug-in architecture for SystemEDGE that allows you to develop complex extended objects (including tables) and full-blown MIBs.

To extend the agent, start by editing the *sysedge.cf* file. This file tells the agent to which extended OIDs it must respond. The format of a command in this file is:

```
extension LeafNumber Type Access ''Command''
```

The keyword extension tells the agent that this configuration entry is an extension that belongs to the *extensionGroup*. *LeafNumber* is the extension object number—i.e., the number you assign to the object in the *extensionGroup* table. *Type* is the SNMP type for the OID. Valid types are Integer, Counter, Gauge, Octetstring, TimeTicks, Objectid, and IPAddress. *Access* is either Read-Only or Read-Write. And finally, *Command* is the script or program the agent will execute when this particular OID is queried by an NMS. We'll talk more about this shortly. Here are some examples of extension objects:

```
extension 1 Integer Read-Only '/usr/local/bin/Script.sh'
extension 2 Gauge Read-Only '/usr/local/bin/Script.pl'
extension 33 Counter Read-Write '/usr/local/bin/Program'
```

The first item defines a read-only OID of type Integer. The OID is *1.3.6.1.4.1.546. 14.1.0*. The agent will execute */usr/local/bin/exampleScript.sh* when this OID is queried. The second entry is similar, except its type is Gauge and its numeric OID is *1.3. 6.1.4.1.546.14.2.0*. The third example simply shows that *LeafNumber* doesn't have to be sequential; you can use any number you want, provided that it is unique.

Extending the agent allows you to write your own scripts that do whatever you want: you can get information about devices or programs that are not SNMP capable, as long as you can write a script that queries them for their status. In the preceding example, */usr/local/bin/Script.sh*, */usr/local/bin/Script.pl*, and */usr/local/bin/Program* are all examples of scripts the agent will execute when the OID assigned to each script is queried. Two requirements must be met by any script or program:

- All set, get, and getnext requests must generate output. For get and getnext, the output from the script should be the actual value of the object requested. This means that the script or program that fetches the required information must return a single value. For a set request, the script should return the object's new value. The request will fail if there is no output. (Note that for a set request, a script may succeed in changing the state of the device even if it produces no output and the agent considers the script to have failed.)

- The script or program should print whatever information it needs to return (based on the type of request), followed by a newline character. The agent parses only up to this character. If a newline is the first character the agent encounters, the agent generates an error and returns this to the NMS or SNMP application.

The agent sends three arguments to the script or program it executes: the *LeafNumber*, the request type (GET, GETNEXT, or SET, in capital letters), and a string that represents some value to be set (the third argument is used only for SET requests). The following skeletal Perl script, called *skel.pl*, shows how you can use all three arguments:

```
#!/usr/local/bin/perl

if ($ARGV[0] == 1) {
    # OID queried is 1.3.6.1.4.1.546.14.1.0
    if ($ARGV[1] eq "SET") {
        # use $ARGV[2] to set the value of something and return the set value,
        # followed by a newline character, to the agent
    } elsif (($ARGV[1] eq "GET") || ($ARGV[1] eq "GETNEXT")) {
        # get the information to which this OID pertains, then return it,
        # followed by a newline character, to the agent
    }
} else {
    return 0;
    # return 0, since I don't know what to do with this OID
}
```

All you have to do is add the logic that takes some action to retrieve (or set) the appropriate value and return the correct value to the agent. The corresponding entry in *sysedge.cf* might look something like this:

```
extension 1 Integer Read-Write '/usr/local/bin/skel.pl'
```

What we've done so far gives the agent the ability to respond to requests for a new kind of data. We still need to solve the other part of the puzzle: telling the management station that some new kind of data is available for it to retrieve. This requires creating an entry in a MIB file.* After adding this entry to the file, you must recompile the MIB into your NMS system so that the NMS will know the access and type of each of the extended objects in the MIB for which it is to perform queries. Here is a MIB entry that corresponds to the previous agent extension:

```
skeletonVariable OBJECT-TYPE
    SYNTAX Integer
    ACCESS Read-Write
    DESCRIPTION
        "This is an example object."
::= { extensionGroup 1 }
```

Once this is compiled into the NMS, you can query the object by specifying its full name (*iso.org.dod.internet.private.enterprises.empire.extensionGroup.skeletonVariable.0*). Alternatively, you can use the numeric OID; for example:

```
$ snmpget server.ora.com public .1.3.6.1.4.1.546.14.1.0
```

---

* Concord recommends that you keep all your extended MIB objects in a separate file, away from the System-EDGE MIB file. This makes it easier for you to recompile it into your NMS.

Security can be a concern when writing your own extension scripts. On Unix systems, it's a good idea to create a separate user and group to execute your extensions, instead of allowing the root user to run your scripts.

Added Extensibility for Windows

While the *extensionGroup* is supported on all platforms, the Windows version of SystemEDGE allows you to extend SystemEDGE with objects taken from the registry and performance registry. You can gain access to configuration data and performance data, which are normally viewed using *regedit* and *perfmon*. The Windows extension group is defined as *iso.org.dod.internet.private.enterprises.empire.nt.ntRegPerf (1.3.6.1.4.1.546.5.7)*. As with the Unix extensions, these extensions are defined in the *sysedge.cf* file.

To configure a registry extension, add a line with the following syntax to *sysedge.cf*:

```
ntregperf LeafNumber Type Registry ''Key'' ''Value''
```

The keyword `ntregperf` defines this as a registry or performance extension object. `LeafNumber` and `Type` are the same as for Unix extensions. The keyword `Registry` identifies this entry as a registry extension. Registry extensions are read-only. `Key` is a quoted string that specifies the registry key to be accessed. `Value` is the value you want to read from the key. Here is an example:

```
ntregperf 1 OctetString Registry
'SYSTEM\CurrentControlSet\Control\CrashControl' 'DumpFile'
```

This creates a registry extension object that returns the path to the crash-control dump file. The OID is *1.3.6.1.4.1.546.5.7.1.0 (iso.org.dod.internet.private.enterprises. empire.nt.ntRegPerf.1.0)*.

To configure a performance extension, use the following syntax:

```
ntregperf LeafNumber Type Performance ''Object'' ''Counter'' ''PerfInstance''
```

Here again, `ntregperf` is the keyword that indicates this is a registry/performance extension object. `LeafNumber` and `Type` should be familiar to you. The keyword `Performance` indicates that we're reading a value from the performance registry; performance extensions are read-only. `Object` specifies the performance object to be accessed. `Counter` specifies the object's performance counter value to be accessed. Finally, `PerfInstance` specifies the performance counter instance to be accessed. This should be identical to what's listed with *perfmon*. Here's a typical performance extension:

```
ntregperf 2 Counter Performance 'TCP' 'Segments Sent/sec' '1'
```

You can use this extension to watch the total number of TCP segments transmitted by the system. Its OID is *1.3.6.1.4.1.546.5.7.2.0 (iso.org.dod.internet.private.enterprises.empire.nt.ntRegPerf.2.0)*. Keep in mind that you should create a MIB entry (in a MIB file) for any extensions you create, similar to the entry we defined earlier for *skeletonVariable*.

The examples in this section should be enough to get you up and running with an extended SystemEDGE agent. Be sure to read the SystemEDGE manual for a complete treatment of this topic.

OpenView's Extensible Agent

Before you start playing around with OpenView's extensible agent, make sure that you have its master agent (*snmpdm*) configured and running properly. You must also obtain an enterprise number, because extending the OpenView agent requires writing your own MIB definitions, and the objects you define must be part of the *enterprises* subtree.* Chapter 2 describes how to obtain an enterprise number.

MIBs are written using the SMI, of which there are two versions: SMIv1, defined in RFCs 1155 and 1212; and SMIv2, defined in RFCs 2578, 2579, and 2580. RFC 1155 notes that "ASN.1 constructs are used to define the structure, although the full generality of ASN.1 is not permitted." While OpenView's extensible agent file, *snmpd. extend,* uses ASN.1 to define objects, it requires some additional entries to create a usable object. *snmpd.extend* also does not support some of the SNMPv2 SMI constructs. In this chapter, we will discuss only those constructs that are supported.

By default, the configuration file for the extensible agent in the Unix version of OpenView is */etc/SnmpAgent.d/snmp.extend*. To jump right in, copy the sample file to this location and then restart the agent:

```
$ cp /opt/OV/prg_samples/eagent/snmpd.extend /etc/SnmpAgent.d/
$ /etc/rc2.d/S98SnmpExtAgt stop
$ /etc/rc2.d/S98SnmpExtAgt start
```

You should see no errors and you should get an exit code of 0 (zero). If errors occur, check the *snmpd.log* file.† If the agent starts successfully, try walking one of the objects monitored by the extensible agent. The following command checks the status of the mail queue:

```
$ snmpwalk sunserver1  .1.3.6.1.4.1.4242.2.2.0
4242.2.2.0 : OCTET STRING- (ascii):    Mail queue is empty
```

We're off to a good start. We have successfully started and polled the extensible agent.

The key to OpenView's *snmpd.extend* file is the DESCRIPTION. If this seems a little weird, it is! Executing commands from within the DESCRIPTION section is peculiar to this agent, not part of the SNMP design. The DESCRIPTION tells the agent where to look to read, write, and run files. You can put a whole slew of parameters within the

---

* Do not use our enterprise number. Obtaining your own private enterprise number is easy and free. Using our number will only confuse you and others later in the game.

† On Solaris and HP-UX machines, this file is located in */var/adm/snmpd.log*.

DESCRIPTION, but we'll tackle only a few of the more common ones. Here's the syntax for the *snmpd.extend* file:

```
your-label-here DEFINITIONS ::= BEGIN

-- insert your comments here

enterprise-name  OBJECT IDENTIFIER ::= { OID-label(1) OID-label{2) 3 }
subtree-name1    OBJECT IDENTIFIER ::= { OID-label(3) 4 }
subtree-name2    OBJECT IDENTIFIER ::= { OID-label(123) 56 }

data-Identifier
This is sometimes called a leaf node, node, object, or MIB.
 OBJECT-TYPE
     SYNTAX Integer | Counter | Gauge | DisplayString
These are just to name a few supported datatypes.

    ACCESS read-only | read-write
    STATUS mandatory | optional | obsolete | deprecated
For now we will always use mandatory as our STATUS.

    DESCRIPTION
        "
        Enter Your Description Here
        READ-COMMAND: /your/command/here passed1 passed2
        READ-COMMAND-TIMEOUT: timeout_in_seconds (defaults to 3)
        FILE-COMMAND: /your/file-command/here passed1 passed2
        FILE-COMMAND-FREQUENCY: frequency_in_seconds (defaults to 10)
        FILE-NAME: /your/filename/here
        "
    ::= { parent-subtree-name subidentifier }

END
```

We can glean some style guidelines from RFC 2578. While there are many guidelines, some more useful than others, one thing stands out: case does matter. Much of ASN.1 is case sensitive. All ASN.1 keywords and macros should be in uppercase: OBJECT-TYPE, SYNTAX, DESCRIPTION, etc. Your *data-Identifiers* (i.e., object names) should start in lowercase and contain no spaces. If you have read any of the RFC MIBs or done any polling, you should have noticed that all the object names obey this convention. Try to use descriptive names and keep your names well under the 64-character limit; RFC 2578 states that anything over 32 characters is not recommended. If you define an object under an existing subtree, you should use this subtree-name, or parent-name, before each new object-name you create. The *ip* subtree in *mib-2* (RFC 1213) provides an example of good practice:

```
ip          OBJECT IDENTIFIER ::= { mib-2 4 }

ipForwarding OBJECT-TYPE
...
::= { ip 1 }
```

```
ipDefaultTTL OBJECT-TYPE
...
::= { ip 2 }
```

This file starts by defining the *ip* subtree. The names of objects within that subtree start with *ip* and use *ip* as the parent-subtree-name. As useful as this recommended practice is, there are times when it isn't appropriate. For example, this practice makes it difficult to move your objects to different parents while you are building a MIB file.

Here's a working *snmpd.extend* file that contains three definitions: *psZombieNum*, *prtDiagExitC*, and *whosOnCall*. I have placed all these objects within my own private enterprise (*2789*, which I have named *mauro*). Figure 10-2 shows this portion of my private subtree.

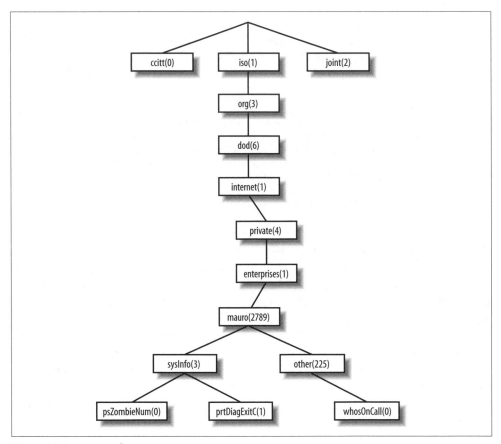

Figure 10-2. mauro subtree

You can now walk the tree and see what my new objects look like; my tree starts at the OID *.1.3.6.1.4.1.2789*, which is equivalent to *.iso.org.dod.internet.private.enterprises. mauro*. I can organize my own subtree any way I want, so I've split it into two branches beneath *mauro*: *mauro.sysInfo* (2789.3) will hold information about the status of the system itself (*psZombieNum* and *prtDiagExitC*), and *mauro.other* (2789.255) will hold additional information (*whosOnCall*). If you look further down, you can see the three leaf nodes I define in this file:

```
SampleExt DEFINITIONS ::= BEGIN

-- comments appear here behind the dashes

internet      OBJECT IDENTIFIER ::= { iso(1) org(3) dod(6) 1 }
enterprises   OBJECT IDENTIFIER ::= { internet(1) private(4) 1 }
mauro         OBJECT IDENTIFIER ::= { enterprises(1) 2789 }

-- Now that we have defined mauro, let's define some objects

sysInfo       OBJECT IDENTIFIER ::= { mauro 3 }
other         OBJECT IDENTIFIER ::= { mauro 255 }

psZombieNum OBJECT-TYPE
  SYNTAX   INTEGER
  ACCESS   read-only
  STATUS   mandatory
  DESCRIPTION
    "Search through ps and return the number of zombies.
    READ-COMMAND: VALUE=`ps -ef | grep -v grep | grep -c  \<defunct\>`; echo $VALUE
    "
 ::= { sysInfo 0 }

prtDiagExitC OBJECT-TYPE
    SYNTAX   INTEGER
    ACCESS   read-only
    STATUS   mandatory
    DESCRIPTION
        "On Solaris, prtdiag shows us system diagnostic information. The
        manpage states that if this command exits with a non-zero value,
        we have a problem. This is a great polling mechanism for some
        systems.
        READ-COMMAND: /usr/platform/`uname -m`/sbin/prtdiag > /dev/null; echo $?"
    ::= { sysInfo 1 }

whosOnCall OBJECT-TYPE
    SYNTAX   OctetString
    ACCESS   read-write
    STATUS   mandatory
    DESCRIPTION
        "This file contains the name of the person who will be on call
        today. The helpdesk uses this file. Only the helpdesk and
        managers should update this file. If you are sick or unable to
        be on call, please contact your manager and/or the helpdesk.
        FILE-NAME: /opt/local/oncall/today.txt"
    ::= { other 0 }

END
```

The first two objects, *psZombieNum* and *prtDiagExitC*, both use the `READ-COMMAND` in the `DESCRIPTION`. This tells the agent to execute the named command and send any output the command produces to the NMS. By default, the program must complete within three seconds and have an exit value of 0 (zero). You can increase the timeout by adding a `READ-COMMAND-TIMEOUT`:

```
READ-COMMAND: /some/fs/somecommand.pl
READ-COMMAND-TIMEOUT: 10
```

This tells the agent to wait 10 seconds instead of 3 for a reply before killing the process and returning an error.

The last object, *whosOnCall*, uses a `FILE-NAME` in the `DESCRIPTION`. This tells the agent to return the first line of the file, program, script, etc., specified after `FILE-NAME`. Later we will learn how to manipulate this file.

Now that we've created a MIB file with our new definitions, we need to load the new MIB into OpenView. This step isn't strictly necessary, but it's much more convenient to work with textual names than to deal with numeric IDs. To do this, use xnmloadmib, discussed in Chapter 5. After we load the MIB file containing our three new objects, we should see their names in the MIB browser and be able to poll them by name.

Once you have copied the MIB file into the appropriate directory and forced the extensible agent, *extsubagt*, to reread its configuration (by using kill –HUP), try walking the new objects using OpenView's snmpwalk program:

```
$ snmpwalk sunserver2 -c public .1.3.6.1.4.1.2789
mauro.sysInfo.psZombieNum.0 : INTEGER: 0
mauro.sysInfo.prtDiagExitC.0 : INTEGER: 2
```

Notice anything strange about our return values? We didn't get anything for *whosOnCall*. Nothing was returned for this object because we haven't created the *oncall.txt* file whose contents we're trying to read. We must first create this file and insert some data into the file. There are two ways of doing this. Obviously, you can create the file with your favorite text editor. But the clever way is to use snmpset:

```
$ snmpset -c private sunserver2 \
.1.3.6.1.4.1.2789.255.0.0 octetstring "david jones"
mauro.Other.whosOnCall.0 : OCTET STRING- (ascii):      david jones
```

This command tells the SNMP agent to put david jones in the file */opt/local/oncall/today.txt*. The filename is defined by the `FILE-NAME: /opt/local/oncall/today.txt` command that we wrote in the extended MIB. The additional *.0* at the end of the OID tells the agent we want the first (and only) instance of *whosOnCall*. (We could have used *.iso.org.dod.internet.private.enterprises.mauro.other.whosOnCall.0* rather than the numeric OID.) Furthermore, the snmpset command specifies the datatype octetstring, which matches the OctetString syntax we defined in the MIB. This datatype lets us insert string values into the file. Finally, we're allowed to set the value of this object with snmpset because we have read-write access to the object, as specified in the MIB.

If you choose to use an editor to create the file, keep in mind that anything after the first line of the file is ignored. If you want to read multiple lines, you have to use a table; tables are covered in the next section.

Now let's add another object to the MIB for our extended agent. We'll use a modification of the example OpenView gives us. We'll create an object named *fmailList-Msgs* (2) that summarizes the messages in the mail queue. This object will live in a new subtree, named *fmail* (4), under the private *mauro* subtree. So the name of our object will be *mauro.fmail.fmailListMsgs* or, in numeric form, *.1.3.6.1.4.1.2789.4.2*. First, we need to define the *fmail* branch under the *mauro* subtree. To do this, add the following line to *snmpd.extend*:

```
fmail           OBJECT IDENTIFIER ::= { mauro 4 }
```

We picked 4 for the branch number, but we could have chosen any number that doesn't conflict with our other branches (3 and 255). After we define *fmail,* we can insert the definition for *fmailListMsgs* into *snmpd.extend*, placing it before the END statement:

```
fmailListMsgs OBJECT-TYPE
    SYNTAX DisplayString
    ACCESS read-only
    STATUS mandatory
    DESCRIPTION
        "List of messages on the mail queue.
         READ-COMMAND: /usr/lib/sendmail -bp
         READ-COMMAND-TIMEOUT: 10"
    ::= { fmail 2 }
```

When polled, *fmailListMsgs* runs the command sendmail –bp, which prints a summary of the mail queue. When all this is done, you can use your management station or a tool such as snmpget to read the value of *mauro.fmail.fmailListMsgs* and see the status of the outgoing mail queue.

Tables

Tables allow the agent to return multiple lines of output (or other sets of values) from the commands it executes. At its most elaborate, a table allows the agent to return something like a spreadsheet. We can retrieve this spreadsheet using snmp-walk—a process that's significantly easier than issuing separate get operations to retrieve the data one value at a time. One table we've already seen is *.iso.org.dod. internet.mgmt.mib-2.interfaces.ifTable*, which is defined in MIB-II and contains information about all of a device's interfaces.

Every table contains an integer index, which is a unique key that distinguishes the rows in the table. The index starts with 1, for the first row, and increases by one for each following row. The index is used as an instance identifier for the columns in the table; given any column, the index lets you select the data (i.e., the row) you want. Let's look at a small table, represented by the text file *animal.db*:

```
1        Tweety        Bird    Chirp   2
2        Madison       Dog     Bark    4
3        "Big Ben"     Bear    Grrr    5
```

Our goal is to make this table readable via SNMP, using OpenView's extensible agent. This file is already in the format required by the agent. Each column is delimited by whitespace; a newline marks the end of each row. Data that includes an internal space is surrounded by quotes. OpenView doesn't allow column headings in the table, but we will want to think about the names of the objects in each row. Logically, the column headings are nothing more than the names of the objects we will retrieve from the table. In other words, each row of our table consists of five objects:

animalIndex

> An index that specifies the row in the table. The first row is 1, as you'd expect for SNMP tables. The SYNTAX for this object is therefore INTEGER.

animalName

> The animal's name. This is a text string, so the SYNTAX of this object will be DisplayString.

animalSpecies

> The animal's species (another text string, represented as a DisplayString).

animalNoise

> The noise the animal makes (another DisplayString).

animalDanger

> An indication of how dangerous the animal is. This is another INTEGER, whose value can be from 1 to 6. This is called an "enumerated integer"; we're allowed to assign textual mnemonics to the integer values.

At this point, we have just about everything we need to know to write the MIB that allows us to read the table. For example, we know that we want an object named *animalNoise.2* to access the *animalNoise* object in the second row of the table; this object has the value Bark. It's easy to see how this notation can be used to locate any object in the table. Now let's write the MIB definition for the table:

```
TableExtExample DEFINITIONS ::= BEGIN

internet        OBJECT IDENTIFIER ::= { iso(1) org(3) dod(6) 1 }
enterprises     OBJECT IDENTIFIER ::= { internet(1) private(4) 1 }
mauro           OBJECT IDENTIFIER ::= { enterprises(1) 2789 }
other           OBJECT IDENTIFIER ::= { mauro 255 }

AnimalEntry ::=
    SEQUENCE {
    animalIndex INTEGER,
    animalName DisplayString,
    animalSpecies DisplayString,
    animalNoise DisplayString,
    animalDanger INTEGER
    }
```

```
animalTable OBJECT-TYPE
    SYNTAX SEQUENCE OF AnimalEntry
    ACCESS not-accessible
    STATUS mandatory
    DESCRIPTION
        "This is a table of animals that shows:
        Name
        Species
        Noise
        Danger Level
        FILE-NAME: /opt/local/animal.db"
    ::= { other 247 }

animalEntry OBJECT-TYPE
    SYNTAX AnimalEntry
    ACCESS not-accessible
    STATUS mandatory
    DESCRIPTION
        "List of animalNum"
    INDEX { animalIndex }
    ::= { animalTable 1 }

animalIndex OBJECT-TYPE
    SYNTAX INTEGER
    ACCESS read-only
    STATUS mandatory
    DESCRIPTION
        "The unique index number we will use for each row"
    ::= { animalEntry 1 }

animalName OBJECT-TYPE
    SYNTAX DisplayString
    ACCESS read-only
    STATUS mandatory
    DESCRIPTION
        "My pet name for each animal"
    ::= { animalEntry 2 }

animalSpecies OBJECT-TYPE
    SYNTAX DisplayString
    ACCESS read-only
    STATUS mandatory
    DESCRIPTION
        "The animal's species"
    ::= { animalEntry 3 }

animalNoise OBJECT-TYPE
    SYNTAX DisplayString
    ACCESS read-only
    STATUS mandatory
    DESCRIPTION
        "The noise or sound the animal makes"
    ::= { animalEntry 4 }
```

```
animalDanger OBJECT-TYPE
    SYNTAX INTEGER {
        no-Danger(1),
        can-Harm(2),
        some-Damage(3),
        will-Wound(4),
        severe-Pain(5),
        will-Kill(6)
    }
    ACCESS read-write
    STATUS mandatory
    DESCRIPTION
        "The level of danger that we may face with the particular animal"
    ::= { animalEntry 5 }

END
```

The table starts with a definition of the *animalTable* object, which gives us our DESCRIPTION and tells the agent where the *animal.db* file is located. The SYNTAX is SEQUENCE OF AnimalEntry. *AnimalEntry* (watch the case) gives us a quick view of all our columns. You can leave *AnimalEntry* out, but we recommend that you include it since it documents the structure of the table.

The table is actually built from *animalEntry* elements—because object names are case sensitive, this object is different from *AnimalEntry*. *animalEntry* tells us what object we should use for our index or key; the object used as the key is in brackets after the INDEX keyword.

The definitions of the remaining objects are similar to the definitions we've already seen. The parent-subtree for all of these objects is *animalEntry*, which effectively builds a table row from each of these objects. The only object that's particularly interesting is *animalDanger*, which uses an extension of the INTEGER datatype. As we noted before, this object is an enumerated integer, which allows us to associate textual labels with integer values. The values you can use in an enumerated type should be a series of consecutive integers, starting with 1.* For example, the *animalDanger* object defines six values, ranging from 1 to 6, with strings like no-danger associated with the values.

You can save this table definition in a file and use the xnmloadmib command to load it into OpenView. Once you've done that and created the *animal.db* file with a text editor, you can walk the table:

```
$ snmpwalk sunserver1 .1.3.6.1.4.1.mauro.other.animalTable
animalEntry.animalIndex.1 : INTEGER: 1
animalEntry.animalIndex.2 : INTEGER: 2
animalEntry.animalIndex.3 : INTEGER: 3
animalEntry.animalName.1 : DISPLAY STRING-(ascii): Tweety
```

---

* Some SNMPv1 SMI-compliant MIB compilers will not allow an enumerated type of 0 (zero).

```
animalEntry.animalName.2 : DISPLAY STRING-(ascii): Madison
animalEntry.animalName.3 : DISPLAY STRING-(ascii): Big Ben
animalEntry.animalSpecies.1 : DISPLAY STRING-(ascii): Bird
animalEntry.animalSpecies.2 : DISPLAY STRING-(ascii): Dog
animalEntry.animalSpecies.3 : DISPLAY STRING-(ascii): Bear
animalEntry.animalNoise.1 : DISPLAY STRING-(ascii): Chirp
animalEntry.animalNoise.2 : DISPLAY STRING-(ascii): Bark
animalEntry.animalNoise.3 : DISPLAY STRING-(ascii): Grrr
animalEntry.animalDanger.1 : INTEGER: can-Harm
animalEntry.animalDanger.2 : INTEGER: will-Wound
animalEntry.animalDanger.3 : INTEGER: severe-Pain
```

snmpwalk goes through the table a column at a time, reporting all the data in a column before proceeding to the next. This is confusing—it would be easier if snmpwalk read the table a row at a time. As it is, you have to hop from line to line when you are trying to read a row; for example, to find out everything about Tweety, you need to look at every third line (all the *.1* items) in the output.

Two more things are worth noticing in the snmpwalk output. The first set of values that snmpwalk reports are the index values (*animalIndex*). It then appends each index value to each OID to perform the rest of the walk. Second, the *animalDanger* output reports strings, such as can-Harm, rather than integers. The conversion from integers to strings takes place because we defined the *animalDanger* object as an enumerated integer, which associates a set of possible values with strings.

Of course, just reading a table doesn't do a whole lot of good. Let's say that we need to update this file periodically to reflect changes in the animals' behavior. The *animalDanger* object has an ACCESS of read-write, which allows us to set its value and update the database file using our SNMP tools. Imagine that the dog in row 2 turns very mean. We need to turn its danger level to 5 (severe-Pain). We could edit the file by hand, but it's easier to issue an snmpset:

```
$ snmpset -c private sunserver2 \
mauro.other.animalTable.animalEntry.animalDanger.2 integer "5"
mauro.other.animalTable.animalEntry.animalDanger.2 : INTEGER: severe-Pain
```

Now let's go back and verify that the variable has been updated:[*]

```
$ snmpget sunserver2 \
mauro.other.animalTable.animalEntry.animalDanger.2
mauro.other.animalTable.animalEntry.animalDanger.2 : INTEGER: severe-Pain
```

Once the snmpset is complete, check the file to see how it has changed. In addition to changing the dog's danger level, it has enclosed all strings within quotes:

```
1 "Tweety" "Bird" "Chirp" 2
2 "Madison" "Dog" "Bark" 5
3 "Big Ben" "Bear" "Grrr" 5
```

---

[*] We could already deduce that the set was successful when snmpset didn't give us an error. This example does, however, show how you can snmpget a single instance within a table.

There are even more possibilities for keeping the file up-to-date. For example, you could use a system program or application to edit this file. A cron job could kick off every hour or so and update the file. This strategy would let you generate the file using a SQL query to a database such as Oracle. You could then put the query's results in a file and poll the file with SNMP to read the results. One problem with this strategy is that you must ensure that your application and SNMP polling periods are in sync. Make sure you poll the file *after* Oracle has updated it, or you will be viewing old data.

An effective way to ensure that the file is up-to-date when you read it is to use FILE-COMMAND within the table's definition. This tells the agent to run a program that updates the table before returning any values. Let's assume that we've written a script named *get_animal_status.pl* that determines the status of the animals and updates the database accordingly. Here's how we'd integrate that script into our table definition:

```
animalTable OBJECT-TYPE
    SYNTAX    SEQUENCE OF AnimalEntry
    ACCESS    not-accessible
    STATUS    mandatory
    DESCRIPTION
        "This is a table of animals that shows:
        Name
        Species
        Noise
        Danger Level
        FILE-COMMAND: /opt/local/get_animal_status.pl
        FILE-NAME: /opt/local/animal.db"
    ::= { other 247 }
```

The command must finish within 10 seconds or the agent will kill the process and return the old values from the table. By default, the agent runs the program specified by FILE-COMMAND only if it has not gotten a request in the last 10 seconds. For example, let's say you issue two snmpget commands, two seconds apart. For the first snmpget, the agent runs the program and returns the data from the table with any changes. The second time, the agent won't run the program to update the data—it will return the old data, assuming that nothing has changed. This is effectively a form of caching. You can increase the amount of time the agent keeps its cache by specifying a value, in seconds, after FILE-COMMAND-FREQUENCY. For example, if you want to update the file only every 20 minutes (at most), include the following commands in your table definition:

```
FILE-COMMAND: /opt/local/get_animal_status.pl
FILE-COMMAND-FREQUENCY: 1200
FILE-NAME: /opt/local/animal.db"
```

This chapter has given you a brief introduction to three of the more popular extensible SNMP agents on the market. While a thorough treatment of every configurable option for each agent is beyond the scope of this chapter, it should help you to understand how to use extensible agents. With an extensible agent, the possibilities are almost endless.

## CHAPTER 11

Adapting SNMP to Fit Your Environment

SNMP can make your life as a system administrator a lot easier by performing many of the tasks that you'd either have to do by hand or automate by writing some clever script. It's relatively easy to take care of most everyday system monitoring: SNMP can poll for disk-space utilization, notify you when mirrors are syncing, or record who is logging in or out of the system. This chapter introduces some interesting scripts for automating common system administration tasks. The SNMP scripts in this chapter represent just a few of the things SNMP allows you to do; use them as a launching pad for your own ideas.

General Trap-Generation Program

Chapter 9 contained some scripts for collecting SNMP information using Perl, Open-View's snmptrap program, and some other tools. Here's how we used snmptrap to generate a trap giving us information about some problems with the database:

```
$ /opt/OV/bin/snmptrap -c public nms .1.3.6.1.4.1.2789.2500 "" 6 3003 "" \
.1.3.6.1.4.1.2500.3003.1 octetstringascii "Oracle" \
.1.3.6.1.4.1.2500.3003.2 octetstringascii "Backup Not Running" \
.1.3.6.1.4.1.2500.3003.3 octetstringascii "Call the DBA Now for Help"
```

The way you send a trap in Perl is a little more involved, but it's still easy to do:

```
#!/usr/local/bin/perl
# Filename: /opt/local/perl_scripts/snmptrap.pl

use SNMP_util "0.54";  # This will load the BER and SNMP_Session

snmptrap("public\@nms:162", ".1.3.6.1.4.1.2789", "sunserver1",
        6, 1247, ".1.3.6.1.4.1.2789.1247.1", "int", "2448816");
```

In this chapter, we won't look so much at how to write commands like these, but at how to use them in clever ways. We might want to include commands like these in startup scripts, or invoke them via hooks into other programs. We'll start by writing some code that records successful logins.

The scripts in this chapter, and all of the code examples in this book, can be downloaded from *http://www.oreilly.com/catalog/esnmp2*.

Who's Logging into My Machine? (I-Am-In)

When Unix users log in, the system automatically executes a profile; for users of the Bourne, Korn, or *bash* shells, the systemwide profile is named */etc/profile*. There's a similar file for users of *csh* and *tcsh* (*/etc/login*). We can use SNMP to record logins by adding a trap to these profiles. By itself this isn't all that interesting, because Unix already keeps a log of user logins. But let's say that you're monitoring a few dozen machines and don't want to check each machine's log. Adding a trap to the system-wide profile lets you monitor logins to all your systems from one place. It also makes your logging more secure. It's not too difficult for an intelligent user to delete the *wtmp* file that stores Unix login records. Using SNMP to do the logging stores the information on another host, over which you should have better control.[*]

To generate the trap, invoke the external program */opt/local/mib_ programs/os/iamin* in */etc/profile* (you can call the same program within */etc/login*). Here is the code for *iamin*:

```
#!/usr/local/bin/perl
#
# Filename: /opt/local/mib_programs/os/iamin

chomp ($WHO = `/bin/who am i \| awk \{\'print \$1\'\}`);

exit 123 unless ($WHO ne '');

chomp ($WHOAMI = `/usr/ucb/whoami`);
chomp ($TTY = `/bin/tty`);
chomp ($FROM = `/bin/last \-1 $WHO \| /bin/awk \{\'print \$3\'\}`);

if ($FROM =~ /Sun|Mon|Tue|Wed|Thu|Fri|Sat/) { $FROM = "N/A"; }

# DEBUG BELOW
# print "WHO :$WHO:\n"; print "WHOAMI :$WHOAMI:\n"; print "FROM :$FROM:\n";

if ("$WHOAMI" ne "$WHO") { $WHO = "$WHO\-\>$WHOAMI"; }

# Sending a trap using Net-SNMP
#
system "/usr/local/bin/snmptrap nms public .1.3.6.1.4.1.2789.2500 '' 6 1502 ''
.1.3.6.1.4.1.2789.2500.1502.1 s \"$WHO\"
.1.3.6.1.4.1.2789.2500.1502.2 s \"$FROM\"
```

---

[*] Yes, a clever user could intercept and modify SNMP packets or rewrite the shell profile, or do any number of things to defeat logging. We're not really interested in making it impossible to defeat logging; we just want to make it more difficult.

```
.1.3.6.1.4.1.2789.2500.1502.3 s \"$TTY\"";

# Sending a trap using Perl
#
#use SNMP_util "0.54";  # This will load the BER and SNMP_Session for us
#snmptrap("public\@nms:162", ".1.3.6.1.4.1.2789.2500", mylocalhostname, 6, 1502,
#".1.3.6.1.4.1.2789.2500.1502.1", "string", "$WHO",
#".1.3.6.1.4.1.2789.2500.1502.2", "string", "$FROM",
#".1.3.6.1.4.1.2789.2500.1502.3", "string", "$TTY");

# Sending a trap using OpenView's snmptrap
#
#system "/opt/OV/bin/snmptrap -c public nms .1.3.6.1.4.1.2789.2500 \"\" 6 1502 \"\"
#.1.3.6.1.4.1.2789.2500.1502.1 octetstringascii \"$WHO\"
#.1.3.6.1.4.1.2789.2500.1502.2 octetstringascii \"$FROM\"
#.1.3.6.1.4.1.2789.2500.1502.3 octetstringascii \"$TTY\"";
#


#
print "\n##############\n";
print "#   NOTICE   \# - You have been logged: :$WHO: :$FROM: :$TTY: \n"; #
print "##############\n\n";
```

This script is a bit meatier than expected because we need to weed out a number of bogus entries. For instance, many programs run within a shell and hence invoke the same shell profiles. Therefore, we have to figure out whether the profile is being invoked by a human user; if not, we quit.* The next step is to figure out more about the user's identity; i.e., where she is logging in from and what her real identity is— we don't want to be confused by someone who uses su to switch to another identity. The third part of the program sends the trap with all the newly found information (who the user is, the host from which she is logging in, and what TTY she is on). We've included trap-generation code using the Net-SNMP utilities, the native Perl module, and OpenView's utilities. Take your pick and use the version with which you're most comfortable. The last portion of this program tells the user that she has been logged.

This script isn't without its problems. The user can always break out of the script before it is done, bypassing logging. You can counter this attempt by using *trap*(1), which responds to different signals. This forces the user to complete this program, not letting her stop midstream. This strategy creates its own problems, since the root user doesn't have any way to bypass the check. In a sense, this is good: we want to be particularly careful about root logins. But what happens if you're trying to investigate a network failure or DNS problem? In this case, the script will hang while DNS tries to look up the host from which you're logging in. This can be very frustrating.

---

* This will also fail if the user is su'ing to another user. In a well-designed environment, users really shouldn't have to su all that often—using sudo or designing appropriate groups should greatly reduce the need to su.

Before implementing a script like this, look at your environment and decide which profiles you should lock.

Any of the packages for receiving traps can be used to listen for the traps generated by this program.

Throw Core

Programs frequently leave core dumps behind. A core file contains all the process information pertinent to debugging. It usually gets written when a program dies abnormally. While there are ways to limit the size of a dump or prevent core dumps entirely, there are still times when they're needed temporarily. Therefore, most Unix systems have some sort of cron script that automatically searches for core files and deletes them. Let's add some intelligence to these scripts to let us track what files are found, their sizes, and the names of the processes that created them.

The following Perl program is divided into four parts: it searches for a file with a given name (defaults to the name *core*), gets the file's statistics, deletes the file,* and then sends a trap. Most of the processing is performed natively by Perl, but we use the command ls –l $FILENAME to include the pertinent core file information within the SNMP trap. This command allows our operators to see information about the file in a format that's easy to recognize. We also use the file command, which determines a file's type and its creator. Unless you know who created the file, you won't have the chance to fix the real problem.

```
#!/usr/local/bin/perl

# Finds and deletes core files. It sends traps upon completion and
# errors. Arguments are:
# -path directory    : search directory (and subdirectories); default /
# -lookfor filename  : filename to search for; default core
# -debug value       : debug level

while ($ARGV[0] =~ /^-/)
{
    if    ($ARGV[0] eq "-path")    { shift; $PATH    = $ARGV[0]; }
    elsif ($ARGV[0] eq "-lookfor") { shift; $LOOKFOR = $ARGV[0]; }
    elsif ($ARGV[0] eq "-debug")   { shift; $DEBUG   = $ARGV[0]; }
    shift;
}


################################################################
######################### Begin Main ########################
################################################################
```

---

* Before you start deleting core files, you should figure out who or what is dropping them and see if the owner wants these files. In some cases, this core file may be their only means of debugging.

```perl
require "find.pl";      # This gives us the find function.

$LOOKFOR = "core" unless ($LOOKFOR); # If we don't have something
                                     # in $LOOKFOR, default to core

$PATH    = "/"    unless ($PATH);    # Let's use / if we don't get
                                     # one on the command line

(-d $PATH) || die "$PATH is NOT a valid dir!";    # We can search
                                                  # only valid
                                                  # directories

&find("$PATH");

##################################################################
###################### Begin SubRoutines ######################
##################################################################

sub wanted
{
    if (/^$LOOKFOR$/)
        {
            if (!(-d $name)) # Skip the directories named core
            {
                &get_stats;
                &can_file;
                &send_trap;
            }
        }
}

sub can_file
{
    print "Deleting :$_: :$name:\n" unless (!($DEBUG));
    $RES = unlink "$name";
    if ($RES != 1) { $ERROR = 1; }
}

sub get_stats
{
    chop ($STATS = `ls -l $name`);
    chop ($FILE_STATS = `/bin/file $name`);

    $STATS =~ s/\s+/ /g;
    $FILE_STATS =~ s/\s+/ /g;
}

sub send_trap
{
    if ($ERROR == 0) { $SPEC = 1535; }
    else             { $SPEC = 1536; }
    print "STATS: $STATS\n" unless (!($DEBUG));
    print "FILE_STATS: $FILE_STATS\n" unless (!($DEBUG));
```

```
# Sending a trap using Net-SNMP
#
#system "/usr/local/bin/snmptrap nms public .1.3.6.1.4.1.2789.2500 '' 6 $SPEC ''
#.1.3.6.1.4.1.2789.2500.1535.1 s \"$name\"
#.1.3.6.1.4.1.2789.2500.1535.2 s \"$STATS\"
#.1.3.6.1.4.1.2789.2500.1535.3 s \"$FILE_STATS\"";

# Sending a trap using Perl
#
use SNMP_util "0.54";  # This will load the BER and SNMP_Session for us
snmptrap("public\@nms:162", ".1.3.6.1.4.1.2789.2500", mylocalhostname, 6, $SPEC,
".1.3.6.1.4.1.2789.2500.1535.1", "string", "$name",
".1.3.6.1.4.1.2789.2500.1535.2", "string", "$STATS",
".1.3.6.1.4.1.2789.2500.1535.3", "string", "$FILE_STATS");

# Sending a trap using OpenView's snmptrap
#
#system "/opt/OV/bin/snmptrap -c public nms
#.1.3.6.1.4.1.2789.2500 \"\" 6 $SPEC \"\"
#.1.3.6.1.4.1.2789.2500.1535.1 octetstringascii \"$name\"
#.1.3.6.1.4.1.2789.2500.1535.2 octetstringascii \"$STATS\"
#.1.3.6.1.4.1.2789.2500.1535.3 octetstringascii \"$FILE_STATS\"";
}
```

The logic is simple, though it's somewhat hard to see since most of it happens implicitly. The key is the call to find( ), which sets up lots of things. It descends into every directory underneath the directory specified by $PATH and automatically sets $_ (so the if statement at the beginning of the wanted( ) subroutine works). Furthermore, it defines the variable name to be the full pathname to the current file; this allows us to test whether the current file is really a directory, which we wouldn't want to delete.

Therefore, we loop through all the files, looking for files with the name specified on the command line (or named *core*, if no –lookfor option is specified). When we find one, we store its statistics, delete the file, and send a trap to the NMS reporting the file's name and other information. We use the variable SPEC to store the specific trap ID. We use two specific IDs: 1535 if the file was deleted successfully and 1536 if we tried to delete the file but couldn't. Again, we wrote the trap code to use either native Perl, Net-SNMP, or OpenView. Uncomment the version of your choice. We pack the trap with three variable bindings, which contain the name of the file, the results of ls –l on the file, and the results of running */bin/file*. Together, these give us a fair amount of information about the file we deleted. Note that we had to define object IDs for all three of these variables; furthermore, although we placed these object IDs under 1535, nothing prevents us from using the same objects when we send specific trap 1536.

Now we have a program to delete core files and send traps telling us about what was deleted; the next step is to tell our trap receiver what to do with these incoming traps. Let's assume that we're using OpenView. To inform it about these traps, we have to add two entries to *trapd.conf*, mapping these traps to events. Here they are:

```
EVENT foundNDelCore .1.3.6.1.4.1.2789.2500.0.1535 "Status Alarms" Warning
FORMAT Core File Found :$1: File Has Been Deleted - LS :$2: FILE :$3:
SDESC
This event is called when a server using cronjob looks for core
files and deletes them.

$1 - octetstringascii   - Name of file
$2 - octetstringascii   - ls -l listing on the file
$3 - octetstringascii   - file $name
EDESC
#
#
#
EVENT foundNNotDelCore .1.3.6.1.4.1.2789.2500.0.1536 "Status Alarms" Minor
FORMAT Core File Found :$1:
File Has Not Been Deleted For Some Reason - LS :$2: FILE :$3:
SDESC
This event is called when a server using cronjob looks for core
files and then CANNOT delete them for some reason.

$1 - octetstringascii   - Name of file
$2 - octetstringascii   - ls -l listing on the file
$3 - octetstringascii   - file $name
EDESC
#
#
#
```

For each trap, we have an EVENT statement specifying an event name, the trap's specific ID, the category into which the event will be sorted, and the severity. The FORMAT statement defines a message to be used when we receive the trap; it can be spread over several lines and can use the parameters $1, $2, etc. to refer to the variable bindings that are included in the trap.

Although it would be a good idea, we don't need to add our variable bindings to our private MIB file; *trapd.conf* contains enough information for OpenView to interpret the contents of the trap.

Here are some sample traps[*] generated by the *throwcore* script:

```
Core File Found :/usr/sap/HQD/DVEBMGS00/work/core: File Has Been \
Deleted - LS :-rw-rw---- 1 hqdadm sapsys 355042304 Apr 27 17:04 \
/usr/sap/HQD/DVEBMGS00/work/core: \
FILE :/usr/sap/HQD/DVEBMGS00/work/core: ELF 32-bit MSB core file \
SPARC Version 1, from 'disp+work':

Core File Found :/usr/sap/HQI/DVEBMGS10/work/core: File Has Been \
Deleted - LS :-rw-r--r-- 1 hqiadm sapsys 421499988 Apr 28 14:29 \
/usr/sap/HQI/DVEBMGS10/work/core: \
FILE :/usr/sap/HQI/DVEBMGS10/work/core: ELF 32-bit MSB core file \
SPARC Version 1, from 'disp+work':
```

---

[*] We've removed most of the host and date/time information.

Here is root's *crontab*, which runs the *throwcore* script at specific intervals. Notice that we use the –path switch, which allows us to check the development area every hour:

```
# Check for core files every night and every hour on special dirs
27 * * * * /opt/local/mib_programs/scripts/throwcore.pl -path /usr/sap
23 2 * * * /opt/local/mib_programs/scripts/throwcore.pl
```

Veritas Disk Check

The Veritas Volume Manager is a package that allows you to manipulate disks and their partitions. It gives you the ability to add and remove mirrors, work with RAID arrays, and resize partitions, to name a few things. Although Veritas is a specialized and expensive package that is usually found at large data centers, don't assume that you can skip this section. The point isn't to show you how to monitor Veritas, but to show you how you can provide meaningful traps using a typical status program. You should be able to extract the ideas from the script we present here and use them within your own context.

Veritas Volume Manager (vxvm) comes with a utility called vxprint. This program displays records from the Volume Manager configuration and shows the status of each of your local disks. If there is an error, such as a bad disk or broken mirror, this command will report it. A healthy vxprint on the *rootvol* (/) looks like this:

```
$ vxprint -h rootvol
Disk group: rootdg

TY NAME         ASSOC       KSTATE   LENGTH  PLOFFS  STATE   TUTILO  PUTILO
v  rootvol      root        ENABLED  922320  -       ACTIVE  -       -
pl rootvol-01   rootvol     ENABLED  922320  -       ACTIVE  -       -
sd rootdisk-B0  rootvol-01  ENABLED  1       0       -       -       Block0
sd rootdisk-02  rootvol-01  ENABLED  922319  1       -       -       -
pl rootvol-02   rootvol     ENABLED  922320  -       ACTIVE  -       -
sd disk01-01    rootvol-02  ENABLED  922320  0       -       -       -
```

The KSTATE (kernel state) and STATE columns give us a behind-the-scenes look at our disks, mirrors, etc. Without explaining the output in detail, a KSTATE of ENABLED is a good sign; a STATE of ACTIVE or – indicates that there are no problems. We can take this output and pipe it into a script that sends SNMP traps when errors are encountered. We can send different traps of an appropriate severity, based on the type of error that vxprint reported. Here's a script that runs vxprint and analyzes the results:

```
#!/usr/local/bin/perl -wc

$VXPRINT_LOC   = "/usr/sbin/vxprint";
$HOSTNAME      = `/bin/uname -n`; chop $HOSTNAME;

while ($ARGV[0] =~ /^-/)
{
    if    ($ARGV[0] eq "-debug")        { shift; $DEBUG = $ARGV[0]; }
    elsif ($ARGV[0] eq "-state_active") { $SHOW_STATE_ACTIVE = 1; }
```

```perl
        shift;
}

#########################################################################
############################ Begin Main ############################
#########################################################################

&get_vxprint;  # Get it, process it, and send traps if errors found!

#########################################################################
######################### Begin SubRoutines #########################
#########################################################################

sub get_vxprint
{

    open(VXPRINT,"$VXPRINT_LOC |") || die "Can't Open $VXPRINT_LOC";
    while($VXLINE=<VXPRINT>)
    {
        print $VXLINE unless ($DEBUG < 2);
        if ($VXLINE ne "\n")
        {
            &is_a_disk_group_name;
            &split_vxprint_output;

            if (($TY ne "TY")   &&
                ($TY ne "Disk") &&
                ($TY ne "dg")   &&
                ($TY ne "dm"))
            {
                if (($SHOW_STATE_ACTIVE) && ($STATE eq "ACTIVE"))
                {
                    print "ACTIVE: $VXLINE";
                }
                if (($STATE ne "ACTIVE") &&
                    ($STATE ne "DISABLED") &&
                    ($STATE ne "SYNC") &&
                    ($STATE ne "CLEAN") &&
                    ($STATE ne "SPARE") &&
                    ($STATE ne "-")      &&
                    ($STATE ne ""))
                {
                    &send_error_msgs;
                }
                elsif (($KSTATE ne "ENABLED") &&
                       ($KSTATE ne "DISABLED") &&
                       ($KSTATE ne "-")       &&
                       ($KSTATE ne ""))
                {
                    &send_error_msgs;
                }
            } # end if (($TY
        }   # end if ($VXLINE
    }       # end while($VXLINE
```

```
}               # end sub get_vxprint

sub is_a_disk_group_name
{
    if ($VXLINE =~ /^Disk\sgroup\:\s(\w+)\n/)
    {
        $DISK_GROUP = $1;
        print "Found Disk Group :$1:\n" unless (!($DEBUG));
        return 1;
    }
}

sub split_vxprint_output
{
($TY, $NAME, $ASSOC, $KSTATE,
    $LENGTH, $PLOFFS, $STATE, $TUTILO,
    $PUTILO) = split(/\s+/,$VXLINE);

    if ($DEBUG) {
        print "SPLIT: $TY $NAME $ASSOC $KSTATE ";
        print "$LENGTH $PLOFFS $STATE $TUTILO $PUTILO:\n";
            }
}

sub send_snmp_trap
{
    $SNMP_TRAP_LOC          = "/opt/OV/bin/snmptrap";
    $SNMP_COMM_NAME         = "public";
    $SNMP_TRAP_HOST         = "nms";

    $SNMP_ENTERPRISE_ID     = ".1.3.6.1.4.1.2789.2500";
    $SNMP_GEN_TRAP          = "6";
    $SNMP_SPECIFIC_TRAP     = "1000";

    chop($SNMP_TIME_STAMP       = "1" . `date +%H%S`);
    $SNMP_EVENT_IDENT_ONE   = ".1.3.6.1.4.1.2789.2500.1000.1";
    $SNMP_EVENT_VTYPE_ONE   = "octetstringascii";
    $SNMP_EVENT_VAR_ONE     = "$HOSTNAME";

    $SNMP_EVENT_IDENT_TWO   = ".1.3.6.1.4.1.2789.2500.1000.2";
    $SNMP_EVENT_VTYPE_TWO   = "octetstringascii";
    $SNMP_EVENT_VAR_TWO     = "$NAME";

    $SNMP_EVENT_IDENT_THREE = ".1.3.6.1.4.1.2789.2500.1000.3";
    $SNMP_EVENT_VTYPE_THREE = "octetstringascii";
    $SNMP_EVENT_VAR_THREE   = "$STATE";

    $SNMP_EVENT_IDENT_FOUR  = ".1.3.6.1.4.1.2789.2500.1000.4";
    $SNMP_EVENT_VTYPE_FOUR  = "octetstringascii";
    $SNMP_EVENT_VAR_FOUR    = "$DISK_GROUP";

    $SNMP_TRAP = "$SNMP_TRAP_LOC \-c $SNMP_COMM_NAME $SNMP_TRAP_HOST
    $SNMP_ENTERPRISE_ID \"\" $SNMP_GEN_TRAP $SNMP_SPECIFIC_TRAP $SNMP_TIME_STAMP
    $SNMP_EVENT_IDENT_ONE    $SNMP_EVENT_VTYPE_ONE    \"$SNMP_EVENT_VAR_ONE\"
```

```
$SNMP_EVENT_IDENT_TWO   $SNMP_EVENT_VTYPE_TWO   \"$SNMP_EVENT_VAR_TWO\"
$SNMP_EVENT_IDENT_THREE $SNMP_EVENT_VTYPE_THREE \"$SNMP_EVENT_VAR_THREE\"
$SNMP_EVENT_IDENT_FOUR  $SNMP_EVENT_VTYPE_FOUR  \"$SNMP_EVENT_VAR_FOUR\"";

# Sending a trap using Net-SNMP
#
#system "/usr/local/bin/snmptrap $SNMP_TRAP_HOST $SNMP_COMM_NAME
#$SNMP_ENTERPRISE_ID '' $SNMP_GEN_TRAP $SNMP_SPECIFIC_TRAP ''
#$SNMP_EVENT_IDENT_ONE s \"$SNMP_EVENT_VAR_ONE\"
#$SNMP_EVENT_IDENT_TWO s \"$SNMP_EVENT_VAR_TWO\"
#$SNMP_EVENT_IDENT_THREE s \"$SNMP_EVENT_VAR_THREE\"
#$SNMP_EVENT_IDENT_FOUR s \"$SNMP_EVENT_VAR_FOUR\"";

# Sending a trap using Perl
#
#use SNMP_util "0.54";  # This will load the BER and SNMP_Session for us
#snmptrap("$SNMP_COMM_NAME\@$SNMP_TRAP_HOST:162", "$SNMP_ENTERPRISE_ID",
#mylocalhostname, $SNMP_GEN_TRAP, $SNMP_SPECIFIC_TRAP,
#"$SNMP_EVENT_IDENT_ONE", "string", "$SNMP_EVENT_VAR_ONE",
#"$SNMP_EVENT_IDENT_TWO", "string", "$SNMP_EVENT_VAR_TWO",
#"$SNMP_EVENT_IDENT_THREE", "string", "$SNMP_EVENT_VAR_THREE",
#"$SNMP_EVENT_IDENT_FOUR", "string", "$SNMP_EVENT_VAR_FOUR");

# Sending a trap using OpenView's snmptrap (using VARs from above)
#
if($SEND_SNMP_TRAP) {
    print "Problem Running SnmpTrap with Result ";
    print ":$SEND_SNMP_TRAP: :$SNMP_TRAP:\n";
}

sub send_error_msgs
{
    $TY =~ s/^v/Volume/;
    $TY =~ s/^pl/Plex/;
    $TY =~ s/^sd/SubDisk/;

    print "VXfs Problem: Host:[$HOSTNAME] State:[$STATE] DiskGroup:[$DISK_GROUP]
        Type:[$TY] FileSystem:[$NAME] Assoc:[$ASSOC] Kstate:[$KSTATE]\n"
        unless (!($DEBUG));

    &send_snmp_trap;
}
```

Knowing what the output of vxprint should look like, we can formulate Perl statements that figure out when to generate a trap. That task makes up most of the get_vxprint subroutine. We also know what types of error messages will be produced. Our script tries to ignore all the information from the healthy disks and sort the error messages. For example, if the STATE field contains NEEDSYNC, the disk mirrors are probably not synchronized and the volume needs some sort of attention. The script doesn't handle this particular case explicitly, but it is caught with the default entry.

The actual mechanism for sending the trap is tied up in a large number of variables. Basically, though, we use any of the trap utilities we've discussed; the enterprise ID is *.1.3.6.1.4.1.2789.2500*; the specific trap ID is *1000*; and we include four variable bindings, which report the hostname, the volume name, the volume's state, and the disk group.

As with the previous script, it's a simple matter to run this script periodically and watch the results on whatever network management software you're using. It's also easy to see how you could develop similar scripts that generate reports from other status programs.

Disk-Space Checker

OpenView's agent has a *fileSystemTable* object that contains statistics about disk utilization and other filesystem parameters. At first glance, it looks extremely useful: you can use it to find out filesystem names, blocks free, etc. But it has some quirks, and we'll need to play a few tricks to use this table effectively. Walking *fileSystemTable.fileSystemEntry.fileSystemDir* (*.1.3.6.1.4.1.11.2.3.1.2.2.1.10*) lists the filesystems that are currently mounted:[*]

```
[root][nms] /opt/OV/local/bin/disk_space> snmpwalk spruce \
.1.3.6.1.4.1.11.2.3.1.2.2.1.10
fileSystem.fileSystemTable.fileSystemEntry.fileSystemDir.14680064.1
: DISPLAY STRING- (ascii):  /
fileSystem.fileSystemTable.fileSystemEntry.fileSystemDir.14680067.1
: DISPLAY STRING- (ascii):  /var
fileSystem.fileSystemTable.fileSystemEntry.fileSystemDir.14680068.1
: DISPLAY STRING- (ascii):  /export
fileSystem.fileSystemTable.fileSystemEntry.fileSystemDir.14680069.1
: DISPLAY STRING- (ascii):  /opt
fileSystem.fileSystemTable.fileSystemEntry.fileSystemDir.14680070.1
: DISPLAY STRING- (ascii):  /usr
fileSystem.fileSystemTable.fileSystemEntry.fileSystemDir.41156608.1
: DISPLAY STRING- (ascii):  /proc
fileSystem.fileSystemTable.fileSystemEntry.fileSystemDir.41680896.1
: DISPLAY STRING- (ascii):  /dev/fd
fileSystem.fileSystemTable.fileSystemEntry.fileSystemDir.42991617.1
: DISPLAY STRING- (ascii):  /net
fileSystem.fileSystemTable.fileSystemEntry.fileSystemDir.42991618.1
: DISPLAY STRING- (ascii):  /home
fileSystem.fileSystemTable.fileSystemEntry.fileSystemDir.42991619.1
: DISPLAY STRING- (ascii):  /xfn
```

Let's think about how we'd write a program that checks for available disk space. At first glance, it looks like this will be easy. But this table contains a number of objects

---

[*] We've truncated the leading *.iso.org.dod.internet.private.enterprises.hp.nm.system.general* to the walk results for space reasons.

that aren't filesystems in the normal sense; /proc, for example, provides access to the processes running on the system and doesn't represent storage. This raises problems if we start polling for free blocks: /proc isn't going to have any free blocks, and /dev/ fd, which represents a floppy disk, will have free blocks only if a disk happens to be in the drive. You'd expect /home to behave like a normal filesystem, but on this server it's automounted, which means that its behavior is unpredictable; if it's not in use, it might not be mounted. Therefore, if we polled for free blocks using the *fileSystem.fileSystemTable.fileSystemEntry.fileSystemBavail* object, the last five instances might return 0 under normal conditions. So, the results we'd get from polling all the entries in the filesystem table aren't meaningful without further interpretation. At a minimum, we need to figure out which filesystems are important to us and which aren't. This is probably going to require being clever about the instance numbers.

When we discovered this problem, we noticed that all the filesystems we wanted to check happened to have instance numbers with the same leading digits; i.e., *fileSystemDir.14680064.1*, *fileSystemDir.14680067.1*, *fileSystemDir.14680068.1*, etc. That observation proved to be less useful than it seemed—with time, we learned that not only do other servers have different leading instance numbers, but also, on any server the instance numbers could change. Even if the instance number changes, though, the leading instance digits seem to stay the same for all disks or filesystems of the same type. For example, disk arrays might have instance numbers like *fileSystemDir. 12312310.1*, *fileSystemDir.12312311.1*, *fileSystemDir.12312312.1*, and so on. Your internal disks might have instance numbers like *fileSystemDir.12388817.1*, *fileSystemDir.12388818.1*, *fileSystemDir.12388819.1*, and so on.

So, working with the instance numbers is possible, but painful—there is still nothing static that can be easily polled. There's no easy way to say "Give me the statistics for all the local filesystems," or even "Give me the statistics for /usr." We were forced to write a program that would do a fair amount of instance-number processing, making guesses based on the behavior we observed. We had to use *snmpwalk* to figure out the instance numbers for the filesystems we cared about before doing anything more interesting. By comparing the initial digits of the instance numbers, we were able to figure out which filesystems were local, which were networked, and which were "special purpose" (like /proc). Here's the result:

```
#!/usr/local/bin/perl
# filename: polling.pl
# options:
#    -min n    : send trap if less than n 1024-byte blocks free
#    -table f  : table of servers to watch (defaults to ./default)
#    -server s : specifies a single server to poll
#    -inst n   : number of leading instance-number digits to compare
#    -debug n  : debug level

$|++;

$SNMPWALK_LOC  = "/opt/OV/bin/snmpwalk -r 5";
```

```
$SNMPGET_LOC    = "/opt/OV/bin/snmpget";
$HOME_LOC       = "/opt/OV/local/bin/disk_space";
$LOCK_FILE_LOC = "$HOME_LOC/lock_files";
$GREP_LOC       = "/bin/grep";
$TOUCH_LOC      = "/bin/touch";
$PING_LOC       = "/usr/sbin/ping";        # Ping Location
$PING_TIMEOUT  = 7;                        # Seconds to wait for a ping

$MIB_C = ".1.3.6.1.4.1.11.2.3.1.2.2.1.6";      # fileSystemBavail
$MIB_BSIZE = ".1.3.6.1.4.1.11.2.3.1.2.2.1.7";  # fileSystemBsize
$MIB_DIR = ".1.3.6.1.4.1.11.2.3.1.2.2.1.10";   # fileSystemDir

while ($ARGV[0] =~ /^-/)
{
    if    ($ARGV[0] eq "-min")    { shift; $MIN = $ARGV[0]; }   # In 1024 blocks
    elsif ($ARGV[0] eq "-table")  { shift; $TABLE = $ARGV[0]; }
    elsif ($ARGV[0] eq "-server") { shift; $SERVER = $ARGV[0]; }
    elsif ($ARGV[0] eq "-inst")   { shift; $INST_LENGTH = $ARGV[0]; }
    elsif ($ARGV[0] eq "-debug")  { shift; $DEBUG = $ARGV[0]; }
    shift;
}


###################################################################
######################### Begin Main ##########################
###################################################################

$ALLSERVERS  = 1 unless ($SERVER);
$INST_LENGTH = 5 unless ($INST_LENGTH);

$TABLE = "default" unless ($TABLE);

open(TABLE,"$HOME_LOC/$TABLE") || die "Can't Open File $TABLE";
while($LINE=<TABLE>)
{
    if ($LINE ne "\n")
    {
    chop $LINE;
    ($HOST,$IGNORE1,$IGNORE2,$IGNORE3) = split(/\:/,$LINE);

    if (&ping_server_bad("$HOST")) { warn "Can't Ping Server
      :$HOST:" unless (!($DEBUG)); }
    else
    {
        &find_inst;

        if ($DEBUG > 99)
        {
        print "HOST:$HOST: IGNORE1 :$IGNORE1: IGNORE2 :$IGNORE2:
            IGNORE3 :$IGNORE3:\n";
        print "Running :$SNMPWALK_LOC $HOST $MIB_C \| $GREP_LOC
            \.$GINST:\n";
        }

        $IGNORE1 = "C1ANT5MAT9CHT4HIS"
```

```
          unless ($IGNORE1); # If we don't have anything then let's set
$IGNORE2 = "CA2N4T6M8A1T3C5H7THIS"
          unless ($IGNORE2); # to something that we can never match.
$IGNORE3 = "CAN3TMA7TCH2THI6S" unless ($IGNORE3);

if (($SERVER eq "$HOST") || ($ALLSERVERS))
{
  open(WALKER,"$SNMPWALK_LOC $HOST $MIB_C \| $GREP_LOC
     \.$GINST |") || die "Can't Walk $HOST $MIB_C\n";
  while($WLINE=<WALKER>)
  {
      chop $WLINE;
      ($MIB,$TYPE,$VALUE) = split(/\:/,$WLINE);
      $MIB =~ s/\s+//g;
      $MIB =~ /(\d+\.\d+)$/;

      $INST = $1;

      open(SNMPGET,"$SNMPGET_LOC $HOST $MIB_DIR.$INST |");
      while($DLINE=<SNMPGET>)
      {
          ($NULL,$NULL,$DNAME) = split(/\:/,$DLINE);
      }

      $DNAME =~ s/\s+//g;

      close SNMPGET;

      open(SNMPGET,"$SNMPGET_LOC $HOST $MIB_BSIZE.$INST |");
      while($BLINE=<SNMPGET>)
      {
      ($NULL,$NULL,$BSIZE) = split(/\:/,$BLINE);
      }

      close SNMPGET;

      $BSIZE =~ s/\s+//g;

      $LOCK_RES = &inst_found; $LOCK_RES = "\[ $LOCK_RES \]";

      print "LOCK_RES :$LOCK_RES:\n" unless ($DEBUG < 99);

      $VALUE = $VALUE * $BSIZE / 1024; # Put it in 1024 blocks

      if (($DNAME =~ /.*$IGNORE1.*/) ||
         ($DNAME =~ /.*$IGNORE2.*/) ||
         ($DNAME =~ /.*$IGNORE3.*/))
      {
          $DNAME = "$DNAME "ignored"";
      }

      else
      {
          if (($VALUE <= $MIN) && ($LOCK_RES eq "\[ 0 \]"))
```

```perl
                        {
                            &write_lock;
                            &send_snmp_trap(0);
                        }

                        elsif (($VALUE > $MIN) && ($LOCK_RES eq "\[ 1 \]"))
                        {
                            &remove_lock;
                            &send_snmp_trap(1);
                        }
                    }

                    $VALUE = $VALUE / $BSIZE * 1024; # Display it as the
                                                     # original block size

                    write unless (!($DEBUG));

                } # end while($WLINE=<WALKER>)
            }       # end if (($SERVER eq "$HOST") || ($ALLSERVERS))
        }           # end else from if (&ping_server_bad("$HOST"))

    }               # end if ($LINE ne "\n")
}                   # end while($LINE=<TABLE>)


################################################################
##################### Begin SubRoutines #####################
################################################################

format STDOUT_TOP =
Server      MountPoint        BlocksLeft     BlockSize     MIB        LockFile
---------   ----------------  ------------   -----------   ---------  ----------
.

format STDOUT =
@<<<<<<<<   @<<<<<<<<<<<<<<<  @<<<<<<<<<<<   @<<<<<<<<<<   @<<<<<<<<  @<<<<<<<<<
$HOST,      $DNAME,           $VALUE,        $BSIZE,       $INST,     $LOCK_RES
.

sub inst_found
{
    if (-e "$LOCK_FILE_LOC/$HOST\.$INST") { return 1; }
    else { return 0; }
}

sub remove_lock
{
    if ($DEBUG > 99) { print "Removing Lockfile $LOCK_FILE_LOC/$HOST\.$INST\n"; }
    unlink "$LOCK_FILE_LOC/$HOST\.$INST";
}

sub write_lock
{
    if ($DEBUG > 99) { print "Writing Lockfile
        $TOUCH_LOC $LOCK_FILE_LOC/$HOST\.$INST\n"; }
```

```
    system "$TOUCH_LOC $LOCK_FILE_LOC/$HOST\.$INST";
}


##################################################################
## send_snmp_trap ##
####################
##
# This subroutine allows you to send diff traps depending on the
#  passed parm and gives you a chance to send both good and bad
#  traps.
#
# $1 - integer - This will be added to the specific event ID.
#
# If we created two traps:
#  2789.2500.0.1000 = Major
#  2789.2500.0.1001 = Good
#
# If we declare:
#  $SNMP_SPECIFIC_TRAP      = "1000";
#
# We could send the 1st by using:
#  send_snmp_trap(0);   # Here is the math (1000 + 0 = 1000)
#  And to send the second one:
#  send_snmp_trap(1);   # Here is the math (1000 + 1 = 1001)
#
# This way you could set up multiple traps with diff errors using
#  the same function for all.
#
##
##################################################################

sub send_snmp_trap
{
    $TOTAL_TRAPS_CREATED     = 2;  # Let's do some checking/reminding
                                   # here. This number should be the
                                   # total number of traps that you
                                   # created on the nms.

    $SNMP_ENTERPRISE_ID      = ".1.3.6.1.4.1.2789.2500";
    $SNMP_SPECIFIC_TRAP      = "1500";

    $PASSED_PARM             = $_[0];
    $SNMP_SPECIFIC_TRAP     += $PASSED_PARM;

    $SNMP_TRAP_LOC           = "/opt/OV/bin/snmptrap";
    $SNMP_COMM_NAME          = "public";
    $SNMP_TRAP_HOST          = "nms";

    $SNMP_GEN_TRAP           = "6";

    chop($SNMP_TIME_STAMP        = "1" . `date +%H%S`);

    $SNMP_EVENT_IDENT_ONE    = ".1.3.6.1.4.1.2789.2500.$SNMP_SPECIFIC_TRAP.1";
    $SNMP_EVENT_VTYPE_ONE    = "octetstringascii";
```

```
$SNMP_EVENT_VAR_ONE       = "$DNAME";

$SNMP_EVENT_IDENT_TWO     = ".1.3.6.1.4.1.2789.2500.$SNMP_SPECIFIC_TRAP.2";
$SNMP_EVENT_VTYPE_TWO     = "integer";
$SNMP_EVENT_VAR_TWO       = "$VALUE";

$SNMP_EVENT_IDENT_THREE   = ".1.3.6.1.4.1.2789.2500.$SNMP_SPECIFIC_TRAP.3";
$SNMP_EVENT_VTYPE_THREE   = "integer";
$SNMP_EVENT_VAR_THREE     = "$BSIZE";

$SNMP_EVENT_IDENT_FOUR    = ".1.3.6.1.4.1.2789.2500.$SNMP_SPECIFIC_TRAP.4";
$SNMP_EVENT_VTYPE_FOUR    = "octetstringascii";
$SNMP_EVENT_VAR_FOUR      = "$INST";

$SNMP_EVENT_IDENT_FIVE    = ".1.3.6.1.4.1.2789.2500.$SNMP_SPECIFIC_TRAP.5";
$SNMP_EVENT_VTYPE_FIVE    = "integer";
$SNMP_EVENT_VAR_FIVE      = "$MIN";

$SNMP_TRAP = "$SNMP_TRAP_LOC \-c $SNMP_COMM_NAME $SNMP_TRAP_HOST
  $SNMP_ENTERPRISE_ID \"$HOST\" $SNMP_GEN_TRAP $SNMP_SPECIFIC_TRAP
  $SNMP_TIME_STAMP
  $SNMP_EVENT_IDENT_ONE    $SNMP_EVENT_VTYPE_ONE    \"$SNMP_EVENT_VAR_ONE\"
  $SNMP_EVENT_IDENT_TWO    $SNMP_EVENT_VTYPE_TWO    \"$SNMP_EVENT_VAR_TWO\"
  $SNMP_EVENT_IDENT_THREE  $SNMP_EVENT_VTYPE_THREE  \"$SNMP_EVENT_VAR_THREE\"
  $SNMP_EVENT_IDENT_FOUR   $SNMP_EVENT_VTYPE_FOUR   \"$SNMP_EVENT_VAR_FOUR\"
  $SNMP_EVENT_IDENT_FIVE   $SNMP_EVENT_VTYPE_FIVE   \"$SNMP_EVENT_VAR_FIVE\"";

if (!($PASSED_PARM < $TOTAL_TRAPS_CREATED))
{
   die "ERROR SNMPTrap with a Specific Number \>
       $TOTAL_TRAPS_CREATED\nSNMP_TRAP:$SNMP_TRAP:\n";
}

# Sending a trap using Net-SNMP
#
#system "/usr/local/bin/snmptrap $SNMP_TRAP_HOST $SNMP_COMM_NAME
#$SNMP_ENTERPRISE_ID '' $SNMP_GEN_TRAP $SNMP_SPECIFIC_TRAP ''
#$SNMP_EVENT_IDENT_ONE s \"$SNMP_EVENT_VAR_ONE\"
#$SNMP_EVENT_IDENT_TWO i \"$SNMP_EVENT_VAR_TWO\"
#$SNMP_EVENT_IDENT_THREE i \"$SNMP_EVENT_VAR_THREE\"
#$SNMP_EVENT_IDENT_FOUR s \"$SNMP_EVENT_VAR_FOUR\"";
#$SNMP_EVENT_IDENT_FIVE i \"$SNMP_EVENT_VAR_FIVE\"";

# Sending a trap using Perl
#
#use SNMP_util "0.54";  # This will load the BER and SNMP_Session for us
#snmptrap("$SNMP_COMM_NAME\@$SNMP_TRAP_HOST:162", "$SNMP_ENTERPRISE_ID",
#mylocalhostname, $SNMP_GEN_TRAP, $SNMP_SPECIFIC_TRAP,
#"$SNMP_EVENT_IDENT_ONE", "string", "$SNMP_EVENT_VAR_ONE",
#"$SNMP_EVENT_IDENT_TWO", "int", "$SNMP_EVENT_VAR_TWO",
#"$SNMP_EVENT_IDENT_THREE", "int", "$SNMP_EVENT_VAR_THREE",
#"$SNMP_EVENT_IDENT_FOUR", "string", "$SNMP_EVENT_VAR_FOUR",
#"$SNMP_EVENT_IDENT_FIVE", "int", "$SNMP_EVENT_VAR_FIVE");
```

```
        # Sending a trap using OpenView's snmptrap (using VARs from above)
        #
        if($SEND_SNMP_TRAP) {
            print "ERROR Running SnmpTrap Result ";
            print ":$SEND_SNMP_TRAP: :$SNMP_TRAP:\n"
        }

sub find_inst
{
    open(SNMPWALK2,"$SNMPWALK_LOC $HOST $MIB_DIR |") ||
                                    die "Can't Find Inst for $HOST\n";
    while($DLINE=<SNMPWALK2>)
    {
      chomp $DLINE;
      ($DIRTY_INST,$NULL,$DIRTY_NAME) = split(/\:/,$DLINE);
      $DIRTY_NAME =~ s/\s+//g;   # Lose the whitespace, folks!
      print "DIRTY_INST :$DIRTY_INST:\nDIRTY_NAME :$DIRTY_NAME:\n"
                            unless (!($DEBUG>99));
        if ($DIRTY_NAME eq "/")
        {
            $DIRTY_INST =~ /fileSystemDir\.(\d*)\.1/;
            $GINST = $1;
            $LENGTH = (length($GINST) - $INST_LENGTH);
            while ($LENGTH--) { chop $GINST; }
            close SNMPWALK;
            print "Found Inst DIRTY_INST :$DIRTY_INST: DIRTY_NAME\
                :$DIRTY_NAME: GINST :$GINST:\n"
                            unless (!($DEBUG > 99));
            return 0;
        }
    }

    close SNMPWALK2;
    die "Can't Find Inst for HOST :$HOST:";
}

sub ping_server_bad
{
    local $SERVER  = $_[0];
    $RES = system "$PING_LOC $SERVER $PING_TIMEOUT \> /dev/null";
    print "Res from Ping :$RES: \- :$PING_LOC $SERVER:\n"
                                        unless (!($DEBUG));
    return $RES;
}
```

The script contains a handful of useful features:

- We use an external ASCII file for a list of servers to poll. We specify the file by using the switch –table FILENAME. If no –table switch is given, the file named *default* in the current directory is used.

- We can specify a single server name (which must appear in the preceding file) to poll using the switch –server SERVER_NAME.

- We can ignore up to three filesystems per server. For example, we might want to ignore filesystems that are being used for software development.

- The script polls only servers that respond to a ping. We don't want to get filesystem traps from a server that is down or not on the network.

- We can set the minimum threshold for each list of servers in 1024-byte blocks using the –min blocks option.

- The script sends a trap when a server's threshold has been met and sends another trap when the state goes back to normal.

- We use lockfiles to prevent the server from sending out too many redundant traps.* When a threshold has been met, a file named *hostname.instance* is created. We send a trap only if the lockfile doesn't exist. When the space frees up, we delete the lockfile, allowing us to generate a trap the next time free storage falls below the threshold.

- We can set the number of leading instance digits used to grab the appropriate filesystem with the –inst switch. Unfortunately, the number of instance digits you can safely use to isolate a local filesystem varies from installation to installation. The default is five, but a lower value may be appropriate.

- The script displays a useful table when we invoke it with the –debug flag.

The script starts by reading the table of servers in which we're interested. It pings the servers and ignores those that don't respond. It then calls the subroutine find_inst, which incorporates most of the instance-number logic. This subroutine walks the filesystem table to find a list of all the filesystems and their instance numbers. It extracts the entry for the root filesystem (/), which we know exists, and which we assume is a local disk. (We can't assume that the root filesystem will be listed first; we do assume that you won't use a script like this to monitor diskless workstations.) We then store the first INST_LENGTH digits of the instance number in the variable GINST, and return.

Back in the main program, we ask for the number of blocks available for each filesystem; we compare the instance number to GINST, which selects the local filesystems (i.e., the filesystems with an instance number whose initial digits match the instance number for /). We then ask for the total number of blocks, which allows us to compare the space available against our thresholds. If the value is less than our minimum, we send one of the two enterprise-specific traps we've defined for this program, 1500, which indicates that the filesystem's free space is below the threshold. If the free space has returned to a safe level, we send trap 1501, which is an "out of danger" notification. Some additional logic uses a lockfile to prevent the script from bombarding the NMS with repeated notifications; we send, at most, one warn-

---

* A few times we missed the fact that a system filled up because a trap was lost during transmission. Using cron, we frequently delete everything in the *lock* directory. This resubmits the entries, if any, at that time.

ing a day and send an "out of danger" only if we've previously sent a warning. In either case, we stuff the trap with useful information: a number of variable bindings specifying the filesystem, the available space, its total capacity, its instance number, and the threshold we've set. Later, we'll see how to map these traps into OpenView categories.

Let's put the program to work by creating a table called *default* that lists the servers we are interested in watching:

```
db_serv0
db_serv1
db_serv2
```

Now we can run the script with the –debug option to show us a table of the results. The following command asks for all filesystems on the server *db_serv0* with fewer than 50,000 blocks (50 MB) free:

```
$ /opt/OV/local/bin/disk_space/polling.pl -min 50000 -server db_serv0 -debug 1
Res from Ping :0: - :/usr/sbin/ping db_serv0:
Server       MountPoint           BlocksLeft BlockSize  MIB             LockFile
----------   ------------------   ---------- ---------  --------------- --------
db_serv0   /                      207766     1024       38010880.1      [ 0 ]
db_serv0   /usr                   334091     1024       38010886.1      [ 0 ]
db_serv0   /opt                   937538     1024       38010887.1      [ 0 ]
db_serv0   /var                   414964     1024       38010888.1      [ 0 ]
db_serv0   /db1                   324954     1024       38010889.1      [ 0 ]
```

Notice that we didn't need to specify a table explicitly; since we omitted the –table option, the *polling.pl* script used the default file we put in the current directory. The –server switch let us limit the test to the server named *db_serv0*; if we had omitted this option, the script would have checked all servers within the default table. If the free space on any of the filesystems falls under 50,000 1024-byte blocks, the program sends a trap and writes a lockfile with the instance number.

Because SNMP traps use UDP, they are unreliable. This means that some traps may never reach their destination. This could spell disaster—in our situation, we're sending traps to notify a manager that a filesystem is full. We don't want those traps to disappear, especially since we've designed our program so that it doesn't send duplicate notifications. One workaround is to have cron delete some or all of the files in the *lock* directory. We like to delete everything in the *lock* directory every hour; this means that we'll get a notification every hour until some free storage appears in the filesystem. Another plausible policy is to delete only the production-server lockfiles. With this policy, we'll get hourly notification about filesystem capacity problems on the server we care about most; on other machines (e.g., development machines, test machines), we will get only a single notification.

Let's say that the filesystem */db1* is a test system and we don't care if it fills up. We can ignore this filesystem by specifying it in our table. We can list up to three filesystems we would like to ignore after the server name (which must be followed by a colon):

```
db_serv0:db1
```

Running the *polling.pl* script again gives these results:

```
$ /opt/OV/local/bin/disk_space/polling.pl -min 50000 -server db_serv0 -debug 1
Res from Ping :0: - :/usr/sbin/ping db_serv0:
Server       MountPoint          BlocksLeft  BlockSize  MIB              LockFile
----------   ----------------    ----------  ---------  ---------------  --------
db_serv0     /                   207766      1024       38010880.1       [ 0 ]
db_serv0     /usr                334091      1024       38010886.1       [ 0 ]
db_serv0     /opt                937538      1024       38010887.1       [ 0 ]
db_serv0     /var                414964      1024       38010888.1       [ 0 ]
db_serv0     /db1 (ignored)      324954      1024       38010889.1       [ 0 ]
```

When the */db1* filesystem drops below the minimum disk space, the script will not send any traps or create any lockfiles.

Now let's go beyond experimentation. The following *crontab* entries run our program twice every hour:

```
4,34 * * * * /opt/OV/bin/polling.pl -min 50000
5,35 * * * * /opt/OV/bin/polling.pl -min 17000 -table stocks_table
7,37 * * * * /opt/OV/bin/polling.pl -min 25000 -table bonds_table -inst 3
```

Next we need to define how the traps *polling.pl* generates should be handled when they arrive at the NMS. Here's the entry in OpenView's *trapd.conf* file that shows how to handle these traps:

```
EVENT DiskSpaceLow .1.3.6.1.4.1.2789.2500.0.1500 "Threshold Alarms" Major
FORMAT Disk Space For FileSystem :$1: Is Low With :$2:
1024 Blocks Left - Current FS Block Size :$3: - Min Threshold
:$5: - Inst :$4:
SDESC
$1 - octetstringascii   - FileSystem
$2 - integer            - Current Size
$3 - integer            - Block Size
$4 - octetstringascii   - INST
$5 - integer            - Min Threshold Size
EDESC
#
#
#
EVENT DiskSpaceNormal .1.3.6.1.4.1.2789.2500.0.1501 "Threshold Alarms" Normal
FORMAT Disk Space For FileSystem :$1: Is Normal With :$2:
1024 Blocks Left - Current FS Block Size :$3: - Min Threshold
:$5: - Inst :$4:
SDESC
$1 - octetstringascii   - FileSystem
$2 - integer            - Current Size
$3 - integer            - Block Size
$4 - octetstringascii   - INST
$5 - integer            - Min Threshold size
EDESC
```

These entries define two OpenView events: a *DiskSpaceLow* event that is used when a filesystem's capacity is below the threshold and a *DiskSpaceNormal* event. We place both of these in the Threshold Alarms category; the low disk space event has a severity of Major, while the "normal" event has a severity of Normal. If you're using some other package to listen for traps, you'll have to configure it accordingly.

Port Monitor

Most TCP/IP services use static ports to listen for incoming requests. Monitoring these ports allows you to see whether particular servers or services are responding or not. For example, you can tell whether your mail server is alive by periodically poking port 25, which is the port on which an SMTP server listens for requests. Some other ports to monitor are FTP (23), HTTP (80) and POP3 (110).* A freely available program called *netcat* can connect to and interact with a specific port on any device. We can write a wrapper for this program to watch a given port or service; if something happens outside of its normal operation, then we can send a trap. In this section, we'll develop a wrapper that checks the SMTP port (25) on our mail server. The program is very simple, but the results are outstanding!

Before we start to write the program, let's establish what we want to do. Telnet to port 25 of your SMTP server. Once you're connected, you can issue the command HELO mydomain.com. This should give you a response of 250. After you get a response from the mail server, issue the QUIT command, which tells the server you are done. Your session should look something like this:

```
$ telnet mail.ora.com 25
220 smtp.oreilly.com ESMTP O'Reilly & Associates Sendmail 8.11.2 ready
HELO mydomain.com
250 OK
QUIT
221 closing connection
```

The *netcat* program needs to know what commands you want to send to the port you are monitoring. We will be sending only two commands to our mail server, so we'll create a file called *input.txt* that looks like this:

```
HELO mydomain.com
QUIT
```

Next, we should test this file and see what output we get from the server. The actual *netcat* executable is named *nc*; to test the file, run it like this:

```
$ /opt/OV/local/bin/netcat/nc -i 1 mailserver 25 < input.txt
```

This command produces the same results as the telnet session. You won't see the commands in your *input.txt* file echoed, but you should see the server's responses. Once you have verified that netcat works and gives the same response each time,

---

* Check your *services* file for a listing of port numbers and their corresponding services. On Unix systems, this file is usually in the directory */etc*; on Windows it is usually in a directory such as *C:\WINDOWS\System32\ drivers\etc*, though its location may vary depending on the version of Windows you are using.

save a copy of its output to the file *mail_good*. This file will be used to determine what a normal response from your mail server looks like. You can save the output to a file with the following command:

```
$ /opt/OV/local/bin/netcat/nc -i 1 mailserver 25 < input.txt > mail_good
```

An alternate approach is to search for the line numbered 250 in the mail server's output. This code indicates that the server is up and running, though not necessarily processing mail correctly. In any case, searching for 250 shields you from variations in the server's response to your connection.

Here's a script called *mail_poller.pl* that automates the process. Edit the appropriate lines in this script to reflect your local environment. Once you have customized the script, you should be ready to go. There are no command-line arguments. The script generates an output file called *mail_status* that contains a 0 (zero) if the server is OK (i.e., if the output of netcat matches $GOOD_FILE); any number other than 0 indicates that an error has occurred:

```perl
#!/usr/local/bin/perl
# filename: mail_poller.pl

$HOME_LOC      = "/opt/OV/local/bin/netcat";
$NC_LOC        = "/opt/netcat/nc";
$DIFF_LOC      = "/bin/diff";
$ECHO_LOC      = "/bin/echo";

$MAIL_SERVER   = "mail.exampledomain.com";
$MAIL_PORT     =  25;
$INPUT_FILE    = "$HOME_LOC\/input.txt";
$GOOD_FILE     = "$HOME_LOC\/mail_good";
$CURRENT_FILE  = "$HOME_LOC\/mail_current";
$EXIT_FILE     = "$HOME_LOC\/mail_status";

$DEBUG = 0;

print "$NC_LOC -i 1 -w 3 $MAIL_SERVER $MAIL_PORT
    \< $INPUT_FILE \> $CURRENT_FILE\n" unless (!($DEBUG));

$NETCAT_RES = system "$NC_LOC -i 1 -w 3 $MAIL_SERVER $MAIL_PORT
    \< $INPUT_FILE \> $CURRENT_FILE";
$NETCAT_RES = $NETCAT_RES / 256;

if ($NETCAT_RES)
{
    # We had a problem with netcat... maybe a timeout?
    system "$ECHO_LOC $NETCAT_RES > $EXIT_FILE";
    &cleanup;
}

$DIFF_RES = system "$DIFF_LOC $GOOD_FILE $CURRENT_FILE";
$DIFF_RES = $DIFF_RES / 256;

if ($DIFF_RES)
```

```
{
    # looks like things are different!
    system "$ECHO_LOC $DIFF_RES > $EXIT_FILE";
    &cleanup;
}
else
{
    # All systems go!
    system "$ECHO_LOC 0 > $EXIT_FILE";
    &cleanup;
}

sub cleanup
{
    unlink "$CURRENT_FILE";
    exit 0;
}
```

After you run the program, review the results in *mail_status*. If you can, try shutting down the mail server and running the script again. Your file should now contain a nonzero error status.

Once you have made sure the script works in your environment, you can insert an entry in *crontab* to execute this program at whatever interval you would like. In our environment, we use a 10-minute interval:

```
# Check the mail server and create a file that we can poll via OpenView
1,11,21,31,41,51 * * * * /opt/OV/local/bin/netcat/mail_poller.pl
```

Notice we staggered the polling so that we don't check on the hour, half hour, or quarter hour. Once cron has started updating *mail_status* regularly, you can use tools such as the extensible OpenView agent to check the file's contents. You can configure the agent to poll the file regularly and send the results to your management console. The entry in my */etc/SnmpAgent.d/snmpd.extend* looks like this:

```
serviceInfo     OBJECT IDENTIFIER ::= { mauro 5 }

-- BEGIN - serviceInfo
--

serMailPort  OBJECT-TYPE
    SYNTAX   INTEGER
    ACCESS   read-only
    STATUS   mandatory
    DESCRIPTION
        "This file is updated via crontab. It uses netcat to check the
         port and push a value into this file.
         FILE-NAME: /opt/OV/local/bin/netcat/mail_status"
    ::= { serviceInfo 0 }
```

Chapter 10 discusses the syntax of this file. Basically, this entry just defines a MIB object in the *serviceInfo* tree, which is node 5 under my private-enterprise tree. In other words, this object's OID is *mauro.serviceInfo.serMailPort* (2789.5.0). The object can be read by any program that can issue an SNMP get operation. The

DESCRIPTION, as we saw in Chapter 10, specifies a filename from which the agent will read an integer value to use as the value of this object. This program can easily be modified to monitor any port on any number of machines. If you're ambitious, you might want to think about turning the *serMailPort* object into an array that reports the status of all your mail servers.

Service Monitoring

This section presents simple scripts that can help you monitor services like mail, DNS, and web content. Earlier we showed how you can use the netcat tool to verify that, for example, your SMTP server is up and responding. This is all well and good, but there are times when you may need more control over the situation. These times may include when you need to know when a service:

- Has been unreachable X number of times
- Has been unreachable X number of times in timeframe Y
- Is not meeting your company's Service Level Agreement (SLA). For example, your SLA may state that your SMTP or POP3 services will take no longer than 500 milliseconds (half a second) to service requests.

In each of these instances, it would be nice to know ahead of time that things may not be working properly in your environment.

The examples presented in this section use Perl modules to interact with the services directly. By using Perl, you have a great deal of control over how the services are monitored and how and when they send traps. What follows here is a Perl module that all the service monitors in this section use to track things like SLA information:

```
1  #
2  # File: MyStats.pm
3  #
4
5  package MyStats;
6  use Class::Struct;
7  use Exporter;
8  use SNMP_util;
9  our (@ISA, @EXPORT, @EXPORT_OK, %EXPORT_TAGS, $VERSION, $duration, $count,
10       $countAndTime, $sla, %watchers);
11
12  $VERSION = 1.00;
13  @ISA = qw(Exporter);
14
15  #
16  # There are two scenarios we want to track and alert on:
17  # 1. Some resource has been down a certain number of times
18  # 2. Service Level Agreements (SLAs). We are concerned with making sure
19  # services respond and operate within limits set forth in our SLA.
20  #
21
```

```perl
22   struct Count => {
23      name    => '$',
24      count => '$',
25      currentCount => '$',
26      message=> '$',
27   };
28
29   struct SLA => {
30      name => '$',
31      responseTime => '$',
32      count => '$',
33      currentResponseTime => '$',
34      currentCount => '$',
35      message=> '$',
36   };
37
38   $count;
39   $sla;
40   %watchers;
41
42   sub new {
43      my $classname  = shift;
44      my $self       = {};
45      my %arg  = @_;
46      bless($self, $classname);
47      return $self;
48   }
49
50   sub removeWatcher{
51      my $classname  = shift;
52      my ($name) = @_;
53      if(exists($watchers{$name})){
54         delete($watchers{$name});
55      }
56   }
57
58   sub thisExists{
59      my $classname  = shift;
60      my ($name) = @_;
61      return exists($watchers{$name});
62   }
63
64   sub setCountWatcher{
65      my $classname = shift;
66      my ($name,$c,$message) = @_;
67      $count = Count->new( );
68      $count->name($name);
69      $count->count($c);
70      $count->message($message);
71      $watchers{$name} = $count;
72   }
73
74   sub incrCountWatcher{
```

```
75     my $classname = shift;
76     my ($name) = @_;
77     if(exists($watchers{$name})){
78        my $count = $watchers{$name}->{Count::currentCount};
79        $count++;
80        $watchers{$name}->currentCount($count);
81     }
82  }
83
84  sub decrCountWatcher{
85     my $classname = shift;
86     my ($name) = @_;
87     if(exists($watchers{$name})){
88        my $count = $watchers{$name}->{Count::currentCount};
89        if($count > 0){
90           $count--;
91           $watchers{$name}->currentCount($count);
92        }
93     }
94  }
95
96  sub setSLA {
97     my $classname = shift;
98     my ($name,$count,$responseTime,$message) = @_;
99     $sla = SLA->new();
100    $sla->name($name);
101    $sla->count($count);
102    $sla->responseTime(sprintf("%.3f",$responseTime));
103    $sla->currentCount(0);
104    $sla->currentResponseTime(0);
105    $sla->message($message);
106    $watchers{$name} = $sla;
107 }
108
109 sub updateSLA {
110    my $classname = shift;
111    my ($name,$responseTime) = @_;
112    if(exists($watchers{$name})){
113       if($responseTime >= $watchers{$name}->{SLA::responseTime}){
114          $watchers{$name}->currentResponseTime($responseTime);
115          my $count = $watchers{$name}->{SLA::currentCount};
116          $count++;
117          $watchers{$name}->currentCount($count);
118       }elsif($responseTime < $watchers{$name}->{SLA::responseTime} &&
119             $watchers{$name}->{SLA::currentCount} > 0){
120          my $count = $watchers{$name}->{SLA::currentCount};
121          $count--;
122          $watchers{$name}->currentCount($count);
123          $watchers{$name}->currentResponseTime($responseTime);
124       }
125    }
126 }
127
```

```
128   sub sendAlert{
129       my $classname = shift;
130       my $host = "public\@localhost:162";
131       my $agent = "localhost";
132       my $eid = ".1.3.6.1.4.1.2789";
133       my $trapId = 6;
134       my $specificId = 1300;
135       my $oid = ".1.3.6.1.4.1.2789.1247.1";
136       foreach my $key (sort keys %watchers){
137           if($watchers{$key}->isa(Count)){
138               if($watchers{$key}->{Count::currentCount} >=
139                       $watchers{$key}->{Count::count}){
140                   my $message = $watchers{$key}->{Count::message};
141                   print "Sending Count Trap: $message\n";
142                   snmptrap($host, $eid, $agent,
      $trapId,$specificId,$oid,"string",$message);
143                   $watchers{$key}->currentCount(0);
144               }
145           }
146           if($watchers{$key}->isa(SLA)){
147               if($watchers{$key}->{SLA::currentCount} >=
148                       $watchers{$key}->{SLA::count} &&
149                       $watchers{$key}->{SLA::currentResponseTime} >
150                       $watchers{$key}->{SLA::responseTime}){
151                   my $message = $watchers{$key}->{SLA::message};
152                   print "Sending SLA Trap: $message\n";
153                   snmptrap($host, $eid, $agent,
      $trapId,$specificId,$oid,"string",$message);
154                   $watchers{$key}->currentCount(0);
155               }
156           }
157       }
158   }
159
160
161   1;
```

The user of this module can create two types of watchers:

Simple counter

You establish some threshold, and as the item you are monitoring changes (for example, becomes unable to connect to your service), *MyStats.pm* updates the count. When the count exceeds the threshold, an SNMP trap is sent.

SLA

The SLA object allows the user to set a duration and count. For example, if connecting to your SMTP server takes longer than one second (duration) and this happens 10 times (count), send an SNMP trap.

MyStats.pm is a basic implementation, but it is functional as is. Its use will become clearer when we present actual service monitoring scripts.

When monitoring customer-visible services, keep in mind the following:

- Deploy the monitoring scripts in the network where the path from the monitoring point traverses a path similar to that of the customer. This is rarely possible, but it's worth mentioning.

- If this sort of placement isn't possible and you have a network that is outside the particular server farm where your services are running, try to at least have the monitoring traffic go through the same router or firewall that the customer would use.

- If this is still not possible, monitoring your services from the same LAN segment or switch is still better than nothing!

Now let's look at three service monitoring scripts.

Web Content

Many people monitor the hardware their web server runs on without actually monitoring the web content itself. The scripts in this section use the Library for WWW in Perl (LWP) module to interact with a web server's content. The LWP module comes with Perl and you should not have to download a copy. We will present two scripts that perform the following monitoring tasks:

- Monitor content retrieval from a server
- Monitor a web site for dead links

The first example is in the same vein as the other service monitors. The second monitor, however, shows how easy it is to validate a web site's links. This can come in handy when you go live with a total redesign of your corporate web site. If the link to investor information is dead, wrong, or just not working, you will want to know about it pronto. Believe it or not, we have seen this happen over and over again.

This script attempts to get the main page from a URL. It detects whether the connection can be made to the web server and whether the request takes an inordinately long time.

```
162  #!/usr/bin/perl
163  #
164  # File: web-load.pl
165  #
166  use LWP::Simple;
167  use MyStats;
168
169  my $URL = "http://www.oreilly.com";
170  my $count = 3;
171  my $loadTime = 1;
172  my $duration = 3;
173  my $name1 = "URL Watcher1";
174  my $name2 = "URL Watcher2";
175  my $message1 = "$URL has been down $count times";
```

```
176  my $message2 = "$URL took greater than $loadTime second(s) to load. The problem
     persisted for over $duration seconds";
177
178  my $stats = MyStats->new( );
179  $stats->setCountWatcher($name1,$count,$message1);
180  $stats->setSLA($name2,$duration,$loadTime,$message2);
181
182  #
183  # Example taken from O'Reilly's Perl Cookbook 2nd edition
184  #
185  my $start = 0;
186  my $stop = 0;
187  my $sleep = 1;
188  while(1){
189     $start = time( );
190     my $content = get($URL);
191     if(!defined($content)) {
192        # Couldn't get content at all!
193        $stats->incrCountWatcher($name1);
194     }else{
195        $stats->decrCountWatcher($name1);
196        $stop = time( );
197        my $total = sprintf("%.3f",($stop-$start));
198
199        $stats->updateSLA($name2,$total);
200     }
201     $stats->sendAlert( );
202     print "Sleeping...\n";
203     sleep($sleep);
204  }
```

Here are some pertinent points about this script. Note that all the scripts in this section follow the same form when it comes to collecting SLA information and sending traps.

Line 169

This is the base URL you wish to monitor.

Line 170

This value is used to set the count used for simple counting.

Line 171

The $loadTime variable is used for the SLA watcher. This value, expressed as seconds, says "when it takes $loadTime time to do something, then note it."

Line 172

$duration is just like $count, but it's for the SLA watcher.

Lines 173 and 174

These two lines are labels used to uniquely identify the two watchers that this monitor will use. You can have any number of watchers in a monitor, as long as they have a unique name.

Lines 175 and 176

> When a trap is sent for a given watcher, these messages will be the guts of the trap. These message strings are meant to be as informative as possible so that someone can begin to resolve the problem.

Lines 178, 179, and 180

> Line 178 creates a new MyStats instance. Line 179 creates a count watcher while 180 creates an SLA watcher.

Line 188

> We enter a loop and continually monitor the service.

Line 189

> We start a timer.

Line 190

> Here we do the work of getting the URL content.

Lines 191 and 193

> If the content isn't defined, we failed to get the content. Line 193 bumps up the counter for the counter watcher.

Lines 195 through 199

> Since we were able to get content from the server, we decrement the counter on Line 195. We stop the timer on Line 196 by setting a variable to the current time. Line 197 calculates how long it took to get the content to three positions after the decimal. This allows for setting $duration to subsecond values—e.g., 0.1 for one-tenth of a second. Line 199 updates the SLA monitor.

Line 201

> The sendAlert subroutine handles checking to see if any watchers need to have traps sent on their behalf. See the *MyStats.pm* code presented at the beginning of this section to see how sendAlert does its thing.

Line 203

> The script sleeps, wakes up, and repeats.

That's about it. It really is quite simple but can be very effective.

The following script can find bad links. It starts at a given URL and works its way through the href tags:

```perl
#!/usr/bin/perl

#
# File: web-badlinks.pl
#
use HTML::LinkExtor;
use LWP::Simple;
use MyStats;

my $URL = "http://www.oreilly.com";
my $count = 3;
```

```perl
my $loadTime = 1;
my $duration = 3;
my $name1 = "URL Watcher1";
my $name2 = "Bad Link Watcher2";
my $message1 = "$URL has been down $count times";
my $message2 = "This URL is BAD: ";

my $stats = MyStats->new( );
$stats->setCountWatcher($name1,$count,$message1);


#
# Place links in here that you do not want to check
#
my %exemptLinks = (
    # http://www.oreilly.com/partners/index.php  will not get processed.
    "$URL/partners/index.php"=>1
);


#
# Parts of this Example taken from O'Reilly's Perl Cookbook,
# 2nd edition
#
my $start = 0;
my $stop = 0;
my $sleep = 1;
while(1){
    my $parser = HTML::LinkExtor->new(undef, $URL);
    my $html = get($URL);
    if(!defined($html)){
        # Couldn't get html. Server may be down
        $stats->incrCountWatcher($name1);
    }else{
        $stats->decrCountWatcher($name1);
        $parser->parse($html);
        my @links = $parser->links;
        foreach $linkarray (@links) {
            my @element  = @$linkarray;
            my $elt_type = shift @element;
            while (@element) {
                my ($attr_name,$attr_value) = splice(@element, 0, 2);
                next unless($exemptLinks{$attr_value} != 1);
                if ($attr_value->scheme =~ /\b(ftp|https?|file)\b/) {
                    if(!head($attr_value)){
                        if(!$stats->thisExists($attr_value)){
                            my $m = $message2.$attr_value;
                            $stats->setCountWatcher($attr_value,$count,$m);
                        }else{
                            $stats->incrCountWatcher($attr_value);
                        }
                    }
                }
            }
        }
    }
}
```

```
    $stats->sendAlert();
    print "Sleeping..\n";
    sleep($sleep);
}
```

We're not going to go into detail about how this script works. The watchers are set up in a similar fashion to the previous script.

One thing to note is that this script can actually produce false positives. When it comes across a link that requires login credentials, it may wrongly assume the link is bad when in fact it is not. To remedy this, you can add URLs to the %exemptLinks hash and they will be ignored altogether.

Finally, here is some sample output generated by these monitors:

```
$ snmptrapd -f -Lo
2005-05-05 12:49:34 NET-SNMP version 5.2.1 Started.

2005-05-05 12:51:39 localhost.localdomain [127.0.0.1] (via UDP: [127.0.0.1]:37243)
TRAP, SNMP v1, community public
        enterprises.2789 Enterprise Specific Trap (1300) Uptime: 0:00:08.00
        enterprises.2789.1247.1 = STRING: "http://www.oreilly.com took greater than 1
second(s) to load. The problem persisted for over 3 seconds"

2005-05-05 13:52:43 localhost.localdomain [127.0.0.1] (via UDP: [127.0.0.1]:37249)
TRAP, SNMP v1, community public
        enterprises.2789 Enterprise Specific Trap (1300) Uptime: 0:00:10.00
        enterprises.2789.1247.1 = STRING: "This URL is BAD: http://www.oreilly.com/
partners/index.php"
```

SMTP and POP3

The best way to monitor the health of your email service is to actually use it. This means sending and receiving email. The logic flow for monitoring SMTP follows:

1. Start timer.
2. Connect to SMTP server.
3. Send email message to dummy account.
4. Stop timer.
5. Note how long it took to interact with the server.

Steps 1 and 4 form a calculation for how long it took to interact with the SMTP server. If you begin to see a decline in the response time, it could be indicative of a problem. Of course, if in step number 2, you aren't able to connect to the server, this should be noted and a trap should be sent.

Monitoring POP3 has a similar logic flow:

1. Start timer.
2. Connect to POP3 server.

3. Start login timer.

4. Send login credentials.

5. Start retrieval timer.

6. Retrieve email for dummy account.

7. Start delete timer.

8. Delete email from account.

9. Stop all timers.

10. Note how long it took to connect, log in, retrieve, and delete from the POP3 server.

Here we are concerned with measuring several additional aspects of the POP3 server. Knowing how long it took to provide authentication credentials to the server may be useful, as well as knowing how long it took to delete one or more messages.

The scripts used in this section use the Net::SMTP and Net::POP3 modules that come with recent versions of Perl. If you are using an older version of Perl, you should be able to download these modules from *http://www.cpan.org*. The SMTP monitor is a separate script from the POP3 monitor so that you can easily run one script on one machine and the other on a different machine.

Now let's look at the actual code for the SMTP monitor:

```perl
#!/usr/bin/perl

#
# File: smtp.pl
#
use Net::SMTP;
use MyStats;

my $sleep = 1;
my $server = "smtp.oreilly.com";
my $heloSever = "smtp.oreilly.com";
my $timeout = 30;
my $debug = 1;
my $count = 3;
my $loadTime = 1;
my $duration = 3;
my $mailbox = "test1\@oreilly.com";
my $from = "test1-admin\@oreilly.com";
my $data = "This is a test email.\n";
my $name1 = "Mail Server Watcher1";
my $name2 = "Mail Server Watcher2";
my $message1 = "$server has been down $count times";
my $message2 = "Sending email to $mailbox took greater than $loadTime second(s). The
problem persisted for over $duration seconds";

$stats = MyStats->new();
$stats->setCountWatcher($name1,$count,$message1);
```

```perl
    $stats->setSLA($name2,$duration,$loadTime,$message2);

    my $start = 0;
    my $stop = 0;
    while(1){
        $start = time();
        my $smtp = Net::SMTP->new(
            $server,
            Hello=>$heloServer,
            Timeout => $timeout,
            Debug => $debug
            );
        if(!$smtp){
            $stats->incrCountWatcher($name1);
        }else{
            $stats->decrCountWatcher($name1);
            $smtp->mail($mailbox);
            $smtp->to($from);
            $smtp->data();
            $smtp->datasend($data);
            $smtp->dataend();
            $smtp->quit;
            $end = time();
            my $total = sprintf("%.3f",($stop-$start));
            $stats->updateSLA($name2);
        }
        $stats->sendAlert();
        print "Sleeping...\n";
        sleep($sleep);
    }
```

Now the POP3 script:

```perl
#!/usr/bin/perl

#
# File: pop3.pl
#
use Net::POP3;
use MyStats;

my $sleep = 1;
my $server = "pop3.oreilly.com";
my $username = "kschmidt";
my $password = "pword";
my $timeout = 30;
my $count = 3;
my $loadTime = 1;
my $duration = 3;
my $name1 = "POP3 Server Watcher1";
my $name2 = "POP3 Server Watcher2";
my $message1 = "$server has been down $count times";
my $message2 = "Popping email from $server for account $username took greater than
$loadTime second(s). The problem persisted for over $duration seconds";
```

```perl
$stats = MyStats->new( );
$stats->setCountWatcher($name1,$count,$message1);
$stats->setSLA($name2,$duration,$loadTime,$message2);

my $start = 0;
my $stop = 0;
while(1){
    $start = time( );
    my $pop = Net::POP3->new($server, Timeout => $timeout);
    if(!$pop){
        $stats->incrCountWatcher($name1);
    }else{
        $stats->decrCountWatcher($name1);
        if ($pop->login($username, $password) > 0) {
            my $msgnums = $pop->list; # hashref of msgnum => size
            foreach my $msgnum (keys %$msgnums) {
                # At this point we get the message and delete it. If you want to
                # measure getting and deleting independent of each other, you
                # should probably start a new timer, get the messages, stop the
                # timer, start a new timer, delete the messages and stop the
                # timer. You will also want to create two new SLA trackers.
                my $msg = $pop->get($msgnum);
                $pop->delete($msgnum);
            }
        }else{
            # Login failure. You will want to track this.
        }
        $pop->quit;
        $end = time( );
        my $total = sprintf("%.3f",($stop-$start));
        $stats->updateSLA($name2);
    }
    $stats->sendAlert( );
    print "Sleeping..\n";
    sleep($sleep);
}
```

The POP3 script will run continually. As soon as the SMTP script sends an email, the POP3 monitor will spring into action and do its thing.

DNS

One of the services that people often forget to monitor is DNS. Using similar techniques used to monitor web, SMTP, and POP3, we can monitor DNS as well. The Net::DNS Perl module is used in the example and is available from *http://search. cpan.org/~olaf/Net-DNS-0.49/*. While Net::DNS does not require the presence of the *libresolv* library on your Unix system to operate, if it does exist, the package uses it to build the module, which allows for increased performance.

This module is full featured and allows for at least the following:

- Look up a host's address.
- Discover nameserver(s) for a domain.

- Discover Mail Exchange (MX) record(s) for a domain.
- Obtain a domain's Start of Authority (SOA) record.

For our purposes, we will measure how long it takes to perform a DNS query for a host as well as obtain MX records for a domain.

```perl
#!/usr/bin/perl

#
# File: dns.pl
#
use Net::DNS;
use MyStats;

my $sleep = 30;
my $search = "www.oreilly.com";
my $mxSearch = "oreilly.com";
my $count = 3;
my $loadTime = 1;
my $duration = 3;
my $ns = "192.168.0.4";
my $debug = 0;
my $name1 = "DNS Server Watcher1";
my $message1 = "The DNS server $ns took greater than $loadTime second(s) to respond
to queries. The problem persisted for over $duration seconds";

$stats = MyStats->new();
$stats->setSLA($name1,$duration,$loadTime,$message1);

my $start = 0;
my $stop = 0;
while(1){
    $start = time();
    my $res = Net::DNS::Resolver->new(
        nameservers => [$ns],
        debug       => $debug,
    );
    my $query = $res->search($search);
    if ($query) {
        foreach my $rr ($query->answer) {
            next unless $rr->type eq "A";
            print $rr->address, "\n";
        }
    } else {
        # You may want to create a new watcher for search errors
        warn "query failed: ", $res->errorstring, "\n";
    }

    # lookup MX records
    my @mx = mx($res, $mxSearch);
    if(@mx){
        foreach $rr (@mx) {
            print $rr->preference, " ", $rr->exchange, "\n";
        }
```

```
    } else {
        # You may want to create a new watcher for MX errors
        warn "Can't find MX records for $name: ", $res->errorstring, "\n";
    }
    $stop = time( );
    my $total = sprintf("%.3f",($stop-$start));
    $stats->updateSLA($name1);
    $stats->sendAlert( );
    print "Sleeping..\n";
    sleep($sleep);
}
```

More Monitoring Suggestions

Here are some suggestions on how you can enhance these monitors:

- A database such as MySQL can be used to store the response times for every run of a monitor. Over time, a profile of how well a service performs can be developed from the stored information. Additionally, SLA reports can be created that show how often a service was responsive during some time interval.

- For web monitoring, you might want to create a script that can detect the age of dynamically created content. This would allow an administrator to know if some component on the backend is malfunctioning. We suggest getting a copy of O'Reilly's *Perl Cookbook* for ways of using LWP and other modules to accomplish this.

- The bad web link finder can be extended to actually log into pages that require authentication credentials. Again, the *Perl Cookbook* can help with adding this functionality to the script.

Pinging with Cisco

Using ICMP messages (also know as "pinging") to determine if a host is up is a common and simple network monitoring technique. Pinging a small number of hosts is not that challenging. But if you have many hosts that are distributed all over the place, things could get ugly.

If the polling interval used is short enough, you could run into the problem where the nth poll hasn't finished before the nth+1 poll begins. Another problem could be that the machine you want to ping from doesn't have proper routing to the host or hosts you want to monitor.

Cisco routers and some switches support the Cisco ping MIB (download from *ftp://ftp.cisco.com/pub/mibs/v2/CISCO-PING-MIB.my*). Basically, this feature allows you to have routers perform ICMP operations on your behalf. In effect, you can have a distributed ping system.

In this script,[*] we'll use SNMP to configure a Cisco router to perform pings on our behalf:

```perl
#!/usr/bin/perl

use SNMP;

#
# This script was adapted from the one that comes with Net-SNMP
#

my %ipsToPing = (
    "192.168.0.48" => 333,
);

my $router = "192.168.0.130";
my $community = "public";
my $version = 1;

my $sess = new SNMP::Session (DestHost => $router,
        Community => $community,
        Retries => 1,
        Version => $version);

my $ciscoPingEntry = ".1.3.6.1.4.1.9.9.16.1.1.1";
my $ciscoPingEntryStatus = "$ciscoPingEntry.16";
my $ciscoPingEntryOwner = "$ciscoPingEntry.15";
my $ciscoPingProtocol = "$ciscoPingEntry.2";
my $ciscoPingPacketCount = "$ciscoPingEntry.4";
my $ciscoPingPacketSize = "$ciscoPingEntry.5";
my $ciscoPingAddress = "$ciscoPingEntry.3";
my $ciscoPingSentPackets = "$ciscoPingEntry.9";
my $ciscoPingReceivedPackets = "$ciscoPingEntry.10";
my $ciscoPingMinRtt = "$ciscoPingEntry.11";
my $ciscoPingAvgRtt = "$ciscoPingEntry.12";
my $ciscoPingMaxRtt = "$ciscoPingEntry.13";
my $ciscoPingCompleted = "$ciscoPingEntry.14";


#
# Set up Cisco Ping table with targets we want to ping
#
foreach my $target (sort keys %ipsToPing){
    my $row = $ipsToPing{$target};
    # We must encode the IP we want to ping to HEX
    my $dec = pack("C*",split /\./, $target);
    $sess->set([
        # First we clear the entry for this target
        [$ciscoPingEntryStatus, $row, 6, "INTEGER"],
        # Now we create a new entry for this target
```

---

[*] Note that this Perl script uses the SNMP Perl API based on Net-SNMP. See Appendix E for an introduction to this Perl module.

```
                    [$ciscoPingEntryStatus, $row, 5, "INTEGER"],
                    # Set the owner of this entry
                    [$ciscoPingEntryOwner, $row, "kjs", "OCTETSTR"],
                    # Set the protocol to use, in this case "1" is IP
                    [$ciscoPingProtocol, $row, 1, "INTEGER"],
                    # Set the number of packets to send
                    [$ciscoPingPacketCount, $row, 20, "INTEGER"],
                    # Set the packet size
                    [$ciscoPingPacketSize, $row, 150, "INTEGER"],
                    # Finally set the target we want to ping
                    [$ciscoPingAddress, $row, $dec, "OCTETSTR"]]);

        # This enables this target and causes the router to start pinging
        $sess->set([[$ciscoPingEntryStatus, $row, 1, "INTEGER"]]);

        if($sess->{ErrorStr}){
            print "An Error Occurred: $sess->{ErrorStr}\n";
            exit;
        }
    }

    # Give router time to do its thing...
    sleep 30;

    #
    # Get results
    #
    foreach my $target (sort keys %ipsToPing){
        my $row = $ipsToPing{$target};
        my ($sent, $received, $low, $avg, $high, $completed) = $sess->get([
            [$ciscoPingSentPackets, $row], [$ciscoPingReceivedPackets, $row],
            [$ciscoPingMinRtt, $row], [$ciscoPingAvgRtt, $row],
            [$ciscoPingMaxRtt, $row], [$ciscoPingCompleted, $row]]);

        printf "($target)Packet loss: %d% (%d/%d)\n", (100 * ($sent-$received)) / $sent,
            $received, $sent;
        print "Average delay $avg (low: $low high: $high)\n";
        # Here we remove this target's entry from the Cisco Ping Table
        $sess->set([$ciscoPingEntryStatus, $row, 6, "INTEGER"]);
    }
```

Let's look at some details of this script:

- The ipsToPing hash is used to map all the target hosts we want our Cisco router to ping for us. Note that we are mapping the IP address to a number. This number uniquely identifies this IP address. If you want to add other IP addresses, make sure they all have unique numbers. This is because the Cisco ping MIB maintains a table of the hosts it has to ping and each entry in the table needs a unique number.

- Look at the first foreach( ) loop where we go through the ipsToPing hash. This is where we create new entries on the Cisco router. The first item we set is the ciscoPingEntryStatus. It is defined in the Cisco ping MIB as follows:

```
ciscoPingEntryStatus OBJECT-TYPE
        SYNTAX      RowStatus
        MAX-ACCESS read-create
        STATUS      current
        DESCRIPTION
                "The status of this table entry.  Once the entry status is
                set to active, the associate entry cannot be modified until
                the sequence completes (ciscoPingCompleted is true)."
        ::= { ciscoPingEntry 16 }
```

Its SYNTAX is RowStatus. RowStatus is a textual convention in the SNMPv2 textual conventions MIB. Basically, RowStatus is used to control the creation and deletion of table entries and can take the values listed in Table 11-1.

Table 11-1. RowStatus values

Value	Status
1	active
2	notInService
3	notReady
4	createAndGo
5	createAndWait
6	destroy

The first line of the SNMP set is issued against the ciscoPingEntryStatus OID with a value of 6, which is destroy. This removes a previously defined entry in this table for the row representing this target IP. The next line also issues a set against ciscoPingEntryStatus, but this time we create a new entry for the target IP address by using a value of 5. This creates the entry but places the row in a holding pattern. The router will not perform any action until we tell it to. The other parameters to the multipart set are self-explanatory. The action we take, before we leave the loop, is to enable the table entry by setting ciscoPingEntryStatus to 1, which is active. This will cause the Cisco router to begin its ping of the target.

- Once out of the loop, the script pauses for a bit to let the router do its thing. The final foreach( ) loop gathers the statistics that the router has captured for the target we previously configured it to ping. The final set operation in the loop removes this target's entry from the table. It does so by setting ciscoPingEntryStatus to 6, which destroys the row from the table.

Here's sample output from a run of this script:

```
$ ./pingmib.pl
(192.168.0.48)Packet loss: 0% (20/20)
Average delay 1 (low: 1 high: 1)
```

Now here's a look at an SNMP walk of the Cisco ping MIB (note that we ftp'ed the Cisco ping MIB and placed it in the same folder with the rest of the Net-SNMP MIBs):

```
$ snmpwalk -m ALL -IR -v1 -c public 192.168.0.130 ciscoPingMIB
CISCO-PING-MIB::ciscoPingProtocol.333 = INTEGER: ip(1)
CISCO-PING-MIB::ciscoPingAddress.333 = STRING: c0:a8:0:30
CISCO-PING-MIB::ciscoPingPacketCount.333 = INTEGER: 20
CISCO-PING-MIB::ciscoPingPacketSize.333 = INTEGER: 150
CISCO-PING-MIB::ciscoPingPacketTimeout.333 = INTEGER: 2000 milliseconds
CISCO-PING-MIB::ciscoPingDelay.333 = INTEGER: 0 milliseconds
CISCO-PING-MIB::ciscoPingTrapOnCompletion.333 = INTEGER: false(2)
CISCO-PING-MIB::ciscoPingSentPackets.333 = Counter32: 20
CISCO-PING-MIB::ciscoPingReceivedPackets.333 = Counter32: 20
CISCO-PING-MIB::ciscoPingMinRtt.333 = INTEGER: 1 milliseconds
CISCO-PING-MIB::ciscoPingAvgRtt.333 = INTEGER: 1 milliseconds
CISCO-PING-MIB::ciscoPingMaxRtt.333 = INTEGER: 1 milliseconds
CISCO-PING-MIB::ciscoPingCompleted.333 = INTEGER: true(1)
CISCO-PING-MIB::ciscoPingEntryOwner.333 = STRING: kjs
CISCO-PING-MIB::ciscoPingEntryStatus.333 = INTEGER: active(1)
```

To summarize, this script does the following:

1. Processes the ipsToPing hash by first destroying (as a just-in-case) and creating a new row in the table

2. Sleeps to give the router time to do its job

3. Gathers the results from the router, and deletes each row from the table

One enhancement that can be made is to persist each row to the table and let the router continually ping the target or targets. This could be accomplished by creating new entries on the router and setting the following OID:

```
ciscoPingDelay OBJECT-TYPE
        SYNTAX      Integer32 (0..3600000)
        UNITS       "milliseconds"
        MAX-ACCESS  read-create
        STATUS      current
        DESCRIPTION
                "Specifies the minimum amount of time to wait before sending
                the next packet in a sequence after receiving a response or
                declaring a timeout for a previous packet.  The actual delay
                may be greater due to internal task scheduling."
        DEFVAL { 0 }
        ::= { ciscoPingEntry 7 }
```

As the DESCRIPTION notes, ciscoPingDelay specifies a sort of sleep. The router will wait for the specified amount of time (in milliseconds) before it tries to ping the target again. Of course, you would also not want to destroy each row after you get the statistics from the routers, as is done in the earlier script.

Here are a couple of things to watch out for if you use this method:

- If you are the only one using the router to perform pings, creating unique row values is controlled by one person. If more than one person uses the router, you run the risk of stepping on each other's toes if someone picks the same unique row number as you.

- The router can reschedule these pings if it needs to. In other words, if it comes down to the router performing a routing function over a ping function, it's going to pick the routing function.

Simple SNMP Agent

Traditional SNMP agents typically give you all the monitoring and management features you could want. Sometimes you may wish you could write your own SNMP agent. Anyone who has looked at the Net-SNMP agent code knows how complex it is. Well, have no fear! The Net-SNMP package now comes with Perl bindings that allow you to create a Perl SNMP agent in a number of ways:

- Standalone SNMP agent
- AgentX subagent
- Embedded agent within the normal Net-SNMP agent

For this section, we thought it would be interesting to present a fully working Perl agent. This isn't so much to write yet another SNMP agent but rather to show how an SNMP agent operates.

The basic flow through the agent is as follows:

1. Create a new agent object
2. Register the top of the agent's OID tree
3. Register a callback subroutine
4. Sit and wait for requests

It's pretty straightforward, and so is the code itself. First things first, though. You need to get a copy of the Net-SNMP package from *http://www.net-snmp.org*. Follow the instructions for building and installing the package and Perl modules.

The complete agent source follows:

```
205  #!/usr/bin/perl
206
207  #
208  # File: agent.pl
209  #
210
211  use NetSNMP::agent (':all');
212  use NetSNMP::default_store (':all');
213  use NetSNMP::ASN (':all');
214  use NetSNMP::OID;
215  use SNMP;
216
217  my $port = "9161";
218  my $host = ".1.3.6.1.4.1.8072.25";
219  my $hrMemorySize = $host.".2.2";
220
```

```perl
221  sub myHandler{
222      my ($handler, $registration_info, $request_info, $requests) = @_;
223      my $request;
224      for($request = $requests; $request; $request = $request->next()) {
225          my $oid = $request->getOID();
226          if ($request_info->getMode() == MODE_GET) {
227              if ($oid == new NetSNMP::OID($hrMemorySize)) {
228                  my $value = getMemorySize();
229                  $request->setValue(ASN_INTEGER, $value);
230              }
231          } elsif ($request_info->getMode() == MODE_GETNEXT) {
232              if ($oid <= new NetSNMP::OID($host)) {
233                  $request->setOID($hrMemorySize);
234                  my $value = getMemorySize();
235                  $request->setValue(ASN_INTEGER, $value);
236              }
237          }
238      }
239  }
240
241  sub getMemorySize{
242      my $file = "/proc/meminfo";
243      my $total = 0;
244      open(FILE,$file) || die("Unable to open file: $!\n");
245      while(<FILE>){
246          chomp;
247          if($_ =~ /^MemTotal/){
248              # One Linux (Kernel 2.6.8-2-686), the entry looks like:
249              # MemTotal:      1026960 kB
250              ($total) = $_ =~ m/^MemTotal:.*?(\d+).*?kB$/;
251              last;
252          }
253      }
254      close(FILE);
255      return $total;
256  }
257
258  my $agent = new NetSNMP::agent(
259          'Name' => 'snmpd',
260          'Ports' => $port);
261
262  my $regoid = new NetSNMP::OID($host); #Beginning of Host Resources Tree
263  print "regoid: $regoid\n";
264  $regitem = $agent->register("mytest", $regoid, \&myHandler);
265  if($regitem == 0){
266      print "Error registering: $!\n";
267      exit -1;
268  }
269
270  my $running = 1;
271  $SIG{'TERM'} = sub {$running = 0;};
272  $SIG{'INT'} = sub {$running = 0;};
273  while($running) {
```

```
274      $agent->agent_check_and_process(1); # 1 blocks, and 0 does not
275    }
276    print "Good-bye!\n";
```

The agent mimics tracking a small portion of the Host Resources MIB (RFC 1514). While Net-SNMP has support for this MIB, it does serve as a good example of how a real agent works under the covers.

Here are some key points about the agent:

Line 217

This is the port the agent will listen on. You can optionally specify the protocol; e.g., tcp:9161 would have the agent listen on TCP port 9161.

Line 218

$host is the top of the OID tree that this agent implements. *.1.3.6.1.4.1.8072* is the Net-SNMP enterprise OID. We added *.25* to it since this corresponds to the Host Resources top-level OID.

Line 219

$hrMemorySize is the one and only managed variable we will implement. It represents the total memory on the system.

Lines 258 and 259

Line 258 begins the creation of a new agent. Line 259 gives a name to this agent. Note that the underlying Net-SNMP library is going to tack on a *.conf* to this attribute. We used *snmpd* so that the library would find the default *snmpd.conf* and use whatever access permissions are in it. If you don't have a configuration file for the library to use, your agent is effectively useless—it won't respond to any requests.

Line 262

Here we create a new OID object which represents the top of the agent's OID tree. The agent will respond to requests for any objects under this tree.

Line 264

The register method is used to define the subroutine that handles incoming requests. The first argument is a name, the second argument is the OID we created on Line 262, and the third argument is the subroutine name.

Line 274

Here we just sit and wait for requests to come in. The underlying library will call the subroutine we registered on Line 264 for us when a request comes in.

Line 221

This begins the subroutine for handling requests. In this agent, we respond to get and getnext requests, but there is no reason why we couldn't handle set requests as well.

Lines 228 and 234

> These lines call a routine to parse the */proc/meminfo* on Linux to get the total memory on the system. Note that this is not portable. Some operating systems, like Solaris, may support actual kernel calls that can return such information.

Lines 229 and 235

> Here we encode the value obtained from Line 228 or 234 and encode it as an integer. Why an integer? If we look in the Host Resources MIB for hrMemorySize, we see the following:

```
hrMemorySize OBJECT-TYPE
    SYNTAX KBytes
    ACCESS read-only
    STATUS mandatory
    DESCRIPTION
            "The amount of physical main memory contained by
            the host."
    ::= { hrStorage 2 }
```

> The SYNTAX is Kbytes. Kbytes is defined earlier in the MIB as:

```
-- memory size, expressed in units of 1024bytes
KBytes ::=    INTEGER (0..2147483647)
```

> It's an integer under the covers, so that's how we chose to encode the total memory.

That's it. The various modules installed by Net-SNMP have corresponding manpages. They provide good details for general usage.

Switch Port Control

Sometimes it can be handy to turn up or down a switch port. For example, you may want to play a prank on an annoying co-worker. Other times, it may be a case of disabling a host that is infected with a virus and spewing packets all over the network. Whatever the case may be, it can be helpful to have something like this in your toolbox.

Most people attach a serial cable from a laptop to the management port on the switch to configure it or manage it. To manage a switch via SNMP, you generally have to create a VLAN (which may encompass all the ports on the switch). This VLAN is configured with an IP address, which allows for SNMP access and control. The actual ability to manage a port comes via the Bridge MIB (RFC 1493). Most if not all switch vendors implement this MIB. Many vendors also have their own MIB that may enhance or extend the Bridge MIB, but we will focus on the RFC version to keep things generic.

To successfully manage a switch port, you have to know the following bits of information:

- IP address of host on port

- MAC address of host on port
- Switch port number

The key to managing your switch ports is keeping track of which hosts are on which switch ports. Tobias Oetiker, creator of MRTG, created a Perl script called *Cammer* (*http://people.ee.ethz.ch/~oetiker/webtools/mrtg/pub/contrib/cammer*). *Cammer* displays which MAC addresses are on a switch, along with IP address information. It does this by querying the Address Resolution Protocol (ARP) table on a router and then matching this up with what's on your switch. Here's a sample run:

```
$ ./cammer.pl public@switch public@router
Fa0/9       1   00:11:43:17:06:8d   192.168.0.48     dhcp48.domain
Fa0/3       1   00:60:f5:08:4e:3c   192.168.0.1      router.domain
Fa0/8       1   00:60:47:40:fd:14   192.168.0.130    dhcp130.domain
```

When running *Cammer*, you must pass it the community string for your switch and router. The first column is the interface name from the switch. The second column is the VLAN number, followed by the MAC address, IP address, and DNS name of the IP address (if available). Unfortunately, this script is Cisco-specific, but modifying it to operate with other vendors is doable.

For our purposes, we modified the *Cammer* source a little bit. The output now looks like this:

```
$ ./cammer2.pl public@switch public@router
192.168.0.148
          1 (ifIndex = 10, ifName = Fa0/9)  00:11:43:17:06:8d 192.168.0.48     dhcp48.
domain
          1 (ifIndex = 4, ifName = Fa0/3)   00:60:f5:08:4e:3c 192.168.0.1      router.
domain
          1 (ifIndex = 9, ifName = Fa0/8)   00:60:47:40:fd:14 192.168.0.130    dhcp130.
domain
```

The display now shows the *ifIndex* in addition to the *ifName*. The *ifIndex* is used later in the script that does the actual port control. The output from running diff on the original *Cammer* version and the one we modified follows:

```
51d50
<
62a62,65
> my %OID_TO_NONARRAY = ( 'dot1dBasePortIfIndex' =>  "1.3.6.1.2.1.17.1.4.1.2",);
>
>
>
129a133,134
>     my %macsToIfIndex;
>     my %macsToIfName;
132a138
>          #my $sws = SNMPv2c_Session->open ($opt{sw},$opt{swco}.'@'.$vlan,161)
141c147,152
<            $port{$vlan}{$mac}=$port;
---
```

```
>                   my $iid = snmpget($opt{swco}.'@'.$opt{sw},"$OID_TO_
NONARRAY{'dot1dBasePortIfIndex'}.$port");
>                   my $ifname = snmpget($opt{swco}.'@'.$opt{sw},"ifName.$iid");
>                   #my $ifname = snmpget($opt{swco}.'@'.$opt{sw},"$OID_TO_
NONARRAY{'ifName'}.$iid");
>                 $macsToIfIndex{$mac} = $iid;
>                 $macsToIfName{$mac} = $ifname;
>                  $port{$vlan}{$mac}=$port;
145c156,158
<          sub {  my($port,$if) = pretty(@_);
---
>          sub {
>          my($port,$if) = pretty(@_);
>          print "$port,$if\n";
166c179
<       push @{$output{$name}}, sprintf "%4s  %-17s  %-15s  %s
%s",$truevlan,$mac,$ip[0],$host[0],$quest;
---
>       push @{$output{$name}},
sprintf "%4s (ifIndex = %s, ifName = %s)  %-17s %-15s  %s
%s",$truevlan,$macsToIfIndex{$mac},$macsToIfName{$mac},$mac,$ip[0],$host[0],$quest
if($ip[0] ne "");
168a182
>     print "\n$opt{sw}\n";
249d262
<
```

The switch control Perl script that follows uses a few MIB objects from the Bridge MIB:

```perl
#!/usr/bin/perl

use SNMP;

use Getopt::Long;
GetOptions("mac=s"   => \$gMac,
           "index=s" => \$gIndex,
           "action=s" => \$gAction,
           );

($gMac,$gAction,$gIndex) = verifyInput($gMac,$gAction,$gIndex);

&SNMP::initMib();
&SNMP::loadModules(qw/BRIDGE-MIB/);

my $host = "192.168.0.148";
my $roComm = "public";
my $rwComm = "private";

$roSession = new SNMP::Session(DestHost => $host, Community => $roComm,
                               UseSprintValue => 1, Version=>2);
die "session creation error: $SNMP::Session::ErrorStr" unless
   (defined $roSession);
```

```perl
$rwSession = new SNMP::Session(DestHost => $host, Community => $rwComm,
                              UseSprintValue => 1, Version=>2);
die "session creation error: $SNMP::Session::ErrorStr" unless
    (defined $rwSession);

findMac();

sub findMac {
    my($discover) = @_;
    $vars = new SNMP::VarList(['dot1dTpFdbAddress'], ['dot1dTpFdbPort']);
    # get first row
    my ($mac, $port) = $roSession->getnext($vars);
    die $roSession->{ErrorStr} if ($roSession->{ErrorStr});
    while (!$roSession->{ErrorStr} and $$vars[0]->tag eq "dot1dTpFdbAddress"
          || $$vars[0]->tag eq "dot1dBasePortIfIndex"){
        my @tmac = $mac =~ m/(\w{1,2}) (\w{1,2}) (\w{1,2}) (\w{1,2}) (\w{1,2}) (\
w{1,2})/g;
        $mac = sanitizeMac(sprintf("%s:%s:%s:%s:%s:%s",@tmac));
        if($gMac eq $mac){
            # We found it
            my $ifnum = $roSession->get("dot1dBasePortIfIndex\.$port");
            if($ifnum eq $gIndex){
                doAction($gAction,$ifnum);
            }else{
                print "$mac has moved to ifIndex $ifnum\n";
            }
            last;
        }
        # keep going
        ($mac, $port) = $roSession->getnext($vars);
    }
}

sub doAction{
    my ($action,$ifnum) = @_;
    my $ifname = $roSession->get("ifDescr\.$ifnum");
    if($action eq "up"){
        print "Turning $ifname $action (ifNum is $ifnum)..\n";
        $rwSession->set([["ifAdminStatus", $ifnum, 1, "INTEGER"]]);
    }elsif($action eq "down"){
        print "Turning $ifname $action (ifNum is $ifnum)...\n";
        $rwSession->set([["ifAdminStatus", $ifnum, 2, "INTEGER"]]);
    }
    if($rwSession->{ErrorStr}){
        print "An error occurred during processing: $rwSession->{ErrorStr}\n";
    }
}

sub sanitizeMac{
    my($mac) = @_;
    my @tmac = split(/:/,$mac);
    foreach my $byte (0..$#tmac){
        $tmac[$byte] =~ s/^0//g;
        $tmac[$byte] = lc($tmac[$byte]);
    }
```

```
    $mac = sprintf("%s:%s:%s:%s:%s:%s",@tmac);
    return $mac;
}


sub verifyInput{
    my($mac,$action,$index) = @_;
    if(($mac eq "" && $action eq "" && $index eq "")) {
        usage();
        exit;
    }
    if($action eq ""){
        usage();
        exit;
    }
    $mac = sanitizeMac($mac);
    $action = lc($action);
    if($action ne "up" && $action ne "down"){
        usage();
        exit;
    }
    return ($mac,$action,$index);
}

sub usage{
    print "Usage:\t$0 --mac=0:f:0:d:55:a --index=10 --action=up\n";
    print "\tSpecify a MAC adddress and the index in the interfaces MIB tree where
this port lives on the switch. Action can be EITHER \"up\" OR \"down\"\n";
}
```

Here are some key points about this script:

- The MAC address that is passed to the script is normalized to a common format.

- The findMac() routine makes use of the *dot1dTpFdbAddress*, *dot1dTpFdbPort*, and *dot1dBasePortIfIndex* OIDs. Here are their MIB definitions:

```
dot1dTpFdbAddress OBJECT-TYPE
                SYNTAX   MacAddress
                ACCESS   read-only
                STATUS   mandatory
                DESCRIPTION
                        "A unicast MAC address for which the bridge has
                        forwarding and/or filtering information."
                REFERENCE
                        "IEEE 802.1D-1990: Section 3.9.1, 3.9.2"
                ::= { dot1dTpFdbEntry 1 }

dot1dTpFdbPort OBJECT-TYPE
                SYNTAX   INTEGER
                ACCESS   read-only
                STATUS   mandatory
                DESCRIPTION
                        "Either the value '0', or the port number of the
                        port on which a frame having a source address
                        equal to the value of the corresponding instance
```

```
                    of dot1dTpFdbAddress has been seen.  A value of
                    '0' indicates that the port number has not been
                    learned but that the bridge does have some
                    forwarding/filtering information about this
                    address (e.g., in the dot1dStaticTable).
                    Implementors are encouraged to assign the port
                    value to this object whenever it is learned even
                    for addresses for which the corresponding value of
                    dot1dTpFdbStatus is not learned(3)."
        ::= { dot1dTpFdbEntry 2 }

dot1dBasePortIfIndex OBJECT-TYPE
            SYNTAX  INTEGER
            ACCESS  read-only
            STATUS  mandatory
            DESCRIPTION
                    "The value of the instance of the ifIndex object,
                    defined in MIB-II, for the interface corresponding
                    to this port."
            ::= { dot1dBasePortEntry 2 }
```

dot1dTpFdbAddress gathers all the MAC addresses on the switch for which it has forwarding information. *dot1dTpFdbPort* gets the corresponding port number and *dot1dBasePortIfIndex* is the port to *ifIndex* mapping. findMac( ) keeps going until it finds a MAC address that matches the one specified on the command line. Once found, it looks to see if the *dot1dBasePortIfIndex* value matches the one specified by the user. If it does, it performs the action. If it doesn't, it displays a message and exits.

• The doAction( ) method performs the actual port control operation. It uses the *ifAdminStatus* OID to set the port to up or down.

Here are some sample runs of the script:

```
$ ./swcontrol.pl --mac=00:11:43:17:06:8d --index=10 --action=up
Turning FastEthernet0/9 up (ifNum is 10)..
$ ./swcontrol.pl --mac=00:11:43:17:06:8d --index=10 --action=down
Turning FastEthernet0/9 down (ifNum is 10)...
$ ./swcontrol.pl --mac=00:11:43:17:06:8d --index=11 --action=up
0:11:43:17:6:8d has moved to ifIndex 10
$
```

The last run shows output when the wrong index is used on the command line. This index check is used as a safety since *ifIndex* values can shift or move at any time. When this happens, you may need to rerun *Cammer* to update your mappings.

Finally, here are some ways to enhance this script:

• *Cammer* needs to be run on a somewhat regular basis, since hosts can move (especially laptops).

• *Cammer* could be extended to store its results in a database. The switch control script could then be made to read from the database to get the proper index information.

Wireless Networking

This section will show how to gather management statistics from wireless access points using the 802.11 MIB. The IEEE 802.11 MIB is freely available from many sites, including *http://www.cs.ucla.edu/~hywong1/doc/IEEE802dot11-MIB.my*. The MIB itself is pretty dense. A detailed discussion of this MIB is beyond the scope of this chapter. Instead, we will present a script that can gather certain data points from your WAP. Consider the following script.

```perl
#!/usr/bin/perl

use SNMP;
$SNMP::use_sprint_value = 1;
&SNMP::loadModules('IEEE802dot11-MIB');

my $host = "192.168.1.4";
my $sess = new SNMP::Session(DestHost => $host,
                             Version => 2,
                             Community => "public");

my %wapStats;
my $var = new SNMP::Varbind(['dot11CurrentChannel']);
do {
  $val = $sess->getnext($var);
  my $channel = $var->[$SNMP::Varbind::val_f];
  my $ifIndex = $var->[$SNMP::Varbind::iid_f];
  my($ssid, $mac, $manufacturer, $model, $rtsFailureCount,
  $ackFailureCount, $fcsErrorCount) = $sess->get([
        ['dot11DesiredSSID',$ifIndex],
        ['dot11MACAddress',$ifIndex],
        ['dot11ManufacturerID',$ifIndex],
        ['dot11ProductID',$ifIndex],
        ['dot11RTSFailureCount',$ifIndex],
        ['dot11ACKFailureCount',$ifIndex],
        ['dot11FCSErrorCount',$ifIndex]
        ]);
  $wapStats{$ifIndex} = "$channel,$ssid,$mac,$manufacturer,"
  $wapStats{$ifIndex} .= "$model,$rtsFailureCount,$ackFailureCount,$fcsErrorCount";
}unless($sess->{ErrorNum});

foreach my $key (sort keys %wapStats){
        my($channel, $ssid, $mac, $manufacturer, $model,
        $rtsFailureCount, $ackFailureCount, $fcsErrorCount) =
                split(/,/,$wapStats{$key});

        print "WAP $ssid with MAC Address $mac (Manufacturer: $manufacturer, Model:
$model, Channel: $channel, ifIndex: $key)\n";
        print "\tdot11RTSFailureCount: $rtsFailureCount\n";
        print "\tdot11ACKFailureCount: $ackFailureCount\n";
        print "\tdot11FCSErrorCount: $fcsErrorCount\n";
}
```

First, notice that we're using the Net-SNMP Perl module. Second, note the MIB module we load:

```
&SNMP::loadModules('IEEE802dot11-MIB');
```

This is critical. It allows us to use textual object names in the script as opposed to numeric OIDs. The first thing we do is set up a variable binding for *dot11CurrentChannel*. This is defined in the 802.11 MIB as:

```
dot11CurrentChannel OBJECT-TYPE
        SYNTAX INTEGER (1..14)
        MAX-ACCESS read-write
        STATUS current
        DESCRIPTION
            "The current operating frequency channel of the DSSS
            PHY. Valid channel numbers are as defined in 15.4.6.2"
     ::= {    dot11PhyDSSSEntry 1 }
```

This is the channel ID currently in use. This entry is in a table that contains other objects. We're concerned only with the channel right now. Also note that this table is indexed by *ifIndex*, which is the same object you might remember from the *interfaces* subtree. We perform a getnext on this object that returns the channel and the *ifIndex*. We then perform a get of seven objects. The first four are the SSID, MAC address, manufacturer ID, and product ID, respectively. The remaining three may seem obscure. It will become apparent why we chose these in a few moments. First, here are the last three objects from the MIB:

```
dot11RTSFailureCount OBJECT-TYPE
        SYNTAX Counter32
        MAX-ACCESS read-only
        STATUS current
        DESCRIPTION


        "This counter shall increment when a CTS is not received in
        response to an RTS."

    ::= { dot11CountersEntry 8 }

dot11ACKFailureCount OBJECT-TYPE
        SYNTAX Counter32
        MAX-ACCESS read-only
        STATUS current
        DESCRIPTION

            "This counter shall increment when an ACK is not received
            when expected."

    ::= {    dot11CountersEntry 9 }

dot11FCSErrorCount OBJECT-TYPE
        SYNTAX Counter32
        MAX-ACCESS read-only
```

```
STATUS current
DESCRIPTION

        "This counter shall increment when an FCS error is
        detected in a received MPDU."

    ::= {  dot11CountersEntry 12 }
```

Before we expand on these objects, let's look at the output from this script:

```
$ ./wapstats.pl
WAP "thehouse2" with MAC Address 0:f:b5:3:fd:6f (Manufacturer: NETGEAR, Model: WG302,
Channel: 10, ifIndex: 1)
        dot11RTSFailureCount: 0
        dot11ACKFailureCount: 0
        dot11FCSErrorCount: 0
```

As you can see, we get some identifying information for WAP. Of course, you can expand on this script and gather other parts of the 802.11 MIB or other statistics from the *interfaces* MIB.

Now, what about these three objects? The first one, *dot11RTSFailureCount*, basically means that a clear to send (CTS) was never received when a ready to send (RTS) was sent. *dot11ACKFailureCount*, according to Matthew Gast, author of O'Reilly's *802.11 Wireless Networks: The Definitive Guide*, "directly tracks the number of inbound acknowledgments lost. Whenever a frame is transmitted that should be acknowledged, and the acknowledgment is not forthcoming, this counter is incremented." *dot11FCSErrorCount* is the frame check sequence (FCS) error count. Basically, the FCS is extra padding in a frame for error control. If this count ever goes up, it could be indicative of problems with the base station subsystem (BSS)—i.e., the radio-related functions of a WAP. As these descriptions imply, these three objects are indicators that something bad is happening.

While at the University of California, Santa Cruz, Max Baker proposed a way of automatically setting a WAP's channel based on a score. The score is made up of the three aforementioned objects. The score he proposes is:

```
Score = .2 * FCS Errors + .4 * RTS Failures + .4 * ACK Failures
```

We can add that score to our script with the following subroutine:

```
sub scoreChannel {
  my($rtsFailureCount, $ackFailureCount, $fcsErrorCount) = @_;
  return (.2 * $fcsErrorCount + .4 * $rtsFailureCount +
    .4 * $ackFailureCount);
}
```

Let's run the *stats* script again with that addition:

```
$ ./wapstats.pl
WAP "thehouse2" with MAC Address 0:f:b5:3:fd:6f (Manufacturer: NETGEAR, Model: WG302,
Channel: 10, ifIndex: 1)
        dot11RTSFailureCount: 0
        dot11ACKFailureCount: 0
```

```
dot11FCSErrorCount: 0
Channel score: 0
```

The lower the score, the better. We can find the lowest-scoring channel in one of two ways:

- Actively monitoring the WAP over time and noting the score for a given channel. The problem with this technique is that you must periodically change the channel number so that other wireless devices can pick it up and begin using it. You then need to monitor these error indicator variables for some period of time, change the channel setting, let people connect to the new channel, gather error variables for a period of time, and keep doing this for as many channels as you can set on your WAP. Changing the channel can also be done via SNMP (more on this in a second).

- Changing the channels, via SNMP, and sitting on each one for about a minute (this is the solution Max proposes). After the minute is up, gather the stats, calculate the score, and move on to the next one. Once you are done, figure out which channel has the lowest score and set the WAP to this channel. The issue with this approach is that you have to coordinate the changing of the channels with someone or something finding the new channel setting and using it. It's similar to the first approach, but since you are monitoring each channel for a brief period, you may want to somehow automate the device that does the actual connection. Note that wireless cards are capable of finding a new channel automatically.

Once you find the lowest-scoring channel, you can force the WAP to use that channel by using the same object we used to discover the channel in the first place: *dot11CurrentChannel*. The following code can be used to set a new channel for a WAP:

```
$sess->set([['dot11CurrentChannel',$ifIndex,$newChannel,"INTEGER"]]);
```

Even wireless devices can be managed via SNMP. With some creativity and thought, you can bring your WAPs into your network management architecture and manage them effectively.

SNMP: The Object-Oriented Way

The SNMP::Info Perl package was developed at the University of California, Santa Cruz. The official web site for this package is *http://snmp-info.sourceforge.net*.

SNMP::Info is based on the Net-SNMP Perl module. It allows you to obtain various information from a device without having to know any OIDs, MIBs, etc., and it does so with object orientation (OO). How does it do this? It supports a well-developed list of MIBs, and it can discover the type of device you are trying to query. If it knows about the device, you can use predefined methods to get interface information and other things. Here's an example script that gathers information about interfaces on a switch:

```perl
#!/usr/bin/perl

use SNMP::Info;

my $info = new SNMP::Info(
                          # Auto Discover more specific Device Class
                          AutoSpecify => 1,
                          Debug       => 0,
                          # The rest is passed to SNMP::Session
                          DestHost    => '192.168.0.148',
                          Community   => 'public',
                          Version     => 2
                         ) or die "Can't connect to device.\n";

my $err = $info->error();
die "SNMP Community or Version probably wrong connecting to device. $err\n" if
defined $err;

$name  = $info->name();
$class = $info->class();
print "SNMP::Info is using this device class : $class\n";

# Find out the Duplex status for the ports
my $interfaces = $info->interfaces();
my $i_duplex   = $info->i_duplex();

# Get CDP Neighbor info
my $c_if       = $info->c_if();
my $c_ip       = $info->c_ip();
my $c_port     = $info->c_port();

# Print out data per port
foreach my $iid (keys %$interfaces){
   my $duplex = $i_duplex->{$iid};
   # Print out physical port name, not snmp iid
   my $port   = $interfaces->{$iid};

   # The CDP Table has table entries different from the interface tables.
   # So we use c_if to get the map from the cdp table to the interface table.

   my %c_map = reverse %$c_if;
   my $c_key = $c_map{$iid};
   my $neighbor_ip   = $c_ip->{$c_key};
   my $neighbor_port = $c_port->{$c_key};

   print "$port: $duplex duplex";
   print " connected to $neighbor_ip / $neighbor_port\n" if defined $remote_ip;
   print "\n";
}
```

And here's the output:

```
$ ./getinterfaceinfo.pl
SNMP::Info is using this device class : SNMP::Info::Layer2::C2900
```

```
FastEthernet0/5: half duplex
FastEthernet0/10: half duplex
FastEthernet0/2: full duplex
FastEthernet0/6: half duplex
FastEthernet0/8: half duplex
FastEthernet0/1: half duplex
FastEthernet0/11: half duplex
Null0:  duplex
VLAN2:  duplex
FastEthernet0/7: half duplex
FastEthernet0/3: half duplex
VLAN1:  duplex
FastEthernet0/9: half duplex
FastEthernet0/12: half duplex
FastEthernet0/4: half duplex
$
```

Let's talk a little bit about the script. First, we create an SNMP::Info object, with such typical parameters as the host we are querying, community string, and SNMP version. The constructor for SNMP::Info also has an `AutoSpecify` parameter, which instructs the session we create to try and discover the device class. This code will get the specific device class:

```
$class = $info->class( );
```

The following code will get all the interfaces from the remote host:

```
my $interfaces = $info->interfaces( );
```

It doesn't get any easier than that. Let's look at what each OO method does, according to the SNMP::Info documentation:

`$info->interfaces( )`

Returns a reference to the map between *ifIndex* in the interface subtree and the physical port. On the 2900 devices, i_name isn't reliable, so we override it to just the description. Next, all dots are changed to forward slashes so that the physical port name is the same as the broadcasted Cisco Discovery Protocol (CDP) port name (e.g., Ethernet0.1 becomes Ethernet0/1).

`$info->i_duplex( )`

Returns a reference to a map of *ifIndex* IDs to the current link duplex.

`$info->c_if( )`

The CDP is a Layer 2 protocol that supplies topology information to other devices that also speak CDP (mostly switches and routers). CDP is implemented in Cisco and some HP devices. c_if( ) returns the CDP interface mapping to the SNMP Interface Table.

`$info->c_ip( )`

Returns a remote CDP IP address.

`$info->c_port( )`

Returns a remote CDP port ID.

The rest of the program is just a foreach loop that runs through all the data structures. Now let's look at another script:

```perl
#!/usr/bin/perl

use SNMP::Info;

my $bridge = new SNMP::Info (
                               AutoSpecify => 1,
                               Debug       => 0,
                               DestHost    => '192.168.0.148',
                               Community   => 'public',
                               Version     => 2
                               );

my $class = $bridge->class();
print " Using device sub class : $class\n";

# Grab Forwarding Tables
my $interfaces = $bridge->interfaces();
my $fw_mac     = $bridge->fw_mac();
my $fw_port    = $bridge->fw_port();
my $bp_index   = $bridge->bp_index();

foreach my $fw_index (keys %$fw_mac){
    my $mac   = $fw_mac->{$fw_index};
    my $bp_id = $fw_port->{$fw_index};
    my $iid   = $bp_index->{$bp_id};
    my $port  = $interfaces->{$iid};

    print "Port:$port forwarding to $mac\n";
}
```

And its output:

```
$ ./bridge.pl
Using device sub class : SNMP::Info::Layer2::C2900
Port:FastEthernet0/12 forwarding to 00:04:9a:da:5e:4c
Port:FastEthernet0/10 forwarding to 00:04:9a:da:5e:4a
Port:FastEthernet0/2 forwarding to 00:0f:1f:d3:c6:3a
Port:FastEthernet0/2 forwarding to 00:11:43:04:a5:25
Port:FastEthernet0/11 forwarding to 00:04:9a:da:5e:4b
Port:FastEthernet0/2 forwarding to 00:0f:20:41:b8:ed
Port:FastEthernet0/2 forwarding to 00:11:43:04:c2:e6
Port:FastEthernet0/2 forwarding to 00:0b:db:d2:d6:10
Port:FastEthernet0/2 forwarding to 00:0f:1f:df:ef:f9
$
```

This script prints port-forwarding information for a bridge. Let's look at some of the methods used in this script:

$bridge->fw_mac()

Returns a reference to a hash of forwarding table MAC addresses as defined in the BRIDGE-MIB object *dot1dTpFdbAddress*.

`$bridge->fw_port( )`

Returns a reference to a hash of learned bridge ports. See *dot1dTpFdbPort* in the BRIDGE-MIB for more detail.

`$bridge->bp_index( )`

Returns a reference to a hash of bridge port table entries mapped back to *ifIndex* entries.

Of course, once we've run these methods, we just use a foreach loop to access the data structures and print the forwarding details.

Extending SNMP::Info

SNMP::Info is great for talking to network devices. But what if you want to, say, talk to Unix systems and obtain more information than what is provided by RFC 1213 and other similar MIBs? Well, luckily the author of SNMP::Info has made it quite easy to extend.

We decided to create a module called HostResources, which makes use of some of the Host Resources objects. Here's the entire Perl module:

```perl
package SNMP::Info::HostResources;

$VERSION = 1.0;

use strict;

use Exporter;
use SNMP::Info;

@SNMP::Info::HostResources::ISA = qw/SNMP::Info Exporter/;
@SNMP::Info::HostResources::EXPORT_OK = qw//;

use vars qw/$VERSION %FUNCS %GLOBALS %MIBS %MUNGE $AUTOLOAD $INIT $DEBUG/;

%MIBS    = (%SNMP::Info::MIBS,
             'HOST-RESOURCES-MIB'  => 'host',
    );

%GLOBALS = (%SNMP::Info::GLOBALS,
             'hr_users' => 'hrSystemNumUsers',
             'hr_processes' => 'hrSystemProcesses',
             'hr_date' => 'hrSystemDate',
             );

%FUNCS   = (%SNMP::Info::FUNCS,
             # HostResources MIB objects
             'hr_sindex'  => 'hrStorageIndex',
             'hr_sdescr'  => 'hrStorageDescr',
             'hr_sused'   => 'hrStorageUsed',
             );
```

```perl
%MUNGE    = (%SNMP::Info::MUNGE,
            'hr_date' => \&munge_hrdate,
           );

sub munge_hrdate {
    my($oct) = @_;
    #
    # hrSystemDate has a syntax of DateAndTime, which is defined in SNMPv2-TC as
    #
    #DateAndTime ::= TEXTUAL-CONVENTION
    # DISPLAY-HINT "2d-1d-1d,1d:1d:1d.1d,1a1d:1d"
    # STATUS        current
    # DESCRIPTION
    #         "A date-time specification.
    #
    #             field  octets  contents               range
    #             -----  ------  --------               -----
    #               1     1-2    year*                  0..65536
    #               2      3     month                  1..12
    #               3      4     day                    1..31
    #               4      5     hour                   0..23
    #               5      6     minutes                0..59
    #               6      7     seconds                0..60
    #                            (use 60 for leap-second)
    #               7      8     deci-seconds           0..9
    #               8      9     direction from UTC     '+' / '-'
    #               9     10     hours from UTC*        0..13
    #              10     11     minutes from UTC       0..59
    #
    #         * Notes:
    #         - the value of year is in network-byte order
    #         - daylight savings time in New Zealand is +13
    #
    #         For example, Tuesday May 26, 1992 at 1:30:15 PM EDT would be
    #         displayed as:
    #
    #                         1992-5-26,13:30:15.0,-4:0
    #
    #         Note that if only local time is known, then timezone
    #         information (fields 8-10) is not present."
    #     SYNTAX      OCTET STRING (SIZE (8 | 11))
    #

    my ($year1, $year2, $month, $day, $hour, $min, $secs, $decisecs,
        $direction, $hoursFromUTC, $minFromUTC) = split(/ /, sprintf("%d %d %d %d %d
%d %d %d %d %d %d",unpack('C*',$oct)));
    my $value = 0;
    $direction = chr($direction);
    $value = $value * 256 + $year1;
    $value = $value * 256 + $year2;
    my $year = $value;
    return
        "$year-$month-$day,$hour:$min:$secs:$decisecs,$direction$hoursFromUTC:
$minFromUTC";
```

```
}

1; # don't forget this line
```

Let's take a look at this module. The first line (package `SNMP::Info::HostResources;`) names the module and the package we are going to be a part of—in this case, SNMP::Info. The `%MIBS` hash configures SNMP::Info with a list of various MIBs you will use in the module. Here we loaded `HOST-RESOURCES-MIB` and gave it the name of the top-level OID in that MIB, host. `%SNMP::Info::MIBS` loads global SNMP::Info MIBs.

The `%GLOBALS` hash lists scalar OIDs that we plan to use—i.e., OIDs that are not part of a column in a table. `%SNMP::Info::GLOBALS` loads SNMP::Info globals. These globals include RFC 1213 objects *sysUptime*, *sysDescr*, etc. *hrSystemNumUsers* is:

```
hrSystemNumUsers OBJECT-TYPE
    SYNTAX      Gauge32
    MAX-ACCESS read-only
    STATUS      current
    DESCRIPTION
        "The number of user sessions for which this host is
        storing state information.  A session is a collection
        of processes requiring a single act of user
        authentication and possibly subject to collective job
        control."
    ::= { hrSystem 5 }
```

hrSystemProcesses is:

```
hrSystemProcesses OBJECT-TYPE
    SYNTAX      Gauge32
    MAX-ACCESS read-only
    STATUS      current
    DESCRIPTION
        "The number of process contexts currently loaded or
        running on this system."
    ::= { hrSystem 6 }
```

hrSystemDate is:

```
hrSystemDate OBJECT-TYPE
    SYNTAX      DateAndTime
    MAX-ACCESS read-write
    STATUS      current
    DESCRIPTION
        "The host's notion of the local date and time of day."
    ::= { hrSystem 2 }
```

The `%FUNCS` hash lists columnar OIDs to query. In this example, we query two items from the *hrStorageTable*. *hrStorageTable* is defined as:

```
hrStorageTable OBJECT-TYPE
    SYNTAX      SEQUENCE OF HrStorageEntry
    MAX-ACCESS not-accessible
    STATUS      current
    DESCRIPTION
```

"The (conceptual) table of logical storage areas on
the host.

An entry shall be placed in the storage table for each
logical area of storage that is allocated and has
fixed resource limits. The amount of storage
represented in an entity is the amount actually usable
by the requesting entity, and excludes loss due to
formatting or file system reference information.

These entries are associated with logical storage
areas, as might be seen by an application, rather than
physical storage entities which are typically seen by
an operating system. Storage such as tapes and
floppies without file systems on them are typically
not allocated in chunks by the operating system to
requesting applications, and therefore shouldn't
appear in this table. Examples of valid storage for
this table include disk partitions, file systems, ram
(for some architectures this is further segmented into
regular memory, extended memory, and so on), backing
store for virtual memory ('swap space').

This table is intended to be a useful diagnostic for
'out of memory' and 'out of buffers' types of
failures. In addition, it can be a useful performance
monitoring tool for tracking memory, disk, or buffer
usage."
    ::= { hrStorage 3 }
```

*hrStorageIndex* is:

```
hrStorageIndex OBJECT-TYPE
    SYNTAX      Integer32 (1..2147483647)
    MAX-ACCESS read-only
    STATUS      current
    DESCRIPTION
        "A unique value for each logical storage area
        contained by the host."
    ::= { hrStorageEntry 1 }
```

hrStorageDescr is:

```
hrStorageDescr OBJECT-TYPE
    SYNTAX      DisplayString
    MAX-ACCESS read-only
    STATUS      current
    DESCRIPTION
        "A description of the type and instance of the storage
        described by this entry."
    ::= { hrStorageEntry 3 }
```

hrStorageUsed is:

```
hrStorageUsed OBJECT-TYPE
    SYNTAX      Integer32 (0..2147483647)
```
```

```
MAX-ACCESS read-only
STATUS      current
DESCRIPTION
    "The amount of the storage represented by this entry
    that is allocated, in units of
    hrStorageAllocationUnits."
::= { hrStorageEntry 6 }
```

We need *hrStorageIndex* as a way to access *hrStorageDescr* and *hrStorageUsed*, which will be indexed based on *hrStorageIndex*.

%MUNGE lists methods, in your module, that will be called based on values in the %GLOBALS or %FUNCS hashes. For example, in the initialization for %MUNGE, we have:

```
'hr_date' => \&munge_hrdate,
```

'hr_date' is also defined in %GLOBALS. Once SNMP::Info performs the actual SNMP operation on the OID for this identifier, it will call munge_hrdate and pass it the value that was retrieved.

The basic reason for having this %MUNGE data structure is to allow for routines to be defined that can perform extended processing. Take the *hrSystemDate* OID. Its SYN-TAX is *DateAndTime*, which is a textual convention defined in the SNMPv2-TC MIB. The actual definition for *DateAndTime* is provided in the subroutine in the module, but basically we are handed a raw OctetString and we must decode the string and format the date and time as specified by this textual convention for *Date-AndTime*. Note that the subroutine returns the converted value. This is an important step, so don't forget it.

Once your module is done, you need to modify some SNMP::Info files. First, copy your new module over to where SNMP::Info is installed:

```
$ cp HostResources.pm /usr/local/share/perl/5.8.4/SNMP/Info/
```

Now edit */usr/local/share/perl/5.8.4/SNMP/Info.pm* and find the following line in the device_type( ) method:

```
return undef unless (defined $layers and length($layers));
```

now comment it out:

```
#return undef unless (defined $layers and length($layers));
```

The reason for this is that some host-based agents may not have sysServices set, which is what this is checking for. In the same method, find the lines that look like this:

```
# These devices don't claim to have Layer1-3 but we like em anyway.
} else {
    $objtype = 'SNMP::Info::Layer2::ZyXEL_DSLAM' if ($desc =~ /8-port .DSL
Module\(Annex .\)/i);
}
```

And make it look like this:

```
    # These devices don't claim to have Layer1-3 but we like em anyway.
    } elsif($desc =~ /linux|unix|windows/i){
        $objtype = 'SNMP::Info::HostResources';
    } else {
        $objtype = 'SNMP::Info::Layer2::ZyXEL_DSLAM' if ($desc =~ /8-port .DSL
Module\(Annex .\)/i);
    }
```

This allows SNMP::Info to create and return a proper HostResources object. Here is an example script which uses this new module:

```perl
#!/usr/bin/perl

use SNMP::Info::HostResources;

my $host = new SNMP::Info (
                            AutoSpecify => 1,
                            Debug       => 0,
                            DestHost    => '127.0.0.1',
                            Community   => 'public',
                            Version     => 2
                          );

my $class = $host->class();
print "Using device sub class : $class\n\n";

my $users = $host->hr_users();
my $processes = $host->hr_processes();
my $date = $host->hr_date();

print "(System date: $date) There are $users users running $processes processes\n\n";

my $storage_index = $host->hr_sindex();
my $storage_descr = $host->hr_sdescr();
my $used = $host->hr_sused();

foreach my $index (keys %$storage_index){
    print "$storage_descr->{$index} is using $used->{$index}\n";
}
```

Note that $host->hr_users() and $host->hr_processes() are called out of *%GLO-BALS*, and $host->hr_sindex() and $host->hr_sdescr() are called out of *%FUNCS*. And here is a sample run:

```
$ ./host.pl
Using device sub class : SNMP::Info::HostResources

(System date: 2005-5-17,13:12:15:0,-4:0)  There are 5 users running 85 processes

/home is using 839925
/ is using 702477
Memory Buffers is using 156044
Swap Space is using 0
/proc/bus/usb is using 0
```

```
Real Memory is using 909092
/sys is using 0
$
```

SNMP::Info is a well-thought-out API. It is perfect for people who may not wish to think about the gory details of OIDs, MIBS, etc. The downside is that if you are going to extend SNMP::Info, you need to know about these details. However, you may be in a situation where you want to allow others to utilize SNMP to write scripts but aren't interested in spending a week teaching people SNMP. You can instead hand someone this module with minimal instruction and they can become productive quite quickly.

Final Words

Our goal in this chapter was twofold: to provide both specific and generic scripts for system administration tasks. More to the point, we wanted to show you what's possible and get you thinking about how you might write scripts that provide elaborate custom monitoring features. If you're thinking creatively about what you can do with SNMP, we've succeeded.

## CHAPTER 12

MRTG

The Multi Router Traffic Grapher (MRTG) is a freely available and fully configurable trend analysis tool that's easy to configure and use. It's a surprisingly small, lightweight package because it doesn't implement a heavyweight user interface. Instead, it generates graphs in the form of GIF or PNG images; these graphs are embedded in standard HTML pages. Therefore, you can view MRTG's output using any web browser and even make its reports visible across your network by using a web server.

Although MRTG is best at displaying usage graphs for router interfaces, it can be configured to graph things like memory usage, load average, and disk usage on server equipment. MRTG is particularly useful for determining when something "peaks out" for an extended period of time, which indicates that you have a capacity problem and need to upgrade. For example, you might find that your T1 interface is maxed out during your peak business hours and you need to upgrade to a bigger circuit, or you might find that you need to add more memory to a server. Likewise, MRTG may let you know that your network connections are operating at a fraction of the available bandwidth and that you can therefore eliminate a few T1 circuits and reduce your telecommunications costs.

Many sites that use MRTG use its default graphing capabilities for capacity planning and provisioning. MRTG doesn't provide the fine-grained statistical tools you need to calculate baseline information or project when your network will need to be upgraded. However, it can be a very useful tool for businesses that don't have the resources to purchase a full-fledged trend analysis package. Baselines and projections are invaluable, but MRTG's graphs can give you similar behavior at a glance; your eyes are very good at spotting typical behavior and trends, even if they can't give you the statistical analysis that managers might like.

MRTG has many options that allow you to customize how it operates. It is beyond the scope of this chapter to discuss every option; instead, we will discuss how to install MRTG and use its default graphing capabilities. We'll also outline how you can configure MRTG to gather system information from a server.

It's important to understand that MRTG is not an NMS solution. Although its graphing capabilities make it look superficially like an NMS, it's really a simple polling engine that's very clever about the output it generates. It performs the same get functions that an NMS would, but its job isn't problem detection and resolution. It doesn't have a facility for generating alarms or processing traps, nor does it have the ability to set objects. It's simply designed to provide a graphical view of how your network is performing. If you're interested in an open source NMS package, you should investigate OpenNMS (*http://www.opennms.org*). This and other open source NMS packages are described in Appendix G.

Using MRTG

Before using MRTG, you have to download and install the software. The primary MRTG web site is *http://www.mrtg.org*. The download link takes you to a directory maintained by MRTG's inventor and primary developer, Tobias Oetiker (*http://people.ee.ethz.ch/~oetiker/webtools/mrtg/pub/*). This directory contains some older MRTG releases, as well as the current one. We downloaded the file *mrtg-2.10.15.tar.gz* (the Unix version) from the list. We will focus on that version in this chapter.

MRTG requires four third-party packages to run: Perl Version 5.004_5 (or newer) and the *gd*, *libpng*, and *zlib* libraries. MRTG comes with a Perl-based implementation of SNMP, so you don't have to worry about getting and installing any SNMP libraries. You can determine what version of Perl you have (and whether it's installed) by typing the command perl –v. This may or may not spit out a bunch of information. If it does, the first line will be the version of Perl you have installed. If you get some sort of "command not found" error, Perl may not be installed. In any event, go to *http://www.perl.com* to get the latest version of Perl.

The *gd* library is used to generate the GIF images that MRTG displays. You can download it from *http://www.boutell.com/gd/*. The other two packages, *libpng* and *zlib*, are also used for various aspects of graphic image creation. They are available from *http://sourceforge.net/projects/libpng/*.

Once you have ensured that Perl, *gd*, *libpng*, and *zlib* are installed on your machine, download and unpack the Unix version of MRTG with the following commands:

```
[root][linuxserver] > cd /usr/local
[root][linuxserver] > tar -zxvf mrtg-2.10.15.tar.gz
```

Once it's unpacked, cd into the directory it created (which should be *mrtg-2.10.15*) and read the installation hints from the *README* file. To build MRTG, you execute three commands:

```
[root][linuxserver] ~/mrtg-2.10.15> ./configure
[root][linuxserver] ~/mrtg-2.10.15> make
[root][linuxserver] ~/mrtg-2.10.15> make install
```

All three of these commands produce a lot of output, which we have omitted. The configure command inspects your system for tools it needs to build MRTG. It will tell you which items are missing and where to go to get them. Running make builds MRTG, but don't bother running this if the configure command failed; MRTG will not build unless everything has been installed and configured properly. Finally, make install installs MRTG and its associated files in the appropriate places. Again, don't bother running make install if the previous make command terminated with errors. The default location for the MRTG executables is */usr/local/mrtg-2/bin*. You may want to add this directory to your search path.

Once you've built MRTG, you need to decide where to put the graphs it generates. Since MRTG's graphs are designed to be viewed with a web browser, they're often stored in a directory that's visible to a web server. However, it really doesn't matter where they go. What's more important is who you want to view the graphs. You probably don't want the world to see your network statistics. On a small network, you can place the graphs in a directory that is out of view of the web server and then use a web browser to view the HTML reports in the local filesystem. In a larger network, other people (e.g., other network staff or management) may need to access the reports; to allow access without publishing your network statistics to the rest of the world, you may want to set up some kind of a secure web server. At any rate, the next set of commands you'll want to execute is something like this:

```
[root][linuxserver] ~/mrtg-2.10.15> mkdir -p /mrtg/images
[root][linuxserver] ~/mrtg-2.10.15> cp ./images/mrtg*.gif /mrtg/images/
```

The first command creates a directory for storing the graphs MRTG creates. The second command copies some MRTG images into the newly created directory for later use in HTML files. For the remainder of this chapter, we will assume that graphs are stored in */mrtg/images*.

You're now ready to set up your first device to poll, which is called a target in MRTG. MRTG uses a configuration file to tell it what devices to poll and what options to apply to the creation of the graphs it will generate. The syntax of the configuration file is complex, but MRTG provides a tool called cfgmaker to help you build it. You'll probably need to edit the file by hand, but it's much easier to start with a working template. Here's how to execute cfgmaker:

```
[root][linuxserver] ~/mrtg-2.10.15> setenv PATH /usr/local/mrtg-2/bin:$PATH
[root][linuxserver] ~/mrtg-2.10.15> mkdir /mrtg/run
[root][linuxserver] ~/mrtg-2.10.15> cfgmaker --global 'WorkDir: /mrtg/images' \
--output /mrtg/run/mrtg.cfg public@10.0.0.1
```

The first argument to cfgmaker sets the WorkDir variable in the configuration file. This tells MRTG where to store any data it gathers from the devices it's going to poll. The second argument specifies where we want cfgmaker's output sent; in this case it's */mrtg/run/mrtg.cfg*. The last argument specifies the device we want to poll and the community string to use when polling that device; its format is *community_ string@device*.

The output from cfgmaker is a mix of commands and HTML. It performs getnext commands on the device you specified on the command line to get an idea of how many interfaces your device has, which ones are up, which are down, etc. It walks the *iso.org.dod.internet.mgmt.mib-2.interfaces* (*1.3.6.1.2.1.2*) tree to discover the total number of interfaces in this table. It then creates logical entries that represent a list of devices to poll, except the list of devices is actually one device with each interface number specified as a target. For example, *TR00ATL* is in the second row of the *interfaces* table on our Cisco router, so cfgmaker created a Target entry called *10.0.0.1_2*. If this interface occupied the third row in the *interfaces* table, the Target entry would be called *10.0.0.1_3*.

Here's a shortened version of our *mrtg.cfg* file:

```
EnableIPv6: no
WorkDir: /mrtg/images

Target[10.0.0.1_2]: 2:public@10.0.0.1:
SetEnv[10.0.0.1_2]: MRTG_INT_IP="10.0.0.1" MRTG_INT_DESCR="Serial0/1"
MaxBytes[10.0.0.1_2]: 192000
Title[10.0.0.1_2]: Traffic Analysis for 2 -- TR00ATL
PageTop[10.0.0.1_2]: <H1>Traffic Analysis for 2 -- TR00ATL</H1>
 <TABLE>
   <TR><TD>System:</TD>      <TD>TR00ATL in </TD></TR>
   <TR><TD>Maintainer:</TD> <TD></TD></TR>
   <TR><TD>Description:</TD><TD>Serial0/1 [TRANSIT] T1 to NewSouth - CID unknown </
TD></TR>
   <TR><TD>ifType:</TD>      <TD>frame-relay (32)</TD></TR>
   <TR><TD>ifName:</TD>      <TD>Se0/1</TD></TR>
   <TR><TD>Max Speed:</TD>  <TD>192.0 kBytes/s</TD></TR>
   <TR><TD>Ip:</TD>          <TD>router1</TD></TR>
 </TABLE>
```

It's worth learning a bit about the format of the configuration file. Comment lines begin with #; in a real configuration file, you'll see many of them. Most of the lines in the file are either commands or snippets of HTML that will be used in MRTG's output files. MRTG commands take the form of *command[key]: options*. For example, the command for the third line is Target, the key is 10.0.0.1_2, and the options are 2: public@10.0.0.1. The key is an identifying string that groups entries in the configuration file and provides a base filename for MRTG to use when generating graphs and HTML files. At a complex site, MRTG might be used to monitor dozens of pieces of equipment, with hundreds of interfaces; the key keeps the configuration file in some semblance of order. The options provide the actual parameters to the command.

This should help you understand the configuration file. The first line specifies the working directory in which MRTG will place its graphs and HTML files. This is a global command, so no key is needed. The working directory is typically somewhere under a web server tree so that MRTG's reports can be visible from a web browser. We've set ours to /mrtg/images/. The third line (Target) tells MRTG which device it should poll. The format for this option is *interface:community_string@device*, or in our case, `2:public@10.0.0.1` The device is specified by its hostname or IP address; we already know about community strings. Since MRTG is only a data-collection tool, the read-only community string will suffice. `interface` specifies which interface on the device to poll, according to the device's *ifTable*. In this case, we're polling interface 4 in the *ifTable*.

The `MaxBytes` line sets up the maximum value for the parameters MRTG is going to read from this interface. By default, MRTG reads *ifInOctets* and *ifOutOctets*. It tries to pick a reasonable maximum value depending on the interface's type, which it should be able to read from the device itself. Since this is an Ethernet interface, MRTG sets `MaxBytes` to `192000`. The `Title` specifies the title for the HTML page generated for the graph. Finally, `PageTop` and the following lines tell MRTG what kind of information to place at the top of the HTML page containing the usage graphs. The command contains actual HTML code, which was generated by cfgmaker.

Altogether, this entry tells MRTG to poll for the default objects (*ifInOctets* and *ifOut-Octets*) on entry 2 in the interface table for the device *10.0.0.1*. Therefore, MRTG will issue get commands for the OIDs *.1.3.6.1.2.1.2.2.1.10.2* (*iso.org.dod.internet.mgmt.mib-2.interfaces.ifTable.ifEntry.ifInOctets.2*) and *.1.3.6.1.2.1.2.2.1.16.2* (*iso.org.dod.internet.mgmt.mib-2.interfaces.ifTable.ifEntry.ifOutOctets.2*). By default, MRTG will generate the following graphs:

- Daily graph with 5-minute averages
- Weekly graph with 30-minute averages
- Monthly graph with 2-hour averages
- Yearly graph with 1-day averages

Once you've finished, try running MRTG by hand to see if there are any problems with the configuration script:

```
[root][linuxserver] ~/mrtg-2.10.15> mrtg /mrtg/run/mrtg.cfg
```

If MRTG has no problems with your configuration file, it will run with no configuration-file errors. If it does have problems, it will give you a fairly verbose description of the problem. The first time you run MRTG, it will complain about not being able to find any logfiles. If you run MRTG three times, you'll see messages similar to these:

```
[root][linuxserver] ~/mrtg-2.10.15> mrtg /mrtg/run/mrtg.cfg
Rateup WARNING: /home/kschmidt/mrtg-2.10.15/bin/rateup could not read the primary log
file for 10.0.0.1_2
Rateup WARNING: /home/kschmidt/mrtg-2.10.15/bin/rateup The backup log file for 10.0.
0.1_2 was invalid as well
Rateup WARNING: /home/kschmidt/mrtg-2.10.15/bin/rateup Can't remove 10.0.0.1_2.old
updating log file
Rateup WARNING: /home/kschmidt/mrtg-2.10.15/bin/rateup Can't rename 10.0.0.1_2.log to
10.0.0.1_2.old updating log file
Rateup WARNING: /home/kschmidt/mrtg-2.10.15/bin/rateup could not read the primary log
file for 10.0.0.1_3
```

```
Rateup WARNING: /home/kschmidt/mrtg-2.10.15/bin/rateup The backup log file for 10.0.
0.1_3 was invalid as well
Rateup WARNING: /home/kschmidt/mrtg-2.10.15/bin/rateup Can't remove 10.0.0.1_3.old
updating log file
Rateup WARNING: /home/kschmidt/mrtg-2.10.15/bin/rateup Can't rename 10.0.0.1_3.log to
10.0.0.1_3.old updating log file

[root][linuxserver] ~/mrtg-2.10.15> mrtg /mrtg/run/mrtg.cfg
Rateup WARNING: /home/kschmidt/mrtg-2.10.15/bin/rateup Can't remove 10.0.0.1_2.old
updating log file
Rateup WARNING: /home/kschmidt/mrtg-2.10.15/bin/rateup Can't remove 10.0.0.1_3.old
updating log file

[root][linuxserver] ~/mrtg-2.10.15> mrtg /mrtg/run/mrtg.cfg
[root][linuxserver] ~/mrtg-2.10.15>
```

As you can see, the first time we ran the program it spat out some errors. The second run produced only two errors, and the last time it ran with no errors. These errors are normal when you run MRTG for the first time; don't worry about them.

Note that you may see the following when you run MRTG from the command line:

```
----------------------------------------------------------------------
ERROR: Mrtg will most likely not work properly when the environment
       variable LANG is set to UTF-8. Please run mrtg in an environment
       where this is not the case. Try the following command to start:

       env LANG=C ./mrtg /mrtg/run/mrtg.cfg
----------------------------------------------------------------------
```

Just follow what it suggests and MRTG will run just fine.

The next step is to make sure MRTG runs every five minutes. There's no need for MRTG to be run by root; any user will do. Add a line like the following to the *crontab* entry for the appropriate user:

```
*/5 * * * * /usr/local/mrtg-2/bin/mrtg /mrtg/run/mrtg.cfg
```

This runs MRTG every five minutes of every day. Note that the */5 notation is Linux-specific; on other Unix systems, you'll have to specify the times explicitly (0,5,10,15,20,25,30,35,40,45,50,55). If your network is fairly large, you might run into problems if MRTG does not finish all its polling duties before the next polling cycle starts. If this is the case, setting a five-minute poll interval may not be a good idea. You may have to experiment to determine a good interval for your environment.

Viewing Graphs

Once you've generated some graphs, you will want to look at them to see the results. To make it easier to view the graphs, MRTG comes with an *indexmaker* script that generates HTML index pages. Here's how to run *indexmaker* for a typical set of graphs:

```
[root][linuxserver] ~/mrtg-2.10.15> indexmaker --title "Cisco to Internet" \
    filter name=~'10.0.0.1'   output /mrtg/images/cisco.html /mrtg/run/mrtg.cfg
```

This command creates one index page with the five-minute average graph for each target you've specified in your *mrtg.cfg* file. Keep in mind that the target is the interface from which you're gathering data. If you have four targets for your router, there will be four graphs in the index file, all pointing to the daily, weekly, monthly, and yearly summary graphs for that target. The - -title option tells *indexmaker* what title to use for the index file. - -filter name=~10.0.0.1 allows you to select some of the targets in the *mrtg.cfg* file by using a regular expression: we told *indexmaker* to find all targets that include the string 10.0.0.1. The - -output option is the name of the index file. The final argument on the command line is the full path to the configuration file. Table 12-1 gives a synopsis of these options as well as some other useful options to *indexmaker*.

Table 12-1. Command-line options to indexmaker

Option	Description
--title	Specify a title for the HTML page.
--filter	Specify the regular expression that will be used to find a specific target from the *mrtg.cfg* file. These matched targets are used to create the HTML report files.
--output	Indicate the full pathname for the HTML file that is to be generated. The default is standard output.
--sort	Sort how the graphs show up on the index page.
--columns	Arrange the graphs on the index page by *x* columns. The default is 2.
--width	Set the width of the graphs. This is not set by default.
--height	Set the height of the graphs. This is not set by default.
--show	Pick which graph to show on the index page. The default is day. Other options include week, month, year, and none.

To display the entire list of options to *indexmaker*, run the command without any options. Figure 12-1 shows how the *cisco.html* file generated by *indexmaker* looks when it's loaded into a web browser.

There are four graphs on the page, one for each of the operational interfaces (interfaces that were up and running when we ran cfgmaker) on our router. This page includes links to other pages that have more detailed information about individual interfaces; Figure 12-2 shows the daily, weekly, monthly, and yearly traffic graphs for the *TR00ATL* interface.

The daily graph (which actually represents a 32-hour period) is the one that most people are interested in viewing. It shows the five-minute average of the traffic on this particular interface. Incoming traffic (*ifInOctets*) is represented by a green line; outgoing traffic (*IfOutOctets*) is represented by a blue line. If we had clicked on one of the other interfaces on the Cisco index page (Figure 12-1), we would have seen a similar graph.

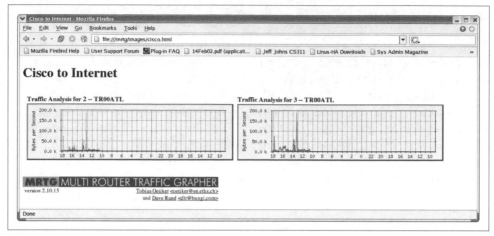

Figure 12-1. Cisco graph overview

That's all there is to viewing the graphs. MRTG stores the raw data it collects in a flat text file but, due to its intelligent log rolling capabilities, the logfiles don't grow out of control; their sizes remain quite manageable even if you use MRTG extensively.

Graphing Other Objects

MRTG polls and graphs the MIB variables *ifInOctets* and *ifOutOctets* by default, but it is possible to poll and graph the values of other objects in addition to polling different kinds of devices. First let's get MRTG collecting input and output octets from a server. To do this, run the following command:

    [root][linuxserver] ~/mrtg-2.10.15> **cfgmaker public@127.0.0.1 >> /mrtg2/run/mrtg.cfg**

This is almost identical to the command we ran earlier in the chapter, except for the community string and target[*] (*public@127.0.0.1*). We appended the output to the *mrtg.cfg* file, as opposed to specifying an output file with the - -output option; this lets us add a new host to the existing configuration file, instead of starting a new file. Because the existing file already specifies a working directory, we also omitted the working directory option (--global 'WorkDir: ... '). This cfgmaker command adds a number of lines like the following to the configuration file:

```
Target[127.0.0.1_2]: 2:public@127.0.0.1:
SetEnv[127.0.0.1_2]: MRTG_INT_IP="" MRTG_INT_DESCR="eth0"
MaxBytes[127.0.0.1_2]: 12500000
Title[127.0.0.1_2]: Traffic Analysis for 2 -- box
PageTop[127.0.0.1_2]: <H1>Traffic Analysis for 2 -- box</H1>
  <TABLE>
```

---

[*] Make sure that your target is running an SNMP agent. See Chapter 6 for a discussion of how to configure several SNMP agents for Unix and Windows.

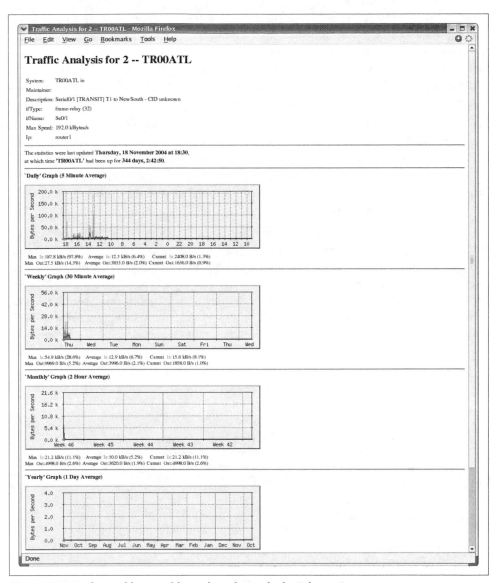

Figure 12-2. Daily, weekly, monthly, and yearly graphs for Ethernet0

```
<TR><TD>System:</TD>      <TD>box in Atlanta,GA</TD></TR>
<TR><TD>Maintainer:</TD> <TD>"kjs@guarded.net"</TD></TR>
<TR><TD>Description:</TD><TD>eth0  </TD></TR>
<TR><TD>ifType:</TD>      <TD>ethernetCsmacd (6)</TD></TR>
<TR><TD>ifName:</TD>      <TD></TD></TR>
<TR><TD>Max Speed:</TD>  <TD>12.5 MBytes/s</TD></TR>
</TABLE>
```

These lines tell MRTG how to poll the server's Ethernet interface. The key used for this interface is 127.0.0.1, and the target number is 2. Why 2? Remember that cfg-maker walks the interface table to determine what entries to add to the configuration file. Therefore, you'll see a set of lines like this for each interface on the device, including the loopback interface. The target numbers are actually indexes into the interface table; on this server, the loopback interface has the index 1.

Now let's create an entry to graph the number of users logged onto the server and the total number of processes running. MRTG is capable of graphing these parameters, but you have to specify explicitly which MIB variables to graph. Furthermore, you have to specify two variables—MRTG won't graph just one. (This is a rather strange limitation, but at least it's consistent: remember that the default graphs show both input and output octets.)

First, let's look at the MIB variables we plan to graph. The two variables, *hrSystem-NumUsers* and *hrSystemProcesses*, are defined as OIDs *1.3.6.1.2.1.25.1.5.6.0* and *1.3.6.1.2.1.25.1.6.0*, respectively. The *.0* at the end of each OID indicates that these two objects are both scalar variables, not part of a table. Both come from the Host Resources MIB (RFC 2790), which defines a set of managed objects for system administration. (Some agents that run on server systems implement this MIB, but unfortunately, the Microsoft and Solaris agents do not.) The definitions for these objects are:

```
hrSystemNumUsers OBJECT-TYPE
    SYNTAX Gauge
    ACCESS read-only
    STATUS mandatory
    DESCRIPTION
        "The number of user sessions for which this host is storing state
        information. A session is a collection of processes requiring a
        single act of user authentication and possibly subject to collective
        job control."
    ::= { hrSystem 5 }

hrSystemProcesses OBJECT-TYPE
    SYNTAX Gauge
    ACCESS read-only
    STATUS mandatory
    DESCRIPTION
        "The number of process contexts currently loaded or running on
        this system."
    ::= { hrSystem 6 }
```

The entry we added to our configuration file looks like this:

```
Target[127.0.0.1_3]: 1.3.6.1.2.1.25.1.5.0&1.3.6.1.2.1.25.1.6.0:public@localhost
MaxBytes[127.0.0.1_3]: 512
Options[127.0.0.1_3]: gauge
Title[127.0.0.1_3]: Number of Users and Processes on localhost
YLegend[127.0.0.1_3]: Users/Processes
LegendI[127.0.0.1_3]: Users:
```

```
LegendO[127.0.0.1_3]: Processes:
PageTop[127.0.0.1_3]: <H1>Number of Users and Processes on localhost</H1>
 <TABLE>
   <TR><TD>System:</TD>      <TD>box in Atlanta,GA</TD></TR>
   <TR><TD>Maintainer:</TD> <TD>"kjs@guarded.net"</TD></TR>
 </TABLE>
```

The first line specifies the device we want MRTG to poll, along with the two OIDs (*hrSystemNumUsers* and *hrSystemProcessess*) we want to graph. This statement is obviously more complex than the Target statement we looked at earlier; its syntax is *OID1&OID2:community_string@device*. The OIDs must be separated by an ampersand character (&). Using this syntax, you can convince MRTG to graph any two scalar-valued MIB variables.

In the next line, we set MaxBytes to 512. This is the maximum value for the graph; values greater than 512 are set to 512. (Forget about bytes; MaxBytes simply defines a maximum value.) For the number of users logged in, this is a high number; there should never be this many people logged onto our system at once. The same goes for the total number of processes running on the system. You can choose values that make sense for your particular environment. If you need separate maximum values for each object, replace MaxBytes with two lines setting MaxBytes1 and MaxBytes2.

The Options command is a new one; it allows you to change how MRTG treats the data it gathers. The only option we have specified is gauge. This instructs MRTG to treat the gathered data as Gauge data, not Counter data. Recall that Counter data is monotonically increasing while Gauge data is not. Since the MIB definitions for both objects specify the Gauge datatype, this option makes sense.

The YLegend, LegendI, and LegendO options are also new. YLegend simply changes the label that is placed on the Y-axis of the graph itself. Since we're graphing the number of users and processes, we set the legend to Users/Processes. It's important for the legend to be short; if it's too long, MRTG silently ignores it and doesn't print anything for the label. LegendI changes the legend used below the graph for the so-called "input variable" (in this case, the number of users logged into the system—remember that MRTG expects to be graphing input and output octets). LegendO changes the legend for the "output variable" (the total number of processes running on the system). The terminology is unfortunate; just remember that MRTG always graphs a pair of objects and that the input legend always refers to the first object and the output legend refers to the second.

Once you have added this entry to your configuration file and saved it, MRTG will start gathering data from the device every time it runs. If you have added the appropriate entry in your *crontab* file, you're all set. Now we'll use *indexmaker* to create intuitive index files for the server graphs, just as we did for the router graphs. The command to create a new index file is similar to the one we used to create the Cisco index file:

```
[root][linuxserver] ~/mrtg-2.10.15> indexmaker --title "Linux Server" \
--filter name=~'127.0.0.1' --output /mrtg/images/linux.html /mrtg/run/mrtg.cfg
```

Figure 12-3 shows the index page for the server graphs. It contains only two graphs: one shows traffic on the Ethernet interface and the other shows the number of running processes versus the number of users logged onto the system.

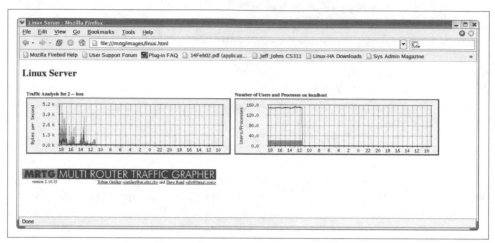

Figure 12-3. Linux server overview graphs

Figure 12-4 shows the daily, weekly, monthly, and yearly graphs for the number of users and processes logged into the system.

Other Data-Gathering Applications

What if you need to monitor devices on your network that don't support SNMP? MRTG is up to the task. For example, you may have a Perl script that gathers usage statistics from some device that doesn't support SNMP. How can you collect and graph this data? Let's make this more concrete. Assume that you have the following script, */usr/local/scripts/hostinfo.pl*, which reports the number of users and the number of processes on the system:

```perl
#!/usr/bin/perl

$who = "/usr/bin/who | wc -l";
$ps = "/bin/ps -ef h | wc -l";

chomp($numUsers = int( `$who` ));
chomp($numProcesses = int( `$ps` ));

print "$numUsers\n";
print "$numProcesses\n";
#
# The following code prints the system uptime and the hostname. These two
# items need to be included in every script that you write and should be the
# very last thing that is printed.
#
```

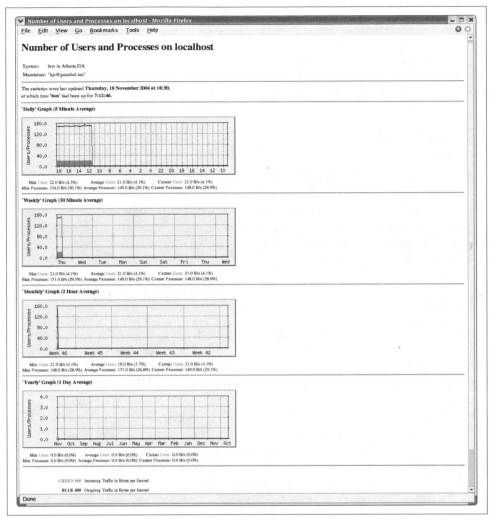

Figure 12-4. Daily, weekly, monthly, and yearly graphs for number of users and processes

```
chomp($uptime =  `/usr/bin/uptime` );
print "$uptime\n";
chomp($hostname =  `/bin/hostname` );
print "$hostname\n";
```

This script prints four variables: the number of users and the number of processes (the data we want MRTG to collect), and the system uptime and hostname (required by MRTG). To get MRTG to run this script, we'll have to edit *mrtg.cfg* by hand. The modification is actually simpler than our previous example. Here's the new entry to *mrtg.cfg*, with the changes shown in bold:

```
Target[linuxserver.users]: `/usr/bin/perl /usr/local/bin/hostinfo.pl`
MaxBytes[linuxserver.users]: 512
```

```
Options[linuxserver.users]: gauge
Title[linuxserver.users]: linuxserver (linuxserver): Number of
users and processes
YLegend[linuxserver.users]: Users/Processes
LegendI[linuxserver.users]:  Users:
LegendO[linuxserver.users]:  Processes:
PageTop[linuxserver.users]: <H1>Number of users and processes
 </H1>
 <TABLE>
   <TR><TD>System:</TD>      <TD>box in Atlanta,GA</TD></TR>
   <TR><TD>Maintainer:</TD> <TD>"kjs@guarded.net"</TD></TR>
 </TABLE>
```

Note the addition of `/usr/bin/perl /usr/local/bin/hostinfo.pl` to the Target command. This line tells MRTG to run the script or program between the backticks. The rest should be familiar. MRTG interprets the first value that the script prints (the number of users) as its input data; the second value (the number of processes) is the output data. When it generates graphs, it applies the appropriate input and output legends (LegendI and LegendO).

Pitfalls

Many SNMP-capable devices change the order of interfaces in the *interfaces* table whenever a new interface card is inserted or an old one is removed. If you run a fairly static router environment (i.e., you hardly ever add or remove cards from your routers), the configuration examples we've shown should work well for you. But in today's fast-paced network environments, stability is rare. MRTG's cfgmaker command provides a command-line option, - -ifref, to help with this problem. It doesn't solve the problem, but it does allow you to generate graphs in which interfaces are labeled with their addresses, descriptions, or names; with this information, you don't have to remember whether interface 1 is your local network interface or your T1 connection. Table 12-2 summarizes the usage of - -ifref.

Table 12-2. Summary of --ifref options

Option	Description
--ifref=ip	Identify each interface by its IP address.
--ifref=eth	Use the Ethernet address to identify the interface.
--ifref=descr	Use the interface description to identify the interface.
--ifref=name	Use the interface name to identify the interface.

Thus, to label interfaces with their IP addresses, run cfgmaker like so:

```
[root][linuxserver] ~/mrtg-2.10.15> cfgmaker --global 'WorkDir: /mrtg/images' \
--output /mrtg/run/mrtg.cfg --ifref=ip public@router
```

Be sure to read the cfgmaker manual that comes with the MRTG documentation.

Getting Help

The MRTG web site, *http://www.mrtg.org*, offers a great deal of information and help. You can subscribe to the MRTG mailing list from this page. MRTG is also discussed frequently in the Usenet newsgroup *comp.dcom.net-management*. Finally, don't ignore MRTG's documentation, which is located in the *doc* subdirectory of the MRTG distribution. The documentation is included in both text and HTML form and is fairly complete and comprehensive.

CHAPTER 13

RRDtool and Cricket

This chapter discusses RRDtool and Cricket. RRDtool, written by the author of MRTG, was meant to be a replacement for MRTG. Instead, MRTG lived on and RRDtool found a place all its own in the world of network performance management. Unlike MRTG, RRDtool has a plethora of frontends written by people all over the world. One of the first and most widely known is Cricket. This chapter shows how to install RRDtool and Cricket on Unix. RRDtool can certainly be used alone, but the goal of this chapter is to demonstrate the easiest and quickest way to get up and running with both tools.

RRDtool

RRDtool is the Round Robin Database Tool. Round robin is a technique that works with a fixed amount of data and a pointer to the current element. Think of a circle with some dots plotted on the edge—these dots are the places where data can be stored. Draw an arrow from the center of the circle to one of the dots—this is the pointer. When the current data is read or written, the pointer moves to the next element. After a while, all the available places are used and the process automatically reuses old locations. This way, the dataset does not grow in size and therefore requires no maintenance. RRDtool works with Round Robin Databases (RRDs). It stores and retrieves data from them.

RRDtool originated from MRTG, which we cover in Chapter 12. MRTG started as a tiny little script for graphing the use of a university's connection to the Internet. MRTG was later used (some might say abused) as a tool for graphing other data sources, including temperature, speed, voltage, number of printouts, and the like.

Most likely you will start to use RRDtool to store and process data collected via SNMP. The data will probably be bytes (or bits) transferred from and to a network or a computer. But it can also be used to display tidal waves, solar radiation, power consumption, the number of visitors at an exhibition, the noise levels near an airport, the temperature at your favorite holiday location, the temperature in the fridge, or whatever your imagination can come up with. It's incredibly flexible.

You need only a sensor to measure the data, and the ability to feed the numbers into RRDtool. RRDtool then lets you create a database, store data in it, retrieve that data, and create graphs in PNG format for display on a web browser. The PNG images are dependent on the data you collect, and they could represent, for instance, an overview of the average network usage, or the peaks that occur.

This chapter focuses on installing RRDtool and Cricket. Cricket is used to gather SNMP data points, store the data in RRDtool, and display the data in graphs.

Installing RRDtool

The latest version of the software can be found at *http://www.rrdtool.org*. RRDtool requires that you install several third-party libraries, including *libart*, *libpng*, *zlib*, *freetype*, and *cgilib*. Luckily, you can find copies of these packages at *http://people.ee. ethz.ch/~oetiker/webtools/rrdtool/pub/libs*. However, if you wish to go directly to home pages for these packages and download them from the source, when you run RRDtool's *configure* script it will tell you what packages you don't have installed and where you can obtain them. You will need Perl installed (if it isn't already) and a C compiler like gcc. Once you have downloaded and untarred the RRDtool distribution, use these three commands to build and install it:

```
[root@machine rrdtool-1.2.9]# ./configure --enable-perl-site-install
[root@machine rrdtool-1.2.9]# make
[root@machine rrdtool-1.2.9]# make install
```

Note the option passed to the configure command. This installs the RRDtool Perl modules, used by Cricket, in the normal Perl site location. These commands produce a good amount of output. Once installed, RRDtool will be, by default, stored in */usr/local/rrdtool-1.2.9*. If you wish to change this directory, run configure like this:

```
[root@machine rrdtool-1.2.9]# ./configure --prefix=/path/to/install
```

That's all you need to do. Next we show how to install, configure, and use Cricket.

Cricket

Cricket can be loosely associated with MRTG because it is an interface to RRDtool. It facilitates the following:

- Data gathering (using SNMP, command-line tools, and so on)
- Creating RRDtool database(s)
- Updating data points in the RRDtool database
- Presenting accumulated data (over time) as graphs in a web page

Cricket allows users to view graphs over the following time periods:

- Daily
- Weekly
- Monthly
- Yearly

The main web site for Cricket is *http://cricket.sourceforge.net*.

Cricket's History

While working for WebTV* in 1998, Jeff Allen originally conceived of Cricket. Jeff wanted to find a way to reduce the complexity of WebTV's MRTG configuration and deployment. At that time, Tobias Oetiker, author of MRTG, released RRDtool. Once Jeff saw RRDtool, he began to see how its design could aid in solving many of WebTV's MRTG woes. MRTG had been known as the tool used for graphing router data. Jeff wanted a new way to graph other things as well, like data from servers.

Cricket's Config Tree

Understanding the *config* tree is critical to understanding how to use and modify Cricket. Everything Cricket knows it learns from the *config* tree. That includes things like which variables to fetch for a certain type of device, how to fetch those variables, which devices to talk to, and the device types. The inheritance property of the *config* tree applies equally to all types of data, making it possible to create a concise description of a large, complicated set of monitored devices.

At the top of the *config* tree is a file called *Defaults*. It contains default values for things like OIDs Cricket polls frequently. The *config* tree is made up of subdirectories which create logical devices, systems, and so on, from which Cricket may be asked to gather data. An example *config* tree might look like Figure 13-1.

In this tree, we have two subtrees—*systemperf* and *routers*. These two subtrees represent groups of targets that are interesting. For example, *systemperf* may be Unix systems from which we wish to gather CPU and disk information, and routers may contain Cisco devices for which we want to gather per-interface usage statistics.

Each subtree has a file called *Targets*. This file contains information about what devices Cricket will actually poll. The filename used is arbitrary since Cricket will discover the file and the contents on its own. Also notice how the *systemperf* subtree has a *Defaults* file and the *routers* subtree does not. This means the *systemperf* subtree can override default values found in the top-level *Defaults* file. Since it has no specialized *Defaults* file, the *routers* subtree uses the top-level default values.

---

* WebTV is now MSN TV.

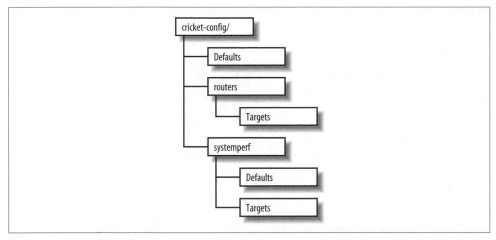

Figure 13-1. Sample config tree

This *config* tree also allows Cricket to parallelize its data-gathering techniques. We'll discuss Cricket parallelization in a little more detail later in the chapter.

Installing Cricket

Cricket requires some Perl modules to be in place before you can begin using it. A list of these modules can be found at *http://cricket.sourceforge.net/support/doc/beginner. html*. Once you have downloaded Cricket, create a user on the system on which you plan to run Cricket. We will use cricket as the username in all of the examples. Here are the initial steps to install Cricket:

```
$ cd ~cricket
$ tar zxvf cricket-1.0.5.tar.gz
$ cd ~cricket/cricket-1.0.5
$ sh configure
$ cd ~cricket
$ ln -s cricket-1.0.5 cricket
```

The sh configure command updates the Perl scripts to point to where your Perl interpreter is installed. The symbolic link makes it easier to install future versions. If you always reference *~cricket/cricket*, nothing should break.

Next, copy the sample Cricket configuration file and edit it:

```
$ cd ~cricket/cricket
$ cp cricket-conf.pl.sample cricket-conf.pl
```

When you edit the file, make sure the variable $gCricketHome points to the home directory for the Cricket user, in our case, */home/cricket*. Next, make sure $gInstallRoot points to the location where you installed Cricket. Here's what our file contains:

```
$gCricketHome = "/home/cricket";
$gInstallRoot = "$gCricketHome/cricket";
```

We show how to configure Cricket to gather information on a Unix host. To set up the initial *config* tree to accomplish this, do the following:

```
$ mkdir cricket-config
$ cp -r cricket/sample-config/systemperf/ cricket-config/
$ cp cricket/sample-config/Defaults cricket-config/
```

Later we'll talk about how to add other devices for Cricket to monitor.

Now we need to get the graphing component of Cricket set up. This requires a running instance of Apache. We created a *public_html* subdirectory in the Cricket user's directory. From there, we need to set up the environment:

```
$ cd ~cricket/public_html
$ mkdir cricket
$ cd cricket
$ ln -s ~cricket/cricket/VERSION .
$ ln -s ~cricket/cricket/grapher.cgi .
$ ln -s ~cricket/cricket/mini-graph.cgi .
$ ln -s ~cricket/cricket/lib .
$ ln -s ~cricket/cricket/images .
```

That's it. We are now ready to configure and begin using Cricket.

Configuring and Using Cricket

Since we will be monitoring a Unix system, we need to set up the Cricket configuration properly. Luckily, Cricket comes with several scripts that make it easy to set up various configurations to monitor many types of devices. Let's look at one we can use to set up our Unix box (assume we are in */home/cricket*):

```
$ cricket/util/systemPerfConf.pl --host 192.168.1.69 \
--community public --auto > cricket-config/systemperf/Targets
```

This command uses SNMP to gather various bits of information about the host and stores these details in *cricket-config/systemperf/Targets*. The --auto configuration switch instructs the script to discover what it can with regard to what MIBs the box may support.

The next step is to compile the configuration into a format that both Cricket and RRDtool can use:

```
$ cricket/compile
[05-Jun-2005 17:39:40 ] Log level changed from warn to info.
[05-Jun-2005 17:39:40 ] Starting compile: Cricket version 1.0.5 (2004-03-28)
[05-Jun-2005 17:39:40 ] Config directory is /home/cricket/cricket-config
[05-Jun-2005 17:39:40 ] Processed 13 nodes (in 3 files) in 0 seconds.
```

This sets the stage for actually gathering data. We can do a quick trial run of the collector by running the following command:

```
$ cricket/collector /systemperf
[05-Jun-2005 17:39:58 ] Log level changed from warn to info.
[05-Jun-2005 17:39:58 ] Starting collector: Cricket version 1.0.5 (2004-03-28)
```

```
[05-Jun-2005 17:39:58 ] Retrieved data for hr_sys (0): 60,5
[05-Jun-2005 17:39:58 ] Retrieved data for ucd_sys ():
455947,168,74908,10090430,24148,522072,546220,0.11,0.08,0.02
[05-Jun-2005 17:39:58 ] Retrieved data for if_lo (1):
15722669,15722669,0,0,93777,93777
[05-Jun-2005 17:39:58 ] Retrieved data for if_eth0 (2):
52684451,22813456,0,0,129146,115315
[05-Jun-2005 17:39:58 ] Retrieved data for if_eth1 (3): 0,0,0,0,0,0
[05-Jun-2005 17:39:58 ] Retrieved data for disk_root (4): 225570,381139
[05-Jun-2005 17:39:58 ] Retrieved data for disk_boot (5): 5912,46636
[05-Jun-2005 17:39:58 ] Retrieved data for disk_home (6): 101004,507980
[05-Jun-2005 17:39:58 ] Retrieved data for disk_usr (7): 242226,1393492
[05-Jun-2005 17:39:58 ] Retrieved data for disk_var (8): 34853,256667
[05-Jun-2005 17:39:58 ] Processed 10 targets in 0 seconds.
```

Notice the argument passed to the collector: /systemperf. This is the directory name under *~cricket/cricket-config/* where the configuration for our Unix box is stored. Now we want to set up the interval at which we will poll our Unix system. Edit the file *~cricket/cricket/subtree-sets*. It should look like the following:

```
# This file lists the subtrees that will be processed together in one
# set. See the comments at the beginning of collect-subtrees for more info.

# This will be passed to collector so it can find the Config Tree.
# If this directory does not start with a slash, it will
# have $HOME prepended.
base:   cricket-config

# this is where logs will be put. (The $HOME rule applies here too.)
logdir: cricket-logs

set normal:
        /routers
        /router-interfaces
```

Change the end of the file so that it looks like this:

```
# This file lists the subtrees that will be processed together in one
# set. See the comments at the beginning of collect-subtrees for more info.

# This will be passed to collector so it can find the Config Tree.
# If this directory does not start with a slash, it will
# have $HOME prepended.
base:   cricket-config

# this is where logs will be put. (The $HOME rule applies here too.)
logdir: cricket-logs

set normal:
        /systemperf
        #/routers
        #/router-interfaces
```

We'll talk about the *routers* and *router-interfaces* subtrees in a moment. Now, as your Cricket user, run *crontab* –e and add the following entry:

```
*/5 * * * * /home/cricket/cricket/collect-subtrees normal
```

This notation works on Linux systems and will run the collect-subtrees command every five minutes. The argument passed to this command (normal) corresponds to the subtree-set in the *subtree-sets* file we just edited. The collect-subtrees command gathers data for all the subtrees configured beneath normal.

Now, you should be ready to access the main Cricket screen. The URL we used is *http://192.168.1.69/~cricket/cricket/grapher.cgi*. Of course, you'll need to insert your own IP address and username in the URL. Figure 13-2 shows the main Cricket screen.

Figure 13-2. Main Cricket screen

Clicking on the systemperf link takes you to a page that looks like Figure 13-3.

What we see here are various links to things like the number of users and processes on the system, traffic statistics for the various network interfaces, and other system-specific variables.

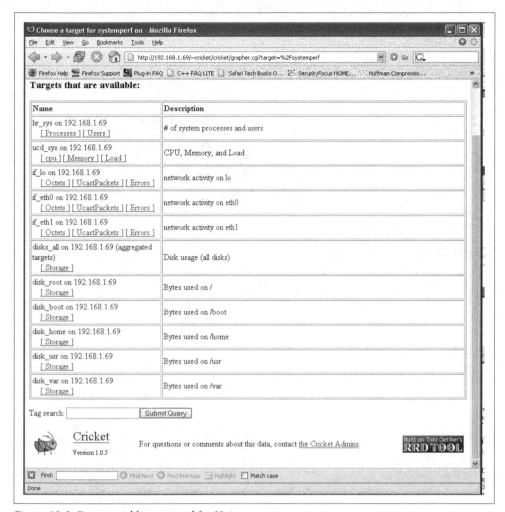

Figure 13-3. Data variables captured for Unix system

Let's now look at some of the graphs that the */systemperf* subtree has created. Figure 13-4 shows a graph of the number of users on the system.

This sort of graph can be useful because it shows, over time, how many users are logged onto the system. Let's say you come into the office on Monday morning and notice that on Saturday night the number of users jumped from its normal number of 5 to 10 for a 15-minute period. No one was supposed to be on the system over the weekend beyond the five you already know about. This could tip you off that your system has been compromised and that you should investigate immediately.

Figure 13-5 shows a graph of processes running on the system.

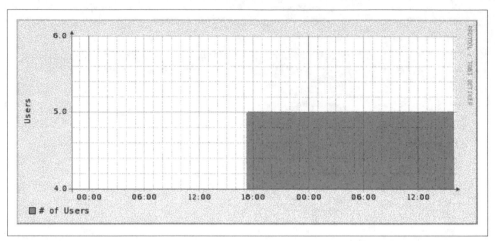

Figure 13-4. Number of users on the system

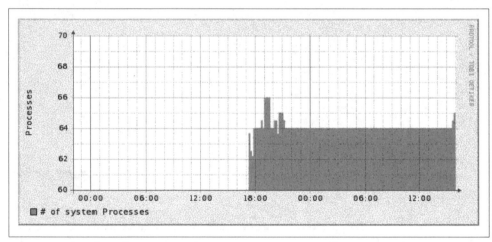

Figure 13-5. Number of processes on the system

Figure 13-5 can be useful to watch how a critical server is utilized. If you are routinely seeing your web server's process load spike very high in the middle of the day, this graph can help pinpoint contributing suspects. Perhaps you are running a database on the server as well and certain users are generating routine reports at that time of the day. This could be your first clue that it is time to move the database off the web server.

Figure 13-6 shows CPU utilization.

Watching CPU utilization can also be very telling. If you see spikes in utilization that remain high for periods of time, you can use the time axis to cross-reference system logs to identify which processes are impacting the system.

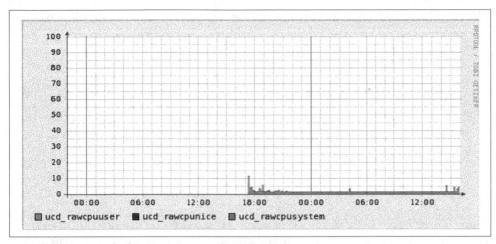

Figure 13-6. CPU utilization

Figure 13-7 shows bits in and out on the system's Ethernet interface. This can be useful, for example, to determine when your system is saturating its connection to the Internet. If the time that the traffic surge occurs is questionable, you might look into whether someone is performing illegal file transfers at 2 a.m.

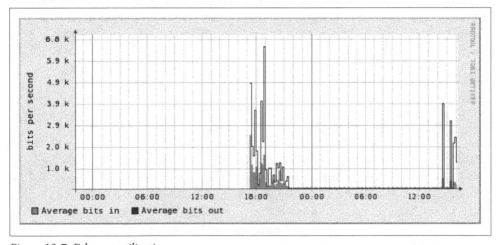

Figure 13-7. Ethernet utilization

Gathering Router Data

A discussion about Cricket wouldn't be complete without explaining how to configure it to gather data from your Cisco routers. We need to set up our *config* tree:

```
$ cd ~cricket
$ cp -r cricket/sample-config/routers/ ./cricket-config/
$ cp -r cricket/sample-config/router-interfaces/ cricket-config/
```

First, the *routers* subtree gathers variables such as temperature, CPU utilization, and so on. You will most certainly want to edit the default values in *cricket-config/routers/Targets*. Here is a sample from this file:

```
target  main-router
    target-type=Cisco-7500-Router
    short-desc  =   "Main router"
```

The target clause is the hostname of the router from which you wish to gather data. `target-type` is the type of Cisco device. Cricket currently supports the following:

- Cisco-2500-Router
- Cisco-3600-Router
- Cisco-7200-Router
- Cisco-7500-Router

It supports only these routers because Cricket uses Cisco-specific private MIB objects to gather temperature, CPU information, and so on.

Finally, `short-desc` is as the name implies: a short description of the device. Try to make this as meaningful as possible in case other people have to interpret this device's graphs. If you have other routers you wish to add to this file, go ahead.

Next we will want to configure the *router-interfaces* subtree. This tree does not have the Cisco-specific version restriction, so most any router can reside under this subtree. The file we are concerned with is *cricket-config/router-interfaces/interfaces*. Here is a sample from this file:

```
target --default--
    router = bsn-router

target Serial0_0_5
    interface-name  =   Serial0/0/5
    short-desc  =   "T1 to Nebraska"
```

The line `router = bsn-router` tells the collector that a router target is defined and each subsequent target configuration denotes an interface on the router—in our case, `bsn-router`—about which Cricket should gather interface statistics. It may seem like a daunting task to keep this file up-to-date. Well, don't fear. As with the *systemperf* example, there is a tool to help gather interface configurations from your routers. Here's a sample run:

```
$ cd ~cricket
$ cricket/util/listInterfaces router public > cricket-config/router-interfaces/ \
interfaces
```

The listInterfaces command discovers all interfaces on the router and creates configurations for each of them. The downside to this is you may end up with router interfaces you don't care to graph. If this is the case, just edit the *interfaces* file and remove the entries you don't want.

Now that we have changed the *config* tree, we must recompile it:

```
$ cricket/compile
```

 This is important to note. Each time you change the *config* tree, you must recompile it. Otherwise, your changes will not take effect.

The final step is to edit the *subtree-sets* file and reinstate these two subtrees:

```
# This file lists the subtrees that will be processed together in one
# set. See the comments at the beginning of collect-subtrees for more info.

# This will be passed to collector so it can find the Config Tree.
# If this directory does not start with a slash, it will
# have $HOME prepended.
base:   cricket-config

# this is where logs will be put. (The $HOME rule applies here too.)
logdir: cricket-logs

set normal:
        /systemperf
        /routers
        /router-interfaces
```

Here we have uncommented the */routers* and */router-interfaces* subtrees. The next time the collect-subtrees command runs, it will begin gathering data for these two new trees.

Figure 13-8 and Figure 13-9 show two router interface graphs.

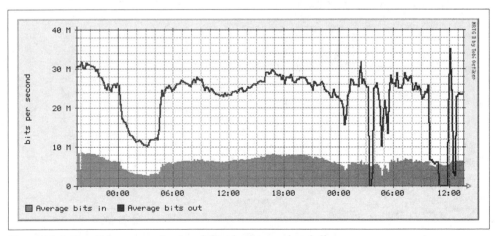

Figure 13-8. Fast Ethernet routing instability during peer handoff

The two graphs show router instability occurring in a service provider's peer network. During the event, about 10 Mb/sec of traffic shifted over to the second peer.

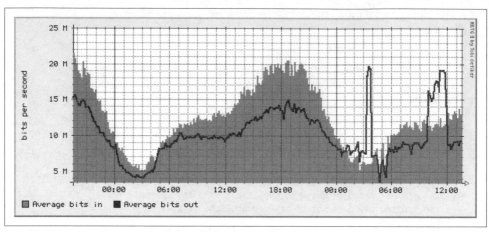

Figure 13-9. Handoff to another peer during router instability

Cricket helped discover the nature of the problem. The outbound traffic failed over to a nonoptimal but functional link. After the instability passed, the traffic returned to normal.

Command-Line Data Sources

Cricket is capable of executing commands instead of issuing SNMP queries. To help you to understand how Cricket does this, we will show how to switch one of the *systemperf* data sources from using SNMP to using a command-line tool.

First, let's look at the *cricket-config/systemperf/Defaults* file. Ellipses (. . .) show where we truncated the file for brevity.

```
target --default--
    server        = ""
    snmp-host     = %server%
    display-name  = "%auto-target-name% on %server%"
    min-size      = 0
    max-size      = undef

OID    hrSystemNumUsers    1.3.6.1.2.1.25.1.5.0

. . .

##### Datasources #########
datasource hrSystemNumUsers
    ds-source     = snmp://%snmp%/hrSystemNumUsers
    rrd-ds-type   = GAUGE

. . .

#### Target Types #########
targetType    hr_System
```

```
    ds    = "hrSystemProcesses, hrSystemNumUsers"
    view  = "Processes: hrSystemProcesses, Users: hrSystemNumUsers"


. . .


#### Graphs ##############
graph    hrSystemNumUsers
    color       = dark-green
    draw-as     = AREA
    y-axis      = "Users"
    units       = "Users"
    legend      = "# of Users"
    precision   = integer
```

The first configuration block is a default setting for target. Cricket uses target as a generic term for a variable or set of variables that will be gathered and/or graphed for a device. The default target sets `snmp-host` to `%server%`, which is defined in our *Targets* file. The `display-name` is set to `"%auto-target-name% on %server%"`. The auto-target-name is set to the target name (more on this in a moment). The `min-size` and `max-size` are used later in the *Defaults* file for graph configuration.

The next section of the *Defaults* file sets various OIDs we wish to use in our data sources. The data sources section sets up each piece of data we wish to gather. Here we show the data source for the number of users on the system. The line:

```
    ds-source    = snmp://%snmp%/hrSystemNumUsers
```

shows the basic syntax for SNMP polling. The convention used is specific to Cricket and resembles a URL. Basically, Cricket will SNMP poll `hrSystemNumUsers`. But how does it know what community string to use? Recall that the top level of the *config* tree has a *Defaults* file. Looking near the top of the file reveals:

```
Target    --default--
    dataDir                = %auto-base%/../cricket-data/%auto-target-path%
    email-program          = /usr/bin/mailx
    rrd-datafile           = %dataDir%/%auto-target-name%.rrd
    rrd-poll-interval      = 300
    persistent-alarms      = false
    snmp-host              = %auto-target-name%
    snmp-community         = public
    snmp-port              = 161
    snmp-timeout           = 2.0
    snmp-retries           = 5
    snmp-backoff           = 1.0
    snmp-version           = 1
    snmp                   = %snmp-community%@%snmp-host%:%snmp-port%:%snmp-timeout%:
%snmp-retries%:%snmp-backoff%:%snmp-version%
    summary-loc            = top
    show-path              = no
```

The *Defaults* file configures variables like community string, port, and version. Set these defaults to suit your requirements. But what if you need to use different community strings, for example, for different *config* subtrees? If this is the case, you can replicate variables like `snmp-community` in the particular subtree's *Defaults* file and Cricket will use them instead of the top-level defaults.

The next section of the *systemperf Defaults* file sets the target types. The target type in the example configuration is `hr_System`. The line:

```
ds      = "hrSystemProcesses, hrSystemNumUsers"
```

defines the data sources that make up this target type: `hrSystemProcesses` and `hrSystemNumUsers`.

Finally, the graph configuration for `hrSystemNumUsers` is shown.

Running a command to gather `hrSystemNumUsers` instead of using SNMP is as easy as changing the following line of code:

```
ds-source      = snmp://%snmp%/hrSystemNumUsers
```

to this:

```
ds-source      = "exec:0:/usr/bin/who | /usr/bin/wc -l"
```

Cricket supports the exec option for the `ds-source` identifier. Basically, it is interpreted like this:

```
exec:output_line_to_grab:command
```

The `output_line_to_grab` argument is meant for commands that may return multiple lines of output. The first line starts at 0, the second line at 1, and so on. The who command returns only one line of output, but notice how the data is returned:

```
$ /usr/bin/who | /usr/bin/wc -l
     5
```

There is whitespace before the 5. This is alright since Cricket will ignore leading whitespace until it finds a floating-point (or integer) number.

> If your Cricket instance will be managing remote devices, running a command like *who* won't work at all. It is presented here merely as an example of how to configure Cricket to run commands. Of course, you can execute scripts or programs that work over a network, which is really the point of allowing arbitrary programs to be run.

Parallelizing Cricket

One advantage to Cricket's *config* tree is that you can break the tree into logical groupings and have Cricket gather data from each tree (or groups of trees) in parallel. Recall our *subtree-sets* file:

```
# This file lists the subtrees that will be processed together in one
# set. See the comments at the beginning of collect-subtrees for more info.

# This will be passed to collector so it can find the Config Tree.
# If this directory does not start with a slash, it will
```

```
# have $HOME prepended.
base:   cricket-config

# this is where logs will be put. (The $HOME rule applies here too.)
logdir: cricket-logs

set normal:
        /systemperf
        /routers
        /router-interfaces
```

If we change the end like this:

```
# This file lists the subtrees that will be processed together in one
# set. See the comments at the beginning of collect-subtrees for more info.

# This will be passed to collector so it can find the Config Tree.
# If this directory does not start with a slash, it will
# have $HOME prepended.
base:   cricket-config

# this is where logs will be put. (The $HOME rule applies here too.)
logdir: cricket-logs

set servers:
        /systemperf

set routers:
        /routers
        /router-interfaces
```

we have created two separate subtree sets: one for servers and the other for routers. The next step is to edit our *crontab* file and change it like this:

```
*/5 * * * * /home/cricket/cricket/collect-subtrees servers
*/5 * * * * /home/cricket/cricket/collect-subtrees routers
```

This will cause two separate collect-subtree commands to run. The first one will collect data for the */systemperf* subtree and the other will collect for the */routers* and */router-interfaces* subtrees.

If you have a machine that is underpowered with respect to CPU and memory, you will want to limit how many of these collect-subtrees you configure. At the very least, try to stagger the times when each one begins. For example, one can start every five minutes, the next every six minutes, and so forth. This technique is also not foolproof, however. Because of variations in how operating systems perform with respect to clock-based activities, you are not guaranteed that something in cron that is scheduled to start every five minutes will start precisely 300 seconds after the last *crontab* entry. It could be off by a few microseconds, a few milliseconds, or even a few seconds. Depending on how many such activities you have scheduled and the limitations of the hardware in question, this could make a difference in performance.

Help with Cricket

This chapter only briefly described how to use Cricket. To learn more about Cricket, check out the following web pages:

http://cricket.sourceforge.net/support/doc/reference.html
    The Cricket Reference Guide describes in detail how to configure Cricket.

http://cricket.sourceforge.net/support/doc/new-devices.html
    This page shows how to add new devices to Cricket.

http://cricket.sourceforge.net/support/doc/
    The main source for Cricket documentation.

## CHAPTER 14

Java and SNMP

So far, we have shown how to use Perl scripts to perform SNMP tasks. In this chapter, we will show how to use Java to create SNMP applications. Java is not widely used in system and network administration circles, but there are those who have made the leap from scripting language to object-oriented language. While Java is an object-oriented language, you don't have to be an object guru to use Java.

Java has similar advantages to Perl. It's platform independent with built-in support for network sockets and threading. One advantage that Java has over Perl is that it can outperform Perl for certain types of tasks. Perl is commonly regarded as being well suited for processing text since its regular expression handling is very good. Java also has regular expression support and can generally outperform Perl in this regard. Java also has the advantage of the HotSpot compiler. HotSpot allows for a long-running Java program to be self-optimized over time. This is something that traditional compiled languages like C and C++ do not have and is also not found in Perl. Another advantage to Java is that creating multithreaded applications is very easy.

SNMP4J

The SNMP API presented in this chapter is SNMP4J. The current version is 1.5 and it works with Java 1.4.1 or later. It is released for free under the Apache software license. You can obtain a copy of SNMP4J from *http://www.snmp4j.org*. The library's design is patterned after the successful SNMP++ C++ library whose early versions were developed by HP.* Because of its roots, SNMP4J has a clean and easy-to-use API. SNMP4J's features include:

- SNMPv3 with MD5 and SHA authentication and DES and AES 128, AES 192, and AES 256 privacy.

---

* HP no longer develops or supports SNMP++. Frank Fock and Jochen Katz have taken SNMP++ and added SNMPv3 support. See *http://www.agentpp.com* for details.

- Pluggable *Message Processing Models* with implementations for MPv1, MPv2c, and MPv3.
- All PDU types.
- Pluggable *transport mappings*. UDP and TCP are supported out of the box.
- Pluggable *timeout model*.
- Synchronous and asynchronous requests.
- Command generator as well as command responder support.
- Java 1.4.1 or later.
- Logging based on Log4J but supports other logging APIs like Java 1.4 Logging.
- Row-based efficient asynchronous *table retrieval* with GETBULK.
- Multithreading support.
- JUnit tests (coming in release 2.0).

SNMP4J has a built-in thread pool model. This means that you can specify the number of threads that respond to and process incoming requests, making your SNMP applications highly efficient.

At this writing, the maintainers of SNMP4J have released an SNMP agent API based on SNMP4J. It is currently in the early alpha stage, so we will not discuss it in this chapter. But for those of you who are interested, keep an eye on the SNMP4J web site to track its development.

A detailed discussion of SNMP4J's API is beyond the scope of this chapter. Instead, we present examples of how to use the library to perform various SNMP operations. You will see that creating SNMP applications is quite easy and requires minimal programming. As a result, you don't have to think as much about using the API and can focus more on creating useful applications that solve whatever problems you face.

Example source code is provided on this book's web site, at *http://www.oreilly.com/ catalog/esnmp2/*. The example sources were built using a command-line tool that is available as a separate download from the SNMP4J web site. Each section in this chapter discusses pertinent aspects of the SNMP operation it is implementing as it pertains to SNMP4J.

SNMP getnext

The SNMP getnext operation is commonly referred to as "walking a MIB." The example source implements a command-line snmpwalk tool similar to that of Net-SNMP's snmpwalk:

```
public class SnmpWalk implements PDUFactory {
...
}
```

Our `SnmpWalk` class implements `PDUFactory`. This means we must implement a method with the following signature:

```
public PDU createPDU(Target target) {
...
}
```

The `createPDU` method is responsible for creating the proper PDU, either an SNMPv2c or SNMPv3 PDU. The type of PDU (the particular SNMP operation) is also configured as part of the version-specific PDU. This is accomplished by setting a member variable that is used when `createPDU( )` is called:

```
private int _pduType = PDU.GETNEXT;
```

The class has two different constructors:

```
public SnmpWalk(String host, String oid){
...
}
public SnmpWalk(String host, String oid, String user, String authProtocol,
   String authPassphrase, String privProtocol, String privPassphrase) {
...
}
```

The first constructor creates an SNMPv2c walk command. The arguments are the host on which an agent is running and the prefix of the OIDs we want to walk. The community string is hardcoded in the application, but ordinarily you will want to pass this as a constructor or expose a setter. The second constructor creates an SNMPv3 walk command. The first two arguments are the same as the first constructor, but the other arguments deal with setting up SNMPv3 security.

Each constructor sets the particular version of SNMP by using one of the following predefined constants:

- `SnmpConstants.version1`
- `SnmpConstants.version2c`
- `SnmpConstants.version3`

The following sequence of code sets up the security name (user), authentication protocol, authentication passphrase, privacy protocol, and privacy passphrase:

```
    _privPassphrase = new OctetString(privPassphrase);
 _authPassphrase = new OctetString(authPassphrase);
 _securityName = new OctetString(user);
    if (authProtocol.equals("MD5")) {
      _authProtocol = AuthMD5.ID;
    } else if (authProtocol.equals("SHA")) {
      _authProtocol = AuthSHA.ID;
    }
 if (privProtocol.equals("DES")) {
      _privProtocol = PrivDES.ID;
    } else if ((privProtocol.equals("AES128")) || (privProtocol.equals("AES"))) {
      _privProtocol = PrivAES128.ID;
```

```
        } else if (privProtocol.equals("AES192")) {
            _privProtocol = PrivAES192.ID;
        } else if (privProtocol.equals("AES256")) {
            _privProtocol = PrivAES256.ID;
        }
```

The privacy passphrase, authentication passphrase, and user are all stored internally as an `OctetString`, which, in contrast with a `String`, implements a character-set–independent 8-bit byte string. The authentication and privacy protocols are stored internally as OIDs. SNMP4J includes constants for all the various protocols and their respective OID value. They are:

- `AuthMD5.ID`
- `AuthSHA.ID`
- `PrivDES.ID`
- `PrivAES128.ID`
- `PrivAES192.ID`
- `PrivAES256.ID`

The next step is to add the OID for walking a `Vector` of `VariableBindings`:

```
    _vbs.add(new VariableBinding(new OID(oid)));
```

Next we create an instance of `UdpAddress`, which represents the host and port we plan to communicate with:

```
    _address = new UdpAddress(host+"/161");
```

The format that is passed to the constructor is `host/port`.

Now that we have the preliminaries set up, the user of the `SnmpWalk` class calls `doWalk( )` to initiate the process. The call to `send( )` sets up all the internals of SNMP:

```
    PDU response = send( );
```

Here is the sequence of calls that occurs before a response `PDU` is returned:

1. `createSnmpSession( )`
2. `createTarget( )`
3. `createPDU( )`
4. `walk(...)`
5. `processWalk( )`

Let's look at each of these method calls. The call to `createSnmpSession( )` creates the underlying SNMP session. If SNMPv3 is used, we add a user to this session with a call to `addUsmUser(snmp)`. This method looks like the following:

```
    private void addUsmUser(Snmp snmp) {
        snmp.getUSM( ).addUser(_securityName,
            new UsmUser(_securityName,
            _authProtocol,
```

```
        _authPassphrase,
        _privProtocol,
        _privPassphrase));
}
```

Here we call the getUSM( ) method for the SNMP session that was created. This in turn allows us to call addUser, where we create a new user entry, with _securityName, followed by a new instance of UsmUser and all the SNMPv3 security-specific parameters passed to the constructor. If you want to create multiple users for this SNMP session, you would repeat these steps until you have added all the users for your session.

Next we create a target by calling createTarget( ). This creates either a UserTarget (SNMPv3) or a CommunityTarget (SNMPv1 and SNMPv2c). Depending on the version used, either the _securityName or the _community variables are set for the respective target. If SNMPv3 is used, the security level is also specified and is set to one of the following constants:

- SecurityLevel.NOAUTH_NOPRIV
- SecurityLevel.AUTH_NOPRIV
- SecurityLevel.AUTH_PRIV

Once we return from createTarget( ), the send( ) method sets the version, address, timeout, and retries for the target. It also places all transport mappings into listen mode:

```
snmp.listen( );
```

This ensures that we respond to SNMP engine discovery requests.

createPDU( ) creates either a ScopedPDU for SNMPv3 or a PDU for SNMPv1 and SNMPv2c. The context name and context engine ID are set for the ScopedPDU. The resulting PDU is returned as the variable request and is used later on by other methods.

Now the walk( ) method is invoked. One of the first things it does is to get the root OID:

```
OID rootOID = request.get(0).getOid( );
```

Since request is a PDU instance, calling get(0) returns a VariableBinding. Calling getOid( ) on a VariableBinding gets its OID for the VariableBinding.

```
ResponseEvent responseEvent = snmp.send(request, target);
response = responseEvent.getResponse( );
```

This code fragment retrieves the lexicographically next object in the MIB tree we wish to walk and gets the response from the target. If the response is null, we never received a response. The pseudocode for walking a MIB tree follows:

```
do {
    Send request to target for top-level OID of where you want to start
```

```
    Check for response from target
} while(!processWalk( ));

function processWalk( ){
    if we have reached the end of the MIB, received an error, or received a
    response which isn't lexicographically in the MIB we are walking, then
    return true

    else print the result from the target. Now encode the
    received OID in the request object, so when we send the next request, the
    target will send us the next OID (lexicographically) in the tree, if
    there is one.
}
```

Once we've processed the target's MIB tree, we print some statistics on how many
requests were sent, how many objects were received, and the total walk time.

That's it in a nutshell. Let's look at a run of the SnmpWalk application. Here's our main
program for exercising the class:

```
public class Main{

public Main( ){
}

public static void main(String[] args){
System.out.println("Doing SNMPv2 walk..");
SnmpWalk walk = new SnmpWalk("127.0.0.1","1.3.6.1.2.1.1");
walk.doWalk( );

System.out.println("Doing SNMPv3 walk..");
walk = new SnmpWalk("127.0.0.1","1.3.6.1.2.1.1",
            "kschmidt","MD5","mysecretpass","DES","mypassphrase");
walk.doWalk( );
}
}
```

The first constructor creates an SNMPv2c PDU, which starts at the *system* (1.3.6.1.2.
1.1) OID and walks from there. The second constructor creates an SNMPv3 PDU
with kschmidt as the security name, MD5 as the authentication protocol, mysecretpass
as the authentication passphrase, DES as the privacy protocol, and mypassphrase as
the privacy passphrase. Here is the command for running this program, along with
its output:

```
$ java -cp SNMP4J.jar:.Main
Doing SNMPv2 walk..
1.3.6.1.2.1.1.1.0 = Linux dhcp48 2.6.8-2-686 #1 Mon Jan 24 03:58:38 EST 2005 i686
1.3.6.1.2.1.1.2.0 = 1.3.6.1.4.1.8072.3.2.10
1.3.6.1.2.1.1.3.0 = 4 days, 4:47:17.53
1.3.6.1.2.1.1.4.0 = myself
1.3.6.1.2.1.1.5.0 = dhcp48
1.3.6.1.2.1.1.6.0 = A bld JM-10119 floor 7
1.3.6.1.2.1.1.8.0 = 0:00:00.08
```

```
1.3.6.1.2.1.1.9.1.2.1 = 1.3.6.1.2.1.31
1.3.6.1.2.1.1.9.1.2.2 = 1.3.6.1.6.3.1
1.3.6.1.2.1.1.9.1.2.3 = 1.3.6.1.2.1.49
1.3.6.1.2.1.1.9.1.2.4 = 1.3.6.1.2.1.4
1.3.6.1.2.1.1.9.1.2.5 = 1.3.6.1.2.1.50
1.3.6.1.2.1.1.9.1.2.6 = 1.3.6.1.6.3.16.2.2.1
1.3.6.1.2.1.1.9.1.2.7 = 1.3.6.1.6.3.10.3.1.1
1.3.6.1.2.1.1.9.1.2.8 = 1.3.6.1.6.3.11.3.1.1
1.3.6.1.2.1.1.9.1.2.9 = 1.3.6.1.6.3.15.2.1.1
1.3.6.1.2.1.1.9.1.3.1 = The MIB module to describe generic objects for network
interface sub-layers
1.3.6.1.2.1.1.9.1.3.2 = The MIB module for SNMPv2 entities
1.3.6.1.2.1.1.9.1.3.3 = The MIB module for managing TCP implementations
1.3.6.1.2.1.1.9.1.3.4 = The MIB module for managing IP and ICMP implementations
1.3.6.1.2.1.1.9.1.3.5 = The MIB module for managing UDP implementations
1.3.6.1.2.1.1.9.1.3.6 = View-based Access Control Model for SNMP.
1.3.6.1.2.1.1.9.1.3.7 = The SNMP Management Architecture MIB.
1.3.6.1.2.1.1.9.1.3.8 = The MIB for Message Processing and Dispatching.
1.3.6.1.2.1.1.9.1.3.9 = The management information definitions for the SNMP User-
based Security Model.
1.3.6.1.2.1.1.9.1.4.1 = 0:00:00.00
1.3.6.1.2.1.1.9.1.4.2 = 0:00:00.00
1.3.6.1.2.1.1.9.1.4.3 = 0:00:00.00
1.3.6.1.2.1.1.9.1.4.4 = 0:00:00.00
1.3.6.1.2.1.1.9.1.4.5 = 0:00:00.00
1.3.6.1.2.1.1.9.1.4.6 = 0:00:00.00
1.3.6.1.2.1.1.9.1.4.7 = 0:00:00.08
1.3.6.1.2.1.1.9.1.4.8 = 0:00:00.08
1.3.6.1.2.1.1.9.1.4.9 = 0:00:00.08

Total requests sent:    35
Total objects received: 35
Total walk time:        55 milliseconds
End of walked subtree '1.3.6.1.2.1.1' reached at:
1.3.6.1.2.1.2.1.0 = 3

Doing SNMPv3 walk..
1.3.6.1.2.1.1.1.0 = Linux dhcp48 2.6.8-2-686 #1 Mon Jan 24 03:58:38 EST 2005 i686
1.3.6.1.2.1.1.2.0 = 1.3.6.1.4.1.8072.3.2.10
1.3.6.1.2.1.1.3.0 = 4 days, 4:47:18.21
1.3.6.1.2.1.1.4.0 = myself
1.3.6.1.2.1.1.5.0 = dhcp48
1.3.6.1.2.1.1.6.0 = A bld JM-10119 floor 7
1.3.6.1.2.1.1.8.0 = 0:00:00.08
1.3.6.1.2.1.1.9.1.2.1 = 1.3.6.1.2.1.31
1.3.6.1.2.1.1.9.1.2.2 = 1.3.6.1.6.3.1
1.3.6.1.2.1.1.9.1.2.3 = 1.3.6.1.2.1.49
1.3.6.1.2.1.1.9.1.2.4 = 1.3.6.1.2.1.4
1.3.6.1.2.1.1.9.1.2.5 = 1.3.6.1.2.1.50
1.3.6.1.2.1.1.9.1.2.6 = 1.3.6.1.6.3.16.2.2.1
1.3.6.1.2.1.1.9.1.2.7 = 1.3.6.1.6.3.10.3.1.1
1.3.6.1.2.1.1.9.1.2.8 = 1.3.6.1.6.3.11.3.1.1
1.3.6.1.2.1.1.9.1.2.9 = 1.3.6.1.6.3.15.2.1.1
```

```
1.3.6.1.2.1.1.9.1.3.1 = The MIB module to describe generic objects for network
interface sub-layers
1.3.6.1.2.1.1.9.1.3.2 = The MIB module for SNMPv2 entities
1.3.6.1.2.1.1.9.1.3.3 = The MIB module for managing TCP implementations
1.3.6.1.2.1.1.9.1.3.4 = The MIB module for managing IP and ICMP implementations
1.3.6.1.2.1.1.9.1.3.5 = The MIB module for managing UDP implementations
1.3.6.1.2.1.1.9.1.3.6 = View-based Access Control Model for SNMP.
1.3.6.1.2.1.1.9.1.3.7 = The SNMP Management Architecture MIB.
1.3.6.1.2.1.1.9.1.3.8 = The MIB for Message Processing and Dispatching.
1.3.6.1.2.1.1.9.1.3.9 = The management information definitions for the SNMP User-
based Security Model.
1.3.6.1.2.1.1.9.1.4.1 = 0:00:00.00
1.3.6.1.2.1.1.9.1.4.2 = 0:00:00.00
1.3.6.1.2.1.1.9.1.4.3 = 0:00:00.00
1.3.6.1.2.1.1.9.1.4.4 = 0:00:00.00
1.3.6.1.2.1.1.9.1.4.5 = 0:00:00.00
1.3.6.1.2.1.1.9.1.4.6 = 0:00:00.00
1.3.6.1.2.1.1.9.1.4.7 = 0:00:00.08
1.3.6.1.2.1.1.9.1.4.8 = 0:00:00.08
1.3.6.1.2.1.1.9.1.4.9 = 0:00:00.08

Total requests sent:    35
Total objects received: 35
Total walk time:        741 milliseconds
End of walked subtree '1.3.6.1.2.1.1' reached at:
1.3.6.1.2.1.2.1.0 = 3
```

That's it. We've covered a lot of ground in a small space, so let's summarize the pertinent parts of what we've accomplished:

- Our SNMP application class implements PDUFactory by implementing a createPDU( ) method.

- The version of SNMP is set, and based on the version, we either use a community string or create a USM entry with a security name and no authentication and privacy, authentication and no privacy, or authentication and privacy.

- The address and port of the target we communicate with is used to create a UdpAddress.

- The SNMP request is sent.

- We create the SNMP session and add the USM user to the session if SNMPv3 is used.

- A target is created. If SNMPv2c is used, a CommunityTarget is created with the community string. Otherwise, a UserTarget is created with the value of _securityName and the proper security level is ascertained and set.

- The createPDU( ) method creates either a ScopedPDU for SNMPv3 or a PDU otherwise.

- From here on out, we walk the MIB tree using the pseudocode algorithm presented earlier.

Each of the remaining examples uses the same basic code for configuring SNMPv2c or SNMPv3. We will point out where the application differs with respect to the actual SNMP operation it implements.

SNMP set

The SnmpSet class looks very similar to the SnmpWalk class. As with the SnmpWalk class, _pduType is set to the appropriate SNMP operation we plan to perform:

```
private int _pduType = PDU.SET;
```

We've introduced a doSet( ) method that operates in a similar manner to the doWalk( ) method of the SnmpWalk class. An SNMP set has the following components:

- An OID
- The syntax for the OID
- A new or different value you wish the OID to take on in the target's SNMP stack

The difference between these classes lies in that third element, the new value you are setting to.

Let's look at the Main class, which uses SnmpSet:

```
public class Main{
  public Main( ){
  }

  public static void main(String[] args){
    System.out.println("Doing SNMPv2 set..");
    SnmpSet set = new SnmpSet("127.0.0.1",
      "1.3.6.1.2.1.1.6.0={s}Right here, right
  now.");
      set.doSet( );

    System.out.println("Doing SNMPv3 set..");
    set = new SnmpSet("127.0.0.1",
      "1.3.6.1.2.1.1.6.0={s}Some place else..",
      "kschmidt","MD5","mysecretpass","DES","mypassphrase");
    set.doSet( );
  }
}
```

The notation we are using to specify the OID, syntax, and value is the same as the notation for the SNMP4J command-line tool. It has the following format:

```
OID={syntax}value_for_OID
```

Table 14-1 lists the different values that syntax can take on, along with the corresponding SNMP4J class that is used to encode *value_for_OID* into that type.

Table 14-1. Syntax values with SNMP4J class names

Syntax value	SNMP4J class	Meaning
i	Integer32	Signed 32-bit integer
u	UnsignedInteger32	Unsigned 32-bit integer
s	OctetString	Octet string
x	OctetString.fromString(value, ':', 16);	Octet string specified as a hex value with bytes separated by colons
d	OctetString.fromString(value, '.', 10);	Octet string specified as a decimal value with bytes separated with dots
b	OctetString.fromString(value, '', 2);	Octet string specified as a binary value with bytes separated with spaces
n	Null	Null value
o	OID	OID value
t	TimeTicks	TimeTicks value
a	IpAddress	IP Address

The getVariableBinding( ) method parses the OID, syntax, and value and encodes the value based on the syntax. Consider the following code:

```
VariableBinding vb = new VariableBinding(new OID(oid));
...
Variable variable;
...
variable = new Integer32(Integer.parseInt(value));
...
vb.setVariable(variable);
...
v.add(vb);
```

This sequence, taken from getVariableBinding( ), shows how to create a new VariableBinding from the OID we want to set, create a new Variable encoded with the proper syntax and value for the OID, and set it within the VariableBinding. The VariableBinding is then added to a Vector, which was created earlier.

The following code shows how the Vector containing the VariableBinding is placed into the request.

```
PDU request = createPDU(_target);
for (int i=0; i< _vbs.size( ); i++) {
  request.add((VariableBinding)_vbs.get(i));
}
```

Since we loop over the Vector, you can add as many VariableBindings as desired to the Vector and they will all get placed in the PDU.

Finally, the SET request is now ready to send:

```
responseEvent = snmp.send(request, _target);
```

When we run the program, the output looks like this:

```
$ java -classpath SNMP4J.jar:. Main
Doing SNMPv2 set..
Received response after 18 millis
Received response: requestID=1713864373, errorIndex=0, errorStatus=Success(0)
1.3.6.1.2.1.1.6.0 = Right here, right now.
Doing SNMPv3 set..
Received response after 618 millis
Received response: requestID=1705592271, errorIndex=0, errorStatus=Success(0)
1.3.6.1.2.1.1.6.0 = Someplace else.
```

Here we set the *sysLocation* (1.3.6.1.2.1.1.6)* to "Right here, right now." using
SNMPv2c and then set it to "Someplace else..." using SNMPv3. We also see the
errorIndex and errorStatus, which both confirm that the set operations succeeded.

Sending Traps and Informs

Now we know how to encode OIDs and their respective syntax and values. This is
exactly what we need to send SNMP traps and informs. The SnmpTrap application is
capable of sending either SNMP traps or informs, depending on the value type of the
parameter passed to the constructor. The PDU type is set to PDU.TRAP by default. If
an inform is to be sent, the PDU type is set to PDU.INFORM.

The doTrap( ) method is invoked and we operate in much the same manner as the
SnmpSet application. We get the variable binding that is sent in the trap or inform.
After getVariableBinding( ) is called, checkTrapVariables( ) is called. Since the first
variable binding in a trap or inform is *sysUpTime* and the second variable binding is
snmpTrapOID for the particular trap or inform we are sending, this method ensures
that these two variables appear before any other bindings we wish to send. Note that
we created a _trapOID member variable for the SnmpTrap class:

```
private OID _trapOID = new OID("1.3.6.1.4.1.2789.2005");
```

Now let's look at the Main class that sends two traps and two informs:

```
public class Main{
  public Main( ){
  }

  public static void main(String[] args){
    System.out.println("Doing SNMPv2 trap..");
    SnmpTrap trap = new SnmpTrap("127.0.0.1",
      "1.3.6.1.4.1.2789.2005.1={s}WWW Server Has Been Restarted",1);
    trap.doTrap( );

    System.out.println("Doing SNMPv3 trap..");
    trap =
      new SnmpTrap("127.0.0.1",
```

---

* Recall that since sysName is a scalar object and not a columnar object, we use the OID *1.3.6.1.2.1.1.6.0* and
not 1.3.6.1.2.1.1.6.

```
    "1.3.6.1.4.1.2789.2005.1={s}WWW Server Has Been Restarted",
    1,"kschmidt","MD5","mysecretpass","DES","mypassphrase");
  trap.doTrap();

  System.out.println("Doing SNMPv2 inform..");
  trap = new SnmpTrap("127.0.0.1",
    "1.3.6.1.4.1.2789.2005.1={s}WWW Server Has Been Restarted",2);
  trap.doTrap();

  System.out.println("Doing SNMPv3 inform..");
  trap =
    new SnmpTrap("127.0.0.1",
    "1.3.6.1.4.1.2789.2005.1={s}WWW Server Has Been Restarted",
    2,"kschmidt","MD5","mysecretpass","DES","mypassphrase");
  trap.doTrap();
  }
}
```

Note that if you pass an integer value 1 to the third parameter of the constructor, a trap is sent. If you pass the value 2, an inform is sent. Here's the output from this application:

```
% java -classpath SNMP4J.jar:. Main
Doing SNMPv2 trap..
TRAP sent successfully
Doing SNMPv3 trap..
TRAP sent successfully
Doing SNMPv2 inform..
Received response after 9 millis
Received response: requestID=1332193165, errorIndex=0, errorStatus=Success(0)
1.3.6.1.4.1.2789.2005.1 = WWW Server Has Been Restarted
1.3.6.1.6.3.1.1.4.1.0 = 1.3.6.1.4.1.2789.2005
Doing SNMPv3 inform..
Received response after 115 millis
Received response: requestID=1931824326, errorIndex=0, errorStatus=Success(0)
1.3.6.1.4.1.2789.2005.1 = WWW Server Has Been Restarted
1.3.6.1.6.3.1.1.4.1.0 = 1.3.6.1.4.1.2789.2005
```

Note that when an inform is sent, a response is received. Recall that SNMP informs are basically traps where the receiver sends an acknowledgement when it receives the PDU.

Receiving Traps and Informs

We've split up the SNMPv2c and SNMPv3 trap receivers into two separate classes, V2TrapReceiver and V3TrapReceiver. These classes implement CommandResponder. This means that we must implement a method that has the following signature:

```
public synchronized void processPdu(CommandResponderEvent e) {
  ...
}
```

The processPdu method is responsible for handling incoming requests. Since SnmpWalk supports SNMPv3, we have to be able to respond to discovery requests from an authoritative SNMP engine.

 With the other SNMP applications, we created transport objects that were a combination of the IP address and port on a remote machine. With a trap or inform receiver, we create a target object, but the IP address is the IP of the local Ethernet interface we wish to bind to, along with the port (default for traps is 162).

Consider the following code sequence:

```
_threadPool = ThreadPool.create("DispatcherPool", _numThreads);
MessageDispatcher mtDispatcher =
new MultiThreadedMessageDispatcher(_threadPool, new MessageDispatcherImpl());

// add message processing models
mtDispatcher.addMessageProcessingModel(new MPv2c());

// add all security protocols
SecurityProtocols.getInstance().addDefaultProtocols();

CommunityTarget target = new CommunityTarget();
if(target != null) {
  target.setCommunity(_comm);
  _target = target;
} else {
  System.out.println("Unable to create Target object");
  System.exit(-1);
}

_snmp = new Snmp(mtDispatcher, _transport);
if(_snmp != null){
  _snmp.addCommandResponder(this);
} else {
  System.out.println("Unable to create Snmp object");
  System.exit(-1);
}
```

This example does the following:

- Creates a thread pool with _numThreads that can respond to incoming traps
- Adds an SNMPv2c message processing model to the MessageDispatcher
- Adds all security protocols by default
- Creates a CommunityTarget and sets the community string
- Creates a new SNMP instance by passing it the mtDispatcher instance
- Adds the class's instance as a CommandResponder to the SNMP instance

Now let's look at the same sequence for SNMPv3:

```
_threadPool = ThreadPool.create("DispatcherPool", _numThreads);

MessageDispatcher mtDispatcher =
  new MultiThreadedMessageDispatcher(_threadPool, new MessageDispatcherImpl());

// add message processing models
mtDispatcher.addMessageProcessingModel(new MPv1());
mtDispatcher.addMessageProcessingModel(new MPv2c());
mtDispatcher.addMessageProcessingModel(new MPv3());

// add all security protocols
SecurityProtocols.getInstance().addDefaultProtocols();
_snmp = new Snmp(mtDispatcher, _transport);
if(_snmp != null){
  _snmp.addCommandResponder(this);
} else {
  System.out.println("Unable to create Target object");
  System.exit(-1);
}

MPv3 mpv3 =
  (MPv3)_snmp.getMessageProcessingModel(MessageProcessingModel.MPv3);
USM usm = new USM(SecurityProtocols.getInstance(),
  new OctetString(mpv3.createLocalEngineID()), 0);
SecurityModels.getInstance().addSecurityModel(usm);
```

No surprises here. We do basically the same operations for SNMPv3, except that we also create a USM entry and a local engine ID in case we receive a discovery request.

The client of this class calls listen() to begin the session:

```
public synchronized void listen() {
  try {
    _transport.listen();
  } catch(IOException ioex) {
    System.out.println("Unable to listen: " + ioex);
    System.exit(-1);
  }

  System.out.println("Waiting for traps..");
  try {
    this.wait();//Wait for traps to come in
  } catch (InterruptedException ex) {
    System.out.println("Interrupted while waiting for traps: " + ex);
    System.exit(-1);
  }
}
```

We place the transport into listen mode by calling _transport.listen(). If this succeeds, this.wait() is called and we block until a trap or inform comes in. When one does, processPdu() is invoked and we handle the request since we created our own implementation of this method.

Since listen( ) is blocked when called, here are two similar Main classes, one for an SNMPv2c receiver and one for an SNMPv3 receiver:

```
public class Main{
    public Main( ){
    }

  public static void main(String[] args){
    V2TrapReceiver v2 = new V2TrapReceiver( );
    v2.listen( );
  }
}


public class Main{
    public Main( ){
    }

  public static void main(String[] args){
    V3TrapReceiver v3 = new V3TrapReceiver( );
    v3.listen( );
  }
}
```

When sending an SNMPv3 trap (we're using the Net-SNMP command-line tools to send traps and informs), use a command like this:

```
$ snmptrap -v3 -u kjs -a MD5 -A "this is private" -x DES -X "this is me" \
127.0.0.1 '' .1.3.6.1.6.3.1.1.5.3 ifIndex i 2 ifAdminStatus i 1 ifOperStatus i 1
Waiting for traps..
TRAP[reqestID=769359741, errorStatus=0, errorIndex=0, VBS[1.3.6.1.2.1.1.3.0 = 64
days, 22:53:05.51; 1.3.6.1.6.3.1.1.4.1.0 = 1.3.6.1.6.3.1.1.5.3; 1.3.6.1.2.1.2.2.1.1 =
2; 1.3.6.1.2.1.2.2.1.7 = 1; 1.3.6.1.2.1.2.2.1.8 = 1]]
```

We see basically the same output when sending an SNMPv2c trap:

```
$ snmptrap -v2c -c public 127.0.0.1 '' .1.3.6.1.6.3.1.1.5.3 \
ifIndex i 2 ifAdminStatus i 1 ifOperStatus i 1
Waiting for traps..
TRAP[reqestID=1476119517, errorStatus=Success(0), errorIndex=0, VBS[1.3.6.1.2.1.1.3.0
= 64 days, 22:56:04.20; 1.3.6.1.6.3.1.1.4.1.0 = 1.3.6.1.6.3.1.1.5.3; 1.3.6.1.2.1.2.2.
1.1 = 2; 1.3.6.1.2.1.2.2.1.7 = 1; 1.3.6.1.2.1.2.2.1.8 = 1]]
```

Receiving informs produces, as you might imagine, similar output to traps:

```
$ snmpinform -v2c -c public 127.0.0.1 '' .1.3.6.1.6.3.1.1.5.3 \
ifIndex i 2 ifAdminStatus i 1 ifOperStatus i 1
Waiting for traps..
INFORM[reqestID=2056364955, errorStatus=Success(0), errorIndex=0, VBS[1.3.6.1.2.1.1.
3.0 = 65 days, 23:41:40.60; 1.3.6.1.6.3.1.1.4.1.0 = 1.3.6.1.6.3.1.1.5.3; 1.3.6.1.2.1.
2.2.1.1 = 2; 1.3.6.1.2.1.2.2.1.7 = 1; 1.3.6.1.2.1.2.2.1.8 = 1]]
```

And finally an SNMPv3 inform:

```
$ snmpinform -v3 -u kjs -a MD5 -A "this is private" -x DES \
-X "this is me" 127.0.0.1 '' .1.3.6.1.6.3.1.1.5.3 ifIndex i 2 \
ifAdminStatus i 1 ifOperStatus i 1
Waiting for traps..
INFORM[reqestID=648331621, errorStatus=0, errorIndex=0, VBS[1.3.6.1.2.1.1.3.0 = 65
days, 23:44:40.18; 1.3.6.1.6.3.1.1.4.1.0 = 1.3.6.1.6.3.1.1.5.3; 1.3.6.1.2.1.2.2.1.1 =
2; 1.3.6.1.2.1.2.2.1.7 = 1; 1.3.6.1.2.1.2.2.1.8 = 1]]
```

One final note: recall that our SnmpTrap class had to encode *sysUpTime* and *snmpTrapOID* as the first two variable bindings in the trap we created. Notice how all the output includes this information, as encoded from the Net-SNMP command-line tools:

```
...VBS[1.3.6.1.2.1.1.3.0 = 65 days, 23:44:40.18;
1.3.6.1.6.3.1.1.4.1.0 = 1.3.6.1.6.3.1.1.5.3;
...]]
```

Resources

The SNMP4J web site, *http://www.snmp4j.org*, has Javadoc (*http://www.snmp4j.org/doc/index.html*) for all the classes in this package. There is also an active mailing list where newcomers can ask questions and get answers to issues that may arise when using this library.

Using Input and Output Octets

To be SNMP-compatible, an IP device must support MIB-II (*iso.org.dod.internet. mgmt.mib-2*) objects. MIB-II contains the *interfaces* table (*mib-2.interfaces.ifTable. ifEntry*), which is one of the most useful objects for network monitoring. This table contains information about the system's network interfaces. Some of its objects are:

ifDescr
> A user-provided description of the interface

ifType
> The interface's type (token ring, Ethernet, etc.)

ifOperStatus
> Whether the interface is up, down, or in some kind of test mode

ifMtu
> The size of the largest packet that can be sent over the interface

ifSpeed
> The maximum bandwidth of the interface

ifPhysAddress
> The low-level (hardware) address of the interface

ifInOctets
> The number of octets received by the interface

ifOutOctets
> The number of octets sent by the interface

We explored various parts of this table in other chapters, but avoided saying too much about *ifInOctets* and *ifOutOctets*. RFC 1213 states that *ifOutOctets* and *ifInOctets* are the total number of octets sent and received on an interface, including framing characters.

In many environments, this information is crucial. Companies such as ISPs make their livelihoods by providing usable bandwidth to their customers, and thus spend huge amounts of time and money monitoring and measuring their interfaces, circuits, etc. When these pipes fill up or get clogged, customers get upset. So, the big question is, how can you monitor bandwidth effectively? Being able to answer this question is often a life-or-death issue.

The information you need to answer this question comes in a few parts. First, you must know what type of line you are trying to monitor. Without this information, the numbers don't mean much. Then you must find the line's maximum speed and determine whether it is used in full- or half-duplex mode. In most cases, you can find both of these pieces of information using SNMP. The *ifSpeed* object defined in MIB-II's *interfaces* table provides "an estimate of the interface's current bandwidth in bits per second." You can poll this object to find the line's maximum speed, or at least what the agent thinks the line's maximum speed should be. Note, though, that you must watch for some pitfalls. For example, Cisco routers have default maximum bandwidths for various types of links, but these defaults may not have much to do with reality: for instance, the default bandwidth for a serial line is 1.544 Mbps, regardless of the actual line speed. To get meaningful data, you must configure the router to report the maximum bandwidth correctly. (Sometimes, network administrators intentionally set the interface bandwidth to an incorrect number to nudge routing paths a different way. If this is the case, you're going to have trouble getting meaningful data out of SNMP.)

It's easier to get reliable information about the line's duplex mode. Serial lines operate in full-duplex mode. This means they can send and receive information at the same time (e.g., a 56 Kbps serial line can upload and download at 56 Kbps simultaneously, for a total of 112 Kbps). Other types of lines, such as 10-baseT Ethernet, can handle only half duplex. In a typical 10-baseT environment, the distinction between uploading and downloading data is meaningless; total bandwidth through the line is limited to 10 Mbps of input and output combined. Some devices have 10/100 cards in them, which makes identification even harder.

Many vendors have private MIBs that return the duplex state. For example, the following Cisco object returns the duplex state for an interface on the model 2900 switch:

iso.org.dod.internet.private.enterprises.cisco.ciscoMgmt.ciscoC2900MIB.c2900MIBObjects. c2900Port.c2900PortTable.c2900PortEntry.c2900PortDuplexStatus.

The table to which this object belongs also contains an object that can be used to switch an interface's duplex state. This object is useful if you have a device that is incorrectly negotiating half duplex instead of full duplex; you can use it to force the port into the correct duplex state.

Once you find the line's maximum speed and duplex mode, you can calculate its utilization percentage. Many NMS products let you create *expressions*, which are named formulas that use MIB objects as variables. OpenView allows you to define expressions in the file *$OV_CONF/mibExpr.conf*. The syntax used in this file is complicated. Expressions are written in postfix notation.* The file contains some entries by default; these expressions are often useful, and may not need any tweaking† to work for your environment. Here is the default definition of the expression If%util:

```
If%util \
"Percent of available bandwidth utilized on an interface\n\
Computed by:\n\
    (Received byte rate + transmitted byte rate) * 8\n\
    ------------------------------------------------\n\
                    interface link speed\n\
then converted to a percentage."\
.1.3.6.1.2.1.2.2.1.10. \
.1.3.6.1.2.1.2.2.1.16. \
+ \
8 \
* \
.1.3.6.1.2.1.2.2.1.5. \
/ \
100 \
*
```

This expression is broken up into three parts: an expression name, comments, and the expression itself. We will use the expression name within xnmgraph for our data-collection definitions. The comments will help us understand what this expression really does. The syntax of the expression is defined in the *mibExpr.conf* (4) manpage. In short, it adds the values of two MIB objects (*ifInOctets* and *ifOutOctets*), multiplies by 8 to get the number of bits traveling through the interface, divides by the interface speed (*ifSpeed*), and converts the result to a percentage. As you can see here, you can break expressions into several lines by using the familiar Unix back-slash-escape at the end of each line.

Once we have defined If%util, we can use it to plot utilization with xnmgraph:

```
$ /opt/OV/bin/xnmgraph -monochrome -c public -poll 5 -title Ifutil_Formula -mib \
If%util:CiscoRouter1a:::::.1.3.6.1.2.1.2.2.1.2:::" CiscoRouter14a
```

This displays a graph of the percent utilization for every interface on the device *CiscoRouter14a*. Note that you can use an expression name as the first of the colon-separated arguments in the xnmgraph command.

Before you start using If%util to measure your entire organization, notice that this expression measures only half-duplex lines—that is, it compares the sum of the input and output octets to the line's capacity. Any full-duplex line graphed with this calculation will look wrong. To prove this point, consider a full-duplex serial line with a maximum speed of 500 Kbps in each direction that is currently sending 125 Kbps and receiving 125 Kbps. The formula for If%util gives us a utilization of 50%,

---

* Also referred to as "reverse Polish notation." Instead of writing "1 + 2", you would write "1 2 +".

† The recommended way to modify *$OV_CONF/mibExpr.conf* is to use xnmcollect with the –delExpr or –load-Expr switch.

which is incorrect: the line is really at 25% of capacity. For a full-duplex line, it makes more sense to make separate computations for incoming and outgoing data. This gives you a better representation of what your network is doing, since in full-duplex mode the incoming data rate isn't affected by the outgoing data. Here are revised expressions for send utilization (WANIF%SendUtil) and receive utilization (WANIF%RecvUtil):

```
WANIf%SendUtil \
"% interface utilization from (ifOutOctets * 8 * 100) / ifSpeed"\
.1.3.6.1.2.1.2.2.1.16. \
8 \
* \
100 \
* \
.1.3.6.1.2.1.2.2.1.5. \
/

WANIf%RecvUtil \
"% interface utilization from (ifInOctets * 8 * 100) / ifSpeed"\
.1.3.6.1.2.1.2.2.1.10. \
8 \
* \
100 \
* \
.1.3.6.1.2.1.2.2.1.5. \
/
```

Now let's take a look at some actual graphs. We graphed different expressions and MIB objects at the same time for a 10-baseT (half-duplex) Ethernet interface. We then created some traffic on the interface and captured the results. Here is the script that generates the graphs:

```
/opt/OV/bin/xnmgraph -monochrome -c public -poll 5 -title \
Cisco_Private_Local_Mib -mib \
".1.3.6.1.4.1.9.2.2.1.1.6:CiscoRouter1a:4:::.1.3.6.1.2.1.2.2.1.2:::,\
.1.3.6.1.4.1.9.2.2.1.1.8:CiscoRouter1a:4:::.1.3.6.1.2.1.2.2.1.2:::" \
CiscoRouter1a &

/opt/OV/bin/xnmgraph -monochrome -c public -poll 5 -title Ifutil_Formula \
-mib "If%util:CiscoRouter1a:4:::.1.3.6.1.2.1.2.2.1.2:::" CiscoRouter1a &

/opt/OV/bin/xnmgraph -monochrome -c public -poll 5 -title \
WANIfRecvUtil_Formula -mib \
"WANIf%RecvUtil:CiscoRouter1a:4:::.1.3.6.1.2.1.2.2.1.2:::" CiscoRouter1a &

/opt/OV/bin/xnmgraph -monochrome -c public -poll 5 -title
WANIfSendUtil_Formula -mib \
"WANIf%SendUtil:CiscoRouter1a:4:::.1.3.6.1.2.1.2.2.1.2:::" CiscoRouter1a &

/opt/OV/bin/xnmgraph -monochrome -c public -poll 5 -title ifInOctets -mib \
".1.3.6.1.2.1.2.2.1.10:CiscoRouter1a:4:::.1.3.6.1.2.1.2.2.1.2:::" \
CiscoRouter1a &
```

```
/opt/OV/bin/xnmgraph -monochrome -c public -poll 5 -title ifOutOctets -mib \
".1.3.6.1.2.1.2.2.1.18.CiscoRouter1a:4:::.1.3.6.1.2.1.2.2.1.2:::" \
CiscoRouter1a &
```

Figure A-1 shows the MIB objects *.iso.org.dod.internet.private.enterprises.cisco.local. linterfaces.lifTable.lifEntry.locIfInBitsSec* and *.iso.org.dod.internet.private.enterprises. cisco.local.linterfaces.lifTable.lifEntry.locIfOutBitsSec.* These are private Cisco MIB objects that report the data rate in and out of an interface, in bits per second.

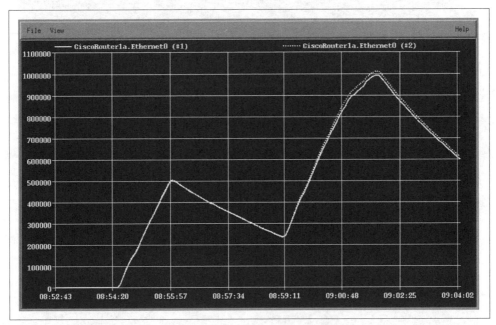

Figure A-1. Graph of Cisco private MIB objects

The next graph, shown in Figure A-2, shows the expression If%util. It's surprisingly different. The difference arises because Cisco uses a five-minute decaying average for these two objects. This can be both good and bad. The decaying average can prevent you from seeing local peaks and valleys in usage. In this example, we see two usage peaks, which the decaying average smears over a longer period of time. When using vendors' private MIBs, be sure to find out how they calculate their numbers.

Figure A-3 and Figure A-4 show the WANIf%RecvUtil and WANIf%SendUtil expressions. Since this is a half-duplex interface, we don't need to look at each direction (in and out) separately, but it may help to verify whether the receive path or the send path is maxed out. Comparing Figure A-3 with Figure A-4 shows that we are sending a bit more traffic than we are receiving.

The standard MIB-II objects *ifInOctets* and *ifOutOctets* are graphed in Figure A-5 and Figure A-6. Remember that these do not show bits per second. Again, these graphs show that we are sending more traffic than we are receiving. The octet graphs

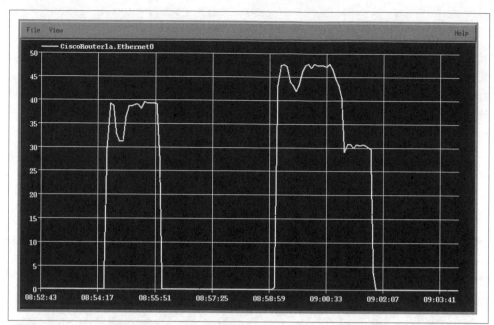

Figure A-2. Graph of If%util

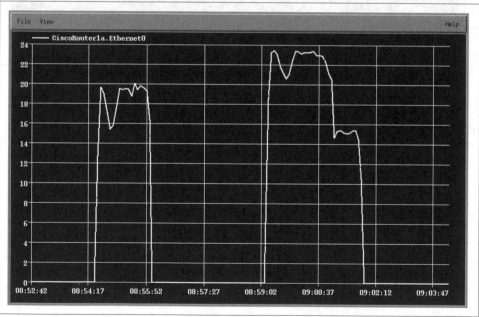

Figure A-3. Graph of WANIf%RecvUtil

in Figure A-5 and Figure A-6 show a real-time picture, like the WAN expressions but unlike Cisco's private MIB objects.

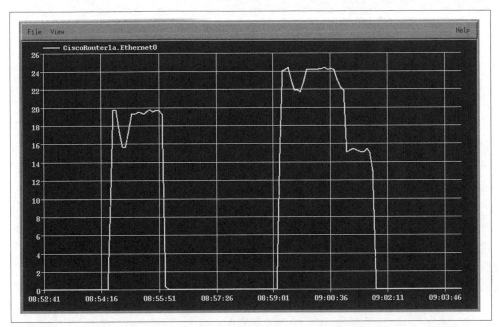

Figure A-4. Graph of WANIf%SendUtil

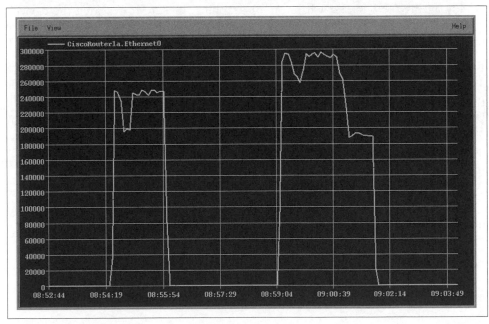

Figure A-5. Graph of ifInOctets

Try to get a feel for what you are looking for before you start writing expressions. Are you trying to find someone who is flooding the network, or are you just looking for a

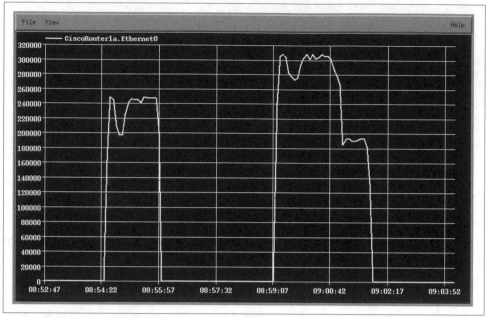

Figure A-6. Graph of ifOutOctets

weekly average? No matter what you are graphing, be sure to research the device's MIB objects before you start generating graphs that may look good but contain meaningless data. Recheck the variables each time you create new graphs.

Keep in mind that some devices have the ability to switch from full to half duplex automatically. You should be aware of your interface's saturation point, which is the point at which no more traffic can be sent or received. This saturation point is indicated in your graphs by a sustained horizontal ceiling line and can really be seen only over extended periods of time. Thus, while there are some horizontal lines in the graphs in this appendix, we are obviously not close to the interface's capacity.

If you plan to use graphs like these, be sure to plan for the average and not for the exceptions (peaks). All networks have traffic spikes here and there; unless you like spending a lot more on telecommunications than you need to, you should plan your network so that it is geared toward servicing your average day-to-day activities, not the occasional peak.

More on OpenView's NNM

By now, you should be familiar with OpenView's NNM and its supporting utilities. Even though many network administrators can get by with the basic OpenView information provided in this book, there is much more to learn. Configuring NNM with your own custom tools makes using it that much better.

While we can't cover all the features of NNM in this appendix, we'll discuss each of the following:

- Using external data with xnmgraph
- Inserting additional menu items into NNM's menu
- Creating NNM profiles for different users
- Using NNM as a centralized communication device

Using External Data

Chapter 8 introduced the xnmgraph command, but only touched on its features. One particularly useful feature is the ability to graph data from external sources. To see how you might graph external data, first generate a graph of any type—one of the graphs we created in Chapter 8 will do—and save the data to a file. Then examine the contents of the file. Each output file contains a short tutorial showing how to reshow the graph. Be sure to look at *$APP_DEFS/Xnmgraph*, which contains xnmgraph's default settings.

Here's a table we created by hand, copying the format of a standard xnmgraph datafile. The data points are organized into streams. A stream is a set of data that will be plotted as a single curve on the graph. All the streams in the file will be combined into a single graph with multiple curves. The StartTime is ignored. The StopTime provides the value for the X (horizontal) axis and the Value provides the value for the Y (vertical) axis:

```
# /tmp/data1
#
```

```
# Stream Number StartTime      StopTime               Value
# ------------- ---------      -------------------    -----
#
# Start of Stream 1
#
   1             0             04.28.2001-12:32:16    7
   1             0             04.28.2001-12:32:20    3
   1             0             04.28.2001-12:32:24    23
   1             0             04.28.2001-12:32:28    4
   1             0             04.28.2001-12:32:31    7
   1             0             04.28.2001-12:32:35    12
   1             0             04.28.2001-12:32:39    1
#
# Start of Stream 2
#
   2             0             04.28.2001-12:32:16    17
   2             0             04.28.2001-12:32:20    21
   2             0             04.28.2001-12:32:24    8
   2             0             04.28.2001-12:32:28    28
   2             0             04.28.2001-12:32:31    2
   2             0             04.28.2001-12:32:35    22
   2             0             04.28.2001-12:32:39    9
```

The following xnmgraph command displays our datafile. Notice that we use stream numbers, preceded by minus signs, instead of object IDs. The minus sign indicates that the stream can take on negative values. If the stream number is preceded by a + or = sign, xnmgraph will take the absolute value of all negative numbers in the datafile.

```
cat /tmp/data1 | xnmgraph -mib "-1:Stream One:::::::,-2:Stream Two:::::::"
```

Figure B-1 shows the result of this command. If your graph looks squished, right-click on it and then left-click on Show All. An option under the View menu lets you generate a black-and-white graph, which is often more effective if you have only a small number of streams.

Now that we can get data into a format that xnmgraph can display, let's see if we can generate some graphs from the output of the Unix *vmstat* utility. *vmstat* should be familiar to all Unix administrators; it provides a lot of information about your memory system, in a cumbersome format. Here's the kind of output *vmstat* produces:

```
procs     memory            page             disk          faults       cpu
 r b w   swap  free  re  mf pi po fr de sr s6 s2 s2 sd   in   sy   cs us sy id
 0 4 0 5431056 33672  1 2371 0  8  8  0  0  0 18 18  2 2161 5583 4490 17 14 69
 0 2 0 5430912 33576  1 2499 0 20 20  0  0  0  1  1  0 2997 8374 7030 25 18 58
 0 2 0 5431296 33824  0  179 4  0  0  0  0  0  0  0  1 2587 3990 6379 18  8 74
 0 0 0 5431240 33792  1 2460 4  8  8  0  0  0  1  1  0 2909 7768 7080 25 18 57
 0 3 0 5431216 33768  1 2359 0 12 12  0  0  0  2  2  0 1934 5057 3818 18 13 70
 0 0 0 5431288 33824  0  136 0  0  0  0  0  0  0  0  1 1842 2190 3803 13  5 82
 0 2 0 5431216 32920  2 1189 0 3196 3176 0 0 0 0  0  4 2734 9980 5642 24 11 65
 0 4 0 5431032 32352  8 1571 0 3100 3044 0 0 0 2  2  5 2763 7767 5817 22 15 63
```

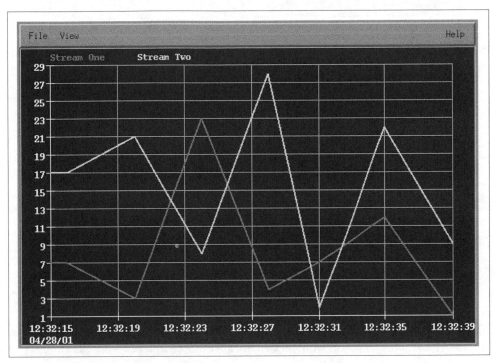

Figure B-1. Sample OpenView graph

Imagine taking 10,000 lines of this output and trying to figure out the trends (min/avg/max) in any given parameter. It's not easy. But with some help from a Perl script, we can massage this data into an xnmgraph input file. Here is what our Perl script looks like:

```
#!/usr/local/bin/perl
# Filename: /usr/local/bin/perl_scripts/cputimes

$|++; # Unbuffer the output!

open(VMSTAT,"/bin/vmstat 2 |") || die "Can't Open VMStat";
while($CLINE=<VMSTAT>)
{
    ($null,$r,$b,$w,$swap,$free,$re,$mf,$pi,$po,$fr,$de,$sr,$aa,$dd1,\
$dd2,$fo,$in,$sy,$cs,$us,$sycpu,$id) = split(/\s+/,$CLINE);

    if (($id) && ($id ne "id"))
    {
        $DATE = `date +%m.%d.%y-%H:%M:%S`;
        chomp $DATE;
        print "1 0 $DATE $us \n";
        print "2 0 $DATE $sycpu \n";
        print "3 0 $DATE $id \n";
    }
    sleep 2;
}
```

This script prints the current CPU usage, as a percentage, in the User ($us), System ($sycpu), and Idle ($ide) states; stream 1 is the User percentage, stream 2 is the System percentage, and stream 3 is the Idle percentage. The first item on each line is the stream number; note that we can interleave the data from the three streams:

```
[root][nms] /> /usr/local/bin/perl_scripts/cputimes
1 0 8.14.99-21:00:22 6
2 0 8.14.99-21:00:22 3
3 0 8.14.99-21:00:22 92
1 0 8.14.99-21:00:24 0
2 0 8.14.99-21:00:24 0
3 0 8.14.99-21:00:24 100
1 0 8.14.99-21:00:26 1
2 0 8.14.99-21:00:26 0
3 0 8.14.99-21:00:26 98
1 0 8.14.99-21:00:28 1
2 0 8.14.99-21:00:28 0
3 0 8.14.99-21:00:28 99
```

The following command generates a graph from the script's output:

```
/usr/local/bin/perl_scripts/cputimes | xnmgraph -title "CPU Time"  -mib \
"+1:User:::::::,+2:System:::::::,+3:Idle:::::::"
```

While this graph is based on live data, it's trivial to save data in an appropriate format and write a script that pulls historical data from your logs and plots it with xnmgraph.

Adding a Menu to NNM

Once you have a toolbox of scripts, adding them to an NNM menu makes them easier to access and execute. This trick can be especially useful if you prefer to use NNM's graphical interface.

The key to adding custom menus is the directory *$OV_REGISTRATION/C*. (*$OV_REGISTRATION* contains directories for all the languages available on your system; C is the directory for the default language and is probably where you should start.) The C directory contains all the files that make up the menu system you see when you run NNM. For example, the file *ovw* contains the familiar options from the main window (New, Open, Refresh, etc.).

Let's look at the *$OV_REGISTRATION/C/ovsnmp/xnmloadadmib* file. It's fairly easy to see how to hook an external command into a menu. Let's jump right in and create a menu that is two levels deep with two menu choices:

```
Application "Graph Menu"
{
        Menubar <100> "Local_Graphs" _p
        {
          <100> "Network"         _N f.menu "network_menu";
        }
```

```
Menu "network_menu"
{
  <90> "5 Minute CPU"    _M f.action "5mincpu";
  <90> "Bits In and Out For All Up Interfaces"  \
                     _B f.action "bit_for_all_up";
}

Action "5mincpu" {
  Command "/opt/OV/local/scripts/Cisco_5min_cpu \
                            \"${OVwSelections}\"";
  MinSelected    1;
  MaxSelected    7;
  SelectionRule  (isSNMPSupported || isSNMPProxied) ;
}

Action "bit_for_all_up" {
  Command "/opt/OV/local/scripts/Cisco_Line_Up_Bits \
                            \"${OVwSelections}\"";
  MinSelected    1;
  MaxSelected    3;
  SelectionRule  (isSNMPSupported || isSNMPProxied) ;
}
}
```

Create a file within *$OV_REGISTRATION/C* and insert the previous code listing.
Once this is done, run ovw with the -verify switch, which checks for errors.* You may
see errors or warnings about your new menu item, but if you're successful, you'll see
an item that looks like the menu in Figure B-2.

NNM can be picky with registration files. If you can't see your menu,
try the ovw –verify trick. If it reveals no errors, take some entries out
and restart ovw. Keep doing this until your items appear. You should
also break up your menu items into multiple files. Do not put all your
menus and actions into one file. The more files you have, the easier it
will be to diagnose and troubleshoot your new menu items.

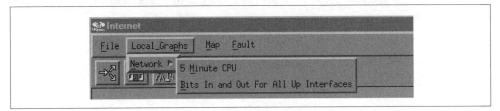

Figure B-2. A new menu

---

* Do not leave any backup files within any of the directories, because NNM takes each file seriously. Backup
or redundant files will produce warnings when you run ovw.

Let's talk about some commonalties within our registration file:

- Each menu and menu item is associated with a keyboard shortcut that allows the user to access it. The trigger character is preceded by an underscore. For example, from the Local_Graphs Network menu, you can press M to go to the 5 Minute CPU item.

- Each menu item has a precedence number within angle brackets. This allows you to control the order in which items appear. Items with the highest precedence appear first in a menu; items with the same precedence are listed in the order in which they appear in the file. For example, if we reduce the precedence of the 5 Minute CPU menu item from <90> to <80>, it will appear after the Bits In and Out menu item because the higher-precedence item comes first.

The Menubar entry contains the menus that will appear in the top NNM menu bar. We used the function f.menu to call a submenu. The following code shows how we could have used f.action to call an action directly:

```
Menubar <precedence> "menubar Label" _MnemonicChar
    {
        <precedence> "SubMenu Label" _MnemonicChar f.menu "menu-name"
        <precedence> "Action Name" _MnemonicChar f.action "action-name"
    }
```

A Menu looks and behaves like the menu bar (or menu) that contains it, with a few differences. Menus don't declare mnemonic characters or precedence; these are defined by the containing menu or menu bar. The menu-name is the linking name that appears after f.menu:

```
Menu "menu-name"
    {
        <precedence> "SubMenu Label" _MnemonicChar f.menu  "menu-name"
        <precedence> "Action Name" _MnemonicChar f.action "action-name"
    }
```

Actions are called just like Menus. The action-name is the linking name of an action that gets called when selected from a previous item (either a Menu or a Menubar):

```
Action "action-name"
    {
        Command "/opt/OV/local/scripts/Cisco_5min_cpu \"${OVwSelections}\"";
        MinSelected    1;
        MaxSelected    7;
        SelectionRule  (isSNMPSupported || isSNMPProxied) ;
    }
```

There are a few additional parameters in our Action declaration:

- Command specifies which program or script should be executed. At the end of the command string, the \"${OVwSelections}\" passes all currently selected objects to the program as arguments.

- `MinSelected` declares how many nodes must be selected before this item becomes available. If nothing is selected, the corresponding menu choice will be grayed out and unclickable.

- `MaxSelected` works the same way, but declares the maximum number of objects that can be selected.

- `SelectionRule` uses capability fields* within a logical statement. These rules declare what is necessary for the selection to be deemed a "good selection."

`Action` declarations can contain many additional parameters, as can registration files. The examples we've given should be enough to get you going in the right direction. The *OVwRegIntro* (5) manpage defines the syntax of the registration files in detail; read this page carefully if you're serious about adding custom menu items.

Profiles for Different Users

Some users may have specific ways in which they want to use NNM. For example, an operator who is watching the network for problems may need a fairly limited set of menus and tools; a senior network engineer might want a substantially larger set of options. You can use the *$OV_REGISTRATION* directory and the $OVwRegDir environment variable to customize NNM on a per-user basis.

The previous section showed how to add menus by modifying files in the *$OV_REG-ISTRATION/C* directory. By default, this is the directory NNM uses when it starts. However, you can create as many profiles as you need under the *$OV_REGISTRA-TION* directory. Once you have created another profile directory, you can change the $OVwRegDir environment variable to point to that new directory. Then, when NNM starts, it will use the new profile.

One way to set up user-specific profiles is to create an account that anyone can use for starting an NNM session. With this account, the network map is opened in read-only† mode and has only the minimal menus (File → Exit, Map → Refresh, Fault → Alarms, etc.). Create a new profile for this account in the directory *$OV_REGISTRA-TION/skel* by copying all the files in the default profile *$OV_REGISTRATION/C* to the new *skel* directory. Then modify this profile by removing most of the menu choices, thus preventing the operator from being able to run any external commands.‡ To start NNM using this profile, you must point the $OVwRegDir environ-

---

* Check out *$OV_FIELDS* for more definitions of capability fields.

† When starting NNM via the command line, use *$OV_BIN/ovw -ro* to open the default map in read-only mode. This will prevent the user from making any map changes (moves, adds, deletes, etc.).

‡ Just because a map is opened in read-only mode does *not* mean that users cannot make changes to the back end of NNM. A user who has the ability to launch the menu items can make changes just like the superuser can. The best way to prevent these changes is to take out all configuration menu options.

ment variable to the new profile directory. To test the new profile, give the following Bourne shell commands:

```
[root][nms] /> OVwRegDir=/etc/opt/OV/share/registration/skel
[root][nms] /> export OVwRegDir
[root][nms] /> $OV_BIN/ovw
```

Once you're confident that this new profile works, create an account for running NNM with minimal permissions, and in the startup script for that account, set *$OVwRegDir* appropriately (i.e., to point to your skeleton configuration). Then make sure that users can't run NNM from their normal accounts—perhaps by limiting execute access for NNM to a particular group, which will force users not in that group to use the special account when they want to run NNM. You should also make sure that the users you don't trust can't modify the *$OV_REGISTRATION* directory or its subdirectories.

Using NNM for Communications

One of the more exotic ways to use SNMP is as a tool for passing messages back and forth. For example, it's certainly useful to know that the Oracle database has gone down, but it's even more useful to send messages to key users notifying them that the database has crashed or that it's going down for maintenance at the end of the day. In a small environment, it's easy to come up with hacks that provide various kinds of notification. But in a large company with many offices, it's useful to have a standard way for communicating with other departments. NNM's Event Categories is the perfect tool to use as a centralized communication device.

Imagine a web interface that allows you to send traps to Event Categories. Filling out a simple form in a browser automatically generates a trap that is posted to the appropriate categories. Figure B-3 shows such an interface.

What types of questions does everyone (you, managers, users, etc.) ask when there's a problem? The most typical ones are:

Who is in charge?
    Name, phone, pager

What is going on?
    Reboot, upgrade, failure

What servers are affected?
    Production, test, development

What services are affected?
    Mail, news, database, web server

When did this happen?
    e.g., 10 minutes ago, 4 days from now

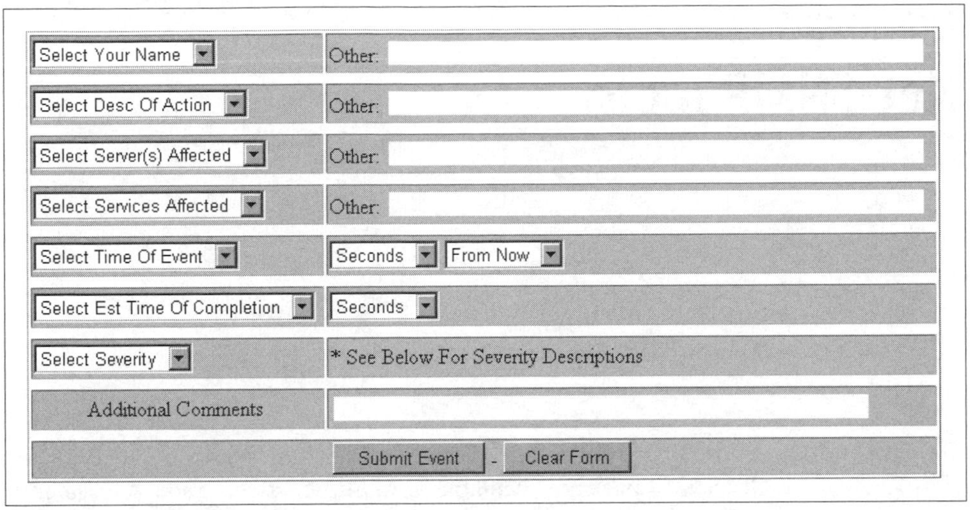

Select Your Name ▾   Other:

Select Desc Of Action ▾   Other:

Select Server(s) Affected ▾   Other:

Select Services Affected ▾   Other:

Select Time Of Event ▾   Seconds ▾ From Now ▾

Select Est Time Of Completion ▾   Seconds ▾

Select Severity ▾   * See Below For Severity Descriptions

Additional Comments

Submit Event - Clear Form

Figure B-3. SNMP web interface

When will this be fixed?
    e.g., immediately, tomorrow

What is the severity?
    Normal, Warning, Minor, Major, Critical

All these questions can be answered using the HTML form in Figure B-3. The CGI script or Java servlet that processes the form can refuse to accept the form until the user has filled in all the fields, guaranteeing that you have complete and consistent information.

Setting up a reporting system like this is not very difficult. You can use any standard web server, a little HTML, and your favorite language for processing the form. Once you parse the output from the form, you can use any of the trap-generation programs we've discussed to send the trap. This trap will then show up in one of NNM's Event Categories. (If you're not using NNM, we've discussed other trap daemons that can be used to receive the trap and notify users. However, NNM is convenient because it will do everything for you.)

The key to this whole setup is getting people to use and watch NNM. If it isn't used by everyone, this mechanism really doesn't accomplish anything. Training users in nontechnical departments to watch NNM for important notifications may not be easy, but if you succeed, you'll have created an elegant mechanism for getting important information to users.

Net-SNMP Tools

This appendix provides brief summaries of the command-line tools included in Version 5.2.1 of the Net-SNMP package (available from *http://net-snmp.sourceforge.net*).

Instead of trying to describe all the options to all the commands, we've focused on those that are most important and useful. We have also pointed out a few cases in which the behavior of the commands differs from the behavior that's described in the manual pages.

Net-SNMP and MIB Files

By default, Net-SNMP reads the MIB files in the directory */usr/local/share/snmp/mibs*. When you install Net-SNMP, it populates this directory with a few dozen MIB files, including the UCD MIB (Net-SNMP used to be called UCD-SNMP) and the RFC 1213 MIB (MIB-II). Net-SNMP uses the MIB files to translate between numeric object IDs and their textual representations. The MIB files also give the tools access to information about each object (its syntax, the type of access allowed, its description, etc.). Adding a vendor-specific MIB file to Net-SNMP is as simple as placing it in the *mibs* directory and setting the environment variable $MIBS to ALL, as discussed in the next section.

Common Command-Line Arguments

For the most part, the Net-SNMP commands follow a similar command structure; they share many options and use roughly the same syntax. For example, in the abstract, an snmpget command looks like this:

```
snmpget options hostname objectID...
```

In other words, the command name is followed by a series of options, the hostname of the system you want to poll, and one or more object IDs. (Note that if you use SNMPv1 or SNMPv2, you can use the –c community option to specify the community string. You can also provide a default hostname in your *snmp.conf* file.) The syntax of snmpset is only slightly different; because snmpset changes object values, it requires you to specify the object's datatype and the new value:

```
snmpset options hostname objectID type value...
```

Table C-1 summarizes some of the most useful options common to all Net-SNMP commands. See the snmpcmd(1) manpage for a complete list.

Table C-1. Summary of command-line options

Option	Description
−m	Specifies which MIB modules you would like the command to load. If you want the command to parse the MIB file for a particular vendor, copy the MIB file to */usr/local/share/snmp/mibs* and invoke the command with the option -m ALL. The argument ALL forces the command to read all the MIB files in the directory. Setting the environment variable $MIBS to ALL achieves the same thing. If you don't want the command to read all the MIB files, you can follow the −m option with a colon-separated list of the MIB files you want parsed.
−M	Allows you to specify a colon-separated list of directories to search for MIB files. This option is useful if you don't want to copy MIB files into the default MIB location. Setting the shell variable $MIBDIRS has the same effect.
−IR	Performs a random-access search through the MIB database for an OID label. By default, the commands assume that you specify an object ID relative to *.iso.org.dod.internet.mgmt.mib-2*. In practice, this option allows you to avoid typing long OIDs for objects that aren't under the *mib-2* subtree. For example, there's a group of objects in the Cisco MIB named *lcpu*. If you use the -IR option, you can retrieve objects in this group without typing the entire OID; the following command is sufficient: `snmpget -IR hostname community lcpu.2`
−On	Prints OIDs numerically (e.g., *.1.3.6.1.2.1.1.3.0)*
−Of	Prints full textual OIDs.
−Os	Prints the entire OID (i.e., starting with *.1*).
−OS	Displays only the final part of the OID, in symbolic form (e.g., *sysUpTime.0*).
−v	Specifies which version of SNMP to use: −v1, −v2c, and −v3 for SNMPv1, SNMPv2 and SNMPv3 respectively.
−h	Displays a help message.
−c	Specifies the community string for SNMPv1 or SNMPv2c.

Net-SNMP Command-Line Tools

This section briefly describes each of the Net-SNMP tools. By default, installing Net-SNMP places all these commands in */usr/local/bin*. All the examples in this section assume that */usr/local/bin* is in your path.

snmpwalk

snmpwalk performs the getnext operation. We've used it throughout the book, so it should be familiar; in this section, we'll use it to demonstrate some of the options introduced in Table C-1.

Let's say you want to perform an snmpwalk against a Cisco router. If you don't have any Cisco MIBs installed, here's what you will see:

```
$ snmpwalk -v2c -c public cisco.oreilly.com .1.3.6.1.4.1.9
SNMPv2-SMI::enterprises.9.2.1.1.0 = "
System Bootstrap, Version 12.2(6r), RELEASE SOFTWARE (fc1)
TAC Support: http://www.cisco.com/tac
Copyright (c) 2001 by cisco Systems, Inc."
SNMPv2-SMI::enterprises.9.2.1.2.0 = "reload"
SNMPv2-SMI::enterprises.9.2.1.3.0 = "cisco"
SNMPv2-SMI::enterprises.9.2.1.4.0 = "oreilly.com"
SNMPv2-SMI::enterprises.9.2.1.5.0 = IpAddress: 127.45.23.1
SNMPv2-SMI::enterprises.9.2.1.6.0 = IpAddress: 0.0.0.0
SNMPv2-SMI::enterprises.9.2.1.8.0 = 131890952
SNMPv2-SMI::enterprises.9.2.1.9.0 = 456
SNMPv2-SMI::enterprises.9.2.1.10.0 = 500
SNMPv2-SMI::enterprises.9.2.1.11.0 = 17767568
SNMPv2-SMI::enterprises.9.2.1.12.0 = 0
SNMPv2-SMI::enterprises.9.2.1.13.0 = 0
SNMPv2-SMI::enterprises.9.2.1.14.0 = 104
SNMPv2-SMI::enterprises.9.2.1.15.0 = 600
...
```

Recall that *.1.3.6.1.4.1* is *.iso.org.dod.internet.private.enterprises*, and 9 is Cisco's private enterprise number. Therefore, the previous command is walking the entire Cisco subtree, which is very large; we've deleted most of its output. The output you see isn't very readable because we haven't yet installed the Cisco MIBs, so the snmpwalk command has no way of providing human-readable object names. We just have to guess what these objects are.

This problem is easy to solve. Copy the Cisco MIBs* to the main Net-SNMP repository (*/usr/local/share/snmp/mibs*) and use the –m ALL command-line option. With this option, snmpwalk parses all the files in the MIB repository. As a result, we get the object IDs in string (human-readable) form, and we can walk the *cisco* subtree by name instead of specifying its complete numeric object ID (*.1.3.6.1.4.1.9*):

```
$ snmpwalk -m ALL -v2c -c public cisco.oreilly.com cisco
CISCO-SMI::enterprises.cisco.local.lcpu.1.0 = "
System Bootstrap, Version 12.2(6r), RELEASE SOFTWARE (fc1)
TAC Support: http://www.cisco.com/tac
Copyright (c) 2001 by cisco Systems, Inc."
CISCO-SMI::local.lcpu.2.0 = "reload"
CISCO-SMI::local.lcpu.3.0 = "cisco"
CISCO-SMI::local.lcpu.4.0 = "oreilly.com"
CISCO-SMI::local.lcpu.5.0 = IpAddress: 127.45.23.1
CISCO-SMI::local.lcpu.6.0 = IpAddress: 0.0.0.0
CISCO-SMI::local.lcpu.8.0 = 131888844
CISCO-SMI::local.lcpu.9.0 = 456
CISCO-SMI::local.lcpu.10.0 = 500
```

---

* You can find many Cisco MIBs at *ftp://ftp.cisco.com/pub/mibs/*.

```
CISCO-SMI::local.lcpu.11.0 = 17767568
CISCO-SMI::local.lcpu.12.0 = 0
CISCO-SMI::local.lcpu.13.0 = 0
CISCO-SMI::local.lcpu.14.0 = 104
CISCO-SMI::local.lcpu.15.0 = 600
...
```

Now let's trim the output by adding the –Os option, which omits the initial part of each OID:

```
$ snmpwalk -v2c -m ALL -Os -c public cisco.oreilly.com cisco
lcpu.1.0 = "
System Bootstrap, Version 12.2(6r),  RELEASE SOFTWARE (fc1)
TAC Support: http://www.cisco.com/tac
Copyright (c) 2001 by cisco Systems, Inc."
lcpu.2.0 = "reload"
lcpu.3.0 = "cisco"
lcpu.4.0 = "oreilly.com"
lcpu.5.0 = IpAddress: 127.45.23.1
lcpu.6.0 = IpAddress: 0.0.0.0
lcpu.8.0 = 131888844
lcpu.9.0 = 456
lcpu.10.0 = 500
lcpu.11.0 = 17767568
lcpu.12.0 = 0
lcpu.13.0 = 0
lcpu.14.0 = 104
lcpu.15.0 = 600
...
```

This output is a little easier to read since it cuts off the redundant part of each OID. Let's take this command one step further:

```
$ snmpwalk -v2c -c public cisco.oreilly.com system
SNMPv2-MIB::sysDescr.0 = " Cisco IOS Software, C2600 Software (C2600-IPBASE-M),
Version 12.3(8)T3, RELEASE SOFTWARE (fc1)
Technical Support: http://www.cisco.com/techsupport
Copyright (c) 1986-2004 by Cisco Systems, Inc.
Compiled Tue 20-Jul-04 17:03 by eaarmas"
SNMPv2-MIB::sysObjectID.0 = OID: DTRConcentratorMIB::catProd.182
EXPRESSION-MIB::sysUpTimeInstance = Timeticks: (344626986) 39 days, 21:17:49.86
SNMPv2-MIB::sysContact.0 = "O'Reilly Data Center"
SNMPv2-MIB::sysName.0 = "cisco.oreilly.com"
SNMPv2-MIB::sysLocation.0 = "Atlanta, GA"
SNMPv2-MIB::sysServices.0 = 6
SNMPv2-MIB::system.8.0 = Timeticks: (0) 0:00:00.00
```

This command walks the *system* subtree. Since the *system* group falls under *mib-2*, there is no need to use –m ALL; *mib-2* is one of the MIBs the Net-SNMP tools load automatically. We see that each line begins with *SNMPv2-MIB*, which is the name of the MIB which describes the *system* tree in SNMPv2. This is the default output for Net-SNMP commands.

snmpget

The snmpget command issues a single *get* operation. Its syntax is:

```
snmpget options hostname objectID...
```

snmpbulkget

SNMPv2 provides an operation called getbulk, which is implemented by the snmp-bulkget command. getbulk allows you to retrieve a chunk of information in one operation, as opposed to a single get or sequence of getnext operations. The syntax of snmpbulkget is:

```
snmpbulkget -v2c options hostname objectID
```

–v2c is required because getbulk is defined by SNMP Version 2.

There are two command-specific options, –Cn*nonrep* and –Cr*rep*. *nonrep* is the number of scalar objects that this command returns; *rep* is the number of instances of each nonscalar object that the command returns. If you omit this option, the default values of *nonrep* and *rep*, 0 and 10, respectively, are used.

snmpbulkwalk

The snmpbulkwalk command uses the getbulk command sequence to retrieve parts of a MIB. This command differs from snmpbulkget in that you can tell it to ignore OIDs that are not increasing. This can be useful because some SNMP agents return OIDs out of order. Use –Cc to specify this behavior. Its syntax is:

```
snmpbulkwalk -v2c options hostname objectID
```

snmpset

The snmpset command is used to change, or set, the value of a MIB object. The command looks like this:

```
snmpset options hostname objectID type value...
```

You can provide any number of objectID/type/value triples; the command executes *set* operations for all the objects you give it. *type* is a single-character abbreviation that indicates the datatype of the object you're setting. Table C-2 lists the valid types.

Table C-2. snmpset object types

Abbreviation	Type
a	IP address
b	Bits
d	Decimal string
D	Double

Table C-2. snmpset object types (continued)

Abbreviation	Type
F	Float
i	Integer
I	Signed int64
o	Object ID
s	String
t	Time ticks
u	Unsigned integer
U	Unsigned int64
x	Hexadecimal string

snmptrap

To send a trap, use the snmptrap command. The syntax for this command is:

```
snmptrap options hostname trap parameters...
```

For Version 1, the following trap parameters are required:

```
enterprise-oid agent trap-type specific-type uptime objectID type value...
```

This command is discussed in detail in Chapter 9. Each object ID/type/value triplet specifies a variable binding to be included with the trap; you may include any number of variable bindings. Note that *agent* and *uptime* are not optional; however, if you provide an empty string ("") as a placeholder, they default to the IP address of the system sending the trap and the system's current uptime.

The parameters are simpler for Version 2 traps, largely because traps (now called *notifications*) are full-fledged MIB objects in their own right. The following parameters are required:

```
snmptrap -v2c options hostname uptime trapoid objectID type value...
```

snmpdelta

The snmpdelta command monitors OIDs and tracks changes in OID values over time. Its syntax is:

```
snmpdelta options hostname objectID...
```

snmpdelta requires you to specify the OID of an integer-valued scalar object—it can't monitor tables. For example, if you want to watch the octets arriving on an interface, you can't just specify *ifInOctets*; you must specify the interface number in addition to the object name (e.g., *ifInOctets.3*). By default, snmpdelta polls the given object every second.

Table C-3 lists some of the snmpdelta-specific options. The documentation for this command has many problems, but if you stick to the options listed here you should be on firm ground.

Table C-3. snmpdelta options

Option	Description
-Cs	Display a timestamp with every set of results.
-Cm	Print the maximum value obtained.
-Cl	Write the output to a file. The filename is in the form *hostname-OID*. For example, if you want to monitor the variables *ifInOctets.3* and *ifOutOctets.3* on the host router, the -Cl option will create two files, *hostname-ifInOctets.3* and *hostname-ifOutOctets.3*, where the output of snmpdelta will be written. (Note that this output has no apparent connection to the configuration, as the documentation claims.)
-Cp	Specify the polling interval (the default is one second).
-CT	Print output in tabular format.

snmpdf

snmpdf works exactly like the Unix df command, except it uses SNMP to query hosts on a network. Its syntax is:

```
snmpdf [-Cu] options... hostname
```

The -Cu option tells the command to consult the old UCD-SNMP private MIB. The Host Resources MIB is used by default.

snmpgetnext

The snmpgetnext command uses the getnext operation to retrieve the next object from a host. For example, if you ask it to perform a getnext for *ifOutOctets.4*, it will retrieve the next object in the MIB tree, which will probably be *ifOutOctets.5*. (If the machine you're polling has only four interfaces, you'll get the next object in the MIB, whatever that happens to be. You should also be aware that there are some obscure situations that create a "hole" in the interface table, so the interface following *.4* might be *.6* or *.7*.) You can use this command to implement your own version of snmpwalk. The syntax is:

```
snmpgetnext options... hostname objectID...
```

There are no options specific to snmpgetnext.

snmpstatus

The snmpstatus command retrieves status information from a host. It prints the following information:

- The IP address of the entity
- A textual description of the entity (*sysDescr.0*)

- The uptime of the entity (*sysUpTime.0*)
- The sum of received packets on all interfaces (*ifInUcastPkts.* + ifInNUcastPkts.**)
- The sum of transmitted packets on all interfaces (*ifOutUcastPkts.* + ifOutNUcastPkts.**)
- The number of IP input packets (*ipInReceives.0*)
- The number of IP output packets (*ipOutRequests.0*)

The syntax of snmpstatus is straightforward, and there are no command-specific options:

```
snmpstatus options... hostname
```

snmptable

The snmptable command uses getnext commands to print the contents of a table in tabular form. Its syntax is:

```
snmptable options... hostname objectID
```

The *objectID* must be the ID of a table (e.g., *ifTable*), not of an object within a table. Table C-4 lists some of the snmptable-specific options.

Table C-4. snmptable options

Option	Description
–Cf *F*	Separate table columns with the string *F*. For example, –Cf : separates columns with a colon, which might make it easier to import the output from snmptable into another program.
–Cw *W*	Set the maximum width of the table to *W*. If the lines are longer than *W*, the table is split into sections. Since tables can have many columns, you almost certainly want to use this option.
–Ci	Prepend the index of the entry to all printed lines.
–Cb	Display a brief heading.
–Ch	Print only column headers.
–CH	Suppress column headers.

snmpusm

The snmpusm command provides simple access to the agent's USM table. This is primarily used for configuring the agent's SNMPv3 features (managing users, setting and changing passphrases, etc.). This command is discussed in Chapter 6.

snmpconf

This command is an interactive Perl script used to create and maintain the Net-SNMP configuration files, *snmp.conf* and *snmpd.conf*. Its syntax is:

```
snmpconf filename
```

filename must be either *snmp.conf* or *snmpd.conf*.

snmpinform

This command can be used to send an SNMPv2 trap. If you send a trap with snmp-inform, it will wait for a response from the recipient. Note that you can send an inform using the snmptrap command if you specify –Ci. The options for snmpinform are identical to those for snmptrap.

snmptranslate

The Net-SNMP package comes with a handy tool called snmptranslate that translates between numerical and human-readable object names. More generally, it can be used to look up information from MIB files. Its syntax is:

```
snmptranslate options objectID
```

snmptranslate does not perform queries against any device, so it doesn't need the *hostname* or *community* parameters. Its sole purpose is to read MIB files and produce output about specific objects. Before looking at examples, it's worth noting that snmptranslate's interpretations of the –O options are, to be kind, interesting. To speak more plainly, they're just plain wrong. The following examples show what actually happens when you use these options—we'll leave the rationalization to you.

Let's say you want to know the enterprise OID for Cisco Systems. The following command does the trick:

```
$ snmptranslate -m ALL -IR -On cisco
.1.3.6.1.4.1.9
```

This tells us that Cisco's enterprise OID is *.1.3.6.1.4.1.9*. Note the use of the –IR option, which tells snmptranslate to do a random-access search for an object named *cisco*. If you leave this option out, snmptranslate will fail because it will try to locate *cisco* under the *mib-2* tree.

Let's say you want to take *.1.3.6.1.4.1.9* and convert it to its full symbolic name. That's easy:

```
$ snmptranslate -m ALL -Of .1.3.6.1.4.1.9
.iso.org.dod.internet.private.enterprises.cisco
```

In this case, –IR isn't needed because we're not performing a random-access search. –Of ensures that we print the full object ID, in symbolic (text) form.

Now, let's say you want to know a little more information about a particular object. The –Td option displays the object's definition as it appears in the MIB file:

```
$ snmptranslate -IR -Td system.sysLocation
SNMPv2-MIB::sysLocation
sysLocation OBJECT-TYPE
  -- FROM        SNMPv2-MIB, RFC1213-MIB
  -- TEXTUAL CONVENTION DisplayString
  SYNTAX        OCTET STRING (0..255)
  DISPLAY-HINT  "255a"
```

```
MAX-ACCESS     read-write
STATUS         current
DESCRIPTION    "The physical location of this node (e.g., 'telephone
               closet, 3rd floor').  If the location is unknown, the
               value is the zero-length string."
::= { iso(1) org(3) dod(6) internet(1) mgmt(2) mib-2(1) system(1) 6 }
```

–Td can save you a lot of work poking through MIB files to find an appropriate definition, particularly when combined with –IR. Furthermore, the last line shows you the entire object ID in both numeric and string forms, not just the object's parent.

The –Tp option prints an entire OID tree. The best way to understand this is to see it:

```
$ snmptranslate -IR -Tp system
+--system(1)
   |
   +-- -R-- String     sysDescr(1)
   |          Textual Convention: DisplayString
   |          Size: 0..255
   +-- -R-- ObjID       sysObjectID(2)
   +-- -R-- TimeTicks sysUpTime(3)
   |  |
   |  +--sysUpTimeInstance(0)
   |
   +-- -RW- String     sysContact(4)
   |          Textual Convention: DisplayString
   |          Size: 0..255
   +-- -RW- String     sysName(5)
   |          Textual Convention: DisplayString
   |          Size: 0..255
   +-- -RW- String     sysLocation(6)
   |          Textual Convention: DisplayString
   |          Size: 0..255
   +-- -R-- INTEGER   sysServices(7)
   |          Range: 0..127
   +-- -R-- TimeTicks sysORLastChange(8)
   |          Textual Convention: TimeStamp
   |
   +--sysORTable(9)
      |
      +--sysOREntry(1)
         | Index: sysORIndex
         |
         +-- ---- INTEGER   sysORIndex(1)
         |          Range: 1..2147483647
         +-- -R-- ObjID       sysORID(2)
         +-- -R-- String     sysORDescr(3)
         |          Textual Convention: DisplayString
         |          Size: 0..255
         +-- -R-- TimeTicks sysORUpTime(4)
                    Textual Convention: TimeStamp
```

We displayed the *system* subtree because it's fairly short. From this output, it's relatively easy to see all the objects underneath *system*, together with their types and textual conventions. This is a great way to see what objects are defined in a MIB as well as their relationships to other objects. The output can be voluminous, but it's still a convenient way to get a map and figure out what objects are likely to be useful.

SNMP RFCs

This appendix provides a brief list of all the SNMP RFCs, along with the status of each RFC. This list (often referred to as the Standards Summary) was taken from *The Simple Times*, an online publication that should be familiar to anyone working with SNMP. It is used with their permission.

SMIv1 Data Definition Language

Full Standards:

> *RFC 1155*—Structure of Management Information
> *RFC 1212*—Concise MIB Definitions

Informational:

> *RFC 1215*—A Convention for Defining Traps

SMIv2 Data Definition Language

Full Standards:

> *RFC 2578*—Structure of Management Information
> *RFC 2579*—Textual Conventions
> *RFC 2580*—Conformance Statements

SNMPv3 Protocol

Draft Standards:

> *RFC 3411*—Architecture for SNMP Frameworks
> *RFC 3412*—Message Processing and Dispatching
> *RFC 3413*—SNMP Applications
> *RFC 3414*—User-Based Security Model

RFC 3415—View-Based Access Control Model
RFC 3416—Protocol Operations for SNMPv2
RFC 3417—Transport Mappings for SNMPv2
RFC 3418—MIB for SNMPv2

Proposed Standard:

RFC 2576—Coexistence Between SNMP Versions

Informational:

RFC 3410—Internet Management Framework

Experimental:

RFC 2786—Diffie-Hellman USM Key Management
RFC 3430—SNMP over TCP

SNMP Agent Extensibility

Proposed Standards:

RFC 2741—AgentX Protocol Version 1
RFC 2742—AgentX MIB

SMIv1 MIB Modules

Full Standards:

RFC 1213—Management Information Base II
RFC 1643—Ethernet-Like Interface Types MIB

Draft Standards:

RFC 1493—Bridge MIB
RFC 1559—DECnet phase IV MIB

Proposed Standards:

RFC 1285—FDDI Interface Type (SMT 6.2) MIB
RFC 1381—X.25 LAPB MIB
RFC 1382—X.25 Packet Layer MIB
RFC 1414—Identification MIB
RFC 1461—X.25 Multiprotocol Interconnect MIB
RFC 1471—PPP Link Control Protocol MIB
RFC 1472—PPP Security Protocol MIB
RFC 1473—PPP IP NCP MIB
RFC 1474—PPP Bridge NCP MIB
RFC 1512—FDDI Interface Type (SMT 7.3) MIB
RFC 1513—RMON Token Ring Extensions MIB

RFC 1515—IEEE 802.3 MAU MIB
RFC 1525—Source Routing Bridge MIB
RFC 1742—AppleTalk MIB

SMIv2 MIB Modules

Full Standards:

RFC 2819—Remote Network Monitoring MIB
RFC 3411—SNMP Framework MIB
RFC 3412—SNMPv3 MPD MIB
RFC 3413—SNMP Applications MIBs
RFC 3414—SNMPv3 USM MIB
RFC 3415—SNMP VACM MIB
RFC 3418—SNMP MIB

Draft Standards:

RFC 1657—BGP Version 4 MIB
RFC 1658—Character Device MIB
RFC 1659—RS-232 Interface Type MIB
RFC 1660—Parallel Printer Interface Type MIB
RFC 1694—SMDS Interface Type MIB
RFC 1724—RIP Version 2 MIB
RFC 1748—IEEE 802.5 Interface Type MIB
RFC 1850—OSPF Version 2 MIB
RFC 2115—Frame Relay DTE Interface Type MIB
RFC 2742—AgentX MIB
RFC 2790—Host Resources MIB
RFC 2863—Interfaces Group MIB

Proposed Standards:

RFC 1666—SNA NAU MIB
RFC 1696—Modem MIB
RFC 1697—RDBMS MIB
RFC 1747—SNA Data Link Control MIB
RFC 1749—802.5 Station Source Routing MIB
RFC 1759—Printer MIB
RFC 2006—Internet Protocol Mobility MIB
RFC 2011—Internet Protocol MIB
RFC 2012—Transmission Control Protocol MIB
RFC 2013—User Datagram Protocol MIB
RFC 2020—IEEE 802.12 Interfaces MIB
RFC 2021—RMON Version 2 MIB
RFC 2024—Data Link Switching MIB

RFC 2051—APPC MIB
RFC 2096—IP Forwarding Table MIB
RFC 2108—IEEE 802.3 Repeater MIB
RFC 2127—ISDN MIB
RFC 2128—Dial Control MIB
RFC 2206—Resource Reservation Protocol MIB
RFC 2213—Integrated Services MIB
RFC 2214—Guaranteed Service MIB
RFC 2232—Dependent LU Requester MIB
RFC 2238—High Performance Routing MIB
RFC 2266—IEEE 802.12 Repeater MIB
RFC 2287—System-Level Application Mgmt MIB
RFC 2320—Classical IP and ARP over ATM MIB
RFC 2417—Multicast over UNI 3.0/3.1/ATM MIB
RFC 2452—IPv6 UDP MIB
RFC 2454—IPv6 TCP MIB
RFC 2455—APPN MIB
RFC 2456—APPN Trap MIB
RFC 2457—APPN Extended Border Node MIB
RFC 2465—IPv6 Textual Conventions MIB
RFC 2466—ICMPv6 MIB
RFC 2493—15 Minute Performance History TCs
RFC 2494—DS0, DS0 Bundle Interface Type MIB
RFC 2495—DS1, E1, DS2, E2 Interface Type MIB
RFC 2496—DS3/E3 Interface Type MIB
RFC 2512—Accounting MIB for ATM Networks
RFC 2513—Accounting Control MIB
RFC 2514—ATM Textual Conventions and OIDs
RFC 2515—ATM MIB
RFC 2558—SONET/SDH Interface Type MIB
RFC 2561—TN3270E MIB
RFC 2562—TN3270E Response Time MIB
RFC 2564—Application Management MIB
RFC 2576—SNMP Community MIB
RFC 2584—APPN/HPR in IP Networks
RFC 2594—WWW Services MIB
RFC 2605—Directory Server MIB
RFC 2613—RMON for Switched Networks MIB
RFC 2618—RADIUS Authentication Client MIB
RFC 2619—RADIUS Authentication Server MIB
RFC 2667—IP Tunnel MIB
RFC 2662—ADSL MIB
RFC 2665—Ethernet-Like Interface Type MIB

RFC 2668—IEEE 802.3 MAU MIB
RFC 2669—DOCSIS Cable Device MIB
RFC 2670—DOCSIS RF Interface MIB
RFC 2677—Next Hop Resolution Protocol MIB
RFC 2720—Traffic Flow Measurement Meter MIB
RFC 2737—Entity MIB
RFC 2787—Virtual Router Redundancy Protocol MIB
RFC 2788—Network Services Monitoring MIB
RFC 2789—Mail Monitoring MIB
RFC 2873—Fibre Channel Fabric Element MIB
RFC 2856—High Capacity Data Type TCs
RFC 2864—Interfaces Group Inverted Stack MIB
RFC 2895—RMON Protocol Identifier
RFC 2925—Ping, Traceroute, Lookup MIBs
RFC 2932—IPv4 Multicast Routing MIB
RFC 2933—IGMP MIB
RFC 2940—COPS Client MIB
RFC 2954—Frame Relay Service MIB
RFC 2955—Frame Relay/ATM PVC MIB
RFC 2959—Real-Time Transport Protocol MIB
RFC 2981—Event MIB
RFC 2982—Expression MIB
RFC 3014—Notification Log MIB
RFC 3019—Multicast Listener Discovery MIB
RFC 3020—Frame Relay UNI/NNI Multilink MIB
RFC 3055—PSTN/Internet Interworking MIB
RFC 3083—DOCSIS Baseline Privacy Interface MIB
RFC 3144—RMON Interface Monitoring MIB
RFC 3165—Scripting MIB
RFC 3201—Circuit Interface MIB
RFC 3202—Frame Relay Service Level MIB
RFC 3231—Scheduling MIB
RFC 3273—RMON High Capacity MIB
RFC 3276—HDSL2/SHDSL Line MIB
RFC 3291—Internet Network Address TCs
RFC 3287—RMON Differentiated Services MIB
RFC 3289—DiffServ MIB
RFC 3295—General Switch Mgmt Protocol MIB
RFC 3371—Layer Two Tunneling Protocol MIB
RFC 3395—RMON Protocol Identifier Extensions
RFC 3419—Transport Address TCs
RFC 3433—Entity Sensor MIB
RFC 3434—RMON High Capacity Alarms MIB
RFC 3440—ADSL Extension MIB

Informational:

> *RFC 1628*—Uninterruptible Power Supply MIB
> *RFC 2620*—RADIUS Accounting Client MIB
> *RFC 2621*—RADIUS Accounting Server MIB
> *RFC 2666*—Ethernet Chip Set Identifiers
> *RFC 2707*—Print Job Monitoring MIB
> *RFC 2896*—RMON Protocol Identifier Macros
> *RFC 2922*—Physical Topology MIB

Experimental:

> *RFC 2758*—SLA Performance Monitoring MIB
> *RFC 2786*—Diffie-Hellman USM Key MIB
> *RFC 2934*—IPv4 PIM MIB

IANA-Maintained MIB Modules

Interface Type Textual Convention
> *ftp://ftp.iana.org/mib/iana.mib/ianaiftype.mib*

Address Family Numbers Textual Convention
> *ftp://ftp.iana.org/mib/iana.mib/ianaaddressfamilynumbers.mib*

TN3270E Textual Conventions
> *ftp://ftp.iana.org/mib/iana.mib/ianatn3270etc.mib*

Language Identifiers
> *ftp://ftp.iana.org/mib/iana.mib/ianalanguage.mib*

IP Routing Protocol Textual Conventions
> *ftp://ftp.iana.org/mib/iana.mib/ianaiprouteprotocol.mib*

Related Documents

Informational:

> *RFC 1270*—SNMP Communication Services
> *RFC 1321*—MD5 Message-Digest Algorithm
> *RFC 1470*—Network Management Tool Catalog
> *RFC 2039*—Applicability of Standard MIBs to WWW Server Management
> *RFC 2962*—SNMP Application Level Gateway for Payload Address Translation
> *RFC 2975*—Introduction to Accounting Management
> *RFC 3052*—Service Management Architectures Issues and Review
> *RFC 3198*—Terminology for Policy-Based Management
> *RFC 3216*—SMIng Objectives
> *RFC 3387*—Considerations on IP Quality of Service

Experimental:

RFC 1187—Bulk Table Retrieval with the SNMP
RFC 1224—Techniques for Managing Asynchronously Generated Alerts
RFC 1238—CLNS MIB
RFC 1592—SNMP Distributed Program Interface
RFC 1792—TCP/IPX Connection MIB Specification
RFC 3139—Requirements for Configuration Management of IP-based Networks
RFC 3179—Script MIB Extensibility Protocol 1.1

SNMP Support for Perl

This appendix summarizes two SNMP Perl modules. The first is Mike Mitchell's SNMP_util module, which we have used in most of our Perl scripts throughout this book. This module is distributed with Simon Leinen's SNMP Perl module; Mike's module, together with Simon's, can make SNMP programming a snap. You can get these modules from *http://www.switch.ch/misc/leinen/snmp/perl* or *http://www.cpan.org*.

The second module is the one that comes with Net-SNMP. It allows you to write SNMPv1, SNMPv2, and SNMPv3 Perl scripts since it basically wraps the Net-SNMP C libraries. It comes with the Net-SNMP distribution at *http://www.net-snmp.org*.

For those of you who wish to review the Perl language, you can find an excellent introduction to the language at *http://search.cpan.org/~rgarcia/perl-5.9.2/pod/perlintro.pod*.

SNMP_Util

Perl scripts need two use statements to take advantage of the SNMP Perl module:

```
use BER;
use SNMP_Session;
```

The BER and SNMP_Session modules make up the core of Simon's package. The SNMP_util module discussed in this appendix makes using this package a little easier. It requires only one use statement:

```
use SNMP_util;
```

Mike's package uses the other two modules, so it's not necessary to include all three in your scripts.

MIB Management Routines

The following sections describe a set of routines for working with MIBs.

snmpmapOID( )

The MIB objects in RFC 1213 (MIB-II) and RFC 2955 (Frame Relay) are preloaded by the routines in this package. This means that you can refer to a symbolic name like *sysLocation.0* rather than to its numeric OID (*.1.3.6.1.2.1.1.6*). The snmpmapOID( ) routine allows you to add name-OID pairs to this map. The routine is used as follows:

```
snmpmapOID(text, OID, [text, OID...])
```

All the parameters are strings. *text* is the textual (or symbolic) name that you want to use and *OID* is the numeric object ID of the object to which the name refers. A single call to this routine may specify any number of name-OID pairs.

If snmpmapOID( ) fails, it returns undef, so you can test for errors like this:

```
@return = snmpmapOID(..);
if(!@return) {
    # error
}
```

snmpMIB_to_OID( )

This routine takes the filename of a MIB as an argument. It reads and parses the MIB file and associates the object IDs defined by the MIB with their textual names. It returns the number of mappings it created. A return value of 0 means that no mappings were created; -1 means an error occurred (i.e., it was unable to open the file). The routine is used as follows:

```
snmpMIB_to_OID(filename)
```

snmpLoad_OID_Cache( )

This routine allows you to map textual names to object IDs using a file. The file should consist of a number of lines in the form:

```
textual_name OID
```

This is much faster than calling snmpMIB_to_OID( ) because it doesn't require parsing a MIB file. The only argument to this routine is the name of the file that contains the preparsed data:

```
snmpLoad_OID_Cache(filename)
```

snmpLoad_OID_Cache( ) returns -1 if it can't open the file; a return value of 0 indicates success.

snmpQueue_MIB_File( )

This routine specifies a list of MIB files that will be used for mapping textual names to object IDs. If a name or OID can't be found in the internal map, each MIB file is parsed in turn until a match is found. The routine is used as follows:

```
snmpQueue_MIB_File(filename, [filename])
```

SNMP Operations

The routines for performing SNMP operations correspond to the standard SNMP Version 1 operations* and have the following parameters in common:

community (optional)
> The community string. If no community string is specified, *public* is used.

host (required)
> The hostname or IP address of the device you want to query.

port (optional)
> The port number to which to send the query or trap. The default for all routines except snmptrap( ) is 161. The default for snmptrap( ) is 162.

timeout (optional)
> The timeout in seconds; if no response is received within this period, the operation is considered to have failed and is retried. The default is 2 seconds.

retries (optional)
> The number of retries before the routine returns failure. The default is 5.

backoff (optional)
> The backoff value; for each successive retry, the new timeout period is obtained by multiplying the current timeout with the backoff. The default is 1.

OID (required)
> The object ID or textual name of the object you are querying.

snmpget( )

The syntax of the snmpget( ) routine is:

```
snmpget(community@host:port:timeout:retries:backoff, OID, [OID...])
```

If snmpget( ) fails, it returns undef.

Recall that all the MIB-II objects are preloaded into this Perl module, so the following code is legal:

```
@sysDescr = snmpget("public\@cisco.ora.com", "sysDescr");
```

We did not specify any of the optional parameters (*timeout*, *backoff*, etc.); the default values will be used. This routine lets us request "sysDescr" as shorthand for *sysDescr.0*. When the Perl module builds its mappings of names to object IDs, it automatically appends the trailing *.0* to any scalar objects it finds. Because *sysDescr* is a scalar object defined by MIB-II, and because the MIB-II objects are preloaded, *sysDescr* is mapped to *.1.3.6.1.2.1.1.1.0*. If you request a scalar object from a private MIB, you must append *.0* to the OID.

---

* Simon Leinen's package supports both SNMPv1 and v2; Mike Mitchell's SNMP_util module supports only v1.

Since one call to snmpget( ) can retrieve many objects, the return values are stored in an array. For example:

```
@oids = snmpget("public\@cisco.ora.com", "sysDescr", "sysName");
```

When this function call executes, the value for *sysDescr* will be stored in $oids[0]; the value for *sysName* will be stored in $oids[1]. All the routines in this package share this behavior.

snmpgetnext( )

The snmpgetnext( ) routine performs a getnext operation to retrieve the value of the MIB object that follows the object you pass to it. Its syntax is:

```
snmpgetnext(community@host:port:timeout:retries:backoff, OID, [OID...])
```

If snmpgetnext( ) fails, it returns undef.

As with snmpget( ), you can request many OIDs; the return value from snmpgetnext( ) is an array, with the result of each getnext operation in each successive position in the array. The array you get back from snmpgetnext( ) differs from the array returned by snmpget( ) in that the value of each object is preceded by the object's ID, in the form:

```
OID:value
```

This routine returns both the OID and the value because with the getnext operation, you don't necessarily know what the next object in the MIB tree is.

snmpwalk( )

The snmpwalk( ) routine could easily be implemented with repeated calls to snmpgetnext( ); it traverses the entire object tree, starting with the object passed to it. Its syntax is:

```
snmpwalk(community@host:port:timeout:retries:backoff, OID)
```

If snmpwalk( ) fails, it returns undef.

Unlike many of the routines in this module, snmpwalk( ) allows only one OID as an argument. Like the other routines, it returns an array of values; each element of the array consists of an object's ID followed by its value, separated by a colon. For example, after executing the following code:

```
@system = snmpwalk("public\@cisco.ora.com","system");
```

the contents of the array @system would be something like:

```
1.0:cisco.ora.com Cisco
2.0:1.3.6.1.4.1.0
3.0:23 days, 11:01:57
4.0:Ora Network Admin Staff
5.0:cisco.ora.com
6.0:Atlanta, GA
7.0:4
```

Note that the array doesn't include the entire object ID. We've told snmpwalk( ) to walk the tree starting at the *system* object, which has the OID *.1.3.6.1.2.1.1*. The first child object, and the first item in the array, is *sysName*, which is *.1.3.6.1.2.1.1.1.0*. snmpwalk( ) returns 1.0:cisco.ora.com because it omits the generic part of the OID (in this case, *system*) and prints only the instance-specific part (1.0). Similarly, the next item in the array is *system.2.0*, or *system.sysObjectID.0*; its value is Cisco's enterprise ID.

snmpset( )

The snmpset( ) routine allows you to set the value of an object on an SNMP-managed device. In addition to the standard arguments (hostname, community, etc.), this routine expects three arguments for each object you want it to set: the object's ID, datatype, and value. The syntax for this routine is:

```
snmpset(community@host:port:timeout:retries:backoff,
        OID, type, value, [OID, type, value...])
```

The *type* argument must be one of the following strings:

string
> Represents the string type

int
> Represents the 32-bit integer type

ipaddr
> Represents the IP address type

oid
> Represents the object identifier (OID) type

If snmpset( ) fails, it returns undef.

Performing a *set* from a script is straightforward. The following code sets the value of *sysContact* to "Joe@Ora". If the operation succeeds, snmpset( ) returns the new value for *sysContact*. If the operation fails, the fs variable is not set and snmpset( ) prints an error message:

```
$setResponse =
    snmpset("private\@cisco.ora.com", sysContact,"string","Joe\@Ora");
if ($setResponse) {
    print "SET: sysContact: $setResponse\n";
} else {
    print "No response from cisco.ora.com\n";
}
```

The most common reasons for an snmpset( ) to fail are that the host isn't up, the host isn't running an SNMP agent, or the community string is wrong.

snmptrap( )

The snmptrap( ) routine generates an SNMPv1 trap. Most of the arguments are familiar:

```
snmptrap(community@host:port:timeout:retries:backoff,
         enterpriseOID, agent, generalID, specificID,
         OID, type, value, [OID, type, value...])
```

The *enterpriseOID*, *agent*, *generalID*, and *specificID* arguments are discussed in Chapter 9. Each OID/type/value triplet defines a data binding to be included in the trap. *OID* is the object ID of the variable you want to send, *value* is the value you want to send for this object, and *type* is the object's datatype. *type* must be one of the following three strings:

string
> Represents the string type

int
> Represents the 32-bit integer type

oid
> Represents the object identifier (OID) type

If snmptrap( ) fails, it returns undef. See Chapter 9 for a more detailed discussion of SNMP traps.

Net-SNMP

Note that when you download and build the source distribution for Net-SNMP, you must explicitly tell the configure command to install the Perl modules as well. You do so like this:

```
$ ./configure --with-perl-modules
```

The use statement for this module looks like the following:

```
use SNMP;
```

Beyond this, the actual usage of the Net-SNMP Perl module is broken into two categories, which are discussed next.

MIB Management Routines

By default, when you use this Perl module it will load all the MIB files located in the default location, */usr/local/share/snmp/mibs*. This means you can use names like sysDescr and not have to remember the OIDs for these objects. But if you want to use some private MIB, there are routines that can help you with this. We'll discuss the two more commonly used ones.

&SNMP::loadModules(<mod>,...)

The `&SNMP::loadModules()` method is used to load a particular MIB file. If you simply copy your MIB file to the normal location (*/usr/local/share/snmp/mibs*), the Net-SNMP library will not automatically load it. It has an internal list of MIB files it knows about (these are installed when you build the Net-SNMP package). This routine can be used to load a specific MIB, list of MIBs, or all MIBs. For example, this line of code will load all MIB files, including any you copied to the default location:

```
&SNMP::loadModules('ALL');
```

Alternatively, you could have invoked this routine like so:

```
&SNMP::loadModules('IEEE802dot11-MIB');
```

This loads the 802.11 MIB we installed. How did we know to use `IEEE802dot11-MIB`? If you look at the top of any MIB file, you will see the `BEGIN` clause. For example, this line is at the top of the 802.11 MIB file:

```
IEEE802dot11-MIB DEFINITIONS ::= BEGIN
```

You just use the name of the MIB definition as the argument to the `loadModules` routine.

&SNMP::addMibDirs(<dir>,...)

The `&SNMP::addMibDirs()` routine allows you to add directories to be searched where other MIB files may belong. This is advantageous if you have private MIBs and either you want to store them in the default location, or you don't have write permission for the directory.

SNMP Operations

Unlike `SNMP_Util`, the Net-SNMP library requires a little more work to achieve the same goal. However, it is a flexible package that allows you a full range of control over your application. We'll present several SNMP applications that will highlight the basic usage of this package. To learn more about this module, you can install the Net-SNMP package and read the manual page for the module by running man SNMP.

snmpwalk

The following is a simple implementation of the snmpwalk command:

```
#!/usr/bin/perl

use SNMP;
$SNMP::use_sprint_value = 1;
my $host = "localhost";

$sess = new SNMP::Session( DestHost => $host,
```

```
                              Version => 3,
                              SecName => "kjs",
                              AuthProto => "MD5",
                              AuthPass => "mypassword",
                              PrivProto => "DES",
                              PrivPass => "myotherpassword",
                              SecLevel => "authPriv");

my $var = new SNMP::Varbind([]);

do {
  my $val = $sess->getnext($var);
  print "$var->[$SNMP::Varbind::tag_f].$var->[$SNMP::Varbind::iid_f] = ",
        "$var->[$SNMP::Varbind::val_f]\n";
} until ($sess->{ErrorNum});
```

First off, we set $SNMP::use_sprint_value to 1. This forces the module to use Net-SNMP's snprint_value library function, which helps make output a little more user friendly. Next we create a new SNMP session. There are many options you can pass to the constructor. In this example, we're creating an SNMPv3 session. If you wanted to use just SNMPv2, you could simply do the following:

```
$sess = new SNMP::Session(  DestHost => $host,
                            Community => $comm,
                            Version => 2);
```

The line $var = new SNMP::Varbind([]); creates an empty variable binding. This means we want to walk the entire MIB tree on the host. Next we go into a loop where we call getnext() on the newly created variable binding. We print the tag name for the OID we retrieved, its instance identifier (always 0 for scalar objects), and the value itself. We check to see if $sess->{ErrorNum} is set (which means we have reached the end of the MIB or some other failure has occurred). If no error has occurred, we do the getnext() again.

Here is a sample run of this program:

```
$ ./mibwalk.pl
sysDescr.0 = Linux snort 2.4.7-10 #1 Thu Sep 6 17:27:27 EDT 2001 i686
sysObjectID.0 = linux
sysUpTimeInstance. = 0:0:51:06.71
sysContact.0 = Root <root@localhost>
sysName.0 = machine
sysLocation.0 = Kevin J. Schmidt
....
```

Note that the output has been cut short.

snmpget

Now let's look at how the simple SNMP get operation is implemented:

```
#!/usr/bin/perl

use SNMP;
```

```
$SNMP::use_sprint_value = 1;

my $host = "localhost";

$sess = new SNMP::Session(  DestHost => $host,
                            Version => 3,
                            SecName => "kjs",
                            AuthProto => "MD5",
                            AuthPass => "mypassword",
                            PrivProto => "DES",
                            PrivPass => "myotherpassword",
                            SecLevel => "authPriv");

$var = new SNMP::VarList(['sysDescr',0],['sysUpTime',0]);
my @vars = $sess->get($var);
foreach (@vars) {
    print "$_ \n";
}
```

The main difference here is the use of the SNMP::VarList command:

```
$var = new SNMP::VarList(['sysDescr',0],['sysUpTime',0]);
```

This allows us to specify one or more OIDs we wish to get. The format of each OID you pass to this routine is as follows:

```
[object, iid]
```

The value for *iid* depends on what the object is. If it's a simple scalar, use 0. Otherwise, you have a columnar object and *iid* will need to be the identifier or index for the object.

The call $sess->get($var); returns an array with each respective bucket set to the return value for each object in the order you specified them with the call to VarList.

snmpset

Here's a script that sets the sysName OID:

```
#!/usr/bin/perl

use SNMP;
$SNMP::use_sprint_value = 1;

my $host = "localhost";

$sess = new SNMP::Session(  DestHost => $host,
                            Version => 3,
                            SecName => "kjs",
                            AuthProto => "MD5",
                            AuthPass => "mypassword",
                            PrivProto => "DES",
                            PrivPass => "myotherpassword",
                            SecLevel => "authPriv");

$var = new SNMP::Varbind(['sysName',0]);
```

```
my ($sysDescr) = $sess->get($var);
print "Old name: $sysDescr\n";
$sess->set(['sysName',0,"New Name","OCTETSTR"]);
my ($newSysDescr) = $sess->get($var);
print "New name: $newSysDescr\n";
my $setter = new SNMP::Varbind(['sysName',0,$sysDescr,"OCTETSTR"]);
$sess->set($setter);
my ($newSysDescr) = $sess->get($var);
print "Back to old name: $newSysDescr\n";
```

Note the line:

```
$sess->set(['sysName',0,"New Name","OCTETSTR"]);
```

Here we change sysName to the value "New Name". The set routine takes an extended form of the format we pass to the Varbind routine:

```
[oid, iid, value, type]
```

The *oid* and *iid* we already know about. *value* is whatever you want the *oid* to be changed to. *type* must be one of the following:

OBJECTID

　　Dotted-decimal (e.g., .1.3.6.1.2.1.1.1)

OCTETSTR

　　Perl scalar containing octets

INTEGER

　　Decimal signed integer (or enum)

NETADDR

　　Dotted-decimal

IPADDR

　　Dotted-decimal

COUNTER

　　Decimal unsigned integer

COUNTER64

　　Decimal unsigned integer

GAUGE

　　Decimal unsigned integer

UINTEGER

　　Decimal unsigned integer

TICKS

Decimal unsigned integer

OPAQUE

Perl scalar containing octets

NULL

Perl scalar containing nothing

Also note the lines:

```
my $setter = new SNMP::Varbind(['sysName',0,$sysDescr,"OCTETSTR"]);
$sess->set($setter);
```

This just shows that a Varbind object can be used as an argument to the set routine. Finally, here is the output from this script:

```
$ ./set.pl
Old name: machine
New name: New Name
Back to old name: machine
```

Network Management Software

Many SNMP software packages are available, ranging from programming libraries that let you build your own utilities (using Perl, C/C++, or Java) to expensive, complete network management platforms. This chapter presents a small sampling of some of the more commonly used packages. This should not only give you an idea of what types of packages are out there, but also introduce you to the different levels of packages (from freeware up to enterprise-class software). Management software falls into five categories:

- SNMP agents
- NMS suites
- Element managers (vendor-specific management)
- Trend analysis software
- Supporting software

Unfortunately, deciding what you need isn't as simple as picking one program from each category. If you have a small network and are interested in building your own tools, you probably don't need a complex NMS suite. Whether you need trend analysis software depends, obviously, on whether you're interested in analyzing trends in your network usage. The products available depend in part on the platforms in which you're interested. The minimum you can get by with is an SNMP agent on a device and some software that can retrieve a value from that device (using an SNMP get). Although this is minimal, it's enough to start working, and you can get the software for free.

This appendix presents a broad sampling of some of the leading products in each of these categories. Since there are more packages than we can cover in this book, be sure to check the SNMPLink.org web site (*http://www.snmplink.org/Tools.html*) for network management product listings.

SNMP Agents

As we explained in Chapter 1, the agent is the software that controls all the SNMP communication to and from any SNMP-compatible device. In some devices, such as Cisco routers, the agent software is built into the device itself and requires no installation. On other platforms, you may have to install the agent as an additional software package.

Before you can look at what types of agents you need, you must research what types of devices you have on your network and what types of information you would like to receive from each. Some agents are very basic and return only a limited amount of information, and others can return a wealth of information. To start, determine whether you need to receive information from servers (Unix, Windows, etc.) or network devices (routers, switches, etc.). Generally, out-of-the-box network-type devices provide more information than their server counterparts. On the other hand, network devices do not extend very easily, if at all, in part because network hardware usually doesn't have a disk-based operating environment.* This keeps the end user from accessing the agent to make modifications or extend it. Table F-1 lists some SNMP agents.

 Make sure that you understand what kind of software is running on your servers (email systems, accounting packages, etc.). Many applications will not listen for or respond to SNMP requests but will send out traps. Traps can be very useful for monitoring some of these applications. Also, there are applications for virus scanners, remote logins (pcAnywhere), and UPSs that will send informative traps when an error has been found. Look for this feature the next time you purchase any package or software suite.

Table F-1. SNMP agents

AdventNet SNMP Agent(s)	*http://www.adventnet.com*
Concord eHealth SystemEDGE	*http://www.concord.com*
HP Extensible SNMP Agent	*http://www.openview.hp.com*
MG-SOFT Master Agent	*http://www.mg-soft.com*
Microsoft	*http://www.microsoft.com*
Net-SNMP (formerly the UCD-SNMP project)	*http://net-snmp.sourceforge.net*
Sun Microsystems	*http://www.sun.com*
SNMP Research International	*http://www.int.snmp.com*

---

* See Chapter 11 for a discussion of extensible agents.

NMS Suites

We use the term *suite* to mean a software package that bundles multiple applications into one convenient product. In this section, we discuss NMS software, which is one of the more important pieces of the network management picture. Without it, the agent software in the previous section is virtually useless. NMS products allow you to have a total view of your network, including all the servers, routers, switches, and desktops. In most cases, this view is a graphical representation of your network, with lots of neat labels and icons. These are highly configurable packages and work in almost any network environment. This freedom often comes with a big price tag and a confusing setup process. Some of the products focus more on the network side of management (i.e., devices such as routers, hubs, and switches). Others go a step beyond this and allow you to customize server and workstation agents to integrate nicely into your NMSs. Keep in mind that the bigger packages are for larger, more complicated networks and require extensive training. Be sure to take some time to research the packages before purchasing; if at all possible, get trial versions. Table F-2 lists both commercial and open source NMS suites.

Table F-2. NMS suites

HP OpenView	*http://www.openview.hp.com*
SolarWinds	*http://www.solarwinds.net*
IBM Tivoli	*http://www.ibm.com/software/tivoli*
Castle Rock SNMPc	*http://www.castlerock.com*
BMC Software	*http://www.bmc.com*
Computer Associates Unicenter	*http://www.ca.com*
Veritas NerveCenter	*http://www.veritas.com*
Micromuse Netcool	*http://www.micromuse.com*
GxSNMP	*http://www.gxsnmp.org*
Tkined	*http://wwwhome.cs.utwente.nl/~schoenw/scotty*
OpenNMS	*http://www.opennms.org*
SNMPSTAT monitoring system	*http://snmpstat.sourceforge.net*
Big Brother	*http://www.bb4.org*
Mercury SiteScope	*http://www.mercury.com*
Ipswitch WhatsUp	*http://www.ipswitch.com/products/whatsup/index.html*
Just For Fun (JFF) NMS	*http://www.jffnms.org*
Nagios	*http://www.nagios.org*
NagMIN	*http://nagmin.sourceforge.net*

Element Managers (Vendor-Specific Management)

These software packages are geared toward a certain type of vendor or function; for example, an element manager might be a product that focuses on managing a modem rack. Before purchasing such a package, take a good look at your present environment, how it's likely to grow, and what vendors you are currently using or are likely to use in the future. Because many of these products are vendor specific, it's easy to buy something that turns out to be less useful than you expect. For example, CiscoView (part of the CiscoWorks suite) is a great piece of software; it does lots of fancy things, such as showing you the backs of your routers. However, if you purchase a number of Nortel devices a few months after installing this product, it won't be able to give you a unified view of your network. Some packages do allow you to manage their competitors' equipment; for example, an element manager that monitors switches may be able to handle switches from competing vendors. Before buying any of these products, research where your network is headed, and be sure to ask hard questions about the product's capabilities. Table F-3 lists some of the available element managers.

Table F-3. Element managers

Sun Management Center	*http://www.sun.com/sunmanagementcenter*
CiscoWorks 2000	*http://www.cisco.com*
3Com Total Control	*http://www.3com.com*
Aprisma (now owned by Concord)	*http://www.aprisma.com*
Nortel	*http://www.nortelnetworks.com/solutions/net_mang*

Trend Analysis

When faced with most network problems, it's nice to have some kind of historical record to give you an idea of when things started going wrong. This allows you to go back and review what happened before a problem appeared, and possibly prevent it from recurring. If you want to be proactive about diagnosing problems before they appear, it is essential to know what "normal" means for your network—you need a set of baseline statistics that show you how your network normally behaves. While many of the bigger packages do some trend reporting, they can be clunky and hard to use. They might not even provide you with the kind of information you need. Once you see what a dedicated trend analysis system can do, you will see why it might be worth the time, energy, and money to integrate one into your network monitoring scheme.

If your environment calls for some serious monitoring, you should look into getting RMON probes. RMON probes are a great addition to trend analysis packages, since most trend packages can make use of the kind of data these probes gather. Table F-4 lists some trend analysis packages.

Table F-4. Trend analysis

Concord eHealth	*http://www.concord.com*
Trinagy (formerly DeskTalk Systems, Inc.) TREND	*http://www.desktalk.com*
MRTG	*http://www.mrtg.org*
Cricket	*http://cricket.sourceforge.net*
InfoVista	*http://www.infovista.com*
RTG	*http://rtg.sourceforge.net*
SNARLSNMP	*http://snarl-snmp.sourceforge.net*

Supporting Software

Supporting software is a grab bag that includes all sorts of things that are used in conjunction with the software packages listed earlier. Some of these packages can be used to write standalone SNMP applications. Table F-5 lists several supporting software packages. Most of these are freely available and can be used with little or no previous experience.

Table F-5. Supporting software

Perl	*http://www.perl.com* *http://www.perl.org*
SNMP framework for Python	*http://pysnmp.sourceforge.net*
SNMP Support for Perl	*http://www.switch.ch/misc/leinen/snmp/perl* *http://www.cpan.org*
pwSNMP Visual Basic	*http://sourceforge.net/projects/websignoff*
WILMA	*ftp://ftp.ldv.e-technik.tu-muenchen.de/dist/WILMA/INDEX.html*
Net-SNMP C Library	*http://net-snmp.sourceforge.net*
Net-SNMP Perl Module	*http://www.cpan.org/authors/id/GSM*
A3Com	*http://www.kernel.org/software/A3Com*
SNMP++	*http://www.agentpp.com*
Netcool	*http://www.micromuse.com*
Network Computing Technologies Trap Receiver	*http://www.ncomtech.com*

Open Source Monitoring Software

In this book, we describe various software applications and suites that give us the ability to monitor our networks. Increasingly, open source software is appearing in today's enterprises in place of or in addition to commercial network management software.

When we refer to open source software, we mean that it's free to download and use. While this sounds like shareware or even freeware, it's not. Take some time to review the General Public License (GPL), available at *http://www.gnu.org/copyleft/gpl.html* as well as the Open Source Initiative's site at *http://www.opensource.org*. Furthermore, licenses have many variations; sometimes a project creates its own specific license that you must review (for example, Big Brother's "Better Than Free" license).

All of the software we describe in this appendix is available from SourceForge (*http://www.sourceforge.net*). Additional open source SNMP tools can be found on sites like *http://freshmeat.net*.

Table G-1 lists the applications we discuss in this appendix.

Table G-1. Summary of software covered

Application	URL
Big Brother	*http://sourceforge.net/projects/big-brother*
Nagios	*http://sourceforge.net/projects/nagios*
JFFNMS	*http://sourceforge.net/projects/jffnms*
NINO	*http://sourceforge.net/projects/nino*
OpenNMS	*http://sourceforge.net/projects/opennms*

Big Brother

Big Brother is one of the most established and popular web-based console monitoring packages available. It gives the user a console or dashboard look-and-feel with typical green, yellow, and red dots indicating system status. Big Brother can monitor information such as connectivity (ping), DNS, FTP, and HTTP, to name a few. Additional (free and commercial) plug-ins and agents (with prewritten samples) are also available.

Availability reporting can help you quickly assess a server's or service's uptime. Notifications are somewhat complex and can be based on machine name, time of day, or event or test that failed. There's even support for delaying alerts (to allow nuisance alarms to resolve themselves) and email paging.

A commercial version, Big Brother Professional Edition (PE), that offers encryption and compiled versions for certain platforms is also available.

We recommend running through the demo at *http://demo.bb4.com/bb*. Although the demo shows the Professional Edition, it gives you a good sense of the overall look-and-feel of the application.

The main Big Brother PE screen is a top-level dashboard that displays a grid of green, yellow, and red icons that assess system status. The left column lists the servers and the top row lists various tests and conditions. In short, when things are running well, square green icons display. Otherwise, you might see a flashing red X for a system in trouble, a yellow circle for something that needs attention, a pink swirling icon for a system for which there is no report, a white icon for a system that is unavailable, or a blue circle for a system that is offline.

The column names on the grid (bkp, conn, cont, cpu, dig, disk, and so on) are abbreviations for various tests. Clicking on an icon drills down into the test and shows the results since the last poll.

 While test results are important, the time the test was last taken is more important. Depending on the polling interval, you could be looking at data that is a few seconds old or a few days old. Every system and test can be set up differently. Before you react to any alert, check the live system.

Clicking on the HISTORY button will take you to a screen that shows the historical data for that server and test. It shows a graphical timeline for the last 24 hours (if the system was in trouble for part of that time, the timeline shows various colors). Below that is a table that displays system state by percentage for the last 24 hours. The bottom table shows the last 50 log entries for this test.

Big Brother has come a long way, and now it does even more with the advent of the Professional Edition. The documentation, FAQs, and support list make this a great application to use. Table G-2 summarizes the details about Big Brother.

Table G-2. Big Brother

URL	*http://www.bb4.org* *http://www.quest.com/bigbrother*
License	Better Than Free (*http://www.bb4.org/license-text.html*)

Operating systems	Unix, Linux, and Windows (WS 2003, Windows 2000, and NT 4.0 with SP3)
Written in	Java, JavaScript
User interface	Web-based
Additional requirements	A C compiler and a web server
Notes	Be sure to check out *http://www.deadcat.net* (sponsored by Quest Software) for a wealth of add-ons and plug-ins to help you customize Big Brother for your environment.

Nagios

Nagios is a comprehensive monitoring software package that, if installed and configured properly, can work nicely for many small to large companies. It has all the typical features like status overview, map view, and an alerts screen (just to name a few), but it goes a step further to give you sections on trends, a tactical overview, and process and performance data. Beyond that, Nagios offers some rather advanced features such as 3D maps of your network (using Virtual Reality Markup Language or VRML) and a WAP interface for cell phones.

Nagios is pretty easy to download and compile. The online docs are useful and easy to read. Experienced users recommended that I download and install the Nagios plug-ins as well. These plug-ins are little pieces of software (which must also be compiled) that do most of the actual monitoring checks (check_pop, check_ssh, etc.). In my setup, I used the check_ssh program to ensure that the SSH port (22) was open and available. Before installing Nagios, you must have the Apache web server installed and configured.

While many packages give you the ability to monitor and show typical alerts, Nagios has the ability to monitor servers and services and group them efficiently to generate a variety of related notifications.

After installation, configuring the product took some time. I had to trudge through numerous configuration files (with the help of the documentation) to get everything up and running. Even with the example files, it took a few hours to get a single host and service (check_ssh) working. Despite this, I enjoyed the fact that I could define and customize a wide variety of parameters. Although during installation I was somewhat frustrated to discover that I must modify yet another definition file, I applaud Nagios for its extensibility.

Overall, Nagios does not provide an easy setup and requires some planning and thought. Once that is done, however, Nagios can provide a wealth of information.

Here's a quick sample of what a configuration file might contain. Please keep in mind that this is not a complete configuration but simply a snippet from the one that I used during my setup, excerpted here to give you a feel for Nagios's configuration:

```
define timeperiod{
    timeperiod_name        24x7
    alias                  24x7
    sunday              00:00-24:00
    monday              00:00-24:00
    tuesday              00:00-24:00
    wednesday              00:00-24:00
    thursday              00:00-24:00
    friday              00:00-24:00
    saturday              00:00-24:00
    }
define command{
    command_name     go_logger
    command_line     /usr/bin/logger "Nagios MSG: $HOSTADDRESS$"
    }

define command{
    command_name     check_ssh
    command_line     /usr/local/nagios/libexec/check_ssh -H $HOSTADDRESS$
    }
define service{
    host_name                myhost
    service_description          check_ssh_for_myhost
    check_command            check_ssh
    max_check_attempts       5
    normal_check_interval    5
    retry_check_interval         3
    check_period             24x7
    notification_interval    30
    notification_options         w,c,r
    }
define contact{
    contact_name               root
    alias                      Douglas Mauro
    service_notification_period    24x7
    host_notification_period        24x7
    service_notification_options    w,u,c,r
    host_notification_options        d,u,r
    service_notification_commands    go_logger
    host_notification_commands    go_logger
    email                      root@localhost
}
define contactgroup{
        contactgroup_name    my1stgroup
        alias                my_1st_group
        members              root
}
define hostgroup{
    hostgroup_name    allhosts
    alias             all my hosts
    members          myhost
}

define host{
```

```
host_name              myhost
alias                  my_local_host
address                192.168.40.130
max_check_attempts     5
contact_groups         my1stgroup
notification_interval  30
notification_period    24x7
notification_options   d,u,r
```

All of the Nagios screenshots shown here come from the online docs available at *http://www.nagios.org/about/screenshots.php*.

Figure G-1 shows the status overview. It gives a quick look at host and service status totals along with a service overview for all the different host groups (which you can define).

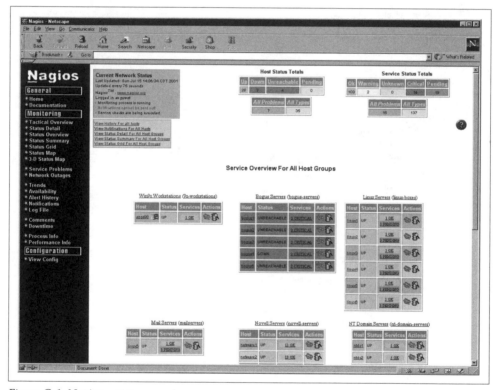

Figure G-1. Nagios – status overview

Figure G-2 shows a high-level color-coded status map. Hovering the mouse over a node pops up detailed information about that particular node. Clicking on a host forwards you to the host's Service Status Details page. The top-right section of the page gives you additional layout options.

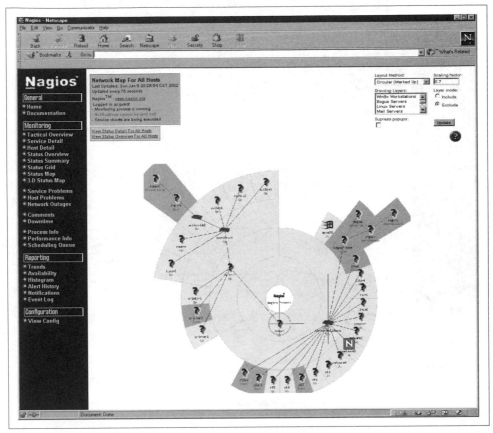

Figure G-2. Nagios status map

Figure G-3 shows the Trends page, which you can see by clicking on the Trends link (on the left) and filling out a report form page. This area allows you to create different reports based on hosts, services, and groups over a given interval (today, the last three months, and so on). The upper-left section of the window links to related reports. This allows you to quickly jump to an availability report for the same object (node, service, etc.) right from this page.

For big shops with strapped budgets and little shops with some extra time on their hands, Nagios is a tool worth looking into. All of the features that Nagios offers (for free) are the same as (if not more than) those in the commercial packages available today.

One feature that would be nice is a live graphing area. Nagios can be forced to immediately poll an object (node, service, and so on), but a live, scrolling graph of something is critical when troubleshooting. Table G-3 summarizes information about Nagios.

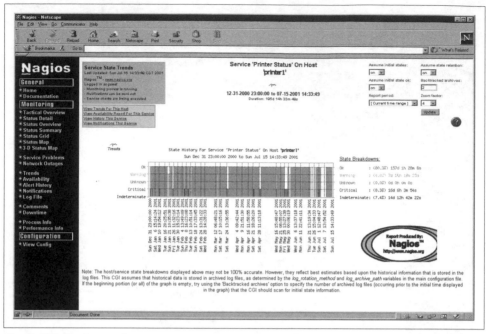

Figure G-3. Nagios trends

Table G-3. Nagios

URL	*http://www.nagios.org*
	http://nagiosplug.sourceforge.net
License	GPL
Operating systems	Unix, Linux
Written in	C
User interface	Web-based
Additional requirements/notes	C compiler, web server (Nagios is set up to install with Apache)

JFFNMS

I enjoyed working through the JFFNMS (Just For Fun NMS) demo—without reading through any documentation first. Intuitive features and navigation make this monitoring package stand out from the crowd.

Supported operating systems include Windows 2000, Windows Server 2003, Windows XP, and, of course, Unix and Linux. JFFNMS is web-based and is written in PHP. It contains typical features such as a status map, events console, and performance graphs (using RRDtool).

The Hosts map view allows you to break down the display into hosts for different customers. A pull-down menu lets you select a single customer's data, further refining the view.

The Performance view shows thumbnail graphs of all the different objects. This screen could serve as a morning wake-up call; it provides a quick way to get a broad view of the health of all your devices.

A few features stand out; the database backend uses MySQL. It has an integrated syslog monitoring facility. JJFNMS provides auto discovery and monitoring capabilities for real-world environments, including APC UPS, Apache and IIS monitoring, and Compaq Insight Manager Monitoring, just to name a few.

JFFNMS offers the ability to set up SLA thresholds. It comes with some useful presets such as logging an event when memory usage goes above 80%.

The maps display the various monitored components with mouse-over pop ups that lead you right to the graphs while continuing to display the events page below.

Another nice feature is the ability to choose different display outputs. You can view the page in HTML, DHTML, graphs, or even plain text! Table G-4 summarizes information about JFFNMS.

Table G-4. JFFNMS

URL	*http://www.jffnms.org*
License	GPL
Operating systems	Unix, Linux, BSD (including Mac OS X), Windows (Server 2003, 2000, XP, 95, 98)
Written in	Perl, PHP, Unix shell
User interface	Web based
Additional requirements	Apache, MySQL, RRDtool, PHP (with the following extensions: snmp, ssl, gd, sockets, mysql or pgsql, pcre, posix, ob, and session), NET-SNMP, GNU Diff, Fping (Unix only)
Optional packages	Graphviz & WebFonts, NMAP PortScanner, JFFNMS Integration Packages, TFTP server

OpenNMS

This web-based management solution focuses on three main areas: polling, performance, and event management. It leverages some other important open source packages, including RRDtool, Tomcat, and Curl (to name a few).

All of the images and screenshots in this section can be found at the OpenNMS web site located at *http://www.opennms.org*.

Figure G-4 shows the main OpenNMS web interface screen. This is the starting area, providing a high-level view into which areas of the network, if any, are experiencing outages. It also serves as a launching area for a variety of reports.

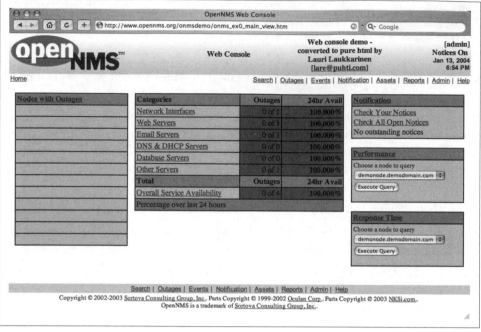

Figure G-4. OpenNMS—main web console screen

One nice feature that OpenNMS provides is notification escalations. Users state that they want to be notified about certain events. When the event occurs, an alert is sent out and the event is set as "outstanding." The user can then log in to the web interface and acknowledge that particular event. If after some (preset) time, the user does not acknowledge the event, OpenNMS escalates the event to another user or group.

Events are displayed in a table format, as shown in Figure G-5. Checkboxes make it easy to acknowledge an event. Admins can raise or lower an event's severity or drill down into more detail about the event.

Reports are displayed in the typical RRDtool fashion (as shown in Figure G-6). There's a report search section that you can use to find reports based on certain criteria as well as the ability to create a list of standard and custom reports for quick execution.

OpenNMS has some great documentation in the form of How-To guides, available on its SourceForge site at *https://sourceforge.net/docman/?group_id=4141*. For example, take a look at these titles:

- How-To Configure OpenNMS Discovery
- How-To Configure Service Level Polling
- How-To Configure SNMP Data Collection
- How-To Configure Events

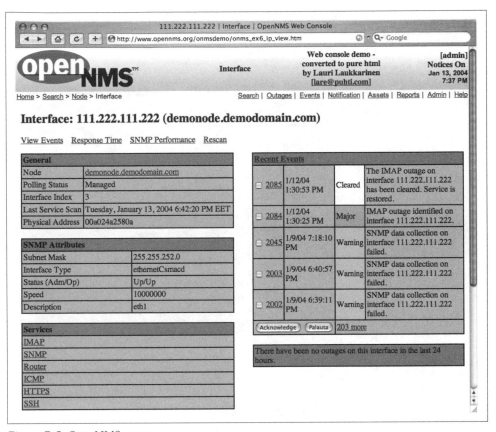

Figure G-5. OpenNMS events screen

I also recommend the OpenNMS Installation Guide. OpenNMS has quite a few prerequisite packages to install, which might deter some admins from trying the application (see Table G-5 for details).

It seems like OpenNMS has been around forever. I think it's safe to say that this group is one of the first (if not the first) to provide a truly open NMS solution. While it doesn't have some of the fancier bells and whistles seen in other packages, it truly makes up for it in the documentation and cross-platform release files. The OpenNMS team has done a very good job at providing an NMS package that is simple yet powerful.

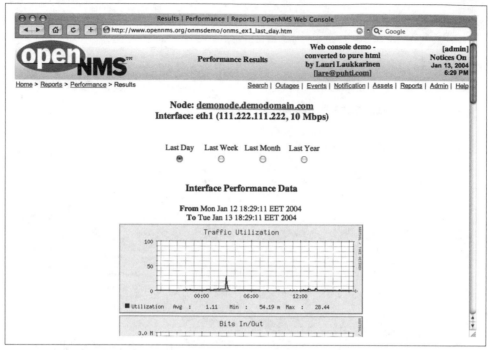

Figure G-6. OpenNMS reporting

Table G-5. OpenNMS

URL	*http://www.opennms.org*
License	GPL
Operating systems	Solaris 8 and Solaris 9 (SPARC and x86), Mac OS X (Panther), Linux (see site for specific distributions)
Written in	Java
User interface	Web-based
Additional requirements	Java, Tomcat 4, RRDtool, PostgreSQL, Curl, Metamail (optional)

NINO

If you're looking for a product that is rich in features and glitz, look no further. NINO (which stands for Nino Is Not OpenView) contains the usual features you've come to expect from NMS software: polling, event console, auto-discovery, support for MySQL databases, reports, and more. However, we'll discuss some standout features that set NINO apart.

You'll find a demo at the NINO web site, *http://nino.sourceforge.net/nino/index.html*. Though it is not all live, it gives a nice overview of all the features and allows you to work with a few active items. Most of the screenshots were captured on a test network.

Most NMS graphs that we've seen are flat images. Some allow you to change the date/time (and click submit), which can be a bit clunky when you are trying to poke around. NINO offers an interactive Java graph that allows you to click and drag the time interval, not only to the left and right, but also up and down to change the scale.

NINO's hostmeter gives you a great view of the status of an object (don't let the *host* in *hostmeter* fool you; it can monitor routers and other devices as well). Using gauges, dials, and graphs, the hostmeter displays disk levels, processes, and CPU usage, among other things.

NINO includes an interactive 3D map of your objects. Using your mouse, you can rotate the collection for a better view; you can also zoom in or out. An auto-rotate feature slowly spins the map, allowing you to see it from every perspective.

Some default sounds come with NINO (and they are on by default). These can be configured to go off when a node goes down or some other important event occurs, to alert you when you are not looking at the screen.

NINO offers a nice MIB search tool that allows you to find keywords within your loaded MIB database. Once keywords are found, the program displays the results within the MIB browser with each hit expanded for easy access.

NINO has still more features worth mentioning:

Service response
> The ability to check the status of services such as FTP, HTTP, and so on.

Easy-to-configure reports
> Reports can be edited with little knowledge of HTML and SQL. In no time I had some custom reports up and running.

Process watching and reporting
> Inside and outside of NINO, you can set watch points on numerous processes.

Skins
> Like many applications today, NINO has skins so that you can change the look-and-feel of the program.

NINO has its share of prerequisite software (see Table G-6). However, on Windows, the installation adds the prerequisites along with the NINO executables. On Linux, admins are expected to install the required packages separately.

Overall, NINO is a great tool for people looking for an NMS with some eye candy. As with many open source tools, a few areas need to be polished. For more in-depth reporting, I had to reference the online guide to understand the relationships between nodes, charts, files, and so on. Nonetheless, NINO is a flexible tool that can make a boring NMS project a lot more fun.

Table G-6. NINO

URL	*http://nino.sourceforge.net/nino/index.html*
License	GPL, Artistic License
Operating systems	Windows (2000, NT, XP, 95, 98), Linux, BSD, Unix, Solaris
Written in	Java, Perl
User interface	Web-based
Additional requirements	Perl 5.8 or higher, MySQL database client and server, Net-SNMP, Apache, Apache mod_perl, Perl DBD/DBI (MySQL) modules, Perl Time Hires module, Perl Net-SNMP modules. On Windows, the install includes all this software.

Network Troubleshooting Primer

SNMP is very good at helping you know when faults occur in your network. For example, if an interface on your router is down or malfunctioning, you may still have network connectivity to the router, so you can use SNMP to further discover what the problem may be.

Sometimes when something bad happens, however, you may only know that some network or system is unreachable. When this happens, it is good to know how to use a few tools of the trade to help diagnose and resolve the issue.

The following points detail the concepts involved in network troubleshooting:

- The process of troubleshooting is systematic in that one must be methodical to properly solve the problem at hand. It requires skills and knowledge including an understanding of your environment, problem-solving skills, and an ability to accurately communicate with others.

- As you begin your troubleshooting task, be sure to change one thing at a time as you test to see whether the problem is resolved. Not doing so can possibly obscure the actual step that resolved the problem, making it difficult to accurately and quickly resolve the same problem when it happens again.

- Documentation is a key step in the process. If you document exactly what the symptoms were, as well as the resolution steps (including any tools that you used in the process), others can learn from this. The next time someone has to solve the same problem, they can do so more quickly and help minimize downtime.

- Don't assume that the problem is due to some convoluted set of circumstances. Always check the obvious first. I cannot count the times when I was a NOC engineer that the problem ended up being a bad cable or something simple.

- Keep in mind that things like firewalls and other security systems can hinder your ability to accurately troubleshoot. For example, a firewall may be configured to disallow packets to the host you are troubleshooting. It pays to understand the security architecture in your environment.

- It is always best to know a few tools well rather than a bunch of tools not so well.
- Testing after the problem is fixed is sometimes overlooked in the frenzy to get something back to operational status. Do not overlook this step.

The remainder of this appendix focuses on some general-purpose tools used in network troubleshooting. Covering these tools in detail is beyond the scope of this appendix. For an excellent treatment of network troubleshooting, see *Network Troubleshooting Tools* by Joseph Sloan (O'Reilly).

ping

ping is probably the most widely used tool for network troubleshooting. It uses ICMP packets to measure how long it takes to send a packet to a remote host and receive a response. ECHO_REQUEST and ECHO_REPLY are used by ping for this purpose. ECHO_REQUEST is used to indicate that a host requests an ICMP reply, and ECHO_REPLY is used to denote a reply to an ICMP request. In theory, all TCP/IP-based devices should respond to an ECHO_REQUEST. In practice, this is not always the case.

ping can be viewed as a layer-three testing tool. If ping doesn't work, suspect layers three and below. If it does work, suspect layers four and higher.

Note that some routers can be configured to block ICMP responses to ICMP packets, so be aware of this.

Here are some general ping error messages you should know about, and an explanation of what they indicate:

- A message similar to "Unknown Host" is usually indicative of a DNS problem. If this type of message is received, try to use the IP address of the remote host you are trying to reach.
- If you receive a host or network unreachable message, it could be due to networking problems like a missing router or misconfigured gateway. A router will respond with an ICMP DESTINATION_HOST_UNREACHABLE message if it has no path to the host.
- If a timeout message is displayed by ping, any number of problems could be to blame, including the simple case that the remote host is not turned on.

Here is some ping output from Windows:

```
C:\> ping www.yahoo.com

Pinging www.yahoo.akadns.net [68.142.226.49] with 32 bytes of data:

Reply from 68.142.226.49: bytes=32 time=34ms TTL=47
Reply from 68.142.226.49: bytes=32 time=26ms TTL=47
Reply from 68.142.226.49: bytes=32 time=29ms TTL=47
```

```
Reply from 68.142.226.49: bytes=32 time=27ms TTL=47

Ping statistics for 68.142.226.49:
    Packets: Sent = 4, Received = 4, Lost = 0 (0% loss),
Approximate round trip times in milli-seconds:
    Minimum = 26ms, Maximum = 34ms, Average = 29ms
```

The ping times look pretty good. Now look at the ping output from Unix:

```
$ ping www.yahoo.com
PING www.yahoo.akadns.net (68.142.226.46) 56(84) bytes of data.
64 bytes from p15.www.re2.yahoo.com (68.142.226.46): icmp_seq=1 ttl=52
time=18.7 ms
64 bytes from p15.www.re2.yahoo.com (68.142.226.46): icmp_seq=2 ttl=53
time=19.8 ms
64 bytes from p15.www.re2.yahoo.com (68.142.226.46): icmp_seq=3 ttl=53
time=19.3 ms
64 bytes from p15.www.re2.yahoo.com (68.142.226.46): icmp_seq=4 ttl=53
time=19.5 ms
^C
--- www.yahoo.akadns.net ping statistics ---
4 packets transmitted, 4 received, 0% packet loss, time 3002ms
rtt min/avg/max/mdev = 18.724/19.342/19.820/0.412 ms
$
```

This set of ping times is higher than the one we saw from Windows. Could this be a problem? Not necessarily. It could be that someone was transferring a large file on the network when we decided to perform our test. Also, some network devices may place ICMP at a lower priority than other protocols, so the response you get may look delayed, but in reality, it was a victim of priority scheduling.

You may be tempted to use the TTL to estimate hop counts, but it isn't an accurate measurement because it may be reset along the path to prevent routing loops.

Finally, here are the basic steps for using ping to troubleshoot network problems:

- Repeatedly run ping to isolate problems. Change the destination IP address as you work your way through each intermediate device between you and the destination.

- Next, to rule out problems with your network interface, your network cable, or the switch or hub you are connected to, try to ping an IP address on your local network.

- Next, to rule out DNS name resolution problems, try to ping the destination by name. If this fails, you can continue to use ping, but you must use the destination's IP address.

- Use traceroute (described later in this appendix) to determine the IP addresses of the intermediate hosts between you and the destination host.

- Responding to a failure at this point depends on who is responsible for the systems beyond your router. If you are responsible, you will need to test the machines beyond the router and work back in your direction from behind the router.

- Running ping over a time interval can help diagnose problems that seem to come and go, for example.

- If you are looking at performance over a long period of time, you will almost certainly want to use the –i option to space your packets in a more network-friendly manner. This is a reasonable approach to take if you are experiencing occasional outages and need to document the time and duration of the outages. You should also be aware that over extended periods of time, you may see changes in the paths the packets follow.

ipconfig and ifconfig

On Unix, you can obtain the machine's network configuration using ifconfig. The command on Windows is ipconfig. To summarize the command:

- Use this tool to obtain the IP address, subnet mask, and default gateway.

- On Windows, use **ipconfig /?** for help.

- On Unix, use **man ifconfig** for help.

- Note that on Linux systems, you may not have permission to run ifconfig. It also may be in a location that isn't in your path—e.g., */sbin/ifconfig*.

Here's a run of ifconfig on a Unix system:

```
$ /sbin/ifconfig -a
eth0      Link encap:Ethernet  HWaddr 00:11:43:17:06:8D
          inet addr:192.168.0.48  Bcast:192.168.0.255  Mask:255.255.255.0
          inet6 addr: fe80::211:43ff:fe17:68d/64 Scope:Link
          UP BROADCAST RUNNING MULTICAST  MTU:1500  Metric:1
          RX packets:282499 errors:0 dropped:0 overruns:0 frame:15
          TX packets:33484 errors:0 dropped:0 overruns:0 carrier:0
          collisions:550 txqueuelen:1000
          RX bytes:43199045 (41.1 MiB)  TX bytes:6730704 (6.4 MiB)
          Interrupt:169

lo        Link encap:Local Loopback
          inet addr:127.0.0.1  Mask:255.0.0.0
          inet6 addr: ::1/128 Scope:Host
          UP LOOPBACK RUNNING  MTU:16436  Metric:1
          RX packets:304 errors:0 dropped:0 overruns:0 frame:0
          TX packets:304 errors:0 dropped:0 overruns:0 carrier:0
          collisions:0 txqueuelen:0
          RX bytes:26811 (26.1 KiB)  TX bytes:26811 (26.1 KiB)

sit0      Link encap:IPv6-in-IPv4
          NOARP  MTU:1480  Metric:1
          RX packets:0 errors:0 dropped:0 overruns:0 frame:0
          TX packets:0 errors:0 dropped:0 overruns:0 carrier:0
          collisions:0 txqueuelen:0
          RX bytes:0 (0.0 b)  TX bytes:0 (0.0 b)
```

Note that along with the IP address and other related information, we see the MAC address, labeled as ether.

Windows output looks like the following:

```
C:\>ipconfig

Windows IP Configuration


Ethernet adapter Local Area Connection:

        Media State . . . . . . . . . . . : Media disconnected

Ethernet adapter Wireless Network Connection 2:

        Connection-specific DNS Suffix  . : hsd1.ga.comcast.net.
        IP Address. . . . . . . . . . . . : 192.168.1.120
        Subnet Mask . . . . . . . . . . . : 255.255.255.0
        Default Gateway . . . . . . . . . : 192.168.1.3
```

arp

The ARP table maps MAC addresses to IP addresses. In other words, it maps layer two to layer three. Only directly connected devices—i.e., on the local network—appear in this table. The arp command found on Windows and Unix systems allows for the addition and deletion of entries. Here is output from the Windows command:

```
C:\> arp -a

Interface: 192.168.1.120 --- 0x10004
  Internet Address      Physical Address      Type
  192.168.1.3           00-09-5b-51-38-26     dynamic
```

Here is output from a Unix system:

```
$ /usr/sbin/arp -a
kahlua.reflex (192.168.0.6) at 00:30:48:20:92:47 [ether] on eth0
barton.reflex (192.168.0.3) at 00:B0:D0:3D:D4:9A [ether] on eth0
myic (192.168.0.147) at 00:0F:1F:04:71:79 [ether] on eth0
jameson.reflex (192.168.0.1) at 00:60:F5:08:4E:3C [ether] on eth0
$
```

Note that on Unix systems, the format of the output from arp can differ.

netstat

This program obtains network information from kernel data structures. The following command displays the routing table on Windows:

```
C:\>netstat -rn

Route Table
```

```
===============================================================
Interface List
0x1 ......................... MS TCP Loopback interface
0x2 ...00 03 47 b8 9d 10 ...... Intel(R) PRO/100 SP Mobile Combo Adapter - SecuR
emote Miniport
0x10004 ...00 09 5b e6 cd 6d ...... NETGEAR WG511 54 Mbps Wireless PC Card
===============================================================
===============================================================
Active Routes:
Network Destination        Netmask          Gateway       Interface  Metric
          0.0.0.0          0.0.0.0      192.168.1.3   192.168.1.120     25
        127.0.0.0        255.0.0.0        127.0.0.1       127.0.0.1      1
      192.168.1.0    255.255.255.0    192.168.1.120   192.168.1.120     25
    192.168.1.120  255.255.255.255        127.0.0.1       127.0.0.1     25
    192.168.1.255  255.255.255.255    192.168.1.120   192.168.1.120     25
        224.0.0.0        240.0.0.0    192.168.1.120   192.168.1.120     25
  255.255.255.255  255.255.255.255    192.168.1.120               2      1
  255.255.255.255  255.255.255.255    192.168.1.120   192.168.1.120      1
Default Gateway:       192.168.1.3
===============================================================
Persistent Routes:
  None
```

And the same command on a Unix system:

```
$ netstat -rn
Kernel IP routing table
Destination     Gateway         Genmask         Flags   MSS Window  irtt Iface
192.168.0.0     0.0.0.0         255.255.255.0   U         0 0          0 eth0
0.0.0.0         192.168.0.1     0.0.0.0         UG        0 0          0 eth0
$
```

Note the third column, Flags. A U indicates the path is up or available, an H indicates the destination is a host rather than a network, and a G indicates a gateway or router. These are the most useful. Others include b, indicating a broadcast address; S, indicating a static or manual addition; and W and c, indicating a route that was generated as a result of cloning. (See the manpage for netstat for more information.)

To display all connections and listening ports, run netstat –a. On Unix, this looks like:

```
$ netstat -a
Active Internet connections (servers and established)
Proto Recv-Q Send-Q Local Address           Foreign Address         State
tcp        0      0 localhost.localdoma:705 *:*                     LISTEN
tcp        0      0 *:sunrpc                *:*                     LISTEN
tcp        0      0 *:www                   *:*                     LISTEN
tcp        0      0 *:ipp                   *:*                     LISTEN
tcp        0      0 localhost.localdom:smtp *:*                     LISTEN
tcp        0      0 localhost.localdoma:ipp localhost.localdo:33628 ESTABLISHED
tcp        0      0 dhcp48:33630            64.233.171.107:www      ESTABLISHED
tcp        0      0 dhcp48:33631            crown:nntp              ESTABLISHED
tcp        0      0 dhcp48:33557            crown:nntp              ESTABLISHED
tcp        1      0 dhcp48:33487            65.39.248.92:www        CLOSE_WAIT
```

```
tcp        0      0 dhcp48:33562     65.161.97.185:www          ESTABLISHED
tcp        0      0 dhcp48:33561     65.161.97.185:www          ESTABLISHED
tcp        0      0 dhcp48:33560     65.161.97.167:www          ESTABLISHED
tcp        0      0 dhcp48:33559     65.161.97.167:www          ESTABLISHED
tcp        0      0 dhcp48:33455     crown:imaps                ESTABLISHED
tcp        0      0 localhost.localdo:33628 localhost.localdoma:ipp ESTABLISHED
tcp        0      0 dhcp48:33606     66.28.46.137:www           ESTABLISHED
tcp        1      0 dhcp48:33475     69.8.203.74:www            CLOSE_WAIT
tcp        0      0 dhcp48:33115     myic:ssh                   ESTABLISHED
tcp6       0      0 *:ssh                 *:*                   LISTEN
udp        0      0 *:bootpc              *:*
udp        0      0 *:sunrpc              *:*
udp        0      0 *:ipp                 *:*
Active UNIX domain sockets (servers and established)
Proto RefCnt Flags       Type      State        I-Node Path
unix  2     [ ACC ]      STREAM    LISTENING    7619
/var/run/dbus/system_bus_socket
unix  2     [ ACC ]      STREAM    LISTENING    7895   /tmp/.X11-unix/X64
unix  2     [ ACC ]      STREAM    LISTENING    8270   /tmp/.X11-unix/X0
unix  2     [ ACC ]      STREAM    LISTENING    8399
/tmp/ssh-wPdEoj4981/agent.4981
unix  2     [ ACC ]      STREAM    LISTENING    8413
/tmp/orbit-kjs/linc-139f-0-4b8cc076635e7
unix  2     [ ACC ]      STREAM    LISTENING    8423
/tmp/orbit-kjs/linc-1375-0-7bd6e96e75bf2
unix  2     [ ACC ]      STREAM    LISTENING    8579   /tmp/.ICE-unix/4981
unix  2     [ ACC ]      STREAM    LISTENING    8587
/tmp/keyring-7SnfPy/socket
$
```

The following line from the output shows an HTTP connection between dhcp48 and 66.28.46.137.

```
tcp        0      0 dhcp48:33606     66.28.46.137:www           ESTABLISHED
```

When a connection is in CLOSE_WAIT, it indicates a recently terminated session:

```
tcp        1      0 dhcp48:33475     69.8.203.74:www            CLOSE_WAIT
```

traceroute and tracert

The traceroute command traces paths through routers. Depending on the system you're using, the name of this command may vary. On the Linux system we used, it's called tcptraceroute:

```
$ /usr/bin/tcptraceroute www.yahoo.com
Selected device eth0, address 192.168.0.48, port 33633 for outgoing packets
Tracing the path to www.yahoo.com (68.142.226.56) on TCP port 80
(www), 30 hops max
1   192.168.0.1    11.811 ms   0.372 ms   0.352 ms
2   69.15.40.49    1.623 ms   1.331 ms   1.331 ms
3   172.16.141.177   3.371 ms   3.314 ms   3.216 ms
4   192.168.14.21   3.629 ms   3.599 ms   3.703 ms
5   192.168.34.10   4.491 ms   4.395 ms   4.447 ms
```

```
 6  ge-9-0-133.hsa1.Atlanta1.Level3.net (209.246.169.33)  4.745 ms
5.025 ms  4.472 ms
 7  ge-6-1-0.bbr1.Atlanta1.Level3.net (64.159.3.5)  9.875 ms  5.234 ms  4.710 ms
 8  ae-0-0.bbr1.Washington1.Level3.net (64.159.0.229)  17.875 ms
18.737 ms  17.529 ms
 9  ge-3-0-0-55.gar1.Washington1.Level3.net (4.68.121.130)  17.824 ms
17.813 ms  18.275 ms
10  63.210.29.230  18.314 ms  18.504 ms  18.742 ms
11  vl4.bas1.re2.yahoo.com (206.190.33.10)  18.549 ms  18.577 ms  18.305 ms
12  p25.www.re2.yahoo.com (68.142.226.56) [open]  18.596 ms  18.499 ms
18.783 ms
$
```

Windows' tracert is identical to traceroute, except it uses ICMP packets rather than UDP packets to discover the paths between routers:

```
C:\>tracert www.yahoo.com

Tracing route to www.yahoo.akadns.net [216.109.117.108]
over a maximum of 30 hops:

  1   10 ms    7 ms    9 ms  10.239.230.1
  2   10 ms    8 ms    9 ms  68.86.109.157
  3   10 ms   10 ms    8 ms  68.86.106.178
  4    9 ms    9 ms    9 ms  68.86.106.182
  5   10 ms    9 ms   10 ms  68.86.106.186
  6   15 ms   17 ms    9 ms  68.86.106.190
  7   10 ms   10 ms    9 ms  68.86.106.158
  8   10 ms   10 ms    8 ms  68.86.107.13
  9   10 ms    9 ms   10 ms  12.124.64.21
 10   11 ms   11 ms   11 ms  tbr1-p013701.attga.ip.att.net [12.123.21.98]
 11   24 ms   24 ms   24 ms  tbr2-cl1.wswdc.ip.att.net [12.122.10.69]
 12   24 ms   24 ms   23 ms  gar1-p390.ascva.ip.att.net [12.123.8.53]
 13    *        *        *    Request timed out.
 14   32 ms   25 ms   24 ms  ae1.p400.msr1.dcn.yahoo.com [216.115.96.181]
 15   25 ms   23 ms   25 ms  ge7-1.bas1-m.dcn.yahoo.com [216.109.120.205]
 16   25 ms   25 ms   25 ms  p23.www.dcn.yahoo.com [216.109.117.108]

Trace complete.
```

Here are some points to remember when using traceroute:

- In the output from both traceroute and tracert, the path was 16 hops.
- Times are printed for each of the three probes sent.
- An asterisk is printed in place of the time when a packet is lost.
- Additional messages can be appended to the end of each line: !H, !N, and !P indicate, respectively, that the host, network, or protocol is unreachable. !F indicates that fragmentation is needed. !S indicates a source route failure.
- The path taken from destination to source may not be the same path taken from source to destination, due to different path routes.

nslookup and dig

nslookup, found on Unix and Windows systems, is used to get IP address information on a host, and vice versa:

```
C:\>nslookup www.yahoo.com
Server:  ns1.mindspring.com
Address:  207.69.188.185

Non-authoritative answer:
Name:    www.yahoo.akadns.net
Addresses:  216.109.118.75, 216.109.118.77, 216.109.118.78, 216.109.118.79
            216.109.118.65, 216.109.118.66, 216.109.118.69, 216.109.118.73
Aliases:  www.yahoo.com

C:\>nslookup 216.109.118.75
Server:  ns1.mindspring.com
Address:  207.69.188.185


Name:    p12.www.dcn.yahoo.com
Address:  216.109.118.75
```

While nslookup has been widely used on Unix systems for many, many years, nslookup is being deprecated on Linux systems. Instead of nslookup, Linux systems now make use of a command called dig (dig stands for Domain Internet Groper).

Let's look at some example usage of dig:

```
$ dig @69.15.40.52 www.yahoo.com

; <<>> DiG 9.2.4 <<>> @69.15.40.52 www.yahoo.com
;; global options:  printcmd
;; Got answer:
;; ->>HEADER<<- opcode: QUERY, status: NOERROR, id: 7406
;; flags: qr rd ra; QUERY: 1, ANSWER: 9, AUTHORITY: 0, ADDITIONAL: 0

;; QUESTION SECTION:
;www.yahoo.com.                 IN      A

;; ANSWER SECTION:
www.yahoo.com.          300     IN      CNAME   www.yahoo.akadns.net.
www.yahoo.akadns.net.   60      IN      A       68.142.226.34
www.yahoo.akadns.net.   60      IN      A       68.142.226.56
www.yahoo.akadns.net.   60      IN      A       68.142.226.44
www.yahoo.akadns.net.   60      IN      A       68.142.226.45
www.yahoo.akadns.net.   60      IN      A       68.142.226.38
www.yahoo.akadns.net.   60      IN      A       68.142.226.47
www.yahoo.akadns.net.   60      IN      A       68.142.226.39
www.yahoo.akadns.net.   60      IN      A       68.142.226.43

;; Query time: 239 msec
;; SERVER: 69.15.40.52#53(69.15.40.52)
;; WHEN: Mon May 16 08:13:18 2005
```

```
;; MSG SIZE  rcvd: 193

$
```

The @ value is optional. You could use a domain name or, as we did, an IP address. It specifies the name server to be queried. The second option is the host we want to look up.

Using the –x option with dig, you can get reverse name lookup:

```
$ dig -x 68.142.226.34

; <<>> DiG 9.2.4 <<>> -x 68.142.226.34
;; global options:  printcmd
;; Got answer:
;; ->>HEADER<<- opcode: QUERY, status: NOERROR, id: 51297
;; flags: qr rd ra; QUERY: 1, ANSWER: 1, AUTHORITY: 0, ADDITIONAL: 0

;; QUESTION SECTION:
;34.226.142.68.in-addr.arpa.      IN      PTR

;; ANSWER SECTION:
34.226.142.68.in-addr.arpa. 1200 IN      PTR      p3.www.re2.yahoo.com.

;; Query time: 79 msec
;; SERVER: 69.15.40.52#53(69.15.40.52)
;; WHEN: Mon May 16 08:13:47 2005
;; MSG SIZE  rcvd: 78
```

With the mx option, dig can be used to obtain the mail exchanger information for a domain:

```
$ dig mx yahoo.com

; <<>> DiG 9.2.4 <<>> mx yahoo.com
;; global options:  printcmd
;; Got answer:
;; ->>HEADER<<- opcode: QUERY, status: NOERROR, id: 25
;; flags: qr rd ra; QUERY: 1, ANSWER: 4, AUTHORITY: 0, ADDITIONAL: 0

;; QUESTION SECTION:
;yahoo.com.                     IN      MX

;; ANSWER SECTION:
yahoo.com.              6557    IN      MX      1 mx3.mail.yahoo.com.
yahoo.com.              6557    IN      MX      5 mx4.mail.yahoo.com.
yahoo.com.              6557    IN      MX      1 mx1.mail.yahoo.com.
yahoo.com.              6557    IN      MX      1 mx2.mail.yahoo.com.

;; Query time: 1 msec
;; SERVER: 69.15.40.52#53(69.15.40.52)
;; WHEN: Mon May 16 08:14:26 2005
;; MSG SIZE  rcvd: 112
```

The soa option can be used to obtain zone authority information:

```
$ dig soa yahoo.com

; <<>> DiG 9.2.4 <<>> soa yahoo.com
;; global options:  printcmd
;; Got answer:
;; ->>HEADER<<- opcode: QUERY, status: NOERROR, id: 41407
;; flags: qr rd ra; QUERY: 1, ANSWER: 1, AUTHORITY: O, ADDITIONAL: O

;; QUESTION SECTION:
;yahoo.com.                     IN      SOA

;; ANSWER SECTION:
yahoo.com.              1800    IN      SOA     ns1.yahoo.com.
hostmaster.yahoo-inc.com. 2005051609 3600 300 604800 600

;; Query time: 21 msec
;; SERVER: 69.15.40.52#53(69.15.40.52)
;; WHEN: Mon May 16 08:14:45 2005
;; MSG SIZE  rcvd: 88
```

See the manual page for more details on this powerful tool.

whois

The whois command is used to obtain domain name registrar information:

```
$ jwhois yahoo.com
Registrant:
        Yahoo! Inc.
        (DOM-272993)
        701 First Avenue Sunnyvale
        CA
        94089 US

    Domain Name: yahoo.com

        Registrar Name: Alldomains.com
        Registrar Whois: whois.alldomains.com
        Registrar Homepage: http://www.alldomains.com

    Administrative Contact:
        Domain Administrator
        (NIC-1382062)
        Yahoo! Inc.
        701 First Avenue Sunnyvale
        CA
        94089 US
        domainadmin@yahoo-inc.com +1.4083493300 Fax- +1.4083493301
    Technical Contact, Zone Contact:
        Domain Administrator
        (NIC-1372925)
        Yahoo! Inc.
        701 First Avenue Sunnyvale
        CA
```

94089 US
domainadmin@yahoo-inc.com +1.4083493300 Fax- +1.4083493301

Created on..............: 1995-Jan-18.
Expires on..............: 2012-Jan-19.
Record last updated on..: 2005-Apr-05 16:34:22.

Domain servers in listed order:

NS4.YAHOO.COM   63.250.206.138
NS5.YAHOO.COM   216.109.116.17
NS1.YAHOO.COM   66.218.71.63
NS2.YAHOO.COM   66.163.169.170
NS3.YAHOO.COM   217.12.4.104

If you are troubleshooting and the path takes you across a network that you have no control over, you can use whois to find out whom to contact for a domain. While this isn't 100% accurate, it is better than nothing.

Ethereal

Finally, we come to Ethereal. This tool is used to capture network packets. It runs on both Unix and Windows. It is intended to run as a GUI application. Figure H-1 shows the packet capture window.

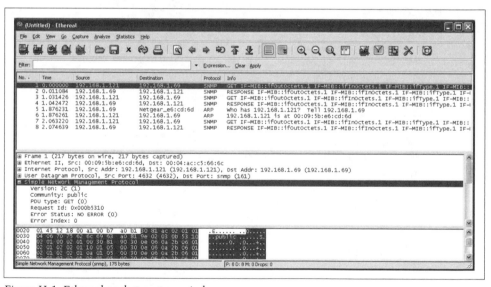

Figure H-1. Ethereal packet capture window

It displays such information as source and destination IP addresses and ports, protocols, and payload data. Each level of the OSI model is represented here, and you can drill down into each layer for further inspection. To learn more about Ethereal, visit *http://www.ethereal.com*.

Index

We'd like to hear your suggestions for improving our indexes. Send email to *index@oreilly.com*.

regular expressions, indexmaker option, 307
reinitialization trap information, 64
remote monitoring, RMON MIB, 70
Remote Network Monitoring, 2
remote-location staffing, 89
report operations, 69
reports
    response time, 10
    trend analysis, 10
Requests for Comments, 2
response time, reporting, 10
retransmissions, overhead and, 19
retrieving values, OpenView and, 144
Retry settings (NNM), 99
reverse engineering, 71
RFCs (Requests for Comments), 2
    documentation, 382
    draft status, 2
    experimental, 2, 377
    historical standards, 2
    list, 377
    process for, 2
    SMIv1 Data Definition Language, 377
    SMIv2 Data Definition Language, 377
    SMIv2 MIB modules, 379
    SNMIv1 MIB modules, 378
    SNMP agent extensibility, 378
    SNMP versions, 2
    SNMPv3, 74
    SNMPv3 protocol, 377
    standard status, 2
risk assessment, chanage management
        and, 12
RMON (Remote Network Monitoring), 2, 6,
        70
    configuration, 158
    events, 158
    groups, 70
    internal polling and, 157–162
    RMON MIB, 6, 70
    versions, 71
Root map
    NNM, 94
    SNMPc, 106
roots in object tree, 24
router-interfaces subtree (Cricket), 326
routers
    access lists, 117
    Cricket, data gathering, 325
    listing commands, 135
    shutting down, 135
    testing, 99
routers subtree (Cricket), 326

rows in tables, 31, 35
RRDtool (Round Robin Database Tool)
    installation, 317
    introduction, 316
    MRTG and, 316

S

scalar objects
    graphing in MRTG, 311
    MIB objects, 39
    OIDs, 39
scope, change management, 12
security
    access, 117
    agent configuration, 116
    authentication-failure traps, 116
    community strings, 22, 116
    events, NNM, 187
    firewalls, 117
    limiting requests to agents, 117, 129
    polling over the Internet, 89
    SNMP weaknesses and, 73, 116
    SNMPv3 and, 73, 117
        Cisco routers, 136
        encryption, 74, 136
        levels, 76
        USM, 76
Security Subsystem, SNMPv3, 74
seed devices, 105, 107
seed files, 99
sending traps, 197–199
    Cisco devices, 135
    forcing hardware, 204
    Net-SNMP, 202
    OpenView, 200
    Perl, 201
    snmptrap (Net-SNMP), 371
    SNMPv3, 75
    Trap Generator (Network Computing
        Technologies), 202
sendmail process, monitoring, 133
servers
    graphing parameters, 310
    web servers, 134
service monitoring, trap generation
        and, 260–268
set operations, 57, 57–62, 141, 388
    error messages, 62
    error responses, 62
    SNMP4J, 341–343
    SNMPv3, 75
sets in filters, 102, 103

About the Authors

Douglas R. Mauro received his bachelor's degree from the University of Albany, New York, and worked as a system administrator for several years before becoming a project engineer with Sun Microsystems, Inc. In addition to his consulting duties with Sun, he authors their internal OneStop Sun Management Center page and has published several InfoDocs with them.

Kevin J. Schmidt currently lives in Lilburn, Georgia. He is a senior software developer at Reflex Security, Inc. (*http://www.reflexsecurity.com*), where he gets to develop software in both Java and C. Prior to Reflex, Kevin spent four years at GuardedNet, Inc. (*http://www.guarded.net*) as a senior software developer and team lead.

Originally from Pensacola, Florida, Kevin moved to Atlanta in late 1996 to work for MindSpring Enterprises (now known as Earthlink, Inc.), a national ISP. He spent four years in network management and was the senior network management architect for Earthlink. He left Earthlink to work at Netrail, a tier-1 Internet backbone provider. While at Netrail, Kevin was in charge of the company's network management architecture.

Kevin's first computer was a Commodore 64. He began running Bulletin Board Systems (BBSs) at age 11 and later became interested in computer networking in general. His other computing interests include Linux, MySQL, programming languages, and theoretical computer science.

Colophon

Our look is the result of reader comments, our own experimentation, and feedback from distribution channels. Distinctive covers complement our distinctive approach to technical topics, breathing personality and life into potentially dry subjects.

The animals on the cover of *Essential SNMP*, Second Edition are red deer (*Cervus elaphus*). Male red deer, also known as *stags* or *harts*, can grow to over 400 pounds. and stand 42–54 inches tall at the shoulder. Females, or *hinds*, are more slightly built and usually reach a weight of only about 200 pounds. The color of the red deer's coat ranges from a warm reddish-brown in the summer to a darker grayish-brown in winter. Calves are spotted at birth, but the spots fade after about two months.

The typical family group consists of a hind, a new calf, a yearling calf, and perhaps a two- or three-year-old stag. Mature stags and hinds live in separate groups for most of the year, with the hinds tending to monopolize the better, more grassy habitats. At the start of the mating season (the rut) in the early fall, the stags split up and join the females. Each eligible stag establishes a harem of up to 20 or more hinds, which he defends vigorously during the rut. During this period, which typically lasts 6–8 weeks, the stags often forego eating and can lose as much as 15% of their body mass.

Red deer are one of the most widely distributed deer species: although they are native to Europe, today they can be found everywhere from New Zealand to North America. They are herbivores, feeding mainly on rough grasses, young tree shoots, and shrubs. Forest-dwellers by nature, they can adapt easily to different climates and terrain. In many of the areas in which they were introduced, red deer are commercially farmed for venison and antler velvet, which has been used in traditional Chinese medicine for over 2,000 years to treat a broad range of ailments, including anemia, arthritic pain and rheumatism, kidney disorders, and stress.

Darren Kelly was the production editor, and Audrey Doyle was the copyeditor for *Essential SNMP*, Second Edition. Carol Marti proofread the book. Genevieve d'Entremont and Colleen Gorman provided quality control. Lydia Onofrei provided production assistance. Johnna VanHoose Dinse wrote the index.

Ellie Volckhausen designed the cover of this book, based on a series design by Edie Freedman. The cover image is a 19th-century engraving from the Dover Pictorial Archive. Karen Montgomery produced the cover layout with Adobe InDesign CS using Adobe's ITC Garamond font.

David Futato designed the interior layout. This book was converted by Andrew Savikas to FrameMaker 5.5.6 with a format conversion tool created by Erik Ray, Jason McIntosh, Neil Walls, and Mike Sierra that uses Perl and XML technologies. The text font is Linotype Birka; the heading font is Adobe Myriad Condensed; and the code font is LucasFont's TheSans Mono Condensed. The illustrations that appear in the book were produced by Robert Romano, Jessamyn Read, and Lesley Borash using Macromedia FreeHand MX and Adobe Photoshop CS. The tip and warning icons were drawn by Christopher Bing. This colophon was written by Rachel Wheeler.

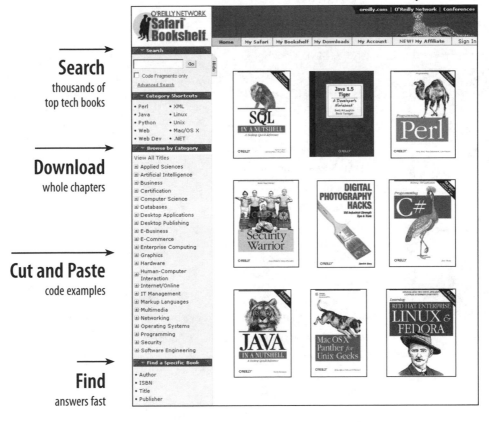

Related Titles from O'Reilly

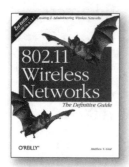

Networking

802.11 Security

802.11 Wireless Networks: The Definitive Guide, *2nd Edition*

Asterisk: The Future of Telephony

BGP

Building Wireless Community Networks, *2nd Edition*

Cisco Cookbook

Cisco IOS Access Lists

Cisco IOS in a Nutshell, *2nd Edition*

DNS & BIND Cookbook

DNS & BIND, 4th Edition

Essential SNMP, *2nd Edition*

IP Routing

IPv6 Essentials

IPv6 Network Administration

LDAP System Administration

Managing NFS and NIS, *2nd Edition*

Network Troubleshooting Tools

RADIUS

sendmail 8.13 Companion

sendmail, *3rd Edition*

sendmail Cookbook

SpamAssassin

Switching to VOIP

TCP/IP Network Administration, *3rd Edition*

Unix Backup and Recovery

Using Samba, *2nd Edition*

Using SANs and NAS

Windows Server 2003 Network Administration

O'REILLY®

Keep in touch with O'Reilly

Download examples from our books

To find example files from a book, go to: *www.oreilly.com/catalog* select the book, and follow the "Examples" link.

Register your O'Reilly books

Register your book at *register.oreilly.com* Why register your books? Once you've registered your O'Reilly books you can:

- Win O'Reilly books, T-shirts or discount coupons in our monthly drawing.
- Get special offers available only to registered O'Reilly customers.
- Get catalogs announcing new books (US and UK only).
- Get email notification of new editions of the O'Reilly books you own.

Join our email lists

Sign up to get topic-specific email announcements of new books and conferences, special offers, and O'Reilly Network technology newsletters at:

elists.oreilly.com

It's easy to customize your free elists subscription so you'll get exactly the O'Reilly news you want.

Get the latest news, tips, and tools

www.oreilly.com

- "Top 100 Sites on the Web"—PC Magazine
- CIO Magazine's Web Business 50 Awards

Our web site contains a library of comprehensive product information (including book excerpts and tables of contents), downloadable software, background articles, interviews with technology leaders, links to relevant sites, book cover art, and more.

Work for O'Reilly

Check out our web site for current employment opportunities:

jobs.oreilly.com

Contact us

O'Reilly Media, Inc.
1005 Gravenstein Hwy North
Sebastopol, CA 95472 USA
Tel: 707-827-7000 or 800-998-9938
     (6am to 5pm PST)
Fax: 707-829-0104

Contact us by email

For answers to problems regarding your order or our products:
order@oreilly.com

To request a copy of our latest catalog:
catalog@oreilly.com

For book content technical questions or corrections: **booktech@oreilly.com**

For educational, library, government, and corporate sales: **corporate@oreilly.com**

To submit new book proposals to our editors and product managers:
proposals@oreilly.com

For information about our international distributors or translation queries:
international@oreilly.com

For information about academic use of O'Reilly books:
adoption@oreilly.com
or visit:
academic.oreilly.com

For a list of our distributors outside of North America check out:
international.oreilly.com/distributors.html

Order a book online

www.oreilly.com/order_new